John Feinstein

THE LEGENDS CLUB

The Legends Club is John Feinstein's thirty-sixth book. He is the author of *A Season on the Brink* and *A Good Walk Spoiled*, both #1 *New York Times* bestsellers, and *Last Shot*, which won the Edgar Allan Poe Award for mystery writing in the Young Adult category. He was inducted into the U.S. Basketball Writers Association Hall of Fame in 2000; the National Sportscasters and Sportswriters Association Hall of Fame in 2012, and the Naismith Memorial Basketball Hall of Fame in 2013. He currently writes for *The Washington Post* and *Golf Digest*, is a regular contributor to the Golf Channel and Comcast Sports Regional Networks, and hosts a college basketball show and a golf show on SiriusXM Radio. He lives in Potomac, Maryland, with his wife, Christine, and is the father of three children, Danny, Brigid, and Jane.

Nonfiction by John Feinstein

THE
LEGENDS CLUB

DEAN SMITH, MIKE KRZYZEWSKI, JIM VALVANO,

and an Epic College Basketball Rivalry

JOHN FEINSTEIN

Anchor Books
A Division of Penguin Random House LLC
New York

The Library of Congress has catalogued the Doubleday edition as follows:
Names: Feinstein, John.
Title: The legends club Dean Smith, Mike Krzyzewski, Jim Valvano,
and an epic college basketball rivalry / John Feinstein.
Description: First edition. New York : Doubleday, 2016.
Identifiers: LCCN 2015029890
Subjects: LCSH: Basketball coaches—United States—Biography.
Basketball teams—North Carolina—History. Sports rivalries—North
Carolina—History. University of North Carolina at Chapel Hill—
Basketball—History. Duke University—Basketball—History.
North Carolina State University—Basketball—History.
Classification: LCC GV884.A1 F45 2016 DDC 796.3230922—dc23
LC record available at http://lccn.loc.gov/2015029890

Anchor Books Trade Paperback ISBN: 978-0-8041-7317-9
eBook ISBN: 978-0-385-53942-5

Author photograph © Christine Bauch Feinstein
Book design by Michael Collica

www.anchorbooks.com

Printed in the United States of America
10 9 8 7 6 5 4 3

This is for Ken Denlinger, who taught me about
college hoops, journalism, and life.

THE
LEGENDS CLUB

INTRODUCTION

In a very real sense, this book was born on February 28, 1976—Dean Smith's forty-fifth birthday.

It was on that afternoon that a very nervous reporter from Duke's student newspaper, *The Chronicle,* timidly introduced himself to the great man in a corner of the North Carolina locker room in Carmichael Auditorium. North Carolina had just finished beating Duke, 91–71, dropping Duke's record to 13–13.

The outcome wasn't a surprise. Carolina was ranked fourth in the country and had run away with the ACC regular season title, finishing 11–1. The Tar Heels were 24–2 and had four players on their roster who would be on the U.S. Olympic team—coached by Dean Smith—that summer: Mitch Kupchak, Walter Davis, Tommy LaGarde, and the great Phil Ford.

Duke had Tate Armstrong.

Who was my excuse to talk to Dean Smith.

Armstrong had been lighting up ACC gyms all winter, a one-man show on a struggling team. Duke coach Bill Foster was in his second season, trying to rebuild the fallen Duke program. Armstrong had just finished his freshman season when Foster arrived and was now a junior. Armstrong did have some help from a superb freshman named Jim Spanarkel, but the Blue Devils were overmatched in the ACC—as their 3–9 conference record proved.

For the season, Armstrong was averaging 24.2 points per game—making an astounding 52 percent of his shots. That was with no three-point shot and no shot clock, and with other teams gearing their defenses to stop him. He was a slender six foot two and spent as much time on the floor after being knocked down as he did in his shooting motion. He had scored 29 points that day against Carolina. I was going to write a column making the case that if ever a player from a team that finished seventh in a seven-team conference deserved consideration for player of the year, it was Armstrong. I might have been just a tad biased.

Smith was talking to another writer when I walked up. When he finished the conversation he'd been having, he looked at me as if to say, "And?" Finding my voice somewhere, I said, "Coach Smith, my name is John Feinstein and I work for *The Chronicle,* the Duke student newspaper . . ."

I had my hand out as I spoke and Smith shook it, stopping me before I could go further by saying, "I know who you are. I read the column you wrote last month saying that Bill [Foster] should copy some of what we do here to rebuild over at Duke. I thought you were very fair to us . . . for someone from Duke."

I had been more than fair. I had been gushy. But that wasn't the point. I was standing in front of Dean Smith and he was telling me *he had read something I had written.*

I was, to put it mildly, stunned. As I've written often in the past, it was later that I learned that the North Carolina basketball office subscribed to every newspaper in North Carolina—the major national papers *and* all the student newspapers in the ACC. An assistant coach was assigned to comb through the papers and clip anything relevant to Carolina for Smith to read. He would put the clips in his briefcase and read them on airplanes.

Still stunned, I somehow got my question out about Armstrong. I'm not sure he ever answered it. Instead, he talked about how proud he was of Ford and Davis, but especially John Kuester, for the defensive job they'd done that day on Armstrong—even if he had scored almost half of Duke's points. Somewhere in the middle of the answer he asked me where I'd grown up. I said New York.

"City?" he asked.

I nodded.

"Well," he said, "I guess that explains why you understand basketball."

Do you think he completely owned me at that moment?

I asked one more question. Early in the game, when it was still close, a couple of calls had gone against Carolina. Some of the students had started a profane chant. It didn't last very long, because Smith walked straight to the scorer's table, took the PA microphone, pointed in the direction of the students, and said, "Stop. Now. We don't do that here. We win with class at Carolina."

They stopped. Instantly.

When I asked about the incident, he smiled again. "I was disappointed that happened," he said. "It won't happen here again." Then he added, "We're not Duke."

And, at that moment, Duke was miles and miles from being North Carolina.

———

If this book was born on that day in 1976, it began to take form in March of 1980 when, in a nine-day period, Duke hired Mike Krzyzewski to replace Bill Foster as basketball coach and North Carolina State hired Jim Valvano to replace Norman Sloan in the same capacity.

Sloan and Foster had each had considerable success: Sloan had won a national championship in 1974 and Foster had taken Duke to the national title game in 1978. But the Aura of Dean had driven both men away—Foster to South Carolina, Sloan to Florida. The two men who succeeded them were kids in the coaching profession—Valvano, thirty-four; Krzyzewski thirty-three. They had coached against each other at Iona and Army, both New York–area schools that were about five hundred miles and worlds away from North Carolina's Research Triangle. Neither had any clue about what the ACC was like or how important Dean Smith was in their new home state.

"If Jimmy and I had landed in a spaceship from Mars instead of on airplanes from New York, we couldn't possibly have had less understanding of what an icon Dean was," Krzyzewski said years later. "We both *thought* we did. We knew Carolina was very good every year, but we had no clue." He shook his head. "I mean, no clue."

They learned quickly—and, in some ways, painfully. Valvano tried to take Smith on with humor, and to some degree it worked. Winning a national championship in 1983 worked better. Krzyzewski confronted Smith head on from the beginning, challenging him first by trying to make it clear to the world he wouldn't back down from him. As with Valvano, he learned that good players and good teams were far more effective.

Valvano, as it turned out, was the hare—dashing ahead with remarkable speed when he first arrived at N.C. State, not only with the national championship but with his completely unbridled personality. Krzyzewski, watching from twenty-five miles away, could only shake his head watching the Valvano rocket ship take off.

"Being honest, I didn't like him at the time," he said. "Or, at the very least, I didn't want to be like him." He smiled. "Of course, being completely honest, I *couldn't* have been like him if I had wanted to be. There was no one else like him."

Krzyzewski was the tortoise, at least compared to Valvano's speed-of-light personality, plodding along, working relentlessly, never losing sight of his goal, which was to build a long-term winner at Duke. Slowly but surely he put together one of the great dynasties in college basketball history. He caught—and passed—Valvano. Amazingly, years later, he caught—and passed—Smith.

And, in 2015, he was still going, having become an icon much the way Smith was an icon. The only real difference I suppose is that a college junior walking around the Duke locker room today isn't likely to encounter Krzyzewski standing off in a corner. But if he did, and if he happened to ask about Smith or Valvano, there would be a remarkable story to be told.

—

Which is why I wanted to write this book.

I wasn't born to write it, but I lived it. I was working for *The Washington Post* when Krzyzewski and Valvano first landed in North Carolina. By then, I knew all three men. I had met Krzyzewski and Valvano at the exact same moment during my senior year, and after arriving at the *Post,* I had written about Smith every chance I got.

In December of 1976 Duke was playing Connecticut (an insignificant game between two insignificant teams in those days) at Madison Square Garden, and as a sports editor of *The Chronicle* I had flown to New York with Bill Foster, Tate Armstrong, and Duke's sports information director, Tom Mickle.

Mickle was bringing Foster and Armstrong in a day early to do some media interviews and I tagged along because it was an excuse to go home for a couple of days. We went straight from the airport to the weekly writers' lunch at Mamma Leone's, a famous Italian restaurant on the West Side of Manhattan. The restaurant has now been closed for more than twenty years, but in 1976 it was still one of *the* tourist stops in the city.

When we walked in, St. John's coach Lou Carnesecca was talking. The last thing he said was, "I don't want to go too long because I know you're all here to listen to Jimmy."

Valvano always went last, even though Carnesecca coached the most popular and important team in the city and Valvano coached at Iona, the Christian Brothers school in Westchester that ranked behind Fordham, Seton Hall, and Rutgers in the college hoops pantheon in the New York area. In fact, Columbia and Army had been higher on the totem pole in the not-too-distant past.

But when it came to the weekly lunches, Valvano was Sinatra and everyone else was the opening act.

Valvano spoke for twenty-five minutes. By the time he was finished—as was the case every week—people were literally holding their sides because they were laughing so hard. He made fun of everyone in the room, including Foster—who had coached him at Rutgers.

When he was finished, Valvano came over to see his old coach—we'd walked in a few minutes late—dragging two of his coaching friends with him: Army's Mike Krzyzewski and Columbia's Tom Penders.

I remembered Krzyzewski as a player because the Bob Knight–coached Army teams he played on were invited to the NIT—which in those days was played entirely in Madison Square Garden—in both 1968 and 1969. In fact, I vividly remembered Krzyzewski shutting down South Carolina's All-American guard John Roche in a stunning upset in the quarterfinals in 1969.

After the introductions, I mentioned that game to Krzyzewski. "You were there?" he said, a big smile on his face. "You must have grown up here then, right?"

That led to a conversation about the differences in growing up in New York compared to Chicago—Krzyzewski's hometown. I remember Valvano jumping in to talk about being a Yankees fan. I admitted to being a Mets fan, which drew a dirty look from Krzyzewski—a Cubs fan who remembered the 1969 baseball season not as fondly as the 1969 basketball season.

Valvano was thirty, Krzyzewski was twenty-nine—not that much older than I was. I liked them both instantly. Little did I know how much they would become a part of my life during the next ten years.

—

I had always wanted to write a book about Dean Smith—almost from the day I first met him. I found him fascinating: brilliant, driven, generous, manipulative, protective, private, and challenging—always challenging. Dean never gave up anything without a fight.

I've written often in the past about the story I wrote about him for *The Washington Post* in 1981. It took me two years to convince him to grant me the kind of lengthy interview I needed to write the kind of profile I wanted to write.

Dean always said no to those requests. He even turned down the great Frank Deford when Deford wanted to profile him for *Sports Illustrated*. Every time I brought it up, Dean would wave a hand—often with a cigarette in it in those days—and say, "Write about the players."

Finally, with the ACC Tournament scheduled to be played in Washington in March of 1981, I decided this was the time to find a way to make Dean talk.

I was fortunate that Rick Brewer, Carolina's longtime sports information director, was on my side. Rick's been a friend of mine since I was in college, and to this day, among the millions who do Dean imitations, Rick probably does the best one. Rick set up a meeting between Dean and me in Dean's hotel room in Charlottesville on a Friday evening, the day before Carolina played Virginia and Ralph Sampson.

Carolina always stays at the best hotel whenever it travels. When other ACC teams went to College Park to play Maryland, they would stay at the Holiday Inn on Route 1 or the Greenbelt Marriott. Carolina always stayed at the Watergate. In New York, it was the Essex House or the Plaza.

In Charlottesville, it was the Boar's Head Inn. Rick and I walked in to find Dean on the phone to the front desk.

"I need someone to come in here and get the fireplace going," he said. "I don't know how to do it."

I realized at that moment that Dean and I had something in common: complete incompetence when it came to making things work. A few years later, I was working in the office at the *Post* on ACC Media Day and needed to track Dean down. I asked my friend Keith Drum if he would give Dean the *Post*'s 800 number and ask him to call me. When Keith found Dean and handed him the number, Dean didn't ask him what I wanted to talk to him about, the way most coaches would. Instead he said, "I'm not sure I know how to dial an eight-hundred number."

He was serious.

Dean, Rick, and I sat down while the guy got the fireplace started. I made my pitch. Dean said I should write about the players.

"I've *written* about the players," I said. "I want to write about you. I'm *going* to write about you one way or the other."

At that moment Dean looked at me and said, "I hear you do me pretty well."

Classic Dean misdirection. Like everyone in the ACC, I imitated Dean.

"I'm okay," I said. "Rick's better."

Dean looked at Brewer and, in that classic, high-pitched, flat midwestern, nasally tone, said in a very surprised voice: "Rick, do *you* do me?"

I've rarely seen Rick Brewer flustered in the almost forty years I've known him. Now, for a split second, he was lost at sea. At last, he found land. "Coach," he said, "*everyone* does you."

Dean finally said he'd think about talking to me and said he'd let me know after the game the next afternoon. I said that was fine, he could call me, since I was driving back that night to cover Maryland–Wake Forest the next day.

"You mean you drove down here just to talk to me?" Dean said.

"Yup."

Dean shook his head. "I wish I'd known that," he said. "I'd have had Rick buy you dinner."

More classic Dean. He'd have had *Rick* buy me dinner.

—

The next day, after losing to Virginia, Dean said yes. Or, specifically, Rick said Dean had said yes. But it had to be done his way: I would come to Chapel Hill and on the Friday of the two-day North-South Doubleheader in Charlotte, and I would drive with Dean to Charlotte. That would give me about two and a half hours to talk to Dean. Then I would drive his car back to Chapel Hill (he'd come home with the team), leave it in his parking space at Carmichael Auditorium, and pick my car up so I could drive to Durham and cover the Maryland-Duke game on Saturday.

The only bad thing about the drive was the cigarette smoke. The interview went very well—Dean was more open and honest than he'd ever been with me—and he agreed to give me names and numbers of the important people in his life. One of them was the Reverend Robert Seymour, Dean's pastor at the Binkley Baptist Church in Chapel Hill.

It was Reverend Seymour who told me the story about Dean helping desegregate Chapel Hill restaurants in 1958 by walking into the Pines, the restaurant where the UNC basketball team ate its pregame meals, with a black member of the church and daring management not to serve them.

Reverend Seymour made it clear to me that this wasn't something taken on lightly. "Segregation was a cherished tradition to many people around here," he said to me. "Dean wasn't *Dean* then. He was an assistant coach. The management would certainly know him, but who knew how they'd react? They might call the police. They might call Coach McGuire and complain. There could have been serious trouble."

Reverend Seymour was a very bright, wise man who clearly was one of the few people who had Dean Smith's ear on a regular basis. "I hear TV announcers talk all the time about courageous comebacks or courageous decisions during a *game,*" he said. "What Dean did that night took real courage."

I couldn't wait to see Dean again to ask him to flesh out the story. I wanted details: Was he nervous or scared? How had he expected management to react? Why hadn't this story been told before?

And so, the next day I walked into Dean's office and asked him the question. He looked at me, clearly unhappy, and said, "Who told you that story?"

I told him it had been Reverend Seymour.

He leaned back in his chair and said, "I wish he hadn't told you that."

I was stunned and said so. "You should be proud of doing something like that," I said.

That was when Dean Smith said something to me that I've repeated often through the years because it says so much about who he was. "John," he said, leaning forward, "you should never be proud of doing the right thing. You should just *do* the right thing."

To this day, the line takes my breath away. The line *was* Dean Smith.

—

On the night of September 24, 2013, Mike Krzyzewski and I were talking about that line and about Dean. We were also talking about the day he and I had met in New York and Jim Valvano's ability to completely take over any room he walked into.

"I was a terrible speaker in those days," Krzyzewski said—something I knew because I'd heard him speak often when he first got to Duke. "I had no confidence. To Jim, speaking publicly was like breathing or walking—he did it without even giving it any thought and knowing he was better than anyone at it. For me, it was a chore."

We were sitting at a table at a dinner in Washington, D.C. Krzyzewski was being honored that night with the Nell and John Wooden Leadership in Coaching Award. The only thing Krzyzewski may have more of than leadership awards is wins. I had been asked to introduce him. So we were sitting next to each other during the dinner.

Krzyzewski is now one of the best public speakers on the planet. He is funny and polished and always prepared—much the same way he's always prepared when he coaches. He's in constant demand from corporate America and charities and doesn't go anywhere for anything less than fifty thousand dollars and a private plane. Usually, it's more than that—except for charity events for friends, which he does often and does for free.

"Jimmy is the reason I became a good speaker," Krzyzewski

said. "When he was sick, we'd sit and swap stories in his hospital room. He started saying to me, 'You're a very good storyteller and you're smart. If you worked at it a little, you could be very good. You could make a lot of money speaking. You *should* make a lot of money speaking.' He pushed me to work at it."

He paused. "Other than Mickie [his wife] and my brother, there's probably no one I've ever been closer to, especially those last few months. We said things to one another that men almost never say to one another. I cherish that time."

As we talked, we were interrupted frequently. People wanted autographs. Or a picture. Or to tell a story about where they were when Duke won a national championship. Krzyzewski treated each person as if the moments he spent with that person were the most important of the night. It's one of his gifts.

During the interruptions, I sat and thought about Valvano and about Dean and about some of the classic games and moments I'd covered and witnessed involving the three of them. When Krzyzewski turned back to me after one more photo, I asked him a question.

"If Jim were here now and saw what you've become, what do you think he'd say?"

Krzyzewski smiled, and I thought I saw his eyes glisten just a tiny bit.

Finally, he said, "He'd say—I told you so."

—

Driving home that night in 2013, all three men were on my mind. What, I wondered, would Valvano have become had he lived longer? Would he have coached again—perhaps in the NBA? Would he have become David Letterman or Jay Leno? That was Krzyzewski's theory. Would he have done something really important, which was what he craved? I still remembered the late-night sessions I'd had with him in his office in the Case Athletics Center at North Carolina State.

It was usually around three A.M. by the time the office cleared out. Valvano would stretch out on his couch and order me to a chair. "You're my therapist," he would say. "I need therapy."

And then he would wander all over the place verbally. Was he chasing money too much? Was he missing his daughters' childhoods? Did he still want to coach basketball? It was all fake, he would say, except the forty minutes during the game and the final score. That was real. Nothing else. And at some point he'd say, "What do I want to be when I grow up?"

The constant search.

I thought about Dean Smith and his extraordinary legacy. I'd never been in his office at three A.M. and he certainly hadn't asked me to be his therapist. But I'd had long talks with him through the years, the best ones when we weren't talking about basketball.

I still remembered going to interview him on Election Day in 1984. When I walked into his office, he handed me a copy of the previous day's *Chronicle*—the student newspaper where I'd started my career as a college freshman. It was open to the editorial page and a headline that said "Ronald Reagan Deserves a Second Term."

"What is going on with your old newspaper?" Dean asked, a huge grin on his face. "Ronald Reagan? Really? You must be *so* embarrassed."

At lunch that day, once Dean had stopped ribbing me about the editorial, we talked more seriously about the state of the country. "Why don't you run against Jesse Helms," I urged—meaning it. "I'd take a leave of absence from my job to come and work for you." I meant that too.

He shook his head. "I'm too liberal to get elected in this state," he said. "Much too liberal."

Twelve years later, I was again in North Carolina on Election Day. This time my lunch with Dean was much more upbeat since we both knew Bill Clinton was going to be reelected. Later that day, I went to practice at Duke and told Krzyzewski how pleased Dean and I were that Clinton was going to win that night.

"Oh yeah," Krzyzewski said. "I forgot. You two liberal left-wingers deserve one another."

I thought about all those things on the drive home from the Wooden dinner: the battles between Mike and Dean; the low moments during Krzyzewski's early days that I'd witnessed first-hand. I remembered looking across the court at him during an awful 40–36 loss to Maryland at home in 1982 and, as he caught my eye, seeing him shake his head in disgust.

"If I'd have been you," he said to me after the game, "I'd have left at halftime."

"I had to work," I said. "I had to stay."

"Me too," he answered. "I still thought about leaving."

I watched in amazement as Krzyzewski went from a seemingly overmatched young coach to a basketball icon: Coach K to almost everyone, a man who has risen to the pinnacle of his sport and won more championships than almost any other coach in history. To this day, I kid Krzyzewski that he needs me around more since I'm one of the few people who still remembers when his name was Mike.

By the time I turned into my driveway on that September evening in 2013, I knew what my next book would be: the story of these three remarkable men. The fact that two of the four coaches on college basketball's Mount Rushmore and a coach who had and has a unique place in basketball history were competing with one another and living alongside one another for an entire decade is an amazing story. The fact that I was there to witness that extended moment in time and was lucky enough to get to know all three men made me—I believed—uniquely qualified to write about all three: about their rivalries and their relationships and how they evolved through time.

I couldn't talk to Dean or Jim but, fortunately, I'm a hoarder and I still had most of my tapes and notebooks from that time long ago. Plus, I was fortunate that their wives were both willing to talk to me at length, as well as Valvano's brothers and many of their former players and assistant coaches. Mike was available to talk and did—at length.

The last time we spoke for an extended time, wrapping up some final details, he spoke emotionally—again—about both Jim and Dean. When we finished, he looked at me and said, "The whole thing really is an extraordinary story. I'm glad you made me think about it all over again."

I'm glad too.

Dean, Jim, and Mike. Or, as their loyal followers would call them, Coach Smith, V, and Coach K. They were hardly the Three Musketeers—their most intense duels were against, not alongside, one another.

But in the end, they *did* become comrades—linked together in basketball lore, forever.

1

Sitting in the tower that had been built for him, Mike Krzyzewski had a spectacular view of his kingdom.

It was a late spring day and, from the sixth floor of the corner of Cameron Indoor Stadium that houses the Duke basketball offices, Krzyzewski could look out his window at the patch of the Duke campus that is called Krzyzewskiville. The sign that tells visitors they have arrived in the township named for the coach sat six floors down and about a hundred yards away from Krzyzewski.

If he wanted to, Krzyzewski could close his eyes and picture what Krzyzewskiville looks like in winter, jammed with tents and students, all waiting for the chance to get inside to watch Duke play North Carolina in what is annually one of *the* games on the college basketball schedule.

Or, if he didn't want to use his imagination at that moment, he could turn to one of the photos on the wall of his office that depicted Krzyzewskiville in winter, every inch of it packed with supplicants.

At this moment, however, Krzyzewski wasn't looking out the window and he wasn't gazing at a photo. He was leaning forward in his chair, his voice soft but filled with emotion.

"I miss them," he said quietly. "I miss them both for different reasons and for the same reason. They were completely different people and they were different as coaches too. But competing against them was always the same—really hard. If you beat them, you knew you'd truly done something, because it was never easy. And when they beat you"—he paused to smile for a moment—"which they did often, it made you really, really want to find a way to beat them the next time.

"They both made me better. If I hadn't had to compete against them, I probably wouldn't be where I am today. That's not me trying to say something nice or say the right thing. It's just a fact."

When Krzyzewski talked about where he was, he wasn't talking about his palatial office, the one jammed with trophies and plaques and magazine covers and photos. He wasn't even talking about preparing for his thirty-fifth season as the basketball coach at Duke University. He was talking about being the winningest coach in college basketball history, about the then four national championships and the two Olympic gold medals.

Now he's simply Coach K to almost everyone in the sport of basketball. But once upon a time he was Mike Krzyzewski, the coach who was greeted on March 19, 1980, the morning after he was hired at Duke, by a headline in the student newspaper that said "Krzyzewski: This Is Not a Typo."

No one knew the name. No one knew how to spell the name. And *no one* knew how to pronounce the name. Lefty Driesell, then the coach at Maryland, gave up early. "I just call him Mike," he said. Even Bob Knight, who coached Krzyzewski for four years in college and hired him as an assistant coach when he got out of the army, got the name wrong. Knight called his former point guard "Kre-shefski." Once, when it was pointed out to him that the correct pronunciation was actually "Je-jevski," Knight shook his head and said, "It's not my fault if he pronounces his name wrong."

Back then, during his early years at Duke, Krzyzewski could only wish that his biggest problem was having his name mispronounced. Every single day he found himself competing against an icon and a rock star. The icon was Dean Smith, who had already coached the U.S. Olympic team by the time Krzyzewski arrived at Duke and had taken the University of North Carolina to five Final Fours even though he was not yet fifty.

Carmichael Auditorium, where North Carolina played home games, was exactly 10.1 miles from Cameron Indoor Stadium.

That alone made it hard to find room to breathe for a young coach moving into the rarefied air of the Atlantic Coast Conference.

There was also the rock star: Jim Valvano, who arrived to coach at North Carolina State nine days after Krzyzewski was hired at Duke. Krzyzewski and Valvano had coached against each other during the previous five years when Krzyzewski had been the coach at Army and Valvano had been the coach at Iona. Krzyzewski's last Army team had gone 9–17, one of the reasons why his hiring stunned almost everyone at Duke and in the basketball world. Iona had been 29–5 during Valvano's final season there and had been the last team to beat Louisville—which would go on to win the national championship. The Gaels, led by Jeff Ruland, a six-foot-eleven-inch brute of a center, beat the Cardinals in Madison Square Garden—by seventeen points.

Valvano, who had always dreamed of coaching, as he called it, "the 9 o'clock game in the Garden" (the second game of a college doubleheader), had his players cut down the nets after they won the game. Valvano was funny—fall-down funny. At one of his first press conferences after taking the N.C. State job he told a story about his early days at Iona.

"I was at a party," he said. "I'm so excited about my new job that I'm running around the room shaking hands with everyone saying, 'Hi, I'm Jim Valvano, Iona College.' I was on a roll. Finally, this woman looks at me and says, 'Young man, aren't you awfully young to own your own college?'"

That sort of story was only a tiny piece of Valvano's humor. "Never, and I mean never, have I met someone who took over every single room he ever walked into like Jim Valvano," Linnea Smith, Dean's wife, said, smiling at the memory. "He didn't own the room, he *became* the room."

Which might explain why, when Mickie Krzyzewski, the wife of the new Duke coach, heard the news that Valvano had been hired at N.C. State, she rolled her eyes and said, "Oh shit. Here we go again."

Her response had nothing to do with her husband's 1–4 record against Valvano and Iona. It had everything to do with the fact that he owned a college. And every room he walked into.

—

Thirty-four years later, Mike Krzyzewski, like everyone who ever knew him, can't help but laugh when he thinks about Valvano.

"He loved to gig Dean," he said, his eyes a little misty but with a huge smile on his face. "And he could do it in a way that no one else could. He actually made Dean *laugh*—which wasn't easy."

Each spring, the Atlantic Coast Conference holds meetings for everyone associated with the league to discuss ongoing business and its past and future. In the 1980s, there were eight schools in the ACC. On the first morning of the meetings, the basketball coaches would get together.

"Dean was always late," remembered Bobby Cremins, who arrived at Georgia Tech one year after Krzyzewski and Valvano were hired at Duke and N.C. State. "I don't know if it was a seniority thing or a control thing, but he'd always come in a few minutes late.

"One year, as usual, everyone is in the room except Dean. Jim says to Mike and me, 'Come on, we're leaving.' We go into the hallway and Jim finds a bellboy. He gives him twenty bucks and tells him to come find us in the bathroom once Dean walks into the meeting. We go and wait in the bathroom.

"A few minutes later, the bellboy comes in and says, 'Coach Smith'"—Cremins actually says "Smit" with his Bronx accent—"'just walked in.' Mike and I are ready to go, but Jimmy says, 'No, no, wait.' So we wait five more minutes—maybe more than that. Then we walk in and Jimmy says, 'Dean, you're here already? You're early!' Dean just cracked up. Couldn't stop laughing."

Valvano made everyone laugh. Smith made opponents cry. It wasn't just the trips to the Final Four or the parade of great players who showed up in Chapel Hill every year. It was the *way* he won games, his teams often digging holes impossible to crawl out of, then somehow finding a way to do it. Around the ACC, games like that were attributed to the Carolina piss factor: you were winning, you were winning, you were about to win, you *knew* you were going to win, and then something insane—a miracle shot, a ball ticking the bottom of a scoreboard, an impossibly bad call— would happen and you would somehow lose and you went home *pissed.*

Even though he had not yet won a national championship, Smith was an iconic figure in the state of North Carolina. He coached at the school most kids in the state grew up rooting for and wanting to play for and the one that had, by far, the most fans. N.C. State had a lot of fans, but not the way Carolina—as it was called by everyone in the ACC—did. Duke had very few fans. It was a private school and drew most of its student body from out of state.

Most alumni of Carolina and State had grown up in North Carolina, gone to school there, and stayed there after graduation. Duke was just the opposite. Many in the state referred to it as "the University of New Jersey" because there were times when it seemed as if half of the school's six thousand undergraduates came from there.

Valvano got his first lesson about Smith's iconic status early. Soon after arriving in Raleigh, he went to get a haircut. The story Valvano told, which he always swore was completely true, went like this:

Barber: "You the fella who replaced ole Norman Sloan?"

Valvano: "Yes I am. Jim Valvano. Nice to meet you."

Barber (ignoring Valvano's introduction but sighing deeply): "Well, I sure hope you have more luck around here than ole Norman did."

Valvano: "Hang on a second. Didn't Norman Sloan win

the national championship a few years ago? Didn't he go twenty-seven and zero one year and fifty-seven and one for two years?"

Barber (chuckling at Valvano's lack of understanding): "Oh sure, he did that. But just imagine what ole Dean Smith would have done with those teams."

Everyone put Smith on a pedestal so high that he often found it embarrassing. He was, by nature, shy and private. If he had never been interviewed during his thirty-six years as Carolina's coach, he would have been thrilled. When the university trustees came to him in 1985 and told him they were planning to name the new twenty-one-thousand-seat basketball palace that was about to open the "Dean E. Smith Center," he balked.

"You should name it for the players," he said.

That name would have been a bit unwieldy.

"They really had to sit down and explain to him why this was the right thing to do," Linnea Smith said. "He was embarrassed by it."

It didn't take long for both Valvano and Krzyzewski to understand what they had walked into when they had moved south. On an early recruiting visit to the home of a player in California named Mark Acres, Krzyzewski had the sense not long after arriving that this was a player he wasn't going to convince to come to Duke.

Still, he had to go through the ritual of trying to sell his school, his program, and himself to the family. Finally, as the evening was winding down, Krzyzewski turned to Acres's mother, who had said nothing all night, and asked her if she had any questions at all about Duke or the basketball program.

She shook her head. "The only thing that matters," she said, "is that Mark goes to college someplace where he can be close to God."

Krzyzewski figured he had nothing to lose. "Well," he said, "if

Mark comes to Duke, God will be coaching ten miles down the road in Chapel Hill, so you might want to think about it."

Mark Acres went to Oral Roberts. Most people in North Carolina would tell you that he was a *lot* farther from God there than he would have been in Durham.

Jim Valvano died in April 1993. He was forty-seven—eleven months older than Krzyzewski—when he died in Duke Hospital on a beautiful spring morning after fighting cancer for eleven months.

Krzyzewski was in the room when Valvano died. He still shudders slightly at the memory. "The doctors had told us it wouldn't be long," he said. "I still remember Jimmy kind of shaking just a little bit, enough that we noticed. And then he was gone."

Gone, but certainly not forgotten. Valvano lives on in video, in memory, and in legend. Every March, during the NCAA Basketball Tournament, he can be seen again and again sprinting around the court in Albuquerque, New Mexico, seconds after North Carolina State had stunned Houston in the 1983 NCAA championship game.

"I was looking for someone to hug," he said whenever he retold the story. "Dereck [Whittenburg] was my designated hugger. I couldn't find him."

The designated hugger is fifty-six now, nine years older than Valvano was when he died. With the score tied at 52–52 and time about to run out, Whittenburg had thrown a desperation shot in the direction of the basket. It came up well short. But, as it started to drop, six-foot-seven-inch Lorenzo Charles leaped above everyone, clasped the ball in his huge hands, and dunked it as the clock went to zero.

"I will never—*ever*—say that was anything but a pass," the designated hugger said one rainy night, sitting in a Raleigh restaurant named for Valvano, directly under a photo of the coach. "If V was here now, he'd tell you we ran the play just like he drew it up."

The designated hugger laughed at the memory.

On Jim Valvano's tombstone are the words he spoke on March 3, 1993—eight weeks before he died—in a speech that has been replayed millions of times through the years: "Take time everyday to laugh, to think, to cry." Valvano said his father, Rocco, had taught him that. "If you do that," he added, "that's a pretty full day."

Fittingly, twenty-two years after Valvano's death, when those who knew him best talk about him, they always laugh, they always cry, and, somewhere along the way, they think too.

"It's been very difficult for the men who have coached basketball at N.C. State since Jim left," said Pam Valvano Strasser, who was Valvano's childhood sweetheart and his wife for twenty-six years. "Because Jim is still alive to so many people. Those are very big shoes to walk in, especially when it feels as if he's still here."

The same can be said—in an entirely different way—for those who have coached basketball at North Carolina since Dean Smith retired in 1997. Roy Williams, who sits now in Smith's chair—but won't park his car in the ex-coach's parking space outside the building named for him—has won two national championships in twelve seasons. Smith won two in thirty-six seasons. But the thought that his name belongs in the same sentence or paragraph, or even on the same page with Smith's, not only wouldn't cross Williams's mind, it would horrify him.

"Everything I've ever done, any success I've ever had, is because of Coach Smith," Williams said one hot summer day. Williams would sooner cut off his arm than call his mentor anything but Coach Smith.

"He didn't just teach me how to coach basketball, he taught me right from wrong. North Carolina basketball *is* Coach Smith. The rest of us have just followed his lead and his lessons."

Smith died on February 7, 2015, after being disabled for several painful years by dementia. Toward the end, only on occasion did Linnea Smith see glimpses into her husband's mind. "Every so often, when there's some kind of positive reinforcement in some way, he might say something or smile or give us an indication that he understands something," she said. "It's a terminal illness. We all understand that. The hardest thing is that he can't tell me how he feels about what's going on around him. To be honest, it's excruciating."

Smith's long decline and death were most excruciating for those who loved him, but also painful for those who knew him—and competed against him. Krzyzewski had more than his share of shouting matches with Smith through the years. Now, though, after all the enmity between the two men, Krzyzewski understands that, in many ways, he *became* Smith. He became the target, the measuring stick for the younger coaches trying to compete with him. Gary Williams, the retired Maryland coach who—like Krzyzewski and Smith—is in the Naismith Memorial Basketball Hall of Fame, spent years trying to figure out how to beat Krzyzewski more often.

"In the end you realize, it wasn't the referees, it wasn't bad luck or anything else," Williams said. "It's really very simple: he's a great, great basketball coach."

That was the conclusion that Krzyzewski finally reached about Smith—though it took him years to get there.

"Whether we admitted it or not, he set the bar for all of us," Krzyzewski said. "I never looked for a bar, I wanted to just make our program as good as I possibly could. But we all learned from him. He set the standard. When he retired and I became the target, I finally understood what it was like to be him when all of us were trying to beat him—trying, really, to *be* him."

Krzyzewski smiled again, his mind's eye clearly seeing those nights when he dueled with Smith and with Valvano.

"Boy were they good," he said. "No matter how much you prepared, no matter how much you believed in your players, you knew every game was going to be a fight to the finish—whether you won or lost.

"I miss those nights. I miss the battles. I miss the two of them."

Once upon a time, that was not the case.

2

The night of December 5, 1980, was unseasonably warm in Greensboro, North Carolina.

To most sports fans around the country, it was football season. The NFL was entering the final month of the regular season. College football teams were preparing for bowl games.

In the state of North Carolina, though, it was already college basketball season. In a sense, it was always basketball season. That sentiment was perhaps best described by Bill Foster, who coached at Duke for six seasons, between 1974 and 1980.

"If you go to the market and buy steak, there's bound to be a story in the paper the next day saying that recruiting must be going well," he said once. "If you just buy hamburger, the story will be that recruiting's not going so well. There's no letup—ever. It's twelve months a year."

Mickie Krzyzewski thought she understood that. She had been living in North Carolina for more than eight months, and just by reading the newspapers, she understood clearly that the job her husband had taken on the previous March was going to be a lot more pressurized than the one he had held for five years when he was the coach at Army.

Mike Krzyzewski's first season at Duke had begun benignly enough, with easy wins over Stetson and South Florida. Those had been warm-up games, scheduled in order to get some kinks out before the Blue Devils and their new coach faced their first real test, a game in the Greensboro Coliseum against archrival North Carolina.

There was only one place in the country where rivals like Duke and North Carolina might meet so early in the season, and that was in the Atlantic Coast Conference, specifically in North Carolina. Every season, long before conference play began, the four schools known collectively as the Big Four made the trip to Greensboro to play a two-night tournament called, cleverly enough, the Big Four. The event had been created in 1971, largely as a money grab for the four athletic departments. All 15,500 seats in the Coliseum were sold for two nights, and since no one had to travel very far (N.C. State had to travel the longest distance, seventy-eight miles) the costs were minimal and the profits were sizeable.

None of that thrilled the four coaches. It was one thing to play a quality opponent early in the season. It was quite another to play an opponent you would meet twice more during conference play and perhaps again in March, in the ACC Tournament. It was also very much another thing to play a game that brought your fans out in full voice when you were still trying to figure out what kind of team you might have.

"I think the players enjoy it," Dean Smith often said. "I know the fans and the media enjoy it. It's us old coaches who aren't so thrilled about it."

Smith, who would turn fifty the following February, was the oldest and by far the most successful of the four coaches in the building that night. Carl Tacy, whose Wake Forest team would play North Carolina State in the second game of the doubleheader, was forty-seven. The two new kids on the block—Jim Valvano and Mike Krzyzewski—were thirty-four and thirty-three.

Mickie Krzyzewski was accustomed to crowds of perhaps a thousand people coming to watch her husband's team play in the old Army field house. There had been more people than that in the building during the first two games he had coached at Duke, but Cameron Indoor Stadium wasn't close to sold out, and the atmosphere had been somewhat louder than the school library, but hardly intimidating.

Now though, as she walked into the Coliseum with Charles

Huestis, one of Duke's vice presidents, it occurred to Mickie Krzy-zewski that this was different from anything she had seen in the eleven years she and Mike had been married.

"Toto, we're not in Kansas anymore," she murmured to herself as she and Huestis watched fans in red and white, black and gold, dark blue and white, and—the most prevalent—light blue and white walk into the building from the massive parking lots that surrounded it. She noticed all manner of people holding signs that said "Need Two" or "Need Four, Will Take Two."

"They scalp tickets for this thing?" she asked Huestis, almost rhetorically.

Huestis, a quiet, pipe-smoking man who had turned sixty earlier that year, just smiled and guided Mickie through the gate and inside.

They walked through the crowded, loud, smoke-filled hallways in search of the quarter of the building where the seats assigned to Duke fans were located. Mickie found herself taking deeper and deeper breaths with every step they took.

"I just wasn't prepared," she said. "I don't know how you could be. Army had played in some bigger arenas, including Madison Square Garden. But this was different. It was all so . . . intense. I didn't think any basketball game could be that intense—*before it started*—much less a game in December."

She and Huestis walked down the steps to their seats and settled in.

"How do you feel?" Huestis asked.

Mickie Krzyzewski smiled. "I feel," she said, "like a virgin."

—

That feeling didn't last very long.

Duke had a good team, led by senior forwards Gene Banks and Kenny Dennard and junior guard Vince Taylor. North Carolina, as always, had a great team, keyed by future Hall of Famer James Worthy, senior All-American Al Wood, and freshman center Sam Perkins, who would go on to score more than 15,000 points in seventeen NBA seasons.

The game swayed back and forth to the very end. With time running down, Duke trailed 78–76 and had the ball. Banks missed a shot and the ball was deflected out-of-bounds—off a Tar Heel hand. Duke would inbound under the Carolina basket.

Except for one thing: the clock had run to zero during the skirmish for the ball underneath the basket. Krzyzewski instantly charged to the scorer's table, convinced there should be at least one second left on the clock to give his team a final chance to tie the game. There were no tenths of a second on the overhead score-board clock in those days, and there was no video replay available, so it was a very tough case to make.

As he continued to argue with the clock operator and the two referees, Krzyzewski saw Smith walking up to him, hand extended.

"Good game," he said.

Krzyzewski ignored the proffered hand. "The goddamn game's not over yet, Dean," he said.

But it was. The officials, having consulted with the clock operator, waved their arms to indicate the game was over and headed for the locker room. There was nothing left for Krzyzewski to do.

He turned to Smith and put out his hand.

Smith was never one for long postgame handshakes. In fact, before the days when teams started lining up to shake hands, he always ordered his assistant coaches and his players to head directly to the locker room when the buzzer went off—win or lose.

"It wasn't about sportsmanship," he said. "It was about avoiding trouble, especially at the end of a close game. A lot of times when we lost, teams would celebrate at midcourt. Tempers could be hot, and you didn't want anything to happen if someone on one side said something to someone on the other side."

The charge to the locker room was always led by Smith's top assistant, Bill Guthridge. Like Smith, Guthridge was from Kansas and had a quick, dry sense of humor. One night, Guthridge was talking to a reporter prior to a game in Chapel Hill between North Carolina and N.C. State, when someone came up to say that the score of the Duke-Maryland game being played down the road in Durham was 74–68.

"Who's winning?" the reporter asked.

"Who do you think?" Guthridge said. "Seventy-four."

Guthridge led the way to the locker room for one reason: he had the key to the door. Even so, Valvano couldn't help but notice Guthridge whizzing by him whenever North Carolina and N.C. State played each other.

"Just once," Valvano would say with his broad grin, "I'd like to tackle him. Problem is, I think he'd just knock me down and keep going."

While Guthridge was leading everyone in light blue to the safety of the locker room, Smith would stay behind to shake hands with the opposing coach. The handshakes rarely lasted very long.

"Dean was usually a 'Good game' and gone guy," Krzyzewski said. "On that night, I didn't let him do it."

In fact, when he finally turned to shake Smith's hand, Krzyzewski wouldn't let it go. Smith, already more than a little annoyed by Krzyzewski's initial response, said nothing when they finally shook hands and started to pull away. Krzyzewski, a little younger and a little bigger, gripped his hand tightly and pulled Smith a few inches in his direction.

"At least acknowledge that it was a hell of a game, Dean," he said.

Smith didn't feel like acknowledging anything at that moment. "I'm going to remember this," he answered.

"Good," Krzyzewski said pointedly. "I hope you do."

The two men glared briefly at each other before parting.

A few feet away, Roy Williams witnessed the exchange. He was North Carolina's number-three assistant coach and, normally, would have been in the locker room. But, because of the potential issue with the clock, he had walked down behind Smith to deal with any questions—Should there be one second left if the game wasn't over? Two seconds? Where would Duke inbound from? Could Carolina substitute?—that might arise as a result of Krzyzewski's attempt to keep the game alive.

As a result, he saw and heard everything that was said.

Many years later, he remembered the exchange quite vividly.

"My first reaction was being kind of angry," he said. "I didn't like the idea that anyone would talk to Coach Smith like that. I have to say, though, looking at Mike at that moment, the thought went through my mind, 'There's no backdown in this guy.' I didn't like what I was hearing and seeing, but I respected it."

Sitting up in the stands, Steve Vacendak, Duke's associate athletic director, turned to his boss, Athletic Director Tom Butters, at the instant when he saw Krzyzewski refuse Smith's initial attempt at a handshake.

"Tom," he said, "we got the right guy."

—

Vacendak had good reason to want Krzyzewski to be the right guy. He was the one who had first brought his name up to Butters the previous spring.

Bill Foster had completely turned a moribund Duke program around after arriving in 1974. Duke had been one of *the* basketball powers in the country in the 1960s under Vic Bubas, winning four ACC titles and reaching the Final Four three times between 1963 and 1966. Bubas had retired in 1969 and turned the program over to a former assistant, Bucky Waters.

Things had not gone well for Waters. After going 12–14 in his fourth season, he was told his contract—which had one year left on it—would not be extended and that he would be, for all intents and purposes, a lame duck going into the 1973–74 season. That fall, a little more than a month before practice was scheduled to start, Waters accepted a job as a fund-raiser for Duke Hospital.

The basketball team was left without a coach. On October 15, when practice officially began, the Blue Devils still didn't have a coach. In a letter to the editor of the student newspaper, Bob

Fleischer, the team's starting center, publicly wondered exactly what was going on with Duke basketball.

What was going on was complicated. Carl James, the athletic director, was trying to pull off what he thought would be a coup: hiring Adolph Rupp, the legendary Kentucky coach, who had been pushed into retirement eighteen months earlier by the school that he had led to four national championships.

Rupp wanted to come to Duke. He wanted to prove, even at the age of seventy-two, that he could still coach. He told James he would take the job, and a press conference was scheduled for the morning of October 18. Word leaked in the *Durham Morning Herald* that Adolph Rupp was going to be the next Duke coach.

It never happened. The night before he was supposed to be introduced in Durham, Rupp called James. His farm director had died very suddenly. Rupp couldn't leave his farm with no one in charge. Regretfully, he told James he couldn't take the job. That left James with a press conference scheduled for 9:30 the next morning to introduce a new coach and no coach to introduce.

Two hours prior to the press conference, James called Neill McGeachy into his office. McGeachy was Waters's top assistant and had been in charge during the first three days of practice. He offered him the job as interim coach. McGeachy didn't want the interim tag. The two men compromised: there would be no interim tag, but McGeachy's contract would be for one year.

Then, after introducing McGeachy as the future of Duke basketball, James began conducting a nationwide search for a new coach. After Duke had finished with a 10–16 record, the worst in school history, McGeachy was told he would not be asked back to coach. A few weeks later, Foster was hired to replace him.

Foster was forty-three and had been successful both at Rutgers and Utah. In 1967, when the National Invitation Tournament was still a big deal, Rutgers had finished third. The point guard on that team was a kid from Seaford, Long Island, New York, named Jim Valvano. He and his classmate Bobby Lloyd, a sweet-shooting guard, were the heart and soul of a team that ended up going 22–7.

In those days, every NIT game was played in Madison Square Garden, and the Scarlet Knights became the tournament darlings—a team from across the Hudson River in New Jersey that showed up to play with a large chunk of the student body there to cheer them on.

In the semifinals, they played Southern Illinois, then a small-college power. The Salukis, led by a lightning-quick point guard named Walt Frazier, had stunned a Bubas-coached Duke team in the quarterfinals. Against Frazier's Salukis, Valvano, normally Lloyd's feeder, became the scorer, making nine straight shots from the field. By halftime he had twenty-one points.

Valvano's brother Bob, who was ten at the time, remembers running out to get some popcorn at one point and hearing two huge roars. "I knew it was Jimmy," he said. "You could tell. He couldn't miss."

"I was unstoppable," Valvano said years later. "Couldn't miss a shot."

At halftime, Southern Illinois coach Jack Hartman made an adjustment, putting Frazier on Valvano.

"Didn't miss a shot in the second half either," Valvano said. "Didn't *take* a shot, because Frazier wouldn't let me touch the ball."

Frazier went on to be considered perhaps the greatest defensive guard in NBA history. Southern Illinois won the game, 79–70, and Valvano and Lloyd closed out their Rutgers careers by beating Marshall in the third-place game.

Foster had actually returned to the NIT in 1974 with Utah, losing the championship game to Purdue. His up-tempo style attracted James, who needed *something* to compete with North Carolina, which had been to four Final Fours in seven seasons, and North Carolina State, which had just finished ole Norman's 57–1 run by winning the national championship, even *without* ole Dean as the team's coach.

Foster turned Duke around. In his fourth season, led by a junior guard named Jim Spanarkel, a sophomore center named Mike Gminski, and a pair of gifted freshmen forwards, Gene Banks and Kenny Dennard, the Blue Devils won the ACC Tournament and reached the NCAA title game. The joyride ended there in a 94–88 loss to Kentucky, but with only one senior on the team—walk-on guard Bruce Bell—Duke was everyone's preseason number-one pick for the 1978–79 season.

That season, as it turned out, was the beginning of the end for Foster. Just as there was nothing Norman Sloan could do to top ole Dean, Foster found that he was constantly hearing about Smith and North Carolina—even after Duke's 27–7 season that had culminated in the trip to the 1978 championship game.

"He was obsessed with Dean twenty-four hours a day," said Bob Wenzel, who had played for Foster at Rutgers and then worked for him as an assistant coach at Duke. "He honestly believed that the only way to compete with him was to drink as much coffee as he could stand and just keep working and working. I think he honestly believed that Dean didn't sleep and that if he slept he'd be losing ground to him.

"There was definitely an aura about Carolina and about Dean. We all felt it. You couldn't *not* feel it."

"I think Bill felt as if the Duke people didn't appreciate what he'd done," said Lou Goetz, who had also played at Rutgers for Foster and had come with him from Utah to Duke as the number-one assistant. "It wasn't *just* about Dean. It was a general feeling that if we slipped even a little, people were ready to jump on him."

Foster was a man blessed with a quick wit and a self-deprecating sense of humor. When Duke, having lost in the opening round of the ACC Tournament in each of Foster's first three seasons, reached the championship game in his fourth season, Foster noted on the morning before the title game that it was snowing in Greensboro.

"They said it would be a snowy March day in Greensboro

before Foster made the ACC final," he said. "Turns out they were right."

But success didn't bring any real satisfaction to Foster or any sense that he could cut back on the coffee and his work hours. In his last three seasons at Duke, his record was 73–24 and Duke won six NCAA Tournament games and two ACC Tournament titles. During those same three seasons, North Carolina was 67–22, didn't win an NCAA Tournament game, and won one ACC Tournament title.

And yet, in spite of all the wins and the fact that Duke could legitimately look Carolina in the eye on the court—the Blue Devils were 5–6 against the Tar Heels in those three seasons— Foster came to believe that almost no one appreciated what he had accomplished or how good a coach he was.

His standard line when people would go on and on about Smith became, "I guess I don't know my basketball history that well. I always thought it was *Nai*smith who invented the sport, not *Dean* Smith."

It wasn't as if Foster was the only person in the ACC who often found Smith's aura difficult to deal with. Lefty Driesell, who coached at Maryland from 1969 to 1986, was convinced that North Carolina always got the benefit of important officiating calls and that Smith would do just about anything to gain an edge.

One year, when Maryland was playing at North Carolina, Driesell's top assistant, Dave Pritchett, walked into the bathroom at halftime and found Driesell balancing himself on top of a toilet, examining the ceiling above it. When the coaches met to talk strategy in the small visitor's locker room, they would walk into the bathroom in order to give the players some space to relax.

"Coach," Pritchett asked. "What in the world are you doing?"

"Looking for a microphone," Driesell answered. "I'm sure Dean's got this place bugged."

In those days, only two officials worked college basketball games. Once, when Driesell was asked if he favored adding a third official, he vehemently shook his head.

"Absolutely not," he said. "If we go to three officials, when I play Dean it'll be eight against five instead of seven against five."

Although Driesell found competing with Smith frustrating, he did manage to retain a sense of humor about it all. That wasn't true of Norman Sloan, who had won a national championship at North Carolina State in 1974 but, like Foster, believed he didn't get the respect he deserved as a coach *because* of Smith. Sloan was a blunt, feisty, combative man who had a quick, occasionally explosive temper. When the Duke students created a rather profane chant one night in Cameron that made fun of his wife, Sloan was so angry that he threatened to pull his team from the court if the chant didn't stop.

After the game, when someone asked Sloan about the chant, he said, "Everyone knows all the Duke students are drunk all the time; what do you expect?"

Sloan was, of course, wrong. Not *all* the Duke students were drunk all the time. Only *some* of them were drunk all the time.

But most of Sloan's anger seemed to be directed at North Carolina and at Smith. He and Driesell were united in their belief that Smith controlled the officials, controlled the conference, and, in fact, controlled the FBI and the CIA. They talked often, and, likely as not, the subject of their conversation was Smith.

"After a while, I thought the name of the coach at North Carolina was That Goddamn Dean," Driesell said once. "Because every morning Norman would call me and say, 'Do you know what that goddamn Dean just did?'"

Years later, when Smith's health began to slip, one of the most frequent callers to check and see how he was doing was Driesell.

"He calls all the time," Linnea Smith said then. "He asks how Dean is doing and how I'm doing. It's really very sweet and kind of him."

It wasn't that way in the 1970s. Keith Drum, then of the *Durham Morning Herald,* often said, "There's a lot of hate in this league." He was talking about the coaches—not the players. Not long after Valvano succeeded Sloan as the coach at N.C. State,

Driesell called an informal meeting of all the ACC coaches not named Smith during the league's spring meetings in Myrtle Beach.

"Look, fellas, we gotta do something about Dean," Driesell said.

"What do you suggest?" Valvano asked. "Should we have him kidnapped?"

This was in the early 1980s. Smith had just won the national championship on his seventh trip to the Final Four. In truth, kidnapping him might have been the best solution. At that moment in time, nothing else seemed to be working. In fact, Dean Smith was the major reason that Valvano had succeeded Sloan and that Krzyzewski had succeeded Foster in the spring of 1980.

And it had all started with Steve Vacendak.

3

Tom Butters had replaced Carl James as Duke's athletic director in the spring of 1977, a little less than a year before Bill Foster turned the basketball program around.

Butters had been a major-league baseball player, pitching for parts of four seasons for the Pittsburgh Pirates between 1962 and 1965. But a serious neck injury suffered in a spring training car accident cut short his pitching career at the age of twenty-seven. He went to work at Ohio Wesleyan, his alma mater, before being offered a job in Duke's development office in the fall of 1967.

Several months later, Duke's baseball coach, J. M. Bly, died suddenly of a heart attack. Eddie Cameron was the athletic director back then. He called Dick Groat, Duke's most famous baseball alumnus, looking for a recommendation on a new coach. Groat had played with Butters in Pittsburgh and knew he was working at Duke.

"The guy you're looking for is working at Duke right now," Groat told Cameron.

Butters became the baseball coach in the spring of 1968. Two years later, quite by accident, he became the athletic department's chief fund-raiser.

"I was getting morning coffee and Eddie [Cameron] was in the coffee room with a guy named Herschel Caldwell, who ran the athletic department's fund-raising arm, which, at the time, was called Blue Trident," Butters said. "They were discussing the fact that Blue Trident was going to raise twenty-five thousand dollars that year.

"I guess Eddie expected me to congratulate them or tell them how remarkable that was because he said to me, 'Tom, you didn't say anything. What do you think about us raising twenty-five thousand dollars?'

"I said, 'I think it's a goddamn shame that you're happy with twenty-five thousand dollars.' Eddie just gave me a look but didn't say anything. A couple of days later he called me and said, 'The president wants to see you.'"

The president was Terry Sanford, the former governor of North Carolina, who had taken over the school in 1969. During his tenure as governor, Sanford's two biggest priorities had been desegregation and improving the quality of schools in the state. He had created a number of new taxes, labeled by his political opponents as "Terry taxes," in order to have the money to more than double funding for the state's public schools.

Sanford had been a close ally of President John F. Kennedy, so close in fact that Kennedy's personal secretary, Evelyn Lincoln, wrote in her memoir that Kennedy had told her three days prior to his death that he was planning to drop Vice President Lyndon B. Johnson from the ticket in 1964 and replace him with Sanford.

Sanford had come to Duke after being Hubert H. Humphrey's campaign manager in the 1968 presidential election. His goal was simple: change Duke's reputation from being the southern safety school for kids from the North who were turned down by Ivy League schools into that of an important nationally known and respected academic institution.

Sanford knew that would take money, and when he heard that someone in the athletic department had claimed it was "a damn shame" that only $25,000 had been raised in the previous year, he asked to meet with him.

If Butters was nothing else during his years at Duke, he was supremely self-confident. Even so, he was more than a little bit nervous when summoned to see Sanford.

"Do you think you can raise a million dollars in the next two to three years?" Sanford asked him.

"I think I can raise that much in a year," Butters answered. Forty-four years after that conversation Butters still wasn't certain exactly *why* he believed he could raise that kind of money.

"I think it was a combination of two things," Butters said. "Belief in myself and absolute belief in Duke."

Butters left Sanford's office with a new job. One of the first things he decided to do was rename the fund-raising arm so that Duke people would understand this was a brand-new entity, not just a continuation of Blue Trident. Ted Mann, the longtime sports information director, suggested reaching way back into Duke's once-glorious football past. In 1938, the Duke football team had been undefeated, untied, and unscored-upon in the regular season. It had finally lost—7–3 to Southern California—on a touchdown in the final minute of the Rose Bowl.

Mann had been the sports information director back then and had dubbed the team "the Iron Dukes." He suggested to Butters that he use that name for his new department. Butters liked the idea and began raising money at a rate that even he found surprising. By the time Carl James left Duke in the spring of 1977, Butters was his number-two man and was named to replace him.

Three years later, even with the basketball team again ranked number-one early in the season, things weren't looking so rosy for Butters. He had fired football coach Mike McGee, an alumnus who had been a star on Duke's last great team, at the end of the 1978 season and replaced him with Shirley "Red" Wilson, a mala-propping good ole boy who'd had success down the road at what was then Elon College.

Wilson said things like, "We're all simonizing our watches for kickoff on Saturday," and once said that the excitement prior to a Duke–North Carolina game was "reaching a Dascenzo." Frank Dascenzo was the sports editor of *The Durham Sun* and was no doubt flattered to be mentioned.

When Wilson was hired, Tom Mickle, who was then Duke's SID, came up with a new slogan for Duke football: "Red Means Go!" The slogan appeared on bumper stickers across the state throughout the fall of 1979. Duke went 2–9 during Wilson's first season, the worst record in the school's long football history. The next year Mickle came up with a new bumper sticker: "Duke Football 1980."

Wilson's failings were not even close to being Butters's biggest problem. While Duke people would have preferred not to be awful in football, the sport that mattered to almost all of them was basketball. Bill Foster had rebuilt the program, and while he may not have been ole Dean, he was by far the most important person in the Duke athletic department.

He was also getting ready to leave.

Foster had made up his mind that there was nothing he could do, short of winning a national championship (maybe), that would earn him the respect he believed he deserved. Jim Carlen, who was both the football coach and the athletic director at South Carolina, was looking for a new basketball coach. Frank McGuire, the man whom Dean Smith had succeeded at North Carolina in 1961, was retiring after sixteen seasons, during which South Carolina had left the ACC to become an independent.

McGuire had been extremely successful at South Carolina. He had won the ACC Tournament title in 1971—South Carolina's last year in the league. The school had decided to bolt from the ACC because the league had a rule in those days requiring that an athlete score at least 800 on the SATs to qualify for a scholarship, and football coach Paul Dietzel believed the rule was hurting his recruiting. McGuire argued against leaving—and lost.

Coaching players he had recruited while South Carolina was still in the ACC, McGuire made the NCAA Tournament the first three years that the Gamecocks played as an independent. But without the ACC, recruiting began to dry up, and by the winter of 1980, McGuire—who was sixty-six—was being pushed toward the door.

Which is where Foster came in. Carlen saw what he had done at Duke and pursued him. Foster liked the attention, but even more than that, he liked the idea of not hearing about Smith on a daily basis from North Carolina fans—not to mention from his own fans.

Foster's belief that Duke was no longer the place for him was cemented—no pun intended—by the fact that it seemed to be taking forever to pave the lot where he and his coaches parked their cars each morning. When he left, the unpaved parking lot became the public symbol of the problems that had led to his departure.

In truth, the rift between him and Butters was much deeper than that by the time Duke finished the regular season 7–7 in the ACC after starting 12–0 prior to conference play. By then, Butters had very much become a Duke man. Terry Sanford had lived up to his promise to change the school's profile nationally, raising millions for the endowment and raiding Ivy League schools for some of their top professors. Butters found it insulting that Foster would even consider leaving Duke for South Carolina.

And so, the week of the ACC Tournament, after a tumultuous meeting with Foster, the two men agreed that Foster would announce his resignation the next week—before the NCAA Tournament began. By the time Duke traveled to Greensboro as the number-six seed in the ACC Tournament, rumors were rife that Foster was leaving.

"We heard it all winter," said Mike Gminski, who was a senior that season and the team's leading scorer. "Obviously, if he left it wasn't going to affect me personally, but I think we all believed that Coach Foster was feeling unbelievable pressure."

Whether it was the rumors that their coach was leaving that fueled them or the embarrassment of a twenty-five-point loss in Chapel Hill in the regular season finale, the Blue Devils became the team they had been early in the year during that weekend in Greensboro. They blew out North Carolina State the first night and did the same to North Carolina in the semifinals. Then they won a dramatic championship game against top-seeded Maryland with the building half empty because a blizzard had hit Greensboro and very few people could get to the Coliseum.

Foster . . . snow . . . the ACC Tournament. Again. Only this snowstorm would be his last hurrah at Duke.

—

While Duke was cutting down the nets on that snowy night, Steve Vacendak was thinking about Mike Krzyzewski.

Vacendak had just returned to his alma mater that week as an associate athletic director. Growing up in Scranton, Pennsylvania, Vacendak was a six-foot-one-inch scoring machine who was recruited by most of the national basketball powers. His decision came down to two schools: Duke and North Carolina.

This was in 1962 and Dean Smith had just finished his first season as the coach at UNC. Vic Bubas was in his third season at Duke and had already had great success. He had taken Duke to the NCAA Tournament for the second time in school history in 1960—reaching the Elite Eight—and his next two teams had gone 22–6 and 20–5.

Even though North Carolina had won the national championship in 1957, Smith had no such résumé. Because of NCAA violations that had occurred while Frank McGuire was the coach, the Tar Heels had been limited to a 17-game schedule in 1961–62 and had gone 8–9.

Even so, Vacendak's final decision on where to go to college wasn't about basketball. "I liked Coach Smith and Coach Bubas," he said. "Dean Smith was one of the most gracious men I've ever met. His attention to detail was amazing. When I visited, he took out a tape measure and measured my arms. I remember he said, 'Your arms are very long for someone your height. You'll get a lot of rebounds for a guard and a lot of loose balls.' I liked that, the attention to detail. I thought that was impressive. He was clearly someone I would enjoy playing for.

"In the end, though, I just felt more comfortable at Duke because it was smaller. It was a very tough decision."

Vacendak had waited until the last possible minute to make up his mind because he was truly torn. He had gone to bed the night before he had to announce where he was going to school still undecided. When he woke up in the morning his gut told him to go to Duke. His high school coach, Jack Gallagher, insisted that he call Smith personally to tell him the news.

"He could not have been nicer about it," Vacendak remembered. "He wished me luck, said he knew I'd chosen a great school and he looked forward to competing against me."

Vacendak played on two ACC championship teams in three years (freshmen were ineligible then) and played in two Final Fours. In 1966, as a senior, he was voted ACC Player of the Year. He played in the ABA for five years before taking a job at Converse in 1971. It was while he was working at Converse that he got a call from Gallagher, his old high school coach.

"Coach Gallagher was friends with Bob Knight," Vacendak said. "He had actually done some scouting for him and had worked and run his summer camps when he was at Army and when he was at Indiana and they stayed in touch. I was living in Annapolis and would go to see Navy play whenever I got the chance. Coach Gallagher said Army was coming down to play, and their coach was a guy named Krzyzewski, who had played for Coach Knight at Army. He suggested I get in touch with him while he was in town."

Vacendak did that, and Krzyzewski invited him to come spend game day with him and his team. Vacendak was blown away by what he saw.

"This was a very young coach; I'm not sure he was even thirty yet," Vacendak said. "But the preparation, the way he connected with his players, was remarkable. There wasn't a single minute when he was talking when all eyes weren't locked on him. I figured some of it was that they were all Army kids, but it clearly went beyond that.

"I thought I knew Navy pretty well, but there was nothing I could have told him or his staff about them that they didn't already know. I remember thinking, 'This guy is going to be a star someday.'"

Vacendak left Converse a couple of years later to get into coaching himself—taking a job at Greensboro College, where he was a one-man staff, taping his players' ankles, planning the travel, doing all the recruiting. He loved it. Which is why, when Butters approached him about coming back to Duke, he was torn.

"I really did like what I was doing," he said. "But it was Duke. It was my school. So, finally, I took it."

One reason Butters wanted Vacendak was that Vacendak wasn't all that eager to take the job. "I've always believed in hiring people who don't necessarily want me to hire them," he said. "I'd rather have someone who ultimately decides he *wants* the job rather than someone who *needs* the job."

Vacendak finished the season at Greensboro and started his new job in time for the ACC Tournament. As Duke was hammering N.C. State on the tournament's first night, Butters turned almost casually to Vacendak and said, "I need to tell you what your first assignment is going to be because you need to get right on it."

Vacendak shrugged. "What is it?"

"I need you to find a new basketball coach."

For a split second Vacendak thought Butters was joking. But there wasn't a hint of a smile on his face. Butters filled Vacendak in on what had been going on. He mentioned one name to him: Jack Hartman, the coach at Kansas State—the same Jack Hartman who had put Walt Frazier on Jim Valvano in the 1967 NIT semifinals, pretty much ending Rutgers's chances of upsetting Southern Illinois.

Hartman had played for the great Henry Iba at Oklahoma State and had taken Iba's defense-first philosophy to heart. He had coached Kansas State to the Elite Eight on three occasions and had gotten the Wildcats to within a whisker of the Final Four in 1975, losing the East Region final to Syracuse in overtime. K-State was about to go to the NCAA Tournament for the fifth time in nine years—an impressive feat in those days when far fewer teams made the tournament.

Butters was impressed. Hartman's only drawback was his age—fifty-four. "Ideally, I want someone for this job who can really coach defense and is young," Butters told Vacendak. "Hartman's not old, but he's not young. I know he can really coach defense."

Vacendak said nothing that night, but he already had a name in mind. On the morning after Duke won the ACC Tournament, Bill Foster announced he was resigning from Duke to take the job at South Carolina, effective whenever Duke played its last NCAA Tournament game.

On Monday morning, Vacendak went to work, compiling a list to present to Butters. When the two men sat down to talk, Vacendak went through five names, all of them familiar to Butters: Hartman—as ordered; Bob Wenzel, who had been Foster's top assistant the previous two seasons after Lou Goetz had become the head coach at Richmond. Wenzel had also played a key role in recruiting the players who had turned the program around. Also on the list was Bob Weltlich, the coach at Mississippi, a Knight disciple who believed in defense first; Tom Davis, another preacher of defense, who was at Boston College; and Paul Webb, who'd had great success at Old Dominion.

Butters knew all the names. Then Vacendak threw out one more. "You said you wanted young," he said. "This guy's young and I've seen him coach. He is hell on wheels when it comes to coaching defense.

"His name's Mike Krzyzewski."

"Who?" Butters asked.

Vacendak repeated the name.

Butters shook his head. "I've never heard of him," he said. "Tell me more."

4

Michael William Krzyzewski was born February 13, 1947—
William and Emily Krzyzewski's second son. He wasn't as big as
his brother, Bill, who was four years older than he was and would
go on to be a Chicago fire captain, but he was a gifted athlete.
From an early age, he played touch football, basketball, and baseball with a group of friends in the schoolyard at Columbus Elementary School on Augusta Boulevard on Chicago's North Side.

William Krzyzewski was an elevator operator. Because there
was still ethnic bias in many areas of Chicago, he used the name
Cross when looking for work. In fact, he had fought in World
War II under the name Cross and would be buried under that
name. Emily Krzyzewski worked as a housekeeper, often at night
at the Chicago Athletic Club, to ensure that there would be
enough money to keep her two boys not only healthy but happy.

Bill was never athletically inclined. "He would have been a
great pulling guard," Mike said. "He was big and strong and he
had great feet. He danced the polka as well as anyone. But when
he walked out the door of our house he turned right and went
to hang out with guys who were into cars and music [Bill played
the saxophone in the school band]. I turned left and went to the
schoolyard to play ball."

The boys who played in the Columbus schoolyard would
later call themselves "the Columbos," and their leader—and
organizer—was Mickey Krzyzewski, which is what they all called
him then and what they all call him now.

"Mickey was always the guy who picked the teams, who
decided what we were going to play and when we were going
to play," said Dennis Mlynski, who has been Krzyzewski's closest

friend since the two met in elementary school at the age of six. "It wasn't necessarily because he was the best player, but because he was a natural leader. If he said we should do something in a certain way, we did."

Krzyzewski was the best basketball player in the group. As a high school freshman, he went out for the football team at Weber High School and made the team—but wasn't on the list of about thirty kids who were given new equipment. That made him angry. "I wasn't the best player, but I was certainly one of the thirty best," he said more than fifty years later, his voice still rising at the memory. "I found out later that a lot of the kids were in CYO programs and they'd been made promises by the coach to get them to go to the school. I was never in a CYO program. So, I got mad and quit."

And he focused solely on basketball. He went from a non-starter on the JV team as a freshman to the starting point guard on the varsity as a sophomore. "It wasn't so much that I grew or anything, it just became what I did, what I worked at," he said. "All day, every day."

By the time he was a senior he was an All-City player and the team's leading scorer. He was recruited by a number of the smaller schools in the Midwest but none of the important D-I schools in the Midwest showed any interest in him.

Then, in June of 1965—his senior year in high school—when he was still undecided about where to go to college, a young coach named Bob Knight came to visit his house. Knight was twenty-four, only three years out of Ohio State, and had just been named the head coach at Army after his boss, Tates Locke, had left to take the job at Miami of Ohio.

Knight had come to Chicago to recruit a player from Loyola Academy. Gene Sullivan, the coach at Loyola, knew that Krzyzewski was still undecided about where to go to college. "The best player in our league played at Weber," he told Knight. "And I don't think he knows where he wants to go to college."

Knight drove to Weber that day and introduced himself to

Krzyzewski's coach, Al Ostrowski. The thought of one of his players going to West Point blew Ostrowski away. He instantly called William and Emily Krzyzewski to tell them that the basketball coach at the United States Military Academy wanted to come to the house to meet them—and their son.

"I remember when he came in, my dad literally couldn't believe this was happening," Krzyzewski said. "Just the thought that West Point might want his son amazed him. Bill hadn't gone to college—he wanted to be an auto mechanic and he got into that and was doing quite well. So any college was going to be a big deal, but West Point? That was beyond belief."

Krzyzewski knew nothing about the school, except that—as Knight explained—he'd be going into the army for four years after graduation if he went there. What he did know was that he had no interest in going into the army when he graduated from college.

"I knew I wanted to coach," Krzyzewski said. "I can't honestly remember not wanting to coach. I knew I wasn't a good enough player to play pro ball, but I did think I could teach and I could lead and it was something I wanted to do. But when Coach Knight came to the house and talked about West Point and having a guaranteed job in the army for four years, my attitude was, 'No f——ing way do I want to be in the army.'"

His parents felt differently. They thought the chance to go to college for free and then serve your country was about as good as it could possibly get for a teenager whose major aptitude seemed to be for playing a game.

"They would talk in the kitchen after dinner every night," Krzyzewski remembered. "They knew I was in the next room listening. They would talk in Polish, but there are no words in Polish for 'stupid' or 'dumb.' I would hear a lot of Polish and then, 'Mike—stupid' or 'Mike—dumb.' It went on like that for a few nights. The message was clear: they couldn't believe they had raised a son so stupid and so dumb that he didn't want to go to a great college and be in the army. Nothing would make them more proud. Where could they have gone wrong?"

Krzyzewski laughed at the memory. "Nowadays, when I hear people say their child has to make up his or her own mind about where to go to college I say, 'No, that's wrong.' If you know things your child doesn't because you're older and smarter, you *owe* it to them to let them know how you feel. If my parents hadn't done that, I have no idea how my life would have turned out—but it wouldn't have been like this.

"I knew exactly what they were doing—but it worked anyway. I finally got angry and I stalked in one night and said, 'Okay, okay, I'll go. If that's what you want, I'll go!' They just looked at me, smiled, and said, 'Good decision.'"

It didn't feel that way when Krzyzewski arrived at West Point for R Day (Reception Day) a few weeks later. For one thing, he got a lot of blank looks when he reported to various places—not because his name was unpronounceable but because he had been a late addition to the incoming class of 1969. By the time Krzyzewski told Knight he wanted to come, it was June and the incoming freshman class was full. Knight went to his boss, Colonel Ray Murphy, who was then the athletic director, looking for help.

"Colonel Murphy knew everything there was to know about West Point," Krzyzewski said. "He knew there was no way to add me to the class, but he also knew that by the end of R Day there would be a number of guys who would take one look at what they were facing and go home. So, he penciled my name in at the bottom of all the lists. When I reported places and gave my name, they couldn't find it alphabetically. Eventually, I figured out what was going on and told them to look at the very bottom of their list. They'd look at me funny but checked my name, and I'd move on."

Like most plebes, Krzyzewski was miserable during the summer of 1965. No one was especially happy to be at West Point. Many were there because Vietnam was ramping up and they figured if they were going to be drafted into the military anyway, they might as well get a free college education and graduate as officers rather than end up as enlisted men. The seniors who would graduate at the end of Krzyzewski's freshman year in June of 1966 would suffer more casualties in Vietnam than any other West Point class.

Somehow, Krzyzewski survived, although he admits he's not sure how he passed the swimming part of his fitness test. "We were supposed to swim the length of the pool with a brick in each hand," Krzyzewski said. "The closest I'd ever come to swimming in my life was when we'd open a fire hydrant during the summer to cool off."

He smiled. "Somewhere at the bottom of that pool are the bricks they gave me. I can tell you for certain they never made it from one end to the other."

Being a cadet was hard. Playing for Knight was harder. Krzyzewski was a three-year starter at point guard on very good teams. Army went to the NIT, which back then was still a big deal, in both his junior and senior seasons. Krzyzewski was the team's captain his senior season even though he never averaged more than eight points a game. He had been the leading scorer in the Chicago Catholic League as a senior, but he was never a scorer in college.

"SOB wouldn't let me shoot," he said, smiling, talking about his college coach. "I *could* shoot the ball. But I couldn't shoot it as well as [fellow guard] Jim Oxley."

During the summer between his junior and senior years, Krzyzewski was on a flight home to Chicago when he met a strikingly pretty dark-haired flight attendant (they were stewardesses back then) named Carol Marsh, whom everyone called Mickey because she had idolized Mickey Mantle growing up outside Washington, D.C. They began dating, and by the time basketball season began, the relationship had become serious.

Mickie—who changed the way she spelled the name once she began using it regularly—showed up one night with a friend when Army was playing at Princeton. The Cadets lost the game in overtime. The next morning, Mickie met Mike at the team hotel for breakfast. The players and coaches were scheduled to take a bus back to West Point a little later that morning. As Mike and Mickie were eating, Knight walked into the restaurant. Seeing his captain enjoying breakfast with his girlfriend only hours after an overtime loss, Knight went ballistic. He told Krzyzewski he was throwing him off the team and that he better figure out a way to get back to West Point because he wasn't welcome on the team bus.

"I had to buy a Greyhound bus ticket to get back to school," Krzyzewski said. "I was really angry. I hadn't done anything wrong. When I got back, I went to see Coach Knight. I told him what he was doing was unfair. I had *not* spent the night with Mickie—I had breakfast with her. I told him he knew how much I cared about the team and about my teammates. I told him I didn't deserve to be treated the way he was treating me."

Knight had no intention of throwing Krzyzewski off the team. Once his captain was finished ranting he told him he was going to give him one more chance to prove himself—as if he hadn't done that for almost four years. Army ended up reaching the semifinals of the NIT that season, upsetting South Carolina in the quarterfinals. South Carolina's best player was All-American guard John Roche. Knight put Krzyzewski on Roche and told him not to switch to another man at any point, regardless of what South Carolina was doing offensively. Krzyzewski held Roche to 11 points and Army won 59–45. The Cadets ended up finishing fourth in the tournament.

After graduation, Krzyzewski went on to play on an All-Army touring team. One of the other players on that team was Fran Dunphy, who had enlisted in the army shortly after graduating from LaSalle. Dunphy would go on to be a hugely successful coach at both Pennsylvania and Temple. Forty-five years later, he still remembered the young Krzyzewski he encountered on that team.

"His knowledge and understanding of the game was on another level from the rest of us," Dunphy said. "I remember thinking, 'This guy won't just be a coach someday, he'll be a great coach.'" Dunphy smiled. "One of the few times I got a call right."

Krzyzewski had married Mickie on the day he graduated from West Point, and they were stationed overseas for two years, although he was never sent to Vietnam. When his five years in the army were over (the minimum time of service had been raised from four years to five during the Vietnam War), Krzyzewski came home, now a father, looking for a job. By then, Knight was at Indiana and had already taken the Hoosiers to a Final Four in 1973, his second season there. Krzyzewski went to meet with Knight about a job as a graduate assistant coach.

"We went to his house," Mickie remembered years later. "I was fascinated by Knight. I wanted to hear everything he had to say to Mike. After a while, though, he wanted to talk to Mike alone, man-to-man. He was the ultimate sexist. He kept dropping hints that Nancy [Knight's wife at the time] should give me a tour of the house or take me outside to see the garden. I kept saying, 'Oh no, I'm fine here, thanks.' Finally, Knight stood up and said, 'Mike and I are going outside. *You* stay here.'

"He and Mike went outside and he said to him, 'Mike, you have everything it takes to be a great basketball coach someday. But I gotta tell you one thing: your wife is a pain in the ass.'"

In spite of that, Krzyzewski got the job. A year later, when Army needed a new coach after going 3–22, Knight recommended his twenty-eight-year-old graduate assistant for the job. Having already coached in a Final Four at Indiana after his stint at West Point, Knight's opinion was taken very seriously by the school's athletic leadership. Krzyzewski got the job.

He turned the program around quickly, winning 11 games his first season and 53 over the next three winters, getting Army back into the NIT. After his fourth season, Krzyzewski was a finalist for the Vanderbilt job, but the school hired Richard Schmidt, who was then an assistant on Terry Holland's staff at Virginia.

"Actually I was hoping he would take Vanderbilt," said Bobby

Dwyer, who had been Krzyzewski's first hire as an assistant coach at Army. "I thought that was a logical step and it was the right time. We'd had success, he'd proven he could coach, and it was a good school academically—the kids we'd be recruiting wouldn't be that different, at least as students, from the ones we'd recruited at Army."

A year later, after going 9–17, Krzyzewski knew the time had come for him to leave—if the right offer came along. "Army's a very hard job for anyone for all the reasons that are obvious," he said. "The academic requirements, the military commitment, what you go through as a cadet—it's a good challenge, especially for a young coach, but it's a challenge. I wanted the chance to coach someplace where a national championship was possible— the way Coach Knight had been able to do it."

By then, Knight had won the 1976 national championship at Indiana—going 32–0 a year after an injury to star forward Scott May had derailed a team that lost in the Elite Eight and finished 31–1.

The chance for Krzyzewski to move up was there in March of 1980: Iowa State was making a coaching change and the school's first choice was Krzyzewski. If not for Steve Vacendak, he might very well have landed there.

—

Vacendak's pitch to Tom Butters after he first brought his name up was simple: Mike Krzyzewski is only thirty-three but he's already a great defensive coach. He played for and coached under Bob Knight, and Butters had always admired Knight's coaching. There was one other thing: unlike any other coach Butters might interview, Krzyzewski would view Duke's academic standards and its recruiting pool as an *escape* from what he had to deal with at Army.

"All the other guys we were bringing in to interview were going to see our admissions standards as a roadblock," Vacendak said. "They were going to feel restricted when they went out to recruit.

Coming from Army, where the academics were equally stringent *and* there was a five-year military commitment when you graduated, Mike was going to feel as if he'd found recruiting Valhalla."

Butters heard Vacendak out and then asked him two questions: "Army?"

Vacendak was ready for that one. "Bob Knight went from Army to Indiana and was in the Final Four in his second year."

The second question was harder: "What was his record this season?"

Vacendak's answer brought Butters up a little short: "He was nine and seventeen. But," he quickly added, "he's seventy-three and fifty-nine in five years and took over after they'd just gone three and twenty-two."

Butters was impressed that Vacendak had done his homework but not sold. "I just had trouble getting the nine and seventeen out of my mind," he said. "We'd been in the Final Four two years earlier and we were about to play in our third straight NCAA Tournament, and I was going to step to a podium and introduce a coach who had been nine and seventeen at Army?"

"You have nothing to lose by talking to him," Vacendak said—still pitching.

Butters looked at his new assistant and laughed. "Just how badly do you want my job?" he asked. "Are you really trying to get me fired by convincing me to hire this guy?"

But he didn't dismiss the idea. He respected Vacendak's understanding of basketball. He decided to find out what Bob Knight thought.

"I'm looking for a basketball coach," Butters said when he reached Knight on the phone. "You have any thoughts?"

Knight had several suggestions—all of them men who had worked under him previously.

"Dave Bliss," he said.

Butters knew Bliss was young (thirty-six) and had enjoyed some success at Oklahoma, although there were rumors that he was about to leave to take the job at SMU.

"Anybody else?" he asked.

"Don DeVoe," Knight said. "Great defensive coach."

Butters knew DeVoe was very good. He had taken Tennessee to back-to-back NCAA Tournaments in his first two seasons there. He wasn't convinced DeVoe would want to leave Tennessee.

Knight brought up Bob Weltlich.

"On the list," Butters said.

"He would be a great hire for you," Knight said.

Butters asked about Jack Hartman. Knight knew him well.

"Terrific coach, but he's not leaving the Midwest," Knight said. "He'll come out there, you'll interview him, you'll like him, and then he'll get a raise and stay at Kansas State."

Butters suspected Knight was right. He waited to see if Knight had any other names he wanted to bring up. He didn't.

"What about Mike Krzyzewski?" Butters asked finally.

Years later, Butters still recalled the next sixty seconds vividly.

"He didn't say a word," Butters said. "There was dead silence. Finally he said, 'Butters, you really like the way I coach, don't you?' I told him I did. He then said, 'Mike Krzyzewski has all of my good qualities and none of my bad.' That stuck with me."

What Butters didn't know was that, at that moment, Knight was pushing Krzyzewski to take the job at Iowa State. Because the Cyclones hadn't made the NCAA Tournament, they were a couple of weeks ahead of Duke in their coaching search and Krzyzewski had already interviewed there.

Butters decided that Vacendak was right: he had nothing to lose by interviewing Krzyzewski. He asked him if he would fly to West Lafayette, Indiana, that Friday. Duke was scheduled to play a second-round NCAA Tournament game there on Saturday. Krzyzewski and Butters met for several hours. When Krzyzewski left, Butters said to Vacendak, "Now I understand what you're talking about."

Vacendak asked Butters what he was going to do next. "I don't know," he said. "I honestly don't know."

Two images kept running through Butters's mind: the smart, intense young man who clearly had a plan and with whom he had spent several hours in his hotel room. That made him smile. The second image wasn't as golden. It was a newspaper headline that said "Butters Hires Army Coach with 9 and 17 Record."

—

Butters finally decided he needed to meet with Krzyzewski again. Duke had beaten Pennsylvania in West Lafayette to advance to the round of sixteen, meaning the Blue Devils would play Kentucky in Lexington—a matchup that had upset Butters so much when the brackets were announced that he had called North Carolina State athletic director Willis Casey, who was a member of the tournament selection committee, to complain about potentially playing Kentucky on its home floor.

Butters asked Krzyzewski if he would fly to Lexington for another meeting. Krzyzewski agreed. Once again the two men met in Butters's hotel room. "The more we talked, the more I liked him," Butters said. "And the more we talked I think Mike became more and more convinced that I wanted to hire him. Or, more specifically, that I *should* hire him."

Krzyzewski was thinking that. By now he was convinced Butters wanted to hire him. What's more, he had put all of his eggs into the Duke basket. He had turned Iowa State down earlier that week, even though Knight had urged him to take it.

"I had called him [Knight] after they made the offer to ask him what he thought," Krzyzewski said. "He said, 'Mike, I think it's time for you to leave Army. I think you need to take this.'

"I understood what he was saying and I thought he was right, that it was time. I knew recruiting at Army wasn't going to get any easier, and this might be my best shot to move up. That's why I'd interviewed for the Vanderbilt job the year before. But the Duke thing was still there in the back of my mind. I knew Weltlich was also interviewing, and I thought that Coach [Knight] might see him as being ahead of me in the pecking order. He was a little older than me [thirty-five], had coached longer because he hadn't spent five years in the army, and was already coaching [at Mississippi] in the SEC."

Krzyzewski decided to ask Colonel Tom Rogers what he thought. He had known Rogers since he had arrived on campus as a cadet in 1965. Rogers had been Knight's OR—officer representative—at the time. Each varsity team at West Point has an OR, an army officer who acts as a liaison between the team and the university. An OR does everything from helping cadets pick classes or find tutors to counseling them when they get into trouble. They often become close to the head coach because their role is so important.

Rogers had become Krzyzewski's OR when Krzyzewski became the coach at Army in 1975. Krzyzewski's father had died suddenly in 1968, during Krzyzewski's junior year, and Knight and Rogers had been the two men he had looked to most for guidance and advice since that time. Krzyzewski told Rogers what Knight had said.

"Iowa State's a good job," Rogers said. "But there will be another job like it out there for you again, if not this year, then next. I think Duke's pretty special. I think you need to ride the Duke thing out to the end."

Krzyzewski's gut told him Rogers was right. He knew Iowa State would be a step up—a good job in a major conference. But he *wanted* the Duke job and he believed he was ready for it. So, he turned Iowa State down and went to meet with Butters for a second time.

As the two men talked back and forth, Krzyzewski began to get frustrated. Butters was repeating questions and Krzyzewski was repeating answers.

"Mr. Butters," he finally said. "What's the problem here? What's the holdup?"

Butters paused and then looked him in the eye. "The problem is you're thirty-three, you're not ready, *and* you were nine and seventeen at Army. How can I hire you?"

Krzyzewski let that sink in. Then he said, "Oh, I'm sorry, I didn't realize you were running scared."

"I should have thrown him out of the room right there," Butters said. "I didn't, because part of me realized he was right."

The two men talked for three hours, and when they shook hands, Butters said he'd be in touch. Duke had managed to beat Kentucky, 55–54, the previous night to reach the Elite Eight. Tired and drained, the Blue Devils ran out of gas on Saturday afternoon and lost to Purdue, 68–60. That loss ended the Bill Foster era.

It was time for Butters to name a new coach.

—

Three days later, on the morning of March 18, Butters went through the formality of parading each of the candidates before Duke's Athletics Council. Technically, Butters needed the council's approval to hire a new coach, but the members were there in almost all cases to rubber-stamp the athletic director's decisions.

"They said, 'You've brought us five good candidates; we'll be satisfied with whatever choice you make,'" Butters said.

That morning, the *Durham Morning Herald* had confidently reported that, while the name of Duke's new basketball coach wasn't known yet, there was no doubt that his last name began with the letter W. The new coach, according to the *Herald,* would be Weltlich, Webb, or Wenzel. The paper didn't mention Tom Davis or Mike Krzyzewski.

After meeting with the council, Butters went to see Chuck Huestis, who was the most athletically inclined of the three-man troika whom President Terry Sanford leaned on to help him run the university. The others were Ken Pye, the school's chancellor, and William Griffith, the vice president for student affairs. Vacendak was also there, and the three men talked about making a final decision.

"I think I'd like to talk to Krzyzewski one more time," Butters said.

"What else can you possibly ask him?" Vacendak said.

"I have no idea," Butters answered. "But ask him if he'll come see me in my office before he goes to the airport."

Krzyzewski brought his wife, Mickie, with him to meet the council members. As instructed, Vacendak escorted them to Butters's office. There were more questions and answers and still no resolution. Vacendak was going to drive the Krzyzewskis to the airport. Before he left, he went in to see his boss one more time.

"Well?" he asked.

"I think he's the best young coach in the country," Butters said. "He's going to be a star . . . someday. I just can't hire him right now."

Vacendak left Butters with one last thought before leaving: "If he's the best young coach in the country, how can you *not* hire him?"

Discouraged, he drove Mike and Mickie to the airport. He and Mike put Mickie on her plane to Washington. She was going there to pick up the two Krzyzewski daughters, who were staying with Mickie's parents. Mike's plane, back to New York, was a little later. Vacendak shook Krzyzewski's hand—apologetically—and began walking in the direction of the airport parking lot. He was almost at the door when he heard himself being paged.

Surprised, he found a phone. It was Butters.

"Bring him back," Butters ordered.

"What?"

"Bring him back; I need to talk to him one more time."

"Tom, you can't do this to the guy. I mean . . ."

"I'm going to offer him the job! Bring him back. But don't tell him why."

Vacendak hung up and looked at his watch. The flight was boarding. There was no time to get back to the gate. He called the airport operator and asked her to page Krzyzewski and tell him *not* to get on the Eastern Air Lines flight that was about to leave for LaGuardia Airport.

Vacendak then sprinted back to the gate and found Krzyzewski waiting for him. "He wasn't pleased," Vacendak said. "He wanted to know what the hell was going on.

"I told him Tom needed to talk to him one more time."

Krzyzewski's response was blunt: "What the f—— can he ask me that I haven't already answered?"

Vacendak knew the answer but kept his word to Butters not to say anything. They drove back to Durham—steam coming out of Krzyzewski's ears. He practically stormed back into Butters's office.

"All I could think was, what now?" he said, laughing at the memory.

Butters was standing behind his desk when Krzyzewski walked in.

"I need to ask you one more question," he said.

"*What* could you possibly have left to ask me?" Krzyzewski said. "You've interviewed me *three* times."

"I know," Butters answered. "But there's one question I haven't asked you. Will you take the job?"

Krzyzewski was stunned for a moment. Then he said, "Of course I'll take the job."

"Don't you want to know what I'm going to pay you?" Butters asked.

Krzyzewski shrugged. "I'm sure you'll be fair," he said.

Years later, he added, "And he wasn't."

Butters offered Krzyzewski a five-year contract for $40,000 a year. There were no agents for coaches back then. Krzyzewski accepted. Twenty-four years later, when the Los Angeles Lakers offered him $40 million to coach their team for five years, Krzyzewski called Butters to ask him what he thought.

"I think you should send me a ten percent finder's fee," Butters said.

"Fine," Krzyzewski said. "If I take the job, I'll send you four thousand dollars."

Within an hour of Krzyzewski accepting the $40,000-a-year offer, Duke had called a press conference to announce his hiring.

If Butters had walked in and introduced John Wooden or Dean Smith as Duke's new coach, the assembled media would not have been any more shocked. They would have been a lot more impressed, but not any more shocked.

"The press conference began at 8:45 P.M.," wrote columnist Frank Vehorn in the *Greensboro Daily News*. "It was a shame it was a Tuesday and not a Monday. Had it been Monday, the press conference would have been held at the exact same time as the TV show 'That's Incredible.' Those two words best described Tom Butters' decision."

Vehorn's sentiments were echoed around the state. Duke's press release introduced "Duke's new Special K." It talked about the fact that Krzyzewski had played for Knight at Army, about how he had "transformed" Army's program in his first two years, and went through his postgraduate coaching record while in the army and his one season under Knight at Indiana.

There was no mention of 9–17.

"Duke was supposed to hire a name coach," another columnist wrote. "Well, it certainly did that—except it wasn't exactly the kind of 'name' Duke fans were expecting."

Butters knew all of that was coming. "I was absolutely convinced that I had made the right choice," he said. "At that moment, though, there were probably three people in the world who agreed with me: Steve, Mike, and Mickie."

—

Mickie Krzyzewski had landed at National Airport that evening shortly before dinnertime and gone to her parents' house to pick up her daughters. Debbie was ten and Lindy was four. Not long after dinner, she began to wonder why she hadn't heard from her husband. His plane had been scheduled to arrive at LaGuardia about an hour after she had gotten to Washington. Normally he would have called before leaving the airport to let her know he'd landed.

Maybe, she thought, he was preoccupied with everything that

had happened at Duke and had gone straight to the car for the one-hour drive back to West Point. That would be unusual for him, but it had been an unusual—and frustrating—day.

By nine o'clock she was starting to get a little bit concerned. She called their house—no answer. Now worried, she called Eastern Air Lines. Had the plane been delayed, canceled—or worse? Nope. The plane had landed right on time.

"Where the hell," Mickie Krzyzewski thought, "is my husband?"

She tried calling his assistant coaches, Bobby Dwyer and Chuck Swenson. They hadn't heard from him. She called Colonel Rogers—nothing.

Finally, just as she was about to become hysterical, the phone rang. It was getting close to midnight. As soon as she heard Mike's voice, Mickie let out a huge sigh of relief and then said, "Where the hell have you been all night?"

"I'm at Duke," he said. "Butters asked me to come back because he had one more question."

Mickie's reaction was exactly the same as Mike's had been several hours earlier: *"One more question? What the hell could he possibly still have to ask you?"*

She was still ranting when Mike broke in. "He asked me if I wanted the job."

Mickie was stunned. "Did you take it?"

Mike was laughing. "Yes, I took it," he said. "That's why I've been so tied up. I'm sorry if you were worried."

Mickie laughed.

"I wasn't worried," she said. "I was hysterical."

Then another thought crossed her mind.

"How much are you getting paid?"

"Forty thousand dollars," he said, and then quickly added, "for five years."

Mickie Krzyzewski sighed. She had known this day would come. She had wished for this day to come because she knew how much Mike wanted it to come.

At that moment, she was a little nervous, a little frenetic thinking about moving her family from West Point to North Carolina, and still a little bit mad at Mike for not calling sooner. She was also thrilled.

"It all worked out in the end," she said years later.

Little did she know that it was just beginning.

5

Twenty-five miles to the east, Willis Casey, Butters's counterpart at North Carolina State, hadn't started the process of looking for a new coach as quickly as Butters had, in large part because he was involved with the NCAA Tournament as a member of the basketball selection committee.

In fact, when Butters had called to complain about Duke drawing Kentucky *at* Kentucky in a potential round-of-sixteen game, Casey had gone right back at him, pointing out that Duke hadn't even been a lock pick to *make* the field before it had won the ACC Tournament.

Casey was not a man who backed down from confrontation. He had come to N.C. State as the swimming coach—the aquatics center at the school now bears his name—and had become the athletic director in 1969. On the day he retired in 1986, Casey told the student newspaper, the *Technician,* that he was a lot different from his image.

"The picture most people have of me is that I'm a mean son-of-a-gun," he said. "But underneath it, I'm really just a teddy bear."

That description would have surprised most who had worked with him or known him during his years at N.C. State. In fact, many people believed that the departure of basketball coach Norman Sloan was brought about by two men: Casey and Dean Smith.

Casey and Sloan both had in-your-face personalities and often clashed, even though Sloan was wildly successful during his fourteen years as the school's basketball coach. He had been hired in the spring of 1966 after coaching at Florida for six seasons. Sloan had grown up in Indiana and was one of six players from the state recruited by the legendary Everett Case to go to school at N.C. State. Case, who had been a high school coach in Indiana, had gone back to his roots to recruit after getting the job at State in 1946. One of Sloan's teammates in college was Vic Bubas, who would go on to be Duke's first great coach in the 1960s.

Sloan had won a national championship in 1974, going 30–1 with a team led by David Thompson. In 1971, State won a massive recruiting war for Thompson, who was from a small town outside Charlotte and was thought to be one of the best high school players anyone had ever seen.

Thompson was so good that both N.C. State and Duke landed on probation during his recruitment. It didn't really matter at Duke, because the Blue Devils had no chance to make the NCAA Tournament during the season they were ineligible. It did matter at N.C. State. During Thompson's sophomore season, the Wolfpack was 27–0 but not eligible to take part in postseason play.

A year later, when Thompson was a junior, the Wolfpack's only loss came in December, against seven-time defending national champion UCLA. The two teams met again in the Final Four—which was in Greensboro—and State won in double overtime. One of college basketball's most famous photos came out of that game, the six-foot-four-inch Thompson leaping to block six-foot-eleven-inch Bill Walton's attempt at a layup during the first overtime. Two nights later, N.C. State beat Marquette to win the national title.

Even after winning the national championship Sloan felt haunted by the specter of Dean Smith—in spite of the fact that he had accomplished the one feat that had eluded Smith. It was Smith, not Sloan, who was selected to coach the 1976 Olympic team, and there were the inevitable whispers among in-state fans and the very much pro-UNC media that the only reason Sloan had won the title was because he had cheated to get Thompson. Sloan didn't hear much of that from Duke supporters for two reasons: there weren't very many of them living in the state, and they were aware of the fact that their basketball program had also been punished by the NCAA during Thompson's recruitment.

Sloan's nickname was Stormin' Norman, in part because of his animated bench behavior but at least as much because of his personality. If Sloan didn't like a question asked by a media member he would instantly let the reporter know what he thought of it—and him.

"What the hell kind of question is that?" he would often demand. And, if he didn't know the offending reporter, he would frequently ask, "Who do you work for?" or "Where exactly are you from?" He saw pro-Carolina/anti-State people lurking behind every camera, notebook, and tape recorder. A lot of the time he was right.

By the late 1970s, the animosity between Sloan and Smith was palpable. Sloan wasn't, by any means, the only ACC coach who had issues with Smith. Sloan and Lefty Driesell were openly hostile at times; others were quieter. Legend has it that Terry Holland, the coach at Virginia, named a dog Dean Smith because, he told friends, "the dog whined all night."

Holland and his wife, Ann, are vehement that the dog was named by their daughter in honor of a friend named Dean who lived down the street. "That's true," Holland said with a smile. "And when the stories started that I'd named it after Dean Smith I told people that wasn't the case." He paused. "I guess I did point out that the dog *had* whined all night when we first got her."

Carl Tacy, the coach at Wake Forest, was the quietest person among the league's seven coaches, but he very much sided with the other coaches when it came to Smith.

All of them talked about how manipulative Smith could be, how he was the master of the subtle shot—at an opponent, at an official, at someone in the media. That wasn't what really frustrated them, though. What frustrated them was far simpler than that: "He was just *so* good," said Bob Wenzel, one of Bill Foster's assistants in those days. "He was the gold standard. Bill Foster was a great coach. So were Norm and Terry and Lefty and Carl Tacy too—look at some of the teams each of them had. But all of them felt like they were chasing Dean, and no matter how successful they were, it was never going to be enough to catch Dean. He had an aura and we all felt it."

That aura, as much as anything, was the reason both Foster and Sloan were willing to listen when non-ACC schools began to recruit them in the winter of 1980. There were two great basketball leagues in those days: the ACC and the Big Ten. The Pacific-8 had UCLA but little else and the SEC was Kentucky and everyone else, although Tennessee had made some inroads when Coach Ray Mears recruited Bernard King and Ernie Grunfeld out of New York City. There was no Big East, and the Big Eight only occasionally popped up on anyone's radar, most often when Kansas had a good team. Many of the top programs were independents— Marquette under Al McGuire, Notre Dame under Digger Phelps, DePaul under Ray Meyer.

Thus it was virtually unheard-of for a coach to voluntarily bolt from the ACC.

"The only way anyone left the league in those days was if they got fired," Krzyzewski said.

The ACC—like Dean Smith—was the gold standard.

—

In the winter of 1980, Sloan had a very good team. Hawkeye Whitney was a senior, a first-team All-ACC player, and Sloan and his staff had recruited three outstanding freshmen: Sidney Lowe and Dereck Whittenburg, who had played together at DeMatha High School outside Washington, D.C., and Thurl Bailey, a graceful six-eleven big man who had played a few miles down the road from Lowe and Whittenburg at Bladensburg High School.

"Honestly, we thought we had it in us to make a deep run in the [NCAA] tournament," Whittenburg said. "We finished tied for second in the ACC in a year when the league was very deep. We thought we could play with anybody."

The ACC *was* deep that year. Maryland, led by Albert King and Buck Williams, won the regular season title. North Carolina and N.C. State tied for second, and Clemson, which would go on to reach the Elite Eight of the NCAA Tournament, had finished fourth. Duke and Virginia—led by freshman Ralph Sampson—had finished tied for fifth. All of those teams, with the exception of Virginia, were invited to play in the NCAA Tournament. Virginia was relegated to the NIT—which it won.

State had finished 20–6 during the regular season. But before the ACC Tournament began, the players heard that their coach was leaving. Sloan had accepted the job at Florida.

"It caught us completely off guard," Whittenburg said. "Sidney, Thurl, and I were freshmen. All of a sudden we had no idea who we were going to be playing for the rest of our college careers."

Lowe knew exactly whom he wanted to play for the rest of his college career: Sloan.

"The main reason I went to N.C. State was Coach Sloan," he said. "Growing up I remember watching his great teams with [David] Thompson, [Monte] Towe, and [Tom] Burleson. Coach Sloan always wore those loud plaid jackets and I liked that—never forgot it. When I met him, I liked him right away. I just liked his directness.

"When I heard he was leaving, I decided I was going with him. I went to his office and told him I was going with him. I remember I was crying. He looked at me and said, 'Sidney, you're going to be a great college player. I'd love to have you at Florida. But I recruited you to play at N.C. State. You stay here—you'll be fine.'"

Lowe wasn't so sure, but he decided to trust Sloan. "If you think about it, what he did was pretty selfless," he said. "I would have gone in a heartbeat. But, even though he was leaving, he still loved N.C. State and honestly thought it was the best place for me to be."

As Lowe retold the story, he smiled, knowing there weren't a lot of people in basketball who viewed Norman Sloan as kind, gentle, or selfless. "I get that," he said. "He was certainly an in-your-face kind of guy. I always liked that about him."

Duke and N.C. State, the two teams with lame-duck coaches, met in the first round. In those days, the ACC Tournament began on Thursday and culminated on Saturday night. The difference between State and Duke going into that first evening was that the Duke players didn't know for certain yet—though they had heard the rumblings—that Foster was leaving. The other difference was that the Blue Devils had gone from a 12–0 start to a 19–8 regular season finish and felt they had a lot to prove.

"We really didn't know what exactly was going on with Coach Foster," said Mike Gminski, who went on to play fourteen years in the NBA. "He was clearly uptight and we weren't playing very well. We all knew *something* was up, especially because it seemed like the parking lot thing kept coming up."

The "parking lot thing" had become symbolic of the rift between Butters and Foster. Years after Foster had left Duke, when his name came up, people who weren't even around in 1980 would say, "Oh yeah, he left because of the parking lot thing."

N.C. State's players knew their coach was leaving; Duke's players had no idea what their coach was going to do. On the court uncertainty prevailed, Duke winning easily 75–62. In spite of the loss, the Wolfpack received a number-four seed into the East Regionals when the NCAA announced its forty-eight-team tournament field that Sunday. Since the first four seeds in each region received first-round byes, State traveled back to Greensboro—the scene of the school's greatest basketball moment six years earlier—to play a second-round game against Iowa, which had won a first-round game against Virginia Commonwealth.

State was no more competitive against Iowa—which would go on to the Final Four—than it had been against Duke, losing 77–64. Just like that, the Norman Sloan era at N.C. State was over. And, with Willis Casey on the road the next two weeks as a basketball committee member, there was no telling when a new coach would be named—or who it would be.

Casey *did* have an idea who he wanted his new coach to be, even though he couldn't start formally interviewing people right away. The man Casey wanted had been born in Durham but was a Maryland graduate who had spent his adult life in the Washington, D.C., area: Morgan Wootten.

Wootten was generally viewed as the best high school basketball coach in the country and was already a legendary figure at DeMatha High School, where he had coached since 1956. He was not yet fifty and had never coached in college but had coached plenty of future college players, including Whittenburg and Lowe.

"We thought it would be great," Whittenburg said. "Playing for Morgan again? We would have loved that."

"When we heard it might be Coach Wootten, I think Dereck and I were relieved," Lowe said. "We both thought, 'If Coach comes, everything will be all right.' But as time went by and he didn't take the job, we began to wonder what was going on."

Wootten was torn. Part of him wanted to give the college game a shot. He had conquered every world there was to conquer at the high school level. In 1965, he had been part of the biggest upset in high school basketball history when DeMatha had ended Power Memorial Academy's 71-game winning streak. Power Memorial was led by seven-foot-one-inch center Lew Alcindor (who was actually closer to seven foot four) and had beaten DeMatha in a close game the previous season.

Prior to the 1965 game, Wootten had his six-foot-eight-inch center, Sid Catlett, play defense in practice holding a tennis racquet over his head so his players would get a sense of what it would be like to shoot over Alcindor—who changed his name to Kareem Abdul-Jabbar in 1971. DeMatha slowed the game down and won, 46–43. To this day, DeMatha's win is still considered the most stunning upset in the history of high school basketball. Given that Alcindor's high school and college basketball teams were a combined 167–4, that's probably not a stretch.

Wootten was tempted by Casey's offer. Even though the coach ran an extremely successful summer basketball camp, Casey was offering him a huge raise: $800,000 over five years. In those days that was very big money. Wootten's son Joe, who followed in his father's footsteps and is now the coach at Bishop O'Connell High School in Arlington, Virginia, was eight at the time. He remembers seeing a headline in *The Washington Post* with the number $800,000 and asking his father if taking the job at N.C. State would mean the family could afford a swimming pool.

"Probably," his dad answered.

"Take it," the eight-year-old boy said.

After deliberating for more than a week, Wootten finally told Casey no. He didn't want to uproot his family, he still enjoyed teaching—he taught history in addition to his coaching responsibilities—and there was really only one job that would be impossible for him to say no to: Maryland.

"It was my school, I wouldn't have to move my family, and I'd have loved that challenge," he said. "But I didn't think Lefty [Driesell] was going anywhere, and we were the same age."

Remarkably, Dean Smith (February 28), Wootten (April 21), and Driesell (December 25) were all born in 1931. Driesell's birthday allowed *The Washington Post*'s superb columnist Ken Denlinger to refer to him once as "God's unique Christmas present to the world in 1931."

Once Wootten said no, Casey was back to square one in his search. Except for a letter that Tom Butters had sent him. As he had suspected—and hoped—Butters had found that the Duke basketball coaching job was coveted by many coaches, especially up-and-coming younger coaches.

One day, Steve Vacendak had walked into Butters's office with a letter that had been sent to Butters but was redirected to him since he was the first stop for any correspondence related to the basketball coaching search.

"I'd gotten a lot of mail," Vacendak said. "I read it all even though we had narrowed the search pretty quickly and I was convinced that Mike [Krzyzewski] was the right choice. But this letter jumped out at me. It was so full of passion, so eloquent, and so different from all the others that I couldn't just toss it on the pile. I thought I had to show it to Tom."

The letter was from Jim Valvano.

Butters was equally impressed. He knew who Valvano was and he knew he had done remarkable work at Iona. But Butters wasn't certain that Valvano's style would fit at Duke, and that spring there had been questions raised (well founded, as it turned out) about whether Jeff Ruland, Valvano's star center, had taken money from an agent. Whether Valvano was culpable or not, Butters wasn't going to hire him.

Still, it was clear to Butters that Valvano was going to be a big-time coach somewhere, sometime. So he forwarded the letter to Willis Casey. Apparently Casey was also impressed because he contacted Valvano right away to see if the State job was of interest to him.

It was.

—

James Thomas Valvano was the second of three sons born to Rocco and Angelina Valvano. He was born on March 10, 1946—three years after Nick and eleven years before Bobby. He was, in many ways, a classic second child: always searching for attention.

"When he was about six, kids in school started giving him a hard time about having a big nose, you know the way kids do," Nick said. "Jim started doing an imitation of Jimmy Durante, who always joked about having a big nose. He was so good at it that the nuns who ran the school began taking him from classroom to classroom to do the bit." Nick Valvano smiled. "I guess you could say they were Jimmy's first comic enablers."

Jim was always the funniest kid in school, but he was also an outstanding athlete, even though he was small for his age until his junior year in high school, when he finally hit a growth spurt. "It didn't matter that he was small," Nick said. "He could play anything. In fact, his best sport might have been baseball."

By the time he hit that growth spurt, Jim was already a three-sport standout at Seaford High School. His dad, who was always his hero, was a high school basketball coach, so sports played a big role in the lives of all the Valvano boys right from the start. Nick went to Rider, where he played basketball and baseball. Jim played basketball at Rutgers, and Bob played basketball at Virginia Wesleyan.

Jim actually went to Rutgers without a scholarship: Bill Foster told him he would almost certainly play on the varsity as a sophomore—freshmen couldn't play varsity sports in those days—but that he couldn't offer him a scholarship. When the guard Foster had recruited ahead of Valvano flunked out of school, Valvano became the point guard on the freshman team. A year later, he and Bob Lloyd were the starters in what would become one of the country's best backcourts.

"It wasn't as if the game came easily to Jim, it really didn't," said Lou Goetz, a teammate, who would go on to be Foster's top assistant at Duke. "He couldn't dribble with his left hand at all. He'd come downcourt, all right hand, the other team knew he was all right hand, and he'd still figure out a way to get the job done and get the ball where it needed to go—which usually meant getting it to Bob."

In 1967, when Valvano and Lloyd were seniors, Lloyd averaged twenty-nine points a game and was a first-team All-American. There were seven consensus first-team All-Americans that season: Lew Alcindor, Elvin Hayes, Wes Unseld, Bob Verga, Clem Haskins, Jimmy Walker, and Lloyd. The first three are in the Basketball Hall of Fame. The first six played for national powers. Lloyd played for Rutgers, which had never appeared in *any* postseason tournament prior to that season.

Lloyd was the star, Valvano was his enabler, and they led Rutgers to the best season in school history.

Valvano majored in English at Rutgers. He wanted to follow

his dad into coaching, and he suspected that would mean being a teacher while he coached at the high school level. He also had a love of reading and an extraordinary memory that allowed him to quote lengthy passages from books he had read years earlier.

"As much as he loved basketball and coaching basketball, he never wanted to think of himself as *just* a basketball coach," Pam Valvano Strasser said. "I think as he got older that became a problem. He believed he could—and should—do more than just coach basketball."

Valvano met Pam Levine when the two were in eighth grade, but they didn't date until the junior prom three years later. Pam had a boyfriend, but he had gone off to college. When Jim asked her to go to the prom she said yes. "I figured it would just be one time," she said. "None of our parents were exactly thrilled but I liked him. He was funny."

Rocco Valvano didn't love the idea of his son dating a Jewish girl. Pam's parents didn't think an Italian Catholic was ideal either. The first date didn't go all that well. Pam picked a restaurant for their preprom dinner that was more expensive than she—or Jim—expected it to be.

"I had to call my dad to bring some money to the restaurant," she said. "Jim didn't have enough to pay the check."

Things got better after that. Pam's boyfriend came home from college to find that she had a new boyfriend. "He didn't take it very well," Pam said. "For a long time he kept insisting that he could make me happy if I gave him a chance. He hadn't done anything wrong, I just liked Jim more. Actually, I *liked* him. I *loved* Jim."

They dated the entire time Jim was at Rutgers. Pam worked in the city, Jim went to college across the river in New Jersey, and they spent their free time together. Jim worked summers to make enough money to buy Pam a respectable engagement ring. Shortly after he graduated in 1967, they were married. By then, Jim was the freshman basketball coach at Rutgers and quite determined to, if not make history, at least cut down the final net someday.

Years later, he would often tell the story about his first game as Rutgers's freshman coach. He had studied old Vince Lombardi speeches and had thrown in some Shakespeare and Carl Sandburg. "I killed it," he would say. "I mean, I knocked it out of the park. It might have been the greatest pregame speech ever given. The players jumped up, ran for the door ready to charge onto the court, and . . . the door was locked. By the time we got it open, everyone was ready for a nap."

The story might have been hyperbolic—the door was unlocked in a matter of seconds—but Valvano's enthusiasm and his players' reaction to his talk were quite real. Unlike Rick Pitino, who would write a book about himself titled *Born to Coach,* Valvano didn't believe that he was born to coach. "I lived to coach," he said once. "My entire focus was to become a great basketball coach. The only real definition of that to me was cutting those nets down. That was what I woke up wanting to do every single morning."

He and Pam set out on what was a typical coaching odyssey. After two years at Rutgers, Jim was hired as the head coach at Johns Hopkins, a school known for producing scholars more than basketball players. After one season resulted in a 10–9 record, Jim decided he wanted to get back to the Division I level and took a job as an assistant coach under Dee Rowe at Connecticut. Rowe was three important things to Valvano: a great teacher of the game, a mentor/father figure, and someone with the kind of basketball connections that would help him advance in the profession. After three years at UConn, Rowe helped Valvano land the head coaching job at Bucknell. Three years after that, Valvano became the owner of his own college when he went to Iona, a tiny Christian Brothers school located in New Rochelle, New York.

Valvano was already a master recruiter, someone who was almost irresistible to parents and their sons once he got inside their home. "He just wasn't like any other coach you had ever met," Terry Gannon said more than thirty years after Valvano had visited his house. "Within ten minutes of walking in the door he was my father's best friend."

Recruiting Jeff Ruland was the kind of coup that just didn't happen at places like Iona. Ruland was six foot eleven and a bull inside. He wasn't your typical recruit in a lot of ways. His mom owned and ran a bar, and there was nothing even a little bit spoiled about him even though he was a star basketball player. He could have played anywhere—both Dean Smith and Bob Knight were dying to have him—but he chose to stay near home and play for Iona—and Valvano.

The Gaels had improved from 11–15 in Valvano's first year to 15–10 in his second. With Ruland on the team, they improved rapidly, going 17–10 and then 23–6 and 29–5 the next two years, making the NCAA Tournament in back-to-back seasons. Valvano had been part of the first Rutgers team to play in postseason as a senior in 1967. In his final two seasons at Iona, he took the school to postseason play for the first time in *its* history, the 1980 team finishing the season ranked nineteenth in the country—unheard-of for such a small college.

Even though he didn't literally own Iona, Valvano came to *own* Iona. He may not have owned the New York City media, but he came close. Every Tuesday, when all the coaches in the area met for lunch with the media at Mamma Leone's, tradition held that St. John's coach Lou Carnesecca, the dean of the city's coaches, would always go last and tell a few funny stories to finish the lunch on a high note.

By Valvano's third season at Iona, Carnesecca was going second to last. "No way was I following Valvano," he said when asked why.

Valvano would do twenty minutes of straight stand-up. Occasionally he'd talk about his team, but most of the time it was to set up a story.

"Guys in the media came to do two things—eat a good meal and listen to Jimmy," said Krzyzewski, who was the coach at Army for the same five years that Valvano was at Iona. "The rest of us knew when we got up to talk that they were just waiting for Jimmy. It was a little bit intimidating."

Valvano's last team was good enough—as evidenced by the one-sided win over Louisville—to go deep into the NCAA Tournament. But the NCAA Tournament committee didn't do Iona any favors, seeding it sixth in the East in spite of its impressive résumé. The Gaels won their first-round game—still Iona's only NCAA Tournament victory—against Holy Cross, but then lost 74–71 to third-seeded Georgetown in a game Valvano never completely got over.

"We just didn't play that well that day," he said. "It was national TV and we knew what it would mean to reach the Sweet Sixteen. I'll always believe if we'd beaten Georgetown we could have gone to the Final Four. We were that good."

Valvano knew there was a good chance Ruland wasn't coming back for his senior year. He also knew it was unlikely he would ever have a team at Iona as good as the one he had just coached. Which is why he wrote the letter to Tom Butters about the opening at Duke.

"I felt like I had maxed out at Iona," Valvano said, several years later. "Even if Jeff had come back for his senior year, it was going to be tough for us to be better than we had been. We'd won twenty-nine games; we'd beaten Louisville in the Garden [and cut down the nets]. We were very good. Jeff had become a truly great college player.

"I think Mike and I were a lot alike in that we were both at places where we knew, realistically, there was a ceiling. Iona's ceiling was higher than Army's, but it was still there."

Valvano came to love N.C. State. When he left the school in 1990 he wondered if he could still live in Raleigh—his home was actually in the suburb of Cary—given all the controversy surrounding his departure.

"At first we thought we'd have to leave," said Pam Valvano Strasser, who to this day lives in Cary, not far from where she and Jim lived. "But two things happened: People were incredibly nice; they stood by us. And Jim and I, the two kids from New York, realized we loved it here."

Why then, had Valvano written to Butters and not to Casey?

"I honestly thought I'd be a good fit at Duke," he said, late one night in 1988. "I thought my sense of humor would have fit right in with their students; I almost could have been one of them. I loved going over there to play. It was fun—whether you were the visitor or the home team."

Valvano's record in Cameron Indoor Stadium was 5–5. Beyond that, though, he clearly enjoyed dueling with the students. In 1984, after Lorenzo Charles, the hero of the 1983 NCAA championship game, had been arrested for participating in the holdup of a Domino's Pizza driver (he and his buddies stole several pizzas, not money), the Duke students had twenty Domino's pizzas delivered to the State bench shortly before tip-off. Valvano paid for the pizzas and handed them out to the students. On another occasion, when the students chanted their familiar "Sit down" chant at Valvano, he did—on the floor. Without missing a beat they changed the chant to "Roll over." He stood up and tipped an invisible hat to them—they'd won that round.

Duke wasn't an option, though, in 1980, and when Casey offered Valvano a deal almost identical to the one that Butters had offered Krzyzewski—$42,000 a year for five years—he took it.

It was March 27, 1980. Krzyzewski had been the coach at Duke for nine days. When Mickie Krzyzewski heard the name of State's new coach, she thought about all the publicity Valvano had been able to generate at Iona with his take-over-the-room sense of humor and his ability to generate attention for himself and his team. That led to her thinking, "Oh shit, here we go again."

Her husband's thoughts were a little different. He wasn't concerned about Valvano's personality. He was thinking about competing with him as a coach.

"My thought was that I couldn't possibly recruit anyone as good as Jeff Ruland when I was at Army," he said. "At Duke, I believed that I could. So, my attitude was, 'Okay, let's go.'"

And so they did.

6

While Bill Foster and Norman Sloan were fleeing from the aura that was Dean Smith in the winter of 1980, things were not totally sanguine in Chapel Hill.

Smith was, without doubt, an icon. He had already taken North Carolina to five Final Fours—twice reaching the national championship game. He had also coached the U.S. Olympic team in 1976—the first active coach to lead an Olympic basketball team. Prior to the Games in Montreal, the United States had felt comfortable putting a retired coach in charge.

But after Henry Iba's 1972 team had lost to the Soviet Union in Munich—on a refereeing call so clearly wrong that the Americans refused to accept their silver medals—it was decided that an active coach was needed. John Wooden was getting ready to retire. The only other possible choice, in the minds of most, was Smith.

The United States—with four North Carolina players on the team—was challenged only once, in a preliminary-round game against Puerto Rico, and rolled to the gold medal.

And yet, in spite of Foster's assertion that people in North Carolina believed that *Dean* Smith, not *Nai*Smith, had invented basketball, there were still some holes in Smith's résumé.

The one that was most notable was the one that was most obvious: he hadn't won a national championship. No one blamed him for losing the national title game to UCLA and Lew Alcindor in 1968—UCLA never lost an NCAA Tournament game during Alcindor's three years in uniform—but the loss in 1977 to Marquette rankled.

The irony was that Smith might have done his best coaching

job in that tournament. Tommy LaGarde, one of the '76 Olympians, was lost for the season in February. Walter Davis, also an Olympian, hurt his hand during the ACC Tournament and played with his fingers taped together the rest of the postseason. And Phil Ford, the third returning Olympian, who most ACC experts agreed was the best point guard they had ever seen, hyperextended his elbow during a round-of-sixteen win over Notre Dame and was limited for the rest of the tournament.

And yet, Smith somehow got the Tar Heels through one down-to-the-wire game after another. They beat Purdue by three and then came from way behind to beat Notre Dame (on St. Patrick's Day, as Smith pointed out to Digger Phelps for years after that). Then they beat Kentucky to reach the Final Four with shooting guard John Kuester running Smith's famed four-corners delay offense because Ford's elbow injury made it impossible for him to handle the ball for lengthy periods.

Kuester was named the MVP of the East Regionals and was asked afterward if it bothered him that he was the only starter on the 1976 team who hadn't made the Olympic team.

"No, not at all," he answered. "I thought Coach Smith did a great job picking the team."

Smith, standing next to him, broke in quickly: "Of course, *I* didn't pick the team, the [Olympic] committee did." He had insisted all along that the presence of four Carolina players on his team had nothing to do with who was coaching the team. No one bought that notion, but given the way the four players performed, their selection really wasn't controversial.

Still playing hurt, the Tar Heels managed to beat Nevada–Las Vegas 84–83 in a wild semifinal in Atlanta thanks to a spectacular 31-point game by freshman forward Mike O'Koren. It was their fifteenth straight victory—almost all of them close—and it put them in the national title game against Marquette, which had been fortunate to beat North Carolina–Charlotte in the semifinals.

Marquette jumped to a 39–27 halftime lead, but as had been

the case throughout the tournament, UNC came back, beginning the second half on a seven-minute 18–4 run to take a 45–43 lead. Marquette appeared to be running out of gas. And yet, after the Warriors tied the score at 45–45 with 12:40 to go, Smith decided to slow the game down. There was no shot clock in those days, and Ford had perfected the four-corners spread offense that Smith had invented years earlier to milk the clock with a lead and force the defense to chase.

Chasing Ford—even at less than 100 percent—was virtually impossible, especially since he never seemed to miss a key free throw. But there was too much time left to simply run out the clock, and Marquette appeared tired.

"We wanted to get them out of their zone," Smith said later. "They had a very big zone [three six-foot-nine-inch players] and we wanted to force them to go man-to-man."

With the score tied, Marquette coach Al McGuire, in his final game as a college coach, saw no reason to change his defense or to chase. The game suddenly slowed to a near halt.

Smith had put senior Bruce Buckley into the game to give O'Koren a breather a couple of moments earlier. O'Koren had scored eight points during Carolina's opening salvo of the second half. Now, with Ford controlling the ball and the floor spread, Smith sent O'Koren to the scorer's table to sub for Buckley on the next dead ball.

Buckley was not a scorer. He came off the bench and played good defense and rebounded. He was a classic UNC bench senior: good student—he would go on to be a lawyer—good kid, someone Smith was proud to have coached. But he wasn't O'Koren, who would score 1,765 points during his college career and was the number-six pick in the 1980 NBA draft. Eddie Fogler, who had graduated from UNC in 1970 and was now the number-two assistant coach, leaned over to his boss and said quietly, "Should we maybe call time to get Mike back in?"

Smith shook his head. He didn't believe in using *any* timeouts, unless absolutely necessary, until the final minutes of a game.

And he wasn't about to call a time-out when it would be clear to everyone in the building he was doing it to sub O'Koren for Buckley.

Buckley was a senior. You just didn't do that to a senior—ever.

Carolina held the ball for almost three minutes. Finally, Ford—still playing hurt—found Buckley on a beautiful backdoor cut. But as Buckley went up for what looked like an open layup, Marquette's Bo Ellis came down the lane and cleanly blocked the shot. Buckley just wasn't quick enough to get the ball out of his hands before Ellis recovered and got there.

The ball went the other way. McGuire milked the clock for more than a minute before guard Jim Boylan came open and scored on a cut similar to the one Buckley had made. The game stayed close until the final minute, but North Carolina never got even again. The Warriors went on to win 67–59.

Thirty-four years later, when North Carolina and Marquette met in an NCAA round-of-sixteen game, Raleigh *News & Observer* columnist Caulton Tudor, who had been in the Omni on that March night in 1977, wrote a column recalling the game. "The game is widely viewed," Tudor wrote, "as Dean Smith's worst moment in 36 years as North Carolina coach."

Smith would have vehemently disagreed with that notion. He was justifiably proud of the run his banged-up team had made to reach the championship game. And there was absolutely no way he would have done anything different on the fateful possession that ended with Ellis blocking Buckley's shot.

"The four-corners got us that far," he said four years later, in 1981, when he was still searching for his first championship. "It made sense to pull them out of the zone."

And Fogler's suggested time-out?

"No. Absolutely not. Even after Ellis blocked the shot there were almost ten minutes left in the game. We had plenty of time to still win. We just didn't."

As for it being Smith's worst moment, that notion was almost laughable. That had come twelve years earlier.

—

On July 15, 1961, the day Dean Smith was named to succeed Frank McGuire as basketball coach at North Carolina, very few people in the sport had any idea who he was. In fact, even though he had been there for three years, there weren't a lot of people in Chapel Hill who knew the name or would have recognized him walking down Franklin Street, the picturesque college town's main street.

That was the way Smith liked it.

"If Dean could have spent his entire coaching career being beamed to and from the practice court and to and from the games without ever talking to anyone in between he'd have been happy," Mike Krzyzewski said. "He loved practice, he loved getting ready for a game and the games. He treasured the relationships he had with his players. The rest of it—publicity, fund-raising, speaking to alumni or anyone else—he would have been delighted if he'd never done it once."

Smith fit the stereotype of a small-town midwestern kid. He had been born in Emporia, Kansas, a prairie town with a population of about twenty thousand that was roughly halfway between Wichita and Topeka. His parents, Alfred and Vesta Smith, were both teachers. Alfred Smith also coached basketball. In fact, his 1934 team was the first to compete in the state championships with an African American on the team.

"I was only three when that happened," Smith said years later. "So, of course, I wasn't aware of it. But when I did find out and had an understanding of what my father had done and the backlash that had occurred as a result, I was very proud of him."

Smith's family moved to the big city—Topeka, the state capital—when he was in high school. He was a good athlete, playing football, basketball, and baseball. "I always liked to play the positions where you were in charge," he said, smiling at the self-awareness of his need to control things. "I was a quarterback, a point guard, and a catcher."

Even then, he was a detailaholic. His younger sister, Joan, told a story once about a football game during which Smith overthrew one of his running backs in the flat and the ball rolled several yards after hitting the ground.

"The running back was named Dean too," she remembered. "He started to run over to pick the ball up and toss it back to the referee. Dean yelled at him to just leave it and let the ref go over and pick it up. He didn't want him to waste any energy chasing the ball down."

Smith went to Kansas, one of *the* powers in college basketball then as now, but not on a basketball scholarship. Instead, he earned an academic scholarship and majored in math. His wizardry with numbers became legendary among coaches and led to a conversation with Bobby Cremins, then the coach at Georgia Tech, at an ACC coaches meeting that everyone in the room talks about to this day.

"Gene Corrigan [then the commissioner] was talking to us about a number of things and Bobby started getting on him about the pressure basketball coaches were facing to make the [NCAA] tournament every year," former Maryland coach Gary Williams remembered. "He said it was unfair for us to be judged just on that because it was so hard to get in.

"Gene said, 'Come on, Bobby, sixty-four teams get in.' And Bobby said, 'Out of how many?' Gene said it was about three hundred. So Bobby turns to Dean and says, 'Dean, you're the math major; what's sixty-four into three hundred?' Dean, of course, says right away that it's twenty-one point three percent. Bobby turns back to Corrigan and asks how many football teams make bowl games. Back then it was, I think, fifty-six. Bobby says, 'Out of how many teams?' Gene says, 'About a hundred.' So Bobby turns back to Dean and says, 'Okay, math major, fifty-six into a hundred, what percent is that?'"

Smith did play basketball in college but was never a starter. By the time he was a senior, Phog Allen, Kansas's legendary coach, had made him an unofficial assistant coach, assigning him to work with the younger players. Kansas played in the Final Four in both 1952 and 1953—beating St. John's in the championship game in '52 before losing, 69–68, to Indiana a year later. Smith always pointed out to people that he *did* play in the '52 game—late—when Kansas pulled away for an 80–63 win.

By the time he was a senior, Smith knew he wanted to coach. He had signed up for Air Force ROTC—the Korean War was in progress—and he had a two-year commitment when he graduated. Just before he was sent to Germany, he met his first wife, Ann, in what friends would later describe as a "classic Dean Smith moment."

"It was at a graduation dance," Smith said. "Ann came with a football player I didn't like. He was very cocky. So, I thought maybe I'd take him down a peg by asking his date to dance. Which I did. We started talking and I realized that I really *liked* her. So, we started dating and we kept in close touch while I was in Germany."

During that time overseas, Smith met Bob Spear, who was about to become the first basketball coach at the brand-new Air Force Academy in Colorado Springs, Colorado. Spear offered him the job as his assistant coach with one caveat: he also had to coach the golf team. Smith accepted. The golf team wasn't very good.

"I knew we were in trouble," Smith said later, "when I realized I was a better player than most of the guys on the team."

He had better luck in basketball. Spear was not only an excellent teacher, he came to be his assistant's number-one advocate. At the 1958 Final Four, when North Carolina coach Frank McGuire was looking for an assistant, Spear recommended Smith. And so, at the age of twenty-seven and with a wife and two very young children, he packed his bags and moved to Chapel Hill.

One of the first things he did upon arriving was look for a church to join. A young minister named Robert Seymour had just become the Binkley Baptist Church's first pastor, and Smith took an instant liking to him. They were close in age and in beliefs. Seymour was very disturbed by the fact that restaurants in Chapel Hill were still segregated. He and Smith decided to do something about it. One night the two of them walked into the Pines, a well-known Chapel Hill restaurant, with an African American divinity student who was a member of the church.

"We just sat down and ordered," Smith said later after Seymour had told a reporter the story. "I guess management made a decision that they didn't want to start trouble with Frank McGuire's assistant coach. They served us dinner and, after that, at least as far as I know, began serving everyone who came to the restaurant—not just white people."

Smith always played down his role in what occurred, but Seymour did not. "What you have to remember is that Dean was not *Dean Smith* in 1958," he said. "He was an assistant basketball coach, new in town. They knew him at the Pines because that's where the basketball team went for team meals [as it still does to this day]. Dean and I had discussed the risks that were involved. He could have been fired for stirring up trouble. I don't think the thought of *not* doing it ever crossed his mind."

As an assistant to Frank McGuire, Smith had no trouble staying comfortably in the background. Billy Cunningham, who would go on to be an All-American at Carolina and an NBA Hall of Fame player, remembers McGuire and Smith coming to his parents' house in Brooklyn when he was being recruited in 1961.

"I remember Dean being there," Cunningham said. "But that's about all I remember about him. It was as if he faded into the living room wall. The pitch was all Frank."

McGuire was a showman, the way Al McGuire (no relation) would be at Marquette and Jim Valvano would be years later. He was a New Yorker who, even after leaving St. John's for North Carolina, continued to recruit New York kids. In basketball circles, the odyssey of city kids to Chapel Hill was called "McGuire's underground railroad."

Sometimes, when he went into a Catholic home, McGuire would bring the local parish priest with him. With the Cunninghams, that wasn't necessary.

"His cousin lived next door to us," Cunningham said, laughing. "After the visit, my dad said to me, 'Okay, Bill, you've got two choices: you can go play for Uncle Frank or go to a Catholic school—your choice.'"

Cunningham went to play for Uncle Frank.

McGuire was not an X's and O's coach by any means. Nor was he a detail guy. He recruited great players and expected them to continue to be great. Smith was the detail guy. He made the practice plans every day; he scouted the opponents. He did all the background things that no one—except the players—would notice.

Three summers after Smith's arrival, McGuire "resigned" as coach. The school was being investigated for numerous NCAA recruiting violations, and Chancellor William Aycock thought it best for McGuire to leave. When the NBA's Philadelphia Warriors were searching for a new head coach, McGuire pursued the job—and got it. On his way out, he recommended to Aycock that the chancellor hire his thirty-year-old assistant coach as his replacement. Since it was July and finding a so-called name coach at that time of year would be difficult, Aycock decided to give Smith a chance.

"When I heard Coach McGuire was leaving my first thought was that I should go someplace else," said Larry Brown, who was a rising junior that summer. "We all knew the NCAA was going to come down on us, so I thought maybe I should go someplace else. I called my mom to see what she thought and she said, 'Coach Smith's already been here. You're staying.'"

Several players did leave. And Smith started his career with one hand tied behind his back. That first season, UNC was allowed to play only two nonconference games and finished 8–9. Scholarship numbers were limited. The second season, Carolina was allowed to play twenty-one games—and finished 15–6.

"We were good that year," Brown said. "Billy [Cunningham] had become a star, and we had figured out that Coach Smith knew what he was doing. If not for darned Duke being so good, we could have made a dent in postseason."

In those days only one conference school could go to the

NCAAs, and darned Duke—which ended up in the Final Four—won the conference tournament. "We were very good that year," Smith said during the last season he coached. "We've had maybe five or six teams I thought were good enough to win the national [title] and that was one of them."

A year later, after Brown and Yogi Poteat had graduated, the Tar Heels slipped back to 12–12. Nowadays, an ACC coach with a three-year record of 35–27 might be in jeopardy of losing his job. There were mitigating circumstances in Smith's case—the NCAA sanctions—but even so, boosters and alumni expect instant success, especially in a program that has recently won a national championship, which UNC had done in 1957 under McGuire.

Cunningham was a senior and a star in 1965. The Tar Heels were 6–3, including a win over Kentucky, when things began to go south. They lost a game at Florida—coached by Norman Sloan, in his first incarnation there—and then lost to Maryland in the first game after Christmas break. That left them 6–5 with a trip to Wake Forest coming up two days later—on January 6.

"We were terrible that night," Cunningham remembered. "Flat, not ready to play. Plus, they were good. Dean didn't do anything wrong. We just didn't show up to play."

The result was a humiliating 107–85 loss. When the bus pulled into the Woollen Gym parking lot after the eighty-mile trip back home that night, the place was deserted—as might be expected late on a cold January night. The only thing the players could see as they wearily stood up to get off the bus was what appeared to be an effigy, hanging from a nearby tree.

Cunningham, the team captain, was the first one off the bus. As soon as he got a good look at the effigy, he knew what had happened: Smith had been hung in effigy by students who had, no doubt, fled when they saw the bus pulling in.

"There wasn't any doubt about what it was or who it was," he said. "When I ran over to the tree I looked up at Winston dorm, which was on the other side of the parking lot, and I could see a lot of faces peering out windows at me. I just ripped the thing down. I was angry and I was embarrassed. It was *our* fault that had happened."

Smith was never comfortable—for obvious reasons—talking about that night. "I *do* remember Billy pulling the effigy down," he said. "I don't remember anyone saying anything at that moment or exactly what I thought."

He smiled for a moment. "I also remember that I think I gave the best pregame talk of my career three days later when we played at Duke."

Coached by Vic Bubas, Duke was *the* team in the ACC during that period. The Blue Devils had reached back-to-back Final Fours in 1963 and 1964 and would return again in 1966. Carolina went into Cameron Indoor Stadium and beat the sixth-ranked Blue Devils 65–62.

"I don't remember his pregame talk," Cunningham said. "I'm not sure any of us heard a word he said. We were all so upset because we'd let him down so badly. If he hadn't said a word, we would have won that game. We owed him that one."

The Tar Heels went 9–3 the rest of that season. That spring, Smith won his first key head-to-head recruiting battle with Bubas, for Larry Miller, a talented six-four swingman from Catasauqua, Pennsylvania. A year later, Charles Scott, the first African American whom Smith successfully recruited, arrived in Chapel Hill. North Carolina won the ACC title in 1967 and advanced to the Final Four. It did the same thing in 1968 and 1969—losing the 1968 title game to Alcindor and UCLA.

The effigy was long gone. The aura had been born.

—

By the time Mike Krzyzewski and Jim Valvano arrived in the Research Triangle to coach at Duke and N.C. State, neither Smith nor anyone else at North Carolina was losing a lot of sleep worrying about who was going to coach at the two neighboring schools.

"We always figured that playing against Duke or N.C. State would be tough," Roy Williams said. "But by then, really, our challenge was winning the national championship. It was the only thing Coach Smith hadn't done yet."

After Tom Butters shocked the basketball world by hiring Krzyzewski, Smith asked Bob Knight, whom he often played golf with in the off-season, about the new coach at Duke.

"I remember he said to us, 'Bob thinks he'll be very good—if he can survive the first few years,'" Williams said. "We all knew that once [Gene] Banks and [Kenny] Dennard graduated after that first year that he'd have to rebuild. The question, Coach Smith said, would be whether Duke would be patient enough to let him do that."

The UNC coaching staff knew more about Valvano because Iona had made a name for itself nationally. Both North Carolina and Indiana—and every other basketball power—had recruited Jeff Ruland, only to see him stay close to home and go to Iona.

The full-court press put on Ruland by Valvano and his relentless assistant, Tom Abatemarco, became legend among coaches. Because of recruiting rules about direct contact with a player, Valvano and Abatemarco couldn't speak to Ruland on a daily basis. Instead, rain, snow, or shine, Abatemarco would drive to Ruland's house every morning and leave a note on the windshield of his car before Ruland left for school.

Eddie Fogler, who spent more time on the road recruiting than the other Carolina coaches, and thus knew more coaches, reported back that Valvano would be a very different sort of opponent than Norm Sloan.

"People liked him," Fogler said with a smile. "Everyone liked Valvano. He was impossible not to like."

Both Valvano and Krzyzewski insisted they weren't going to worry about Smith or North Carolina or the aura when they started their new jobs. "I expect them to be good," Krzyzewski said. "That doesn't mean we can't be good too."

Valvano, being Valvano, explained his approach to competing with Smith differently. "I'll never outcoach Dean Smith," he said. "But maybe I can outlive him."

7

Jim Valvano and North Carolina State actually came close to beating Dean Smith and North Carolina both times the two teams faced each other during the regular season in 1980–81. Carolina won a pair of three-point games, but—naturally—that wasn't the way Valvano told the story in the years that followed.

The way Valvano told it, Carolina won both games in blowouts. He counted on the fact that most of his listeners wouldn't remember the two games.

"So, the second time we get blown out, an old State alumnus comes up to me and he says, 'Coach, I know you're a Yankee and you don't understand about tradition down here, but we *cannot* be losing to the Tar Heels this way.'

"I say to him, 'No, I *do* get it. I know all about the tradition down here and I *promise* you, next season we're going to do a lot better against them.'

"He shakes his head and says, 'Coach, you just don't get it. If you lose to the Tar Heels here in Reynolds [Coliseum] next season, we're going to kill your dog.'

"Okay, I'm just a little nervous now because the guy isn't smiling even a little bit. But I say to him, 'Look, I have to tell you, I don't have a dog, but I hear you loud and clear.'

"He just nods and walks away. Next morning I go to the front door to get my newspaper, and when I open the door there's a basket on my front step. I look under the blanket and there's the cutest little puppy you've ever seen in your life. There's a note attached to the puppy's collar. It says, 'Don't get too attached.'"

The story illustrated the intensity of the Triangle rivalries among N.C. State, North Carolina, and Duke. It was also complete fiction.

"Only story he ever made up," Bob Valvano said. "He came up with it when he decided he wanted to do stand-up comedy. He called me and said, 'I've been working on this all day and this is what I've come up with so far. This is hard work.'"

It was never work for Valvano to be off-the-cuff funny. That was his genius. That first year at State, his team struggled often—finishing 14–13. The Wolfpack faced Carolina for a third time, in the first round of the ACC Tournament, losing 69–54 to end Valvano's first season. It was probably a good thing that the dog was fictional.

Duke and Krzyzewski had better luck. After losing the non-handshake game in Greensboro, the Blue Devils got blown out in Chapel Hill in January. Carolina came to Durham on the final day of the regular season, a Saturday afternoon, for Senior Day. Smith had actually invented Senior Day after succeeding McGuire. The concept was simple: honor those playing their last home game—from stars to walk-ons—by introducing them and by starting every senior on the roster, including walk-ons. On a couple of occasions when Carolina had six seniors, Smith put them all on the floor to start the game and accepted the technical foul for having six men on the court.

"It was a brilliant concept in a lot of different ways," Lou Goetz, the former Foster assistant, said. "You start the walk-ons so you don't have to worry about trying to get them into the box score at the end of the game when it might be close. And you put pressure on the other team because if by some chance one of them hits a shot or makes a play, you look bad *and* it gives the home team some extra momentum.

"Plus there's the added bonus that it's a nice thing to do for the seniors."

Nowadays, Senior Day at most schools has become an almost unbearable parade of managers and their moms and dads; cheerleaders and their moms and dads; players and their moms and dads; and just about every graduating senior who happens to show up at the game. Everyone gets a plaque, a framed team picture—or both.

Smith's concept was simpler than that: make sure all the seniors play so they are recognized the last day they wear a uniform on their home court. Duke's three seniors in 1981 were Jim Suddath, Kenny Dennard, and Eugene Banks. All three had played important roles in the revival of Duke basketball under Bill Foster.

Suddath had been a steady off-the-bench shooter his first three years before becoming a starter as a senior. He was a deeply religious young man who would go on after graduation to become a minister—surprising none of his teammates, who already called him the Reverend while he was still in college. Remarkably, Suddath had roomed with Dennard when the two were freshmen, creating perhaps the ultimate odd-couple pairing in the history of higher education. Dennard spent most of his nights praying that he could convince a coed to come back to the room with him. Often, his prayers were answered.

When Dennard's prayers were answered, Suddath cowered under the covers in the other bed, also praying—for Dennard's soul.

"Poor Jim," Dennard said years later. "He really did want to save me. I was a hopeless cause."

Dennard had been an exception to the rule that said kids from North Carolina didn't go to Duke. He was from King, a suburb of Winston-Salem, and he decided he wanted to go to Duke after his official visit to campus, which if you have five or six hours with nothing to do, he will gladly recount to you to this day.

Dennard was six foot eight, athletic, and mean—on the court. He was a starter from day one, a major upgrade at the small-forward spot.

But the breakthrough recruit was Banks. In the winter of 1977, there were two high school seniors coveted by every major program in the country: Banks and Albert King. There was a third senior who was considered to be very talented but not quite in Banks and King's class: Earvin Johnson, whose nickname was Magic. He decided early on to stay home and go to Michigan State. Which meant most recruiting geeks were focused on King, who was from Brooklyn and was the younger brother of Bernard King; and Banks, who went to West Philadelphia High School.

Banks was a born performer—on and off the basketball court. He was six foot seven and chiseled, without ever lifting a weight, in a way that made him look more like twenty-five than eighteen. His SAT scores were awful, low enough that none of the five schools on his final list—Duke, Penn, Villanova, Notre Dame, and UCLA—could consider admitting him, even as an athlete. Except that all five were willing to take him, largely because of his basketball ability but also because it was clear on meeting him that he was a lot smarter than the numbers reflected.

Foster had to do a major selling job to the Duke admissions board. He pointed out that if ever there was an example of the SAT's cultural bias, it was Gene Banks. "He'll come here and graduate in four years," he told the admissions people.

He didn't add: "And he'll transform the basketball program." That was a given.

On February 7 Bob Wenzel, who had been babysitting Banks all season, got an early-morning phone call from Banks: "Coach," he said. "I've made up my mind. I'm coming to Duke."

The timing was a godsend for Duke and for Foster. Two days earlier, the Blue Devils had blown a seven-point lead in the final minute to lose to Maryland in large part because star point guard Tate Armstrong was out with a broken wrist and the Blue Devils couldn't handle Maryland's pressure. Steve Gray, Armstrong's replacement, threw one pass off his own rim and then dribbled the ball off his foot to seal Duke's fate. That night, Foster tried to fly to Louisville, Kentucky, on a recruiting trip. The plane had to make an emergency landing in high winds, and Foster returned home the next day too sick to get out of bed. When Wenzel called the next morning with the news about Banks, he felt considerably healthier.

After he hung up with Foster, Wenzel called a friend and said four words: "The worm has turned." The friend didn't need to ask what he meant.

Banks's decision was the most important basketball news to hit the Duke campus since Vic Bubas had announced his retirement eight years earlier. But his recruitment wasn't over yet. He couldn't actually sign a letter of intent until April, and UCLA and Notre Dame kept recruiting him very aggressively.

"Their basic pitch was simple," Wenzel remembered. "Duke—you're going to Duke? You'll never be heard from again there—they're terrible."

On the night of March 18 Wenzel went to see Banks play in Washington, at the Knights of Columbus Tournament in the D.C. Armory, right across the street from RFK Stadium. It was an old, dingy gym with lots of history and very little hot water in the showers.

When Banks came up the steps from the locker room after West Philadelphia had beaten Georgetown Prep in a first-round game, he found Notre Dame coach Digger Phelps waiting for him. Phelps and Notre Dame had lost to North Carolina in College Park in the round of sixteen of the NCAA Tournament the previous night, and Phelps had stuck around to see Banks play in downtown D.C. He had brought friends with him: Austin Carr, Bob Whitmore, and Sid Catlett, all Notre Dame graduates, all great college players.

As the four men surrounded Banks, Wenzel stood a few yards away, steam coming out of his ears, knowing he couldn't even think of intervening. He had to let the scene play out.

Phelps introduced the three former stars to a wide-eyed Banks and said, "Gene, if you come to Notre Dame, this is who you'll be following." He glanced in Wenzel's direction. "If you go to Duke, who will you be following there?"

He and the three alums spent several minutes telling Banks about the wonders of Notre Dame while Wenzel stewed. Finally, there were handshakes and hugs all around, and Banks walked over to where Wenzel was standing.

"Coach, are you okay?" he asked.

"I'm fine, Gene, why?"

"Because you're white as a sheet."

Wenzel walked Banks to the West Philadelphia team bus. As they shook hands, Banks said, "Coach, it's fine. I'm coming to Duke."

At that moment, Wenzel felt the color returning to his face.

Four weeks later, Banks officially signed a letter of intent to go to Duke. It was during a recruiting "dead" period, when coaches weren't allowed to have any contact with recruits. Foster was taking no chances. At nine o'clock in the morning, Banks walked to his mailbox and put an envelope in it. Foster, sitting in his car at the end of the block, waited until Banks walked inside his house and then—as previously arranged—drove down to the mailbox, took the envelope out of the box, and looked inside. The letter of intent was there—with Banks's signature on it.

The worm had, in fact, turned.

—

Four years later, Banks made his final appearance in Cameron Indoor Stadium. It had not been an easy year for any of the three seniors. Suddath had been thrilled to find himself starting but never could completely grasp the notion of playing Mike Krzyzewski's man-to-man defense after playing Foster's 2-3 zone throughout his college career.

Banks's and Dennard's adjustment to the new coach had little to do with the defense he played. It was about style—and discipline.

"They were used to laissez-faire from Bill," said Bobby Dwyer, who had come to Duke with Krzyzewski from Army. "Mike wouldn't know laissez-faire if you hit him over the head with it."

The new coach and the veteran players clashed often about

being on time, about how much they partied (and how often), and about going to class. Dennard, whose board scores had been as high as Banks's had been low, had no interest in going to school or graduating. Banks, in spite of riding an academic roller coaster, would fulfill Foster's promise and graduate in four years.

By the time Senior Day rolled around, Krzyzewski and his two senior stars had finally bonded for one reason: all three hated to lose.

As always, Dennard was introduced before Banks. When Banks was introduced he came out carrying roses and laid one on each corner of the court as a tribute to the student body. There is a picture of the two of them hugging a moment later, Dennard with his hands over his eyes. Most people who look at the picture are moved by the sight of Dennard's tears.

"I wasn't crying," Dennard said, looking at the photo many years later. "I was hiding my eyes because I couldn't believe Gene came out and did that corny thing with the roses. But that was Gene. No one ever loved the spotlight more than he did."

Banks lived up to his own hype that day. With Duke down two and one second left, he caught an inbounds pass from Dennard twenty-five feet from the basket and launched a high-arching shot over the outstretched arms of Sam Perkins, who was six foot nine but, according to Dean Smith's measurements, had the arms of someone who was seven-four. The shot came down from the ceiling and splashed through the net, sending the game into overtime.

Linnea Smith was watching the game from a hospital room a few miles away. She had given birth two days earlier to her second child, a daughter named Kelly Marie. The baby was Smith's fifth child—he'd had two daughters and a son with Ann, his first wife, and this was the second daughter for him and Linnea since their marriage in 1976.

Linnea Smith didn't get emotional about basketball games very often. She and Dean had met on an airplane, and, she had learned later, one of the things he liked about her was that she had absolutely no idea who he was. She was a doctor, a psychiatrist, and he had opened the conversation with her by asking about the book she was reading: *The Gospel According to Peanuts.*

Five years and two children into their marriage, Linnea Smith hardly considered herself an expert on basketball, but she knew how intensely competitive her husband was and how much he loathed losing to Duke—especially at Duke. She was in a Durham hospital because that was where her doctor practiced. "Yes," she said with a smile many years later, "my girls have to deal with the fact that they were born in Durham."

Linnea and Dean Smith often talked about the importance of basketball. "We agreed that it wasn't life and death," she said with a smile. "But it *was* deadly serious."

Because she had given birth by C-section, Linnea had to stay in the hospital for forty-eight hours. The plan was for Dean to pick her up en route home from Duke that afternoon after the game.

"I was a complete wreck watching that game," she said. "I had all these hormones from birth racing through my body, and every time Duke scored I was screaming, 'Oh no, we can't lose this game. My poor daughter, what will happen to her if we lose this game?'"

Banks's shot made things even worse. Then, when he scored late in overtime to seal a 66–65 Duke win, Linnea Smith threw her arms in the air and said, "That's it. My daughter's life is ruined."

Kelly Marie's life would turn out fine—she is a doctor now—but the trip home that afternoon wasn't so great. "Not a word," Linnea Smith said. "Neither one of us said a word."

The Senior Day win over Carolina was as joyous for Mickie Krzyzewski as it was devastating for Linnea Smith. It was, without question, the biggest win of Mike's first season at Duke. It raised the Blue Devils' record to 15–11, meaning they were assured of at least a berth in the NIT. Most important, it was a win over Carolina.

"We celebrated," Mickie Krzyzewski said. "Usually when Mike

is excited about something he says it was 'pretty good.' This was better than pretty good."

Nine months later, the Krzyzewski's third child, Jamie, was born. "It had to be that night," Mickie said. "No other possibility that time of year."

Several years later, Kelly and Jamie were in the same piano class. The parents would sit next to each other at recitals. When Mickie told Linnea about Jamie's conception, Linnea laughed.

"It was one basketball game," she said. "I thought my daughter's life was ruined by it. Mickie's daughter was a *result* of it. If you think about it, that's pretty amazing."

—

North Carolina recovered from the loss to Duke to win the ACC Tournament and reach the national championship game, where it lost to Indiana in Philadelphia on the night President Ronald Reagan was shot in Washington.

It can be argued that the atmosphere that night in Philadelphia's Spectrum was the strangest in the history of the tournament. For most of the day, no one really knew how serious the president's condition was. The NCAA basketball committee didn't want the national championship game being played if the president's life was in danger or if—God forbid—news should break that he had died during the game.

"What bothered me," Smith would say years later, "was that they seemed more concerned about looking bad than about doing what was right. They didn't want to move the game because that would affect television. Bob [Knight] and I had no say in it at all. We were simply told what was going on. No one ever asked either one of us what we thought should be done."

The two coaches in the consolation game—LSU's Dale Brown and Virginia's Terry Holland—were given even less say, if that was possible. They were told to start their game as scheduled while the committee continued to debate whether to play the championship game.

"It seemed ridiculous to me," Holland said. "Neither one of us really cared about playing the game or, for that matter, wanted to play it. A year later, they finally got rid of the consolation game, but that year they told us to go out and play. I think they figured if something happened to the president, they could just take us off the court because no one would really notice or care."

There couldn't have been a thousand people watching when the consolation game—which Virginia won—began. It wasn't until that game was over that word came from Washington that the president was out of surgery and doing well. What's more, the rumors that press secretary James Brady had died had proven to be untrue. The committee decided to play the game.

Indiana, led by sophomore guard Isiah Thomas, pulled away to win, 63–50, leaving Smith one game shy of a national title for the third time. This was different, though, than the Marquette game in 1977, because Indiana was clearly the better team.

Al Wood was graduating, but James Worthy, Sam Perkins, Matt Doherty, and Jimmy Black—four of the five starters—would be back. And Carolina appeared to have a very strong freshman class coming to join those four. There were two highly touted guards: Buzz Peterson and Lynwood Robinson. And there was a six-six swingman from Wilmington named Michael Jordan. Word was, he was quite the leaper.

8

On the same March weekend in 1981 that North Carolina was winning the NCAA West Regional in Salt Lake City, Mike Krzyzewski's first season at Duke ended on a snowy night in West Lafayette, Indiana.

A year earlier, Duke's final game under Bill Foster had been a loss to Purdue in the Mideast Region final—the round of eight—of the NCAA Tournament. Lee Rose had been Purdue's coach that day, but after losing to UCLA a week later in the Final Four, Rose left Purdue to become the coach at South Florida. It was a move almost as surprising—maybe even more surprising—than Foster's decision to leave Duke for South Carolina.

Like Duke, Purdue had lost several key players—including center Joe Barry Carroll—and found itself in the NIT under new coach Gene Keady. Duke had won two NIT home games to reach the quarterfinals—the round of eight—but had lost Gene Banks to a broken wrist in the first-round victory over North Carolina A&T. Without Banks, the Blue Devils had managed to beat Alabama at home, but playing at Purdue proved impossible. For the second straight season, the Boilermakers ended a Duke season, this time 81–69, to reach the NIT semifinals in New York.

The day he walked in the door, Krzyzewski had known he would be losing three of his four best players—Banks, Kenny Dennard, and Jim Suddath—after his first season. Returning for his second season would be one of those top four, Vince Taylor, along with Chip Engelland and Tom Emma, both good shooters but limited otherwise—especially on defense.

It would not be a team one wanted to go to war with—especially in an ACC that included North Carolina and Virginia, both Final Four teams in 1981 with key players, including Virginia's seven-foot-four-inch center Ralph Sampson, returning; Maryland under Lefty Driesell; a very solid Wake Forest team; and an up-and-coming North Carolina State team that returned all five starters and a sweet-shooting sixth man named Terry Gannon.

Knowing he needed reinforcements, Krzyzewski had ambitiously pursued some of the top high school seniors in the country. Once the season was over, he was all over the map, chasing five players he thought he had a good chance to get. The best of them was Chris Mullin, a New York City kid whom Krzyzewski had fallen in love with the first time he'd seen him. Not only could Mullin shoot, he had a coach's sense of the game, the kind of court vision you couldn't teach, and a look in his eye that made Krzyzewski believe Mullin was the kind of player you build a program around.

The other four were also highly touted: Uwe Blab, a seven-foot-three-inch German who was going to high school in Effingham, Illinois; Rodney Williams, a talented swingman from Florida; and Jim Miller and Tim Mullen—Miller from West Virginia, Mullen from Virginia. Krzyzewski was hoping that only one of the Miller-Mullen duo would choose Virginia and that Duke would land the other.

In an ideal world, all five would sign with Duke. Realistically, Krzyzewski would have been very happy to get three. If he could only have one—and it was Mullin—he'd be thrilled.

He also knew it was probably a long shot. Mullin was from Brooklyn and, like most New York kids, had grown up a St. John's fan. The Redmen (as they were still called back then) were a national power under Coach Lou Carnesecca and had been in the Elite Eight as recently as 1979—beating Duke in that NCAA Tournament when the Blue Devils were coming off their trip to the championship game the previous season.

One night in the dead of winter, Krzyzewski and assistant coach Chuck Swenson flew to Glens Falls, New York, to watch Mullin play in a two-night tournament. Mullin's play confirmed everything Krzyzewski had thought about him. Teenage boys fall in love with girls who have blond hair and blue eyes. Basketball coaches fall in love with players who have a cerebral court sense and a great jump shot. Krzyzewski was in love.

And, like a lot of teenage boys dealing with the notion of unrequited love, he was depressed.

"Mike had a strict routine when we were on the road recruiting," Swenson said. "Eat dinner—or supper as midwesterners call it—before the game. Go to the game, try to make sure the kid and his coach know you're there. Stop on the way back to the hotel for ice cream. Get to the room, call Mickie, and go to bed. That was it. All the time."

Swenson knew the routine cold because in those days, the head coach and his assistant shared a room on the road. Often as not in a place like Glens Falls it was at a roadside motel.

On this night, though, Krzyzewski hung up the phone with Mickie, looked at Swenson, and said, "Let's go get a brew."

"You mean a beer?" Swenson asked.

"Yeah, that's what I said," Krzyzewski said. "Let's get a beer."

They found a bar and Krzyzewski sipped his brew quietly.

"Usually after we'd seen a player he liked, especially one he liked as much as Mullin, he'd be wound up," Swenson said. "He'd talk about what the kid could do in our offense or how he might make our older kids better—which Mullin certainly would have.

"That night, he was quiet and introspective in a way I wasn't used to seeing. I'd been with him for a while at that stage—four years at Army and then at Duke. It kind of scared me a little. He finally said, 'Chuck, this is the kid we need to get. And I don't know if there's anything we can do to guarantee that we get him.'"

Mullin actually visited Duke on the weekend of what is still referred to in Duke lore as "the Banks game." He saw Cameron at its absolute wildest and clearly loved the atmosphere.

But Krzyzewski's gut was right. Mullin wasn't leaving New York. His buddies all wanted him to go to St. John's. Krzyzewski had done an excellent job "recruiting" Mullin's mom, but in the end it wasn't enough. Mullin, the player Krzyzewski believed would be his first Jeff Ruland, went to play for Carnesecca—where he had a brilliant career and led St. John's to the Final Four in 1985.

One by one, the recruiting blocks fell that spring—all in the wrong direction. Blab liked Krzyzewski but his high school coach was enamored of Bob Knight—so he went to Indiana.

Rodney Williams was coming to Duke. That's what he told Krzyzewski when he asked the coach to come down and speak at his high school's awards banquet in April. The plan was for Krzyzewski to speak and then, when Rodney got up to accept his award as the team's MVP, he would announce that he was signing with Duke.

Krzyzewski flew to Titus, Florida, on the afternoon of the banquet, rented a car, and drove to the school. He was greeted there by Williams's coach, John Smith.

"Coach, I feel really badly about this. Rodney just signed with Florida a couple of hours ago. He won't be at the banquet tonight. I hope, since you're here already, you'll stay and speak."

Krzyzewski wasn't sure what was most upsetting: Williams backing out at the last possible second to mysteriously sign with Florida, his unwillingness even to face him at the banquet, or the coach requesting that he still speak.

He stayed and spoke. "I just decided that I wasn't going to start breaking commitments," he said. "No matter how upset I was at that moment."

Soon after the Williams debacle, Tim Mullen decided on Virginia and so did Jim Miller—on the last day of the signing period. Krzyzewski and Bobby Dwyer had gotten a call the day before saying that Miller was leaning toward Duke.

"Let's not take any chances," Krzyzewski said. "Drive up there tonight, and if it's us, pick up the letter from the mailbox."

Although contact between recruits and coaches was allowed during the signing period, Duke had used up all its allowable visits. That's why Krzyzewski wanted the letter of intent in the mailbox.

Miller lived in the mountains, in the town of Princeton, West Virginia. It would take Dwyer several hours on a lot of back roads to get there. He arrived at about two in the morning and asked for an eight o'clock wake-up call. Miller had said he would make his final decision when he woke up in the morning.

Dwyer's wake-up call came early—a little after seven. Only it wasn't from the front desk. It was Miller. "Coach, I'm really sorry," he said. "I woke up this morning and my gut told me I should go to Virginia."

Dwyer called Krzyzewski. Desperate, Krzyzewski tracked down Miller's mother, who was at a teachers' convention. He knew she wanted her son to go to Duke. "Let me talk to him," Brenda Miller said. "I'll call you back."

An hour later she called back. "Jim's really set on Virginia," she said. "I have to support him. It's his choice. I'm sorry."

Not as sorry as Krzyzewski was at that moment. They were now officially zero for five. There were others willing to sign, notably Danny Meagher, a six-foot-five-inch Canadian who would develop into a productive player—the kind of physical, hard-nosed opponent Dean Smith couldn't stand. But Krzyzewski's first full recruiting season had been, at least in terms of players who could be program cornerstones, a washout.

Soon after Miller had signed with Virginia, Krzyzewski sat down with his staff.

"We blew it this year," he said, remembering what he'd learned as a West Point plebe: when something goes wrong the only acceptable answer when asked about it is, "No excuse, sir!"

So, instead of making excuses or talking about how unlucky they'd gotten, Krzyzewski told his two recruiters that the three of them had collectively blown it. "Next year we're going about it differently," he announced. "We aren't recruiting twenty or twenty-five players. We're recruiting eight—ten at most. And we're going to sign five or six of them."

"What if we don't?" Swenson asked, still smarting from all the near misses.

"We *will*," Krzyzewski said.

That was the end of the meeting.

—

Jim Valvano's first recruiting season at N.C. State had been far more productive. He knew he already had players who could score in Sidney Lowe, Dereck Whittenburg, and Thurl Bailey—the three players recruited by Norm Sloan prior to his final season at State. Valvano wanted to add one outside shooter and a couple of players who could play physically inside. Bailey was six-eleven but was more of a finesse player.

He signed three players: Cozell McQueen, a quick-leaping six-foot-eleven-inch center from South Carolina; Lorenzo Charles, a Brooklyn kid who was six-seven and Charles Barkley wide and strong (though without Barkley's offensive gifts); and Terry Gannon, a six-one shooting guard from Joliet, Illinois. The three signees were an example of Valvano's ability to connect with different personalities. McQueen was a southern kid who told Valvano one of the reasons he liked N.C. State was because he didn't want to go to school in the South. Everything is relative in life. Charles was quiet, a tough-minded New York kid. And Gannon was a coach's son who never thought for one second he would end up going to college in North Carolina.

"I grew up dreaming of playing at Notre Dame," he said. "My dad is an Irish Catholic high school basketball coach [Joliet Catholic High School] and we're a hundred miles away from Notre Dame. He was friends with Digger [Phelps] and we went to South Bend for games all the time. That was where I wanted to go.

"Fortunately for me, there was another guard Digger liked more than he liked me, and he offered him a scholarship early in my senior year. That opened things up. Still, the only program I knew anything about in the ACC was North Carolina. Everyone knew who Dean Smith was. But that was about it.

"Then State starts recruiting me. Jim comes to the house for a home visit. The first thing he said to my father when he opened the door was, 'Who the hell taught you how to give directions?' He'd gotten lost. He was by himself, and he and my dad start talking.

"My dad loved to drink and he loved to gamble. The next thing I know he and my dad are in the next room and Jim's helping him pick games. I'd never met anyone like him. No one's ever met anyone like him. I thought he was crazy but I liked him. One minute he'd be talking pop culture, the next world affairs. Anything but basketball—or at least that's the way it seemed. He was a coach's son. I was a coach's son, so I liked him right away. But it was my dad he recruited. When he left that night my dad said, 'You're going to go play for him.' I'd never seen the campus but the decision was made.

"It was definitely culture shock for me when I got down there. First time I went into a convenience store I said something to the guy behind the counter and he looked at me and said, 'Oh, so you're a Yankee.' It took me a while to get used to that."

Gannon, McQueen, and Charles were all learning on the job during that second season. The three juniors, Whittenburg, Lowe, and Bailey, were coming into their own as ACC players, and the three freshmen all made an impact right away. State improved from 14–13 overall and 4–10 in the ACC to 21–9 in the regular season and 7–7 against ACC teams. That jumped them from seventh place in 1981 to fourth place, which meant they had wrapped up a spot in the NCAA Tournament by the time they arrived in Greensboro for the ACC Tournament.

After winning an ugly first-round game against Maryland, State lost to North Carolina in the semifinals, making Valvano 0–6 against Smith. State went into the NCAA Tournament as a number-seven seed and played a first-round game against tenth-seeded Tennessee-Chattanooga.

"We overlooked them, simple as that," Whittenburg said.

"We just figured we'd show up and win and then have a tough second-round game against Minnesota. They had a really good guard [Willie White, who later played in the NBA], and we got in a hole we could never get out from. When we'd lost to Iowa when we were freshmen, we'd known going in they were good and they just outplayed us. This time, it was our fault. It was sudden and it was disappointing."

Still, the twenty-two wins and the trip to the NCAA Tournament with all the key players returning the next season gave State reason for hope even if their fans were getting restless about the lack of success against North Carolina. Valvano was 3–2 against Krzyzewski, but that didn't excite anyone. If anything, people wanted to know how he'd managed to lose twice to Duke—especially that second season when the Blue Devils were 10–17 and lucky to win 10.

"Honestly, Duke never really crossed our minds," Gannon said. "They probably should have, just because they played so hard. But they didn't have the talent to compete with us at that point."

Duke didn't really have the talent to seriously compete with anyone in the ACC at that point. The Blue Devils were 4–10 in conference play and ended their season by losing 88–53 to Wake Forest in Greensboro.

Duke versus Wake was the dreaded 9:30 game—dreaded because the teams had to sit around until what felt like the middle of the night waiting their turn to play. If the game wasn't close, the Coliseum was always virtually empty by the time it was over, sometime around midnight.

With the game a complete blowout, there couldn't have been more than two thousand people left in the building as the game dragged to a finish. In the final minute, veteran ACC referee Lenny Wirtz twice called meaningless fouls on Wake Forest walk-ons who were about the only ones in the building with any energy left for anything other than going home.

As Wirtz stood in front of the press table while a Duke player went to the free-throw line, Bill Brill, a Duke graduate who had been covering the league since it had been invented in 1953—Brill had graduated in 1952—yelled Wirtz's name. Surprised, Wirtz turned to look at him. The two men had known each other forever.

"Lenny, if you blow that goddamn whistle one more time, I swear to God I'm going to come across this table and shove it down your throat," Brill said.

"Just doing my job," Wirtz said.

A moment later a hapless Wake walk-on and an equally hapless Duke walk-on collided at midcourt. Wirtz glanced at Brill, turned, and ran down the court without blowing his whistle. Thus, he lived to blow it another day.

When Mike Krzyzewski had finished talking to the media he walked over to where Mickie was waiting for him. Mickie began to cry.

"It's okay," he said. "It was just a very bad night."

"That's not why I'm crying," Mickie said. "I'm crying because the season's over."

Mike Krzyzewski looked at his wife and said, "You're kidding, right?"

Years later, Krzyzewski changed the story.

"I said to her, 'Do you still love me?' She looked at me and said, 'Honey, I still love you. I'm just not sure I respect you.'"

It would get worse before it would get better.

9

While N.C. State was showing improvement in the winter of 1982 and Duke was sliding to the worst record in school history, North Carolina had only one question to answer that March: Would the Tar Heels finally deliver a national championship in Dean Smith's twenty-first season as coach?

Carolina had lost two games during the regular season: the first was at home to Wake Forest. The Demon Deacons always gave the Tar Heels trouble because Carl Tacy had a knack for recruiting talented guards who knew how to handle UNC's trapping defenses. The other loss was at Virginia, which still had Ralph Sampson and also had excellent guard play—including Jeff Jones, who came from Owensboro, Kentucky, and had been a player Smith coveted.

"One of my biggest disappointments was not getting him," Smith often said. "He was a terrific player and a better young man."

Jones, who went on to coach at his alma mater and then at American University and Old Dominion, still has the letter Smith sent him after he had decided to go to Virginia. "He was the only coach who recruited me at a school I didn't pick who took the time to do that," Jones said. "I always had great respect for him. I had even more after that."

Smith almost always wrote to recruits he had ardently pursued who decided not to go to North Carolina, to wish them luck. It was an act of extreme grace—most coaches will tell you they'd rather not hear the name of a player who turns them down ever again—but it also paid dividends.

"I can't tell you the number of players and coaches through the years who told me that one reason they were attracted to Carolina was hearing a story about Coach Smith writing a letter like that," Eddie Fogler said. "A lot of those kids grow up to be coaches. Or their coaches remembered the letter when they had another talented player."

Was that Smith's intent in writing?

Fogler smiled. "No, I really don't think so," he said. "But it didn't hurt."

Smith didn't have Jeff Jones to coach during the winter of 1982, but he had a plethora of talent. Junior James Worthy was arguably the best player in the country and would be the number-one pick in that spring's NBA draft. Sam Perkins was a sophomore who was blossoming into a star. Jimmy Black was a senior point guard, exactly the kind of player Smith liked to have running his offense—especially with so many talented scorers in the lineup. Matt Doherty was a hard-nosed swingman from Long Island who could score, guard, and rebound.

There was also a freshman who had been the North Carolina state high school player of the year the previous season: Buzz Peterson.

"I think Michael's probably still mad about that," Peterson said with a grin thirty-three years after he and Michael Jordan had graduated from high school.

Jordan was a little bit of a late bloomer. He and Peterson first met after their junior seasons in high school at North Carolina's basketball camp. Peterson was a star already and had been invited to the two important national camps that existed in those days: the Five-Star Basketball Camp in Pennsylvania and the B/C All-Stars Basketball Camp in Georgia. Jordan had just received an invitation to Five-Star when he and Peterson first met.

"I still remember him saying to me, 'How do I get invited to B/C?'" Peterson said. "He hadn't been invited and he wanted to go there."

As it turned out, Jordan didn't really need to go to B/C. After his week at Five-Star was over, camp owner Howard Garfinkel convinced him to stay a second week—which wasn't the norm.

"There were better players coming that second week," Garfinkel said. "That meant more coaches and more media. I told him if he stayed he was going to explode as a star nationally. Funny thing is, I only took him because Roy Williams [then a UNC assistant] said they'd had him at their camp and I should invite him."

Garfinkel's advice that Jordan stay seven more days was sound. By the time his second week at Five-Star was over, every coach in the country knew about the kid from Laney High School in Wilmington. Still, because Peterson was considered a better shooter (Jordan hadn't yet developed his unstoppable jump shot), he was equally coveted in the fall of 1980.

"We tried to recruit both of them," Bobby Dwyer remembered. "We were a little late getting started when they were both juniors because we didn't get to Duke until March. But we went after them both hard after that." He smiled. "There was just one problem: we had *no* chance with either one."

Both Dwyer and Mike Krzyzewski remember visiting Peterson's house and being given a tour by Buzz. "We walked into his room and the walls were filled with Carolina posters and calendars," Dwyer said. "I remember thinking to myself, 'This is what we're up against trying to recruit in this state.'"

Peterson remembers feeling a little bit sheepish when he saw the look on the faces of the two coaches.

"Carolina always put out a calendar every year with the schedule and a team picture on it," he said. "If you had been to their camp, they would send it to you. I'd been going to the camp since I was ten, so I had every calendar.

"The funny thing is I *really* liked Coach K. He was impressive. I remember thinking, 'They're going to be good in a few years.' But I wasn't interested in a few years, I was interested in *now*. Plus, I don't think there's any way I would have been allowed to go anyplace but Carolina when all was said and done."

In fact, Peterson visited Kentucky and was awed by the facilities and the clear fanaticism everyone in the state had for Kentucky basketball. He also very much liked Leonard Hamilton, who was then Coach Joe B. Hall's top recruiter.

"Carolina had gotten a commitment from a very good guard named Lynwood Robinson," he said. "I knew Michael was going too and I really did like Kentucky. I came home and I told my friend Randy Shepard that I thought I might want to go there," Peterson said. "Next morning, I'm sitting in homeroom and my coach, Rodney Johnson, came into class and said, 'Come with me.' He took me down to his office and he said, 'Are you seriously thinking about going to Kentucky? Really? What's wrong with you?'"

Peterson laughed at the memory. "That afternoon, Coach Smith was at practice. It's about four hours to drive from Chapel Hill to Asheville and he drove. It occurred to me that, one way or the other, I was going to Carolina. Then Michael [who had already committed to UNC at that point] started calling and saying, 'Come on, Buzz, what are you thinking?'"

He ended up thinking he wanted to go to North Carolina. And he was voted the player of the year by the state high school association. "Not exactly sure what they were watching or who they were watching," Peterson said with a grin. "But it's the one thing I've got Michael doesn't have."

Peterson and Jordan were roommates in college and were in each other's weddings. In the spring of 2014, Peterson was fired as the coach at UNC Wilmington. He wasn't out of work for long. The owner of the Charlotte Hornets hired him to be a liaison between the coaching staff and the owner—in effect his eyes and ears on the court and in the locker room.

The owner was Michael Jordan, who had forgiven him—finally—for being the state player of the year thirty-three years earlier.

—

Dean Smith didn't like to start freshmen. He had opposed the NCAA rules change that had made freshmen eligible to play varsity basketball in 1972, and he had strict rules for them. In the Carolina hierarchy, they were the low men on the totem pole. A senior walk-on had rights that a highly touted freshman did not. Smith so believed in the seniority system that water breaks during practice were done according to class. It was routine for a star freshman to carry the equipment bags for walk-on seniors. When the team gathered for pregame meals at the local restaurant that had once been the Pines but was now called Slugs, they gathered in the lobby until everyone had arrived. Then the seniors walked in and sat down, followed by the juniors, sophomores, and—finally—the freshmen.

Freshmen couldn't do media interviews before they played their first game.

And, in the fall of 1981, when *Sports Illustrated* wanted to photograph Carolina's five starters for the cover of their college basketball preview issue, only four of the starters—James Worthy, Sam Perkins, Jimmy Black, and Matt Doherty—appeared. The missing fifth starter was Michael Jordan—because he was a freshman.

Twenty-eight years later, when Jordan was inducted into the Naismith Memorial Basketball Hall of Fame in Springfield, Massachusetts, he brought up his absence from that cover shot as part of a laundry list of slights he felt had motivated him during his career.

Jordan was the fourth freshman to start from day one for a Smith-coached team. The first had been Phil Ford, the second Mike O'Koren, and the third James Worthy. They had been picked second, sixth, and first upon leaving in the NBA draft. Jordan's unofficial coming-out party came in a nationally televised game in the Meadowlands against Kentucky. (Back then, network TV games were a big deal.) The teams were ranked first and second in the country (Carolina number one), which made the pregame hype huge for a December game.

Worthy and Perkins were both terrific, scoring 26 and 21 points respectively in an 82–69 Carolina win. But Jordan, with 19 points on 8-of-13 shooting and a couple of spectacular plays, had everyone talking. During his postgame press conference, Smith got frustrated with all the Jordan questions.

"You know, Michael spends a lot of his time thanking James and Sam and Jimmy Black for getting him such wide-open shots," he said finally. "They're the reason we won this game."

Black had picked up seven assists, Worthy six. Perkins had none, but the larger point was that Jordan had done plenty on his own. Smith knew that. He just didn't want a freshman emerging as his team's star—especially before conference play had begun.

That season turned out to be a historic one in Chapel Hill—for a number of reasons. North Carolina and Virginia, having split their regular season meetings, met in the ACC championship game. With just under eight minutes left, leading 44–43, Smith decided he wanted to pull Virginia out of its zone. He ordered his team into a delay offense, waiting for UVA coach Terry Holland to order his team to go man-to-man in order to pick up the pace of the game.

Holland wouldn't bite. Virginia stayed in its zone, meaning that James Worthy, Sam Perkins, Michael Jordan, Ralph Sampson, Jeff Jones, and Othell Wilson stood and stared at one another for the next seven minutes.

"It was a great game until the last eight minutes," Smith said later. "But then they wouldn't come out of their zone and chase us."

The Carolina people blamed Holland for not chasing. The Virginia people—and most of the basketball world—blamed Smith for bringing a game filled with all-world players to a halt. When the NCAA finally put in a forty-five-second clock three seasons later, most pointed at that game as the turning point in the argument for a clock.

Carolina won 47–45. In the NCAA Tournament, Virginia ended up losing—after point guard Wilson was hurt—to

Alabama-Birmingham in the round of sixteen. Carolina survived a scare from James Madison (52–50) in the second round but rolled from there to Smith's seventh Final Four. The Tar Heels beat Houston, led by Hakeem Olajuwon and Clyde Drexler, in the semifinals to set up a confrontation with Georgetown in the championship game.

The Hoyas star was a freshman, center Patrick Ewing. But they also had experienced guards, notably Eric "Sleepy" Floyd, a great shooter who had been part of the 1980 team that had just missed the Final Four. There was great drama in the coaching matchup. Smith was now on the doorstep of a championship for the fourth time, and standing in his way was John Thompson, one of his closest friends in coaching. Thompson had been one of Smith's assistants on the 1976 Olympic team and the two were good friends.

Both men were concerned about somehow not being as intense as they needed to be while coaching against each other—even with the stakes so high. As always, Smith insisted that winning wasn't *that* big a deal. Walking up the ramp to the locker room after warm-ups he encountered two reporters he knew well.

"How you feeling?" one of them asked.

Smith reached into his shirt pocket for his ever-present cigarettes. Producing the pack, he held it out and said, "Look, I've smoked less tonight than before the Duke game."

Thompson would say later that in the early minutes of the game he wouldn't look at Smith for fear that he would find himself wanting his friend and mentor to finally win the elusive title.

About five minutes into the game, Ewing was fouled. As Ewing walked to the foul line, Thompson could hear Smith talking to Hank Nichols, the lead referee on the game. Ewing's foul-shooting routine was one of the most deliberate in the history of basketball. He would often go over the allotted ten seconds that a shooter had to release a free throw once he was handed the ball. No one ever called the violation because no one could ever remember *any* official calling it.

Now, Thompson could hear Smith's distinctive voice over the din in the New Orleans Superdome. "Now, Hank, I know he takes more than ten seconds a lot, but I don't want you to call it," Smith said. "Don't worry about it. Let him take all the time he needs."

Thompson started laughing. He knew exactly what Smith was doing because he knew Smith. He was trying to gain any tiny little edge he could. He didn't expect Nichols to call a violation on Ewing, but maybe—just maybe—Nichols might at some point say, "Patrick, you're awfully close to ten seconds, be careful." Or maybe—just maybe—he'd become the first ref in history to make the call and Smith could honestly say later, "I specifically told Hank we didn't want that call made."

"It was just Dean being Dean," Thompson said years later. "He never missed a chance to gain any little edge he could. It was part of his genius. But when I heard him say that I thought, 'Hell, he's doing everything he possibly can to win the game. I damn well better do the same.'"

The game turned into a basketball classic. After Georgetown took a 62–61 lead on a Floyd jumper with just over a minute to play, Smith called time-out. He knew that Georgetown was going to sag inside on Worthy and Perkins, and he didn't love the idea of challenging Ewing. Knowing that there would come a moment when Jordan would be open on the wing, Smith patted him on the back coming out of the huddle and said, "Knock it down, Michael."

The notion that a freshman might be the hero wasn't on Smith's mind just then. Sure enough, Jimmy Black caught the ball right of the key, looked inside to Worthy, and spotted Jordan open on the left wing. He reversed the ball to him, and in one motion Jordan was in the air, the ball was out of his hand, and, with seventeen seconds left, it splashed through the net for a 63–62 lead.

Even though he had one time-out left, Thompson didn't use it—not wanting to give Smith a chance to set his defense. Sophomore guard Fred Brown raced downcourt with the ball, and with forward Eric Smith wide open under the basket, Brown turned to pass the ball to the other wing. But the "teammate" he thought he saw there was Worthy, who gratefully grabbed the perfect pass from Brown and raced to the other end of the court, all but running out the clock.

Smith never changed character when the clock hit zero. He engaged in an awkward hug with Thompson—awkward because, at six-ten, Thompson was a foot taller and it was difficult for the two men to reach each other—and then did the ritual on-court postgame interviews.

There was no formal awards ceremony—the NCAA didn't do that until 1991—so the Tar Heels began cutting the nets down. Unlike today, there was no corporate ladder sponsor, so they actually helped one another up to snip the mesh. When Smith was helped up to take his snip, the Superdome was filled with cheers—not just from the Carolina section, but from everywhere. Smith took one quick snip and insisted on coming down.

A few feet away from him, Roy Williams was weeping, and even Eddie Fogler, the tough New Yorker, had tears in his eyes. A few minutes later, as the second net was coming down, someone told Smith that "everyone" wanted him to come back and take the last cut of the net.

Smith shook his head. "Find Jimmy Black," he said. "Let him do it."

Why Black? Because he was the only senior starter. Why, Smith was asked, wouldn't he take the final cut that everyone in the building wanted him to take?

"Because I hope I'll have a chance to do this again," he said. "Jimmy won't have that chance."

When Smith came to meet the media a few moments later he was still totally in character. Three years earlier, *The Charlotte Observer*'s Frank Barrows, who was generally regarded as the best feature writer in the state, had written a lengthy piece on Smith and the "Carolina system." Barrows's thesis had been simple:

everything that Smith did that made Carolina so consistently good kept it from being great—as in great enough to win the national championship.

Barrows researched the piece, which was about five thousand words in length, exhaustively. He spent two full days with Smith and went to Kansas to interview Smith's parents—among many others. In the story, Barrows pointed out that the two most gifted college guards of the 1970s had been Phil Ford and Earvin "Magic" Johnson. "Dean Smith would never be comfortable coaching someone with the nickname 'Magic,'" Barrows asserted.

Ford had played on the North Carolina team that lost the national championship game to Marquette in 1977, in part because he had to play hurt, but also in part because Smith had stuck to his system by going to the four-corners very early and, more important perhaps, by stubbornly sticking to his system and not calling time-out to get Mike O'Koren back into the game in place of backup *senior* Bruce Buckley.

Two years later, as a sophomore, Johnson led Michigan State to the national title. Early in that season, Michigan State had lost to North Carolina in Chapel Hill.

"Magic *did* have eight turnovers in that game," Smith liked to point out.

Ford, no doubt, would never have had eight turnovers in a game.

And so, when Smith met with the media, having finally won the national championship after seven Final Four trips—in a classic game—his opening comment was this: "I guess we proved a very bright writer from Charlotte wrong tonight."

Most in the room had *no* idea what he was talking about. Those who knew Smith knew exactly what he was talking about because he had been openly disdainful of the piece in the past. In 1981, when the subject had come up, he had waved a hand angrily.

"We've done a study," he said. "Did you know that, statistically, it's much harder to get to three Final Fours than it is to win one?" Soon after that he made the comment about Johnson's eight turnovers in Chapel Hill in December 1978.

Clearly, the story had stuck with him, because it was the very first thing he thought about when he finally won his first title.

Twenty-five years later, in an interview with Scott Fowler, an *Observer* columnist, Smith said, "I shouldn't have said it. I shouldn't have gone after Barrows that way. But I just thought the premise of the whole thing was dumb."

Even in saying he was wrong, Smith couldn't completely let go of his anger.

Later that night, Rick Brewer, Carolina's longtime sports information director, was walking down the wide Superdome hallway to the locker room when he saw James Jordan, Michael Jordan's father, stomping the floor repeatedly. Brewer looked to see what might be under James Jordan's foot but saw nothing.

"Mr. Jordan, what are you doing?" he finally asked.

James Jordan looked up with a wide grin on his face. "I'm stomping that monkey once and for all," he said.

"What monkey?" Brewer asked, still baffled.

"That monkey that's been sitting on Coach Smith's shoulder all those years." He looked down at the floor and said, "Yup, it's dead. Michael finally killed it."

10

Both Jim Valvano and Mike Krzyzewski knew they had their work cut out for them after Jimmy Black took down that final cut of the net in the Superdome.

Valvano's hope lay in the improvement he had seen in his team that season and the fact that all five starters would be returning. He had cast his recruiting net far and wide and was in contention for some very talented high school players, the kind he knew he needed to recruit in order to compete with Dean Smith. The Tar Heels would lose Black and James Worthy, who turned pro after his junior season to become the number-one pick in the NBA draft, but they kept reloading. Among the freshmen arriving on campus in the fall of 1982 were Steve Hale, a talented shooting guard from Oklahoma; Curtis Hunter, a McDonald's High School All-American from Durham; and Brad Daugherty, a gifted big man from the mountains in western North Carolina.

Daugherty was seven feet one and good enough to move quickly into the starting lineup, taking the spot vacated by Worthy. He did create one headache for Smith—the kind that could exist only in the Carolina system. Smith didn't like to list players as being seven feet tall. He didn't like the notion that other coaches would be able to refer to "all those seven-footers" that the Tar Heels had on their team. Daugherty was clearly over seven feet tall. Not if you read the Carolina media guide. There, he was listed as six feet eleven and three-quarters. *Not* a seven-footer.

Smith had a rule that allowed a player to round up and add an inch to his height or round down and take off an inch. That was how he justified Daugherty going from seven feet one to six eleven and three-quarters. It was also how Larry Brown had gone from being five ten and a half to six feet as a senior and how Michael Jordan at six-four and a half was listed as six feet six.

"Everyone knows Jordan's only six-four," Pat Riley, then the coach of the Los Angeles Lakers, declared while defending the Portland Trail Blazers' decision to draft Sam Bowie ahead of Jordan in the 1984 NBA draft. "The media doesn't understand the NBA. Dean's players are never as tall as he says they are."

Perhaps not. What those in the media who had seen Jordan play *did* understand that the self-declared genius Riley did not was that Jordan could have been *five*-four and he was going to be a superstar.

With Jordan and Sam Perkins returning, Carolina would have a legitimate chance to win a second straight national title. The Tar Heels main competition in the ACC would again be Virginia, led by Ralph Sampson, who had won a second consecutive national player of the year title in 1982. N.C. State, with Sidney Lowe, Dereck Whittenburg, and Thurl Bailey now seniors, would also be a threat, as would Wake Forest. Maryland, coming off a down year, would be better, thanks in large part to a freshman forward named Len Bias. Duke's hopes for improvement lay in its freshman class. Krzyzewski's changed recruiting tactics after the failures of 1981, and his "will," as Chuck Swenson described it, had produced results.

The best and most important of the Duke signees was Johnny Dawkins, a six-foot-one-inch string bean whose leaping ability was comparable to Jordan's. He was lightning fast, the kind of guard who was almost impossible to stay in front of and, because of his vertical leap, able to get his shot off over almost anyone.

Krzyzewski had targeted Dawkins during his junior season in high school. There was another talented guard named JoJo Buchanan, from Seattle, who was also interested in Duke, but it was Dawkins, who was playing at Mackin, a Catholic school in the Washington suburbs rich in basketball tradition, that Krzyzewski wanted. Maryland wanted him too and so did Notre Dame—among others.

"Historically the best kids from Mackin [notably Austin Carr and Donald 'Duck' Williams] had gone to Notre Dame," Krzyzewski said. "So I knew we'd have our work cut out for us. But [Mackin coach] Paul DeStefano told me we'd be given a fair chance and thought we had a legitimate shot. I believed him. He was a straight shooter. So we went after Johnny very hard."

The first time Krzyzewski saw Dawkins play turned into one of the more important nights of his coaching career. Mackin was playing in the Jelleff League, which was then one of the more revered summer basketball leagues in the country. The Jelleff Boys Club was in northwest D.C., and the games were played on an outside court that was smaller than a regulation court with rickety backboards and rims. But every July the best D.C.-area teams and players came to play in the Jelleff League.

In fact, it can be argued that the most anticipated high school basketball game never played took place there in 1970. Morgan Wootten and DeMatha were the kings of high school basketball in Washington and perhaps the most famous high school team nationally in the years after the famous 1965 upset of Power Memorial. A young coach named John Thompson had built St. Anthony's High School into a local power. DeMatha wouldn't play St. Anthony's. Wootten didn't like Thompson implying he was racist and was "afraid" to play St. Anthony's in downtown Washington.

And so, when the luck of the draw in the 1970 Jelleff League matched DeMatha and St. Anthony's, an estimated five thousand people packed the stands on a warm July night—about twice as many people as the stands would hold. DeMatha won the game 108–26 because neither Thompson nor his team showed up. Instead, St. Anthony's was represented by cheerleaders and football players.

"If he wasn't going to play me in the winter, I wasn't going to play him in the summer," Thompson said years later after winning a national title as the coach at Georgetown. Although Wootten had a plethora of good players during Thompson's twenty-seven years at Georgetown, he almost never recruited any of them.

"Sometimes in life, you can live away from someone," Thompson said once.

Years later, when Thompson had retired and had become a radio talk-show host in Washington, Wootten would appear on the show regularly. "The media made all that stuff up about us not liking each other, didn't they, Morgan?" Thompson liked to say, laughing. "We always respected one another."

Krzyzewski wasn't concerned about Wootten's relationship with Thompson as he sat in the stands watching Dawkins play a Jelleff League game on a hot July night in 1981. At halftime, he was approached by a man he didn't recognize. The man didn't really recognize him either, except by the logo on his shirt that said "Duke Basketball."

At that moment, Krzyzewski was still little more than an unpronounceable name in the college basketball pantheon.

"Are you the Duke coach?" the man asked.

His name was Reginald Kitchen. He was an AAU coach. He wasn't coaching that night because, in the Jelleff League, high school teams played one another.

"I know you're here to see Dawkins," Kitchen said. High school and AAU coaches always knew which players colleges were pursuing. "But one of my players is playing in the next game and you might want to stick around to watch him too. He's only going to be a junior this fall and he's little, but he really knows how to play."

Krzyzewski was staying with his in-laws in Virginia that night and flying home the next day. "It wasn't like I had anything else to do," he said. "I thought I'd be polite and tell him that I'd stay and watch for a while."

"What's his name?" Krzyzewski asked.

"Tommy Amaker. You'll know who he is when you see him."

Krzyzewski already knew he wanted Dawkins. He also knew

that Dawkins's best position would be at the number-two guard spot, even though he was a good enough ball handler to play the point if need be. Krzyzewski got something to drink between games, said hello to Paul DeStefano to make sure that Dawkins knew he was there, and returned to his seat.

Kitchen was right. Krzyzewski knew who Amaker was right away. He was no more than five-nine and might have weighed 135 pounds. But his sense of the game was undeniable. He was waterbug-quick, made it very difficult for the opposing point guard to start his offense, and consistently set up his teammates for open shots. At halftime, Kitchen returned.

"What'd you think?" he said.

"I love him," Krzyzewski said.

"Would you like to meet his mom?" Kitchen said. "She's here."

Alma Amaker was an English teacher in Fairfax County and almost never missed one of her son's games. When Krzyzewski was introduced he shook hands with her and said, "Mrs. Amaker, your son is going to look great in Duke blue." At that moment, Tommy Amaker had no intention of wearing Duke blue. He wanted to go to Maryland. His older sister was already there, and John Lucas, his basketball hero, had played there. He had attended Lefty Driesell's summer camp in College Park for years.

Krzyzewski began planning trips to Washington to see both Dawkins and Amaker. When he couldn't make it up there, Bobby Dwyer was dispatched to make the trip. There were no restrictions then on how many times coaches could see a player in action. Dawkins didn't play a single game his senior year without at least one Duke coach in attendance.

With Dwyer more or less living in the D.C. area, the rest of the country fell—more or less—to Chuck Swenson. At one point, the *Durham Morning Herald* did a story on one of Swenson's trips when, in a four-day period, he flew from Durham to Chicago; Chicago to Phoenix; Phoenix to Los Angeles; L.A. to Seattle; and Seattle to Lincoln, Nebraska, before flying home. Swenson saw five players on that trip: Weldon Williams, Mark Alarie, Jay Bilas,

JoJo Buchanan, and Bill Jackman. All but Buchanan ended up at Duke.

But while Swenson was traveling thousands of air miles, Dawkins remained the number-one target.

"I grew up a Maryland fan," Dawkins said. "My parents were ACC fans, and, of course, if you went to Mackin you had to consider Notre Dame. I remember meeting Coach K for the first time and he was very serious. But he was also very confident. I kind of liked that he was so convinced he was going to succeed even though he hadn't done anything yet."

Dawkins was the key guard in the recruiting mix that winter. Bilas—at least early on—was the key big man. He was six-eight, an excellent student, and willing to consider leaving California. "Honestly, when Duke first contacted me, I didn't know where it was," he said. "I had to find it on a map. I just knew it was in the South, but to me 'the South' meant San Diego. But once I got to know Coach K, I got serious about the possibility of going there. I honestly believed in what he was telling me about the school and about his vision for the program.

"If UCLA hadn't just changed coaches [Larry Brown had left and had been replaced by Larry Farmer when Bilas was a junior in high school] I might have ended up there because if you lived in L.A., UCLA was the holy grail for a basketball player. My parents knew about Duke as a school. I remembered the '78 team with [Jim] Spanarkel and [Gene] Banks. The key for me though wasn't academics, it was the coach. I didn't like my high school coach. For me, it wasn't so much about what the school was but who the coach was."

Bilas liked Lute Olson, who was then the coach at Iowa, and he liked Syracuse's Jim Boeheim. He also really liked Krzyzewski.

By mid-January, Duke was en route to an awful season. Things seemed to hit bottom in a 40–36 loss at home to Maryland. The Terrapins weren't very good. The Blue Devils were worse. Vince Taylor, Tom Emma, and Chip Engelland—the team's three guards—scored 12 points apiece in the game. No one else scored for Duke.

Krzyzewski was sick that night—literally and figuratively. Watching his team play made him feel ill. He was also running a fever. He had planned a trip to Los Angeles on Monday to watch Bilas practice. Because it was a no-contact period and because he wanted Bilas to understand that he was flying coast-to-coast—coach class with a stopover in Chicago—just to see him practice, Krzyzewski called him to ask for a restaurant recommendation. He and Chuck Swenson were going to watch Bilas practice, have dinner, and then fly home on a red-eye.

"Let me check with my parents," Bilas said. "I'll get a name and directions from the school for you and give them to my coach in a note. He can hand them to you after practice."

Krzyzewski followed the plan, taking the restaurant recommendation handoff after he and Swenson had spent some time talking to Bilas's coach. When they got into the rental car, Krzyzewski opened the envelope with the name of the restaurant and the directions. He read the directions to Swenson and then noticed a PS at the bottom of the note.

"Oh, one more thing. I know this isn't as important as the restaurant is but I'm coming to Duke."

Krzyzewski sat and stared at the words for a moment almost not believing what he was seeing.

"It was a huge moment," he remembered years later. "Jay was a big-time recruit. We hadn't gotten a commitment from someone as highly thought of as he was since I had gotten to Duke. All of a sudden, I didn't feel sick or tired anymore."

Bilas had been thinking about visiting Kansas the following weekend. But his father had asked him where he stood in terms of his decision. Jay's answer was, "I'm eighty-five percent Duke, fifteen percent Syracuse."

"Then you shouldn't visit Kansas," his father said. "It's not fair to them."

Jay knew his father was right. And, unlike a lot of athletes, he hadn't enjoyed the recruiting process. "There was very much a used-car feeling about it," he said. "I was tired of it. I liked Coach K. I decided to go with my gut."

—

As important as reading Bilas's note was to Krzyzewski, a bigger moment came six weeks later. It was a Thursday night in late February when his phone rang. It was Dawkins. Krzyzewski had been pushing him to make a decision. He had even told Dawkins at one point that if Buchanan decided to come to Duke, he would take him.

"I knew what had happened to them the year before," Dawkins said. "So I understood how he felt. Of course Digger [Phelps] was also recruiting Buchanan and had told me pretty much the same thing. I knew I wanted to go to Duke. They had been the most involved from the start. They were always at my games. I liked the idea that I would be an important part of what they were doing from the start.

"So I told Coach K I was coming."

Getting Dawkins was a huge breakthrough for Krzyzewski. Bilas was a well-regarded player, but Dawkins was a *star*. Most people had assumed he would end up at Notre Dame or Maryland. One of those people was Maryland coach Lefty Driesell.

"Duke? How can you possibly go to Duke?" Driesell asked Dawkins incredulously when Dawkins called to tell him his decision.

"Well, Coach, I guess I just wanted to go to college the same place you went," Dawkins answered.

Other good players were now committing to Duke: Weldon Williams, a six-six guard out of Chicago, and Bill Jackman, a six-nine perimeter player from Grant, Nebraska, also decided to go to Duke. That left Krzyzewski with two scholarships left. He knew he wanted to give one to Mark Alarie. He wanted the last one to go to David Henderson—although he wasn't certain he'd have the chance to do that.

Alarie had been a Chuck Swenson find. He went to a small private school in Phoenix—Brophy Prep—and was a skinny six-eight as a junior. But Don Meade, whom Swenson described as "the West Coast Howard Garfinkel," meaning he knew everything about every high school player west of the Mississippi, had told him that Alarie was someone worth pursuing. He was athletic and a good student, and was *not* being pursued by any of the power schools.

Swenson flew to Santa Clara to see Alarie play in a summer camp only to learn that he'd broken his hand and wasn't there. "I was upset because I'd flown across the country to see the kid and he wasn't even there," Swenson said. "It was a camp with a lot of big-time players, so I thought I'd really get an idea if he was any good. Chances are, his being hurt was lucky for us. If he'd played in that camp and played well, he'd have drawn a lot more attention to himself. As it was, I decided it was important to see him, so I went to watch him practice—even though his hand was still in a cast. He was shooting left-handed, but you could see he had long arms and quick feet. I thought it was worth going back even though Mike was very committed to Bilas at that point."

Several months later, Swenson finally saw Alarie play—in a pre-Christmas tournament in Sacramento. Swenson liked what he saw. He still has the notes he scrawled during the first half: "Has more inside game than Bilas," he wrote at one point. At another juncture he wrote, "Tough choice between him and Bilas."

Near the end of the first half, Alarie was caught alone on a three-on-one break. The guard in the middle made a perfect pass on the wing to a player almost Alarie's height who soared in for a layup. "The next thing I saw was Alarie's hand above the [backboard] square cleanly knocking the ball away," Swenson said. "He made it look easy. As soon as the half ended I ran to a pay phone in the hallway and called Mike. I said, 'You have to fly to Phoenix as soon as you can to see this kid.'

"Mike was skeptical. For one thing, flying from Durham to Phoenix wasn't easy, and the season had started. I finally said, 'Mike, the kid's better than Bilas.' Mike started shouting at me:

'There's no way he's better than Bilas! What are you talking about?' I stuck to my guns and just kept saying, 'You have to see him.'"

And so Krzyzewski flew to Phoenix to see the kid his insane assistant coach insisted was better than Jay Bilas. "It took him about five minutes," Swenson said. "Maybe less. He turned to me and said, 'We have to get this kid.'"

The bad news was that Stanford was already very involved with Alarie. Brophy Prep kids who were good athletes often went to Stanford. "If you went to Brophy and had the chance to go to Stanford that's where you went," Alarie said. "When they got involved, I honestly figured that's where I was going to go."

Stanford made more sense for Alarie than Duke. His father had died a year earlier at the age of forty-three, leaving Mark and his mother to care for Mark's younger brother, Mike, who had cerebral palsy. Mark knew it was going to be tough on his mom when he went away under any circumstances, but at Stanford, he'd be a short plane flight away.

But Duke had two things in its favor: Rumors were rife in the college basketball world that Stanford coach Dick DiBiaso was going to be fired at season's end. Alarie didn't like the uncertainty of committing to a school without knowing who his coach would be. And then there was Krzyzewski's relentless pursuit of him.

"He made it very clear how much he wanted me to come to Duke," Alarie said. "I remember having a phone conversation with him in February and he said to me, 'Tell me honestly where you're leaning right now.' I told him it was probably eighty to eighty-five percent Stanford and fifteen to twenty percent Duke. He got angry. He said to me, 'I just wish you understood as clearly as I do how good a player you are.' When I thought about it, I knew he was right. I was always a tough self-critic. I finally decided my best chance to become a better player was going to Duke."

By the time Alarie decided to go to Duke, the same high school scouts who had been ridiculing Krzyzewski's strikeout season in 1981 were saying he had signed the best high school class of 1982. But Krzyzewski wanted one more player: Henderson.

The biggest issue was politics. Henderson was from the tiny town of Roxboro, North Carolina, and all four ACC schools in the state had recruited him. In fact, it was while recruiting Henderson that North Carolina assistant coach Eddie Fogler first came to the conclusion that Krzyzewski and Duke were going to be formidable opponents down the road.

"I went to see David play in the first round of the state high school tournament," Fogler said. "I looked around and there were two big-time schools with coaches in the gym: North Carolina with me, and Duke with Krzyzewski. I went back the next night—same thing. I didn't go back the third night. David's high school coach called me and said, 'There was one coach here last night—Krzyzewski.' I realized this guy wasn't going to be outworked by us or anybody else."

The political issue was simple: Duke was also involved with Curtis Hunter, a McDonald's All-American from Durham. Beating Carolina for Hunter would be a major coup for Krzyzewski, especially since most in-state kids Carolina wanted, Carolina got.

"We all liked Henderson better than Hunter," Bobby Dwyer said. "We thought he was a better player and a better kid—not because Curtis was a bad kid but because David was special. But if a kid from Durham who was a McDonald's All-American said yes to us over Carolina, it would be impossible to say no to him. And we only had one scholarship left to give."

The coaches even talked about trying to convince Henderson to go to prep school for a year if Hunter picked Duke. Henderson would not have gone for that. He would have gone to N.C. State. "I grew up a State fan," he said. "When I started being recruited, that's where I thought I'd go. I liked Coach V a lot and I knew the school well. Then Duke got involved.

"I went to a game in Cameron when Duke was playing Wake Forest, and during the game, Coach [Carl] Tacy tripped Danny Meagher as he was running past the Wake bench. I'm sure it was an accident, but Coach K was convinced it wasn't. I remember him running down and yelling at Coach Tacy about it. I thought,

'Hey, this guy stands up for his players no matter what.' That stuck with me."

In mid-April, after the Final Four, with much fanfare, Curtis Hunter announced he would be going to North Carolina. It was probably the only time in history that Duke's coaches celebrated *losing* a recruit.

"By then, we all really loved David," Swenson said. "Nothing had been easy for him. He drove the school bus every day to make extra money. I'll never forget the first time we went to visit his house, the bus was parked outside because he kept it there overnight. Mike, Bobby, and I were in jackets, dress shirts, and ties. We got out of the car and Mike said, 'Take off your jackets and ties.' We were just dressed too formally.

"We all wanted David. First we worried we'd lose him to State. Then we worried we'd lose him to Curtis Hunter."

Krzyzewski, Swenson, and Dwyer drove back to Henderson's house after the Hunter announcement to formally offer him a scholarship and ask him to come to Duke. "When Mike said, 'We'd like to offer you a scholarship,' David had tears in his eyes," Swenson said. "We all did. I'm not sure I've had a moment that meant more to me in coaching because of who David Henderson was. If he'd never have scored a basket, I'd have been glad we got him."

Thirty-two years later, Chuck Swenson's eyes teared up again at the memory.

Eddie Fogler's eyes don't tear up when he thinks back to that winter. "The Duke guys wanted Henderson more than Hunter," he said. "Turns out, they were right."

Duke now had the number-one-rated recruiting class in the country. That was progress.

"It was," Swenson said, "an absolute necessity for us to have any chance to survive."

A highly touted recruiting class guaranteed nothing. What it meant was there was hope. That was a big step for a coach whose team had just finished with the worst record in school history.

11

The goal at Duke going into the 1982–83 season was simple: get better. Try not to go 10–17 again and try not to end the season with a thirty-five-point loss in the ACC Tournament. The presence of the six freshmen was reason to think those modest goals could be achieved.

At North Carolina State, the challenges were completely different—and considerably more difficult. The Wolfpack had won twenty-two games in Jim Valvano's second season, but in the minds of State fans very few of them had any real meaning. The three games against North Carolina—the last in the ACC Tournament semifinals—had produced the same result that the three games against the Tar Heels had produced a year earlier: loss, loss, loss. The scores didn't matter; the outcome did.

After a one-year absence, the team had returned to the NCAA Tournament, but a first-round loss to Tennessee-Chattanooga hardly provided any salve to a fan base that found Valvano charming and funny but, if truth be told, not doing any better than, or even as well as, ole Norman had.

During the David Thompson–Monte Towe–Tom Burleson era, in the midst of the 57–1 run that had climaxed with winning the 1974 national championship, ole Norman's team had beaten ole Dean's team nine straight times. By the time that run began—in 1972—Smith was about to take Carolina to the Final Four for the fourth time in six seasons, which, unless your name was John Wooden, was an unheard-of sort of run.

The nine-game Wolfpack winning string ended during Thompson and Towe's senior year (Burleson had graduated) in 1975 when Carolina won in Chapel Hill and in the ACC Tournament championship game. Ole Dean ended up beating ole Norman ten of the last twelve times their teams played.

Even so, the memory of that nine-game winning streak lingered in Raleigh.

"I heard about it all the time," Valvano remembered several years after his own national title run. "Whenever I spoke to a Wolfpack club or if I was out to dinner it would come up. Sometimes it would be subtle: 'Gosh, those teams we had back in the seventies were great.' Sometimes it was less subtle: 'Remember when David, Tommy, and Monte beat up on the Tar Heels?' And sometimes it was blatant: 'Hey, Coach, you ever going to beat Carolina?'"

It was moments like those that caused Valvano to make up the story about the fan threatening to kill his nonexistent dog. But in more serious moments he knew, having lived in the state for two years, that not beating the Tar Heels was completely unacceptable.

"In some way, to our fans, beating Carolina was as important, maybe more important, than winning the national championship," he said. "It wasn't about Duke. It was never about Duke because back then Mike hadn't gotten it going and we handled them more often than not. But Dean and Carolina had that aura. The whole light-blue thing. I swore when I got there that I wasn't going to get caught up in it. You don't judge the success of your program on how you do against one team—no matter how good that team might be.

"But I knew there were a lot of people who *did* judge us based on one thing: how we did against Carolina. And, yes, there were times it got to me. I always believed that we could be good and they could be good too. But after eighty-two, when we won twenty-two and made the tournament, I didn't hear, 'Hey, nice job, Coach, you won eight more than last year.' I heard, 'When are you going to beat Carolina?'"

Valvano always did a good job publicly deflecting how much losing destroyed him. He deflected it with his humor and with his ability to instantly break down what had happened in a game as if he were watching it replay inside his head as he spoke. But those who knew him best understood that losing, that *any* loss, tore him up and the 0–6 record against Carolina was even worse than that.

"He was always a bad loser—very bad," Pam Valvano Strasser remembered. "He would come home and just want to be alone, need to be alone. It was very hard at times—on me and on the girls. Their dad was away a lot anyway and then he'd be at home but not be there.

"I always cringed when he'd schedule a tough game as the last one before Christmas because if he lost, he wouldn't come downstairs on Christmas morning. I'd stall the girls as long as I could and then I'd go upstairs and say, 'Jim, you have to come down and open presents with your daughters.' He would say, 'I need some more time,' and I'd tell him he didn't have any more time. It was Christmas."

Jim's older brother, Nick, remembered his brother taking losing hard his entire life. "He was small growing up, didn't really grow at all until he was a senior in high school," he said. "He was always trying to prove himself. He was a *great* athlete. He was such a good hitter as a sophomore in high school they couldn't keep him out of the lineup. But his arm was so weak he could barely make the throw from second to first on a double play."

It seemed to Valvano that he was always finding a way to overcome his failings. As a point guard at Rutgers, he could barely dribble the ball at all with his left hand. And yet, he succeeded.

"He'd come down the court and he was all right hand," said Lou Goetz, who was a teammate. "He had this up-and-down way of dribbling as if he wasn't going to go forward at all. But then, somehow, he'd create something, find Bobby Lloyd open, and we'd score. He did what he had to do to be an effective player. And, by senior year, he'd made himself into a good shooter too."

Goetz was two years behind Valvano in school. They were teammates—but never close. Like a lot of people, Goetz was awed by Valvano's humor and showmanship. But he didn't always enjoy it.

"Jimmy would always sit in the back of the bus with a group of guys and do his shtick," Goetz remembered. "He'd do it on the way home, even after losses. Some of us didn't think that was the time for humor. And I promise you there were times when [Coach] Bill Foster didn't think it was the time for humor. I can remember him standing up on more than one occasion and screaming at Jimmy to shut the f—— up."

The bus-ride shticks were a precursor to Valvano's postgame riffs after losses as a coach. They were a defense mechanism. "You got two choices after a loss," he would often say. "You can laugh or you can cry. I didn't want anyone to see me cry."

The desire to cry, though, was always there.

"I can remember days after a loss when I'd see Mrs. V," Sidney Lowe remembered. "I'd say, 'How's he doing?' because we knew how hard he took the losses. She'd just shake her head sometimes and say, 'It's not good today.' The worst, though, was after we'd lose to Carolina. It had been a while but at least Dereck, Thurl, and I had won against them as freshmen. Coach V hadn't done it and neither had any of the underclassmen."

Which is why Valvano felt an almost desperate need to beat North Carolina and—if possible—do better in both the ACC Tournament and in the NCAA Tournament in his third season. He had joked when he first arrived at N.C. State that he knew he would never outcoach Dean Smith but he hoped he could outlive him. It was beginning to look as if that might be the only way for Valvano to finally beat ole Dean.

—

In Chapel Hill that fall, things were far more comfortable. Dean Smith would never admit that winning the national championship changed his life, but it did, if only because he didn't have to have assistant coaches spend time statistically proving it was harder to get to three Final Fours than to win one of them.

There were no more questions about the exclamation point needed to finish the sentence on his career résumé. It now read:

nine ACC Tournament titles, seven Final Fours, an Olympic gold medal, an NIT championship, and—*finally*—a national championship. There was only one active coach whose record could measure up to Smith's and that was Indiana's Bob Knight, who had won two national titles. But Smith hadn't been arrested in Puerto Rico while coaching the U.S. Pan American team in 1979, hadn't stuffed a taunting fan into a garbage can at the Final Four in 1981, and was not considered a sometimes-out-of-control bully.

Smith was proof that you could be a great coach and treat people with respect.

He also had a team that appeared to have an excellent chance to win a second national title in a row. James Worthy and Jimmy Black were gone. But Michael Jordan, now very clearly a star, was back, and so were Sam Perkins and Matt Doherty. What's more, the freshman class—led by Brad Daugherty, Steve Hale, and Curtis Hunter—was, again, dazzling.

Daugherty was one of four Carolina players listed that season at six-ten or more: John Brownlee was six-ten, and Daugherty, Warren Martin, and Timo Makkonen were all at least six-eleven. Naturally, there were *no* seven-footers. Regardless of Daugherty's height, he was only seventeen when he enrolled and clearly had remarkable potential. Hale and Hunter were also McDonald's All-Americans—which was why Duke would have been compelled to take Hunter if he hadn't chosen North Carolina.

The other two teams being picked at the top of the polls that fall were Virginia—which returned two-time national player of the year Ralph Sampson, who at seven-four couldn't possibly be rounded down to under seven feet by Terry Holland—and Houston, which had lost to Carolina in the Final Four and had Hakeem Olajuwon, who was still in many ways learning how to play the game, returning along with All-American forward Clyde Drexler. Georgetown still had Patrick Ewing but had graduated three important seniors and was probably a year away from another Final Four run.

There was a good deal of talent in the ACC outside Virginia and North Carolina. N.C. State's top six players were back. Whittenburg, Lowe, and Bailey returned for their senior seasons along with the three sophomores—Lorenzo Charles, Cozell McQueen, and Terry Gannon—who had played often as freshmen. Joining them was Ernie Myers, a six-foot-five-inch McDonald's All-American whom Valvano had been able to recruit successfully from the Bronx.

Wake Forest had won twenty-one games the previous season and reached the NCAA Tournament. Maryland was coming off its worst season in years but had added Len Bias to pair with Adrian Branch, who had led all ACC freshmen in scoring the previous season. Clemson had been to the Elite Eight of the NCAAs as recently as 1980 but had a very young team that would struggle in a stacked ACC.

Finally, there was Duke and there was Georgia Tech. The Yellow Jackets were in their fourth season in the ACC. Their first two seasons under Dwane Morrison, a chain-smoking, deeply religious man who ended all conversations by saying, "Bless you, brother," had produced one conference victory—total. Out went Morrison and in came Bobby Cremins, who was a Fourth of July baby in 1947—making him a little more than four months younger than Krzyzewski and fifteen months younger than Valvano.

Cremins was a Bronx kid who, like a lot of New York players, had found his way to the South to play for Frank McGuire—after McGuire landed at South Carolina in 1964 following his unsuccessful NBA stint in Philadelphia. "When Coach McGuire came to my house he brought the parish priest and a cop from the local precinct because he knew everybody in the Bronx," Cremins said. "That was pretty much it. I was going even though I had no idea where Columbia, South Carolina, was."

Cremins was a very good player on very good teams led by All-Americans like John Roche, Kevin Joyce (also from the Bronx), Tom Riker, and Tom Owens. Cremins was the guy who did everything on offense and defense. He would also *say* anything. Shortly after getting the Georgia Tech job he told Dean Smith he owed him a huge debt of gratitude.

"We were playing Carolina in Chapel Hill and we're up late in the game," Cremins said. "Dean kept fouling me because I was the worst foul shooter. We won 87–86 because I made all the free throws." Cremins paused for effect. "Next night I lost my virginity because I was such a hero on campus."

In 1969, South Carolina finished second in the ACC and went to the NIT since only one conference team could go to the NCAAs and that was tournament champion North Carolina. In the quarterfinals they played an Army team coached by Bob Knight and captained by a senior guard named Mike Krzyzewski.

Late in the game, with Army leading, McGuire called time-out to tell his players they were going to come out of their zone and go man-to-man to put pressure on the ball and try to create turnovers. Coming out of the huddle, McGuire turned to Cremins and said, "You know who you've got, Bobby?"

"Yeah, sure," Cremins answered. "I've got the kid with the big nose whose name I can't pronounce."

Army and the kid with the unpronounceable name and the big nose won the game.

Cremins got his first head-coaching job at Appalachian State in 1975 and was successful there, going 100–70 in six seasons. In 1980, hearing that there was no clear-cut candidate for the Duke job, he decided to call Tom Butters. Recognizing the name, Butters took the call. Cremins asked if Butters had hired a coach yet because, if not, he was interested.

"We've got a short list," Butters told him. "We're going to make the hire soon."

Cremins asked who was on the list. Butters told him.

"Mike Krzyzewski?" Cremins asked. "The guy from Army? Boy, Tom, you do that, I think you're making a big mistake."

Years later, Cremins laughed at the memory. "I guess it's fair to say Tom knew what he was doing," he said. "It worked out okay for him."

Cremins arrived in the ACC a year later. His first recruiting class included John Salley, a gifted big man from Brooklyn, and Mark Price, a baby-faced guard from Enid, Oklahoma.

"I owe Dean Smit [aka Smith] on that one too," Cremins said. "He and his guys liked Steve Hale. Price would have walked to Chapel Hill to play there. He loved North Carolina. [Cremins actually says 'Naut Cowlina' in his distinctive Bronx accent.] If Dean recruits him, I have no chance—zero. But they liked Hale."

Hale had a very solid college career and is now a doctor. Price became one of the great guards in ACC history and an NBA All-Star. He was six foot one and looked like a freckled-face choirboy, which he was—he sang in his church choir growing up. But he was stunningly quick with the ball and a dead-eye shooter. He and Salley immediately made Georgia Tech a competitive team, and Cremins quickly became a popular figure in the ACC. Whenever he walked on court at Cameron Indoor Stadium, his prematurely gray hair bouncing up and down in the floppy-haired style he favored, the Duke students began chanting "Grecian" on one side of the court and "Formula" on the other side.

Cremins loved it. "Jimmy, Mike, and I were the young guns back then," he said. "Of course for a while it looked like only two of us would survive."

He laughed again. "Guess I got that one wrong too."

12

The so-called number-one recruiting class of 1982 met one another for the first time as a group at Mike Krzyzewski's house late in August after arriving on campus to enroll as Duke freshmen.

Jay Bilas and Mark Alarie had actually crossed paths on occasion during summer league tournaments, and Bilas and Johnny Dawkins had met when Bilas had been in Washington for a few days that summer and Krzyzewski had suggested he look Dawkins up.

Bilas had done that. Dawkins had told Bilas to come to his house and that they'd go to a nearby playground where the best players in the area congregated. When Bilas knocked on the door, Dawkins's little brother answered.

Or so Bilas thought. "This kid came to the door," Bilas said. "He looked about fourteen, maybe fifteen. He was really skinny. I said, 'Hey, is your big brother here?'"

"You mean Johnny?" the kid asked.

"Yeah, Johnny," Bilas said.

"That's me," the kid answered.

"I probably weighed about one forty-five—soaking wet," said Dawkins, who is now the basketball coach at Stanford. "Jay was embarrassed but he shouldn't have been. I looked *young*."

Any doubts Bilas might have had about Dawkins upon first laying eyes on him went away when they got to the courts.

"He was without question the quickest guy I'd ever played with," Bilas said. "He had an explosiveness that you just don't see very often. I had heard that he was very good, but seeing him in person was impressive."

There was more. "There was a play at the end of our first game where it looked like we had lost," Bilas said. "I don't remember exactly what happened, but Johnny got into an argument about it—and won. You don't win arguments on the schoolyard like that but Johnny argued anyway. We ended up winning the game. That told me something about his toughness and competitiveness."

Right from the start, Dawkins was the leader of the freshman group. Some of it was his personality and some of it was that he was the best player. "When he said, 'Let's do something,' we did it," Mark Alarie said.

And so, that first day at Krzyzewski's house, when Dawkins said they were all going to drive to Chapel Hill the next day to play in the pickup games at Woollen Gym, there weren't any questions asked other than, "What time do we leave?"

In those days, teams couldn't formally practice in any way until October 15. Early in the fall, players at top schools would gather to play against one another. The best games were usually the ones played in Carolina's old gym, the same place where Dean Smith had once been hung in effigy outside.

There was a game going on when the Duke freshmen walked in. They sat on the floor at one end of the court, their heads resting against the wall while they watched and waited for a turn to play. As luck would have it, Michael Jordan was playing in the game that was going on as they sat down.

"We'd only been there for a couple of minutes when Jordan caught a pass on the baseline pretty much right in front of us," Alarie remembered. "He made a shot fake and went to the basket and dunked the ball. As he did it, he bumped his head *against the backboard.* I was sitting next to Jay, and I looked at him and we both said the same thing: 'What the f—— have we gotten ourselves into?' It was pretty intimidating."

When the Duke kids got their chance to play, they didn't last long. "Whoever we were playing took care of us pretty quickly," Alarie said. "Maybe I was being paranoid, but as we were walking off the court I thought I heard someone say, 'That's the best recruiting class in the country?' Or maybe *I* was the one thinking it."

There were a lot of people thinking the same thing once the season began. Krzyzewski was a little bit like a chemist that fall looking for a combination that would work. He had four seniors who knew that the future of the program lay with the freshmen but still believed it should be *their* team. There was also the sophomore class, the guys who had been signed the previous spring after all the big names had gone to other places. And there were the freshmen, who believed they should play because, quite simply, they were better than the older guys.

There wasn't a lot of love lost between the seniors and the freshmen. It showed—especially on the court. After winning their first two games against weak opposition, the Blue Devils lost four in a row—unheard-of for an ACC team in December. The good news was that the next four games were at home against teams that couldn't possibly beat Duke.

Except one of them—Wagner—did.

Located in Staten Island, New York, Wagner didn't have one of those dangerous lower-level Division I teams that year. The Seahawks came to Durham with a 2–7 record having just lost at UNLV by 50. They beat Duke, 84–77. At one point early in the second half Dawkins was stripped on back-to-back possessions by Wagner's Bob Mahala. After the game Krzyzewski didn't even know Mahala's name. "We couldn't stop number ten," he said.

That was Mahala. Wagner would go on to finish 10–18, but that night the Seahawks carried their coach, Neil Kennett, off the court. On the night Krzyzewski became college basketball's all-time winningest coach, *Staten Island Advance* columnist Cormac Gordon wrote a column about that game almost twenty-nine years earlier and described Krzyzewski and Kennett crossing paths again at a funeral many years later. According to Gordon, Kennett approached Krzyzewski and said, "Coach, I'm sure you don't remember me . . ."

"I remember you very well," Krzyzewski answered. "Because of you, I haven't taken an opponent lightly in thirty years."

There would be other low moments, but this one was unique

because it was in Cameron—which wasn't close to full that night. The listed attendance was 5,500. When the game was over, those who were there made their feelings known.

"I think we're all probably a little blurry on the game," Bilas said. "But we all remember what we heard going off the court afterwards."

To get to the locker room, the players and coaches had to pass directly below the stands in the corner of the gym where most of the alumni and boosters sat. As they did, they could very clearly hear fans—*their* fans—many of them leaning down over the railing so they were almost in their faces, screaming at all of them in anger.

"It was almost all directed at Coach K," David Henderson remembered. "Some of it was profane, but most of it was, 'You're a loser' and 'You're out of here, pack your bags!' That kind of stuff."

"That was the gist of most of it," Bilas said. "They wanted him gone. It made us angry—at them, but also at ourselves for playing so poorly."

A new joke began making the rounds in the ACC after the Wagner game: if Krzyzewski could do for Duke basketball in three years what he had done for Wagner basketball in forty minutes, he would be a huge success.

There were not a lot of yuks in Durham. The team was divided. Some of the seniors were telling the freshmen they might as well transfer because there was no way Krzyzewski would be around beyond their sophomore years—if that long. By mid-February, Krzyzewski had decided to ride the freshmen the rest of the season because they were the future.

The tension inside the locker room was perhaps best summed up when the team sat down to watch tape after being routed 105–81 by North Carolina in the regular season finale in Cameron. Krzyzewski had started the three remaining seniors: Tom Emma, Chip Engelland, and Mike Tissaw (one, Allen Williams, had left the team at midseason). They were the last of Bill Foster's recruits.

Engelland and Emma had been starters for large chunks of their careers. Tissaw's minutes had gone way down once Bilas and Alarie arrived, but Krzyzewski started him in his final home appearance. On Duke's first possession of the game, Tissaw took an eighteen-foot jump shot—a shot that was about seventeen feet outside his range. As he played back the tape, Krzyzewski stopped it right after Tissaw released the shot.

"You see, when I look at this, Tiss," Krzyzewski said, "all I can think is that you're just saying 'f—— you' to me."

There was a long silence in the room.

"That's because that's exactly what Tiss was saying with that shot," Mark Alarie said thirty-three years later. "It's probably fair to say that's how the seniors felt at that stage of the season."

—

The seniors hated their coach and resented the freshmen. The freshmen felt the resentment and the anger and resented it right back. The coach understood the seniors' frustration on an intellectual level but not on an emotional level.

"There was a lot of bad feeling," Krzyzewski said. "I was a young coach, still learning, and I didn't handle it well. If the blame's on anyone, it's on me. We had no leadership at all in the locker room. Johnny [Dawkins] tried but he was still a freshman trying to learn to play in the ACC, and even for him that was hard. By the time we got to Atlanta we were done."

Not only done—but humiliated. The Blue Devils were matched against Virginia in the opening round of the ACC Tournament, played that year in Atlanta's Omni. Virginia led only 59–50 at halftime, thanks in large part to the fact that Ralph Sampson spent much of the first half on the bench with two fouls.

The game got completely out of hand in the second half and the final score was 109–66. Thirty-two years later, Krzyzewski remembers the score—and most of the night—vividly.

"I was angry with everyone," Krzyzewski said. "In fact I hated almost everyone that night. I hated what I'd let my team become.

We had no leadership—least of all from me—we were bickering, and we didn't play nearly as hard as we should have played.

"I hated my opponent because I thought Terry [Holland] had run up the score. I hated my alumni because I knew they were grumbling behind my back that I should be fired and none of them would look me in the eye. Hate can destroy you or it can fuel you. I knew I had to find a way for it to fuel me."

Krzyzewski and Holland got into a shouting match in the hallway outside the locker room after each had finished his postgame press conference. Holland had expressed frustration with Jay Bilas, saying he believed that the six-eight freshman had been trying to hurt Sampson, his seven-four senior.

"I wasn't trying to hurt anyone," Bilas said, years later. "I was trying not to get humiliated and I failed utterly."

Sampson played only fourteen minutes in the game because of the two first-half fouls and the second-half score. Even in those limited minutes, he scored eighteen points and had twelve rebounds, which might be why—in Krzyzewski's memory—he played *forty* minutes, not fourteen. Years later, in a radio interview with Dan Patrick, he said he had been most angry at Holland that night because Sampson played all forty minutes.

"I guess," he said, after learning Sampson had played only fourteen minutes, "it just *felt* like forty minutes."

In truth, it felt to the Duke people as if the game would never end. When it did, after Holland and Krzyzewski had yelled at each other, Krzyzewski went back to Duke's hotel on the outskirts of Atlanta. Mickie was in the room, in tears, convinced that Butters was going to be forced to fire her husband.

Butters had been set upon by Iron Duke boosters as soon as he walked into the hotel lobby, asking him what he intended to do about the situation.

"There was no way I was going to fire Mike," Butters said. "I was still completely convinced he was the right coach. I heard a lot of anger that night from a lot of people. But there were no death threats . . . yet."

Long after midnight, Bobby Dwyer gathered a small group of Krzyzewski friends and convinced his boss that he needed to get out of the hotel and get something to eat. In pouring rain, the group of eight—including two reporters, one accompanied by his wife; Krzyzewski, Dwyer, and his fiancée; and Duke's sports information director Tom Mickle and his assistant, Johnny Moore—walked into a Denny's.

Water was served. Mickle picked up his water and said, "Here's to forgetting tonight."

Krzyzewski picked up his water glass and looked at the soggy group around him. "Here," he said, "is to never *f——ing* forgetting tonight."

And he never did.

—

While the Duke people headed home from Atlanta to lick their many wounds, North Carolina and North Carolina State were playing the first game of semifinal Saturday at the ACC Tournament.

The Tar Heels' season had gone pretty much as had been expected. They had lost their first two games of the season to ranked teams (St. John's and Missouri) and had then gone 25–4 the rest of the regular season. They had beaten Virginia twice and had lost two ACC games in February: at Maryland and then at N.C. State.

State's victory in Reynolds Coliseum wasn't just critical—Carolina had won the teams' first meeting 99–81 in Chapel Hill to drop Valvano to 0–7 against the Tar Heels—it was cathartic. It was also surprising, because Dereck Whittenburg was still out of the lineup nursing the foot he had broken on January 12 against Virginia. Whittenburg had been on fire in the first half of that game, scoring twenty-seven points—aided by the fact that the ACC was using an experimental three-point line that was literally inside the key.

"I don't want to say the line is close," Valvano said one day.

"But my mom dropped by practice yesterday and *she* made nine of ten from behind the line."

But with State leading Virginia by five and Reynolds Coliseum in a frenzy early in the second half, Whittenburg accidentally stepped on Virginia guard Othell Wilson's foot right in front of the State bench. He went down writhing in pain—his right foot broken for the second time in his career. The doctors said he was done—his college career over. Valvano held out some hope for postseason.

"I knew they were wrong," Whittenburg said. "I'd made it back in six weeks the first time. I knew I could do it again."

Without Whittenburg, State lost that night and then lost four of its next six games to drop to 9–7. It appeared the season was spiraling out of control. Valvano decided to change his offense—going from a lot of high screens designed to set up jump shooters like Whittenburg, Terry Gannon, and Sidney Lowe to a motion offense that opened up the lane. This was especially helpful to freshman Ernie Myers, who was excellent at powering his way to the basket. Myers scored thirty-five points in a rout of Duke ("rout of Duke" was becoming redundant by that point in the season) and State went on a 7–2 skein.

"It was a scary time right after Whitt got hurt," Lowe said. "It was scary for me because I'd never played without him since my sophomore year of high school. There were times, especially right after the injury, when I remember thinking, 'Maybe this isn't going to end the way we want it to.' But then Coach V made some changes in the offense and Ernie began to play really well. In a lot of ways, Ernie saved our season."

On February 19, with Whittenburg almost ready to come back, Carolina came to town. State played an almost perfect game, Lowe dominating the ball in the final minutes when the Tar Heels were trying to rally. A couple of weeks earlier, in a game against Wake Forest, Lowe had been dribbling the clock down and felt a wave of exhaustion.

"First, I tried to give him [Valvano] the tired sign," Lowe said, laughing. "He just looked the other way as if he didn't see me. Then I dribbled over near the bench and shouted, 'Coach, I think I need a blow.'"

Valvano had nodded. "You'll get one, Sidney," he said. "Just as soon as your eligibility is used up."

Lowe understood. He wasn't coming out of any game that was still in doubt. On that euphoric night in Reynolds Coliseum, the thought of a rest never crossed his mind. "No way was I coming out of *that* game," he said. "We were all tired, but none of us wanted to come out."

Lowe and the Wolfpack made it to the finish line, and the fans stormed the court. Back then, court stormings were a big deal. North Carolina was ranked number three in the country, but that wasn't the only reason to storm the court. It was Valvano's first win over Smith and finally broke the seven-game losing streak that had started soon after ole Norman left town.

"It was unbelievably important," Pam Valvano Strasser said years later. "I think Jim honestly was starting to believe he couldn't beat Dean, no matter what. To beat them at all felt like a miracle. To do it without Dereck *was* a miracle."

Eight days later, Whittenburg was ready to play again. State was a different team, though—one that was often fueled by Myers. It took a couple of games for the Wolfpack to adapt from looking to set Myers up to drive the ball to again looking for Whittenburg to shoot the ball from the perimeter. They promptly lost back-to-back games to Virginia and Maryland. That dropped their record to 16–10 overall and 7–6 in the ACC.

They finally got their act together in the final game of the regular season, crushing Wake Forest 130–89 in the final home game for Whittenburg, Lowe, and Bailey.

"That game was important even though it didn't appear to be at the time," Whittenburg said. "It told us how good we could be when we got rolling. I think everyone had forgotten a little bit how well we were playing the night I got hurt. We needed that reminder going into the ACC Tournament. A lot of people had been saying we were dead. I said, 'A dead team doesn't beat someone as good as Wake Forest by forty-one.' We were a long way from dead."

There was some talk going into the ACC Tournament that State—the number-four seed—might get an at-large bid to the tournament if it got to the championship game and lost. North Carolina and Virginia—the Tar Heels were the top seed in the tournament by virtue of their two wins over UVA, even though both teams had finished 12–2—were tournament locks. So was Maryland, which had finished third. Georgia Tech, Duke, and Clemson—the sixth, seventh, and eighth seeds—weren't going anywhere. Wake Forest, the number-five seed, probably needed one win to get in, because it had a stronger overall résumé than the Wolfpack.

N.C. State probably needed to win at least two games and make the finals to get a bid. Valvano wasn't convinced even that would be good enough.

"We can't lose again," Valvano told his team before the tournament. "We need three wins this weekend if we want a bid Sunday night. It's in our hands now. We can't leave it in anyone else's hands. If we lose, it's out of our hands."

—

The Wolfpack was very lucky to win one game that weekend, much less three. It took a critical last-minute steal by Lowe from Wake Forest star Rodney Rogers to allow State to escape with a 71–70 victory on Friday afternoon—the game being played right after North Carolina had opened the tournament with an easy win over Clemson and a few hours before Virginia's humiliation of Duke.

Wake had been leading 70–69 when Lowe stole the ball. He found Lorenzo Charles on the wing, and Charles went to the basket and was fouled. He made both free throws for the winning points. After the game, Lowe was asked if he had thought about waiting for Whittenburg or Bailey to come open or even take the shot himself rather than pass the ball to Charles, whose game at that stage was built around his rebounding and his defense.

"Never occurred to me," Lowe said. "I saw that Lo had a lane to the basket and I knew he could make a play—or free throws."

Years later, Lowe looked back on that play as a harbinger of what was to come. "I think I believed, we all believed, that whoever was on the court could make whatever play we needed to make," he said. "I never thought for a second about *not* giving the ball to Lo. I had complete confidence in him."

Georgia Tech's late-night upset of Maryland set up a semifinal Saturday afternoon that started with Carolina playing N.C. State. There was little reason to believe, especially on a neutral court, that the Wolfpack could repeat the magic it had found in Raleigh three weeks earlier.

Something happened just before the start of the game that afternoon that may not have affected the outcome but did affect Valvano's mood.

"Jim and Dean were talking at midcourt just before they blew the players off the court to introduce the lineups," assistant coach Tom Abatemarco remembered. "Jim always did that with the other coach. It actually helped distract him instead of worrying about every detail—which he did all the time.

"He comes walking back to the bench and I can see he's angry. I said, 'V, what's up?' He starts shaking his head and saying, 'F——ing Dean, f——ing Dean, he just can't stop himself.'

"I asked him what he was talking about and he said, 'Dean just said to me, "So I guess you have to win today *and* tomorrow if you want to have any chance to make the tournament." I know what he's doing. He's trying to get in my head, get me thinking about that instead of the game. Son of a bitch.'

"I started laughing. I said, 'V, guess what, he *did* get inside your head!' He shook his head and said, 'Dammit, you're right. He did.'"

Smith wasn't inside the State players' heads once the game began. With Whittenburg now fully integrated back into the lineup, they were completely convinced that they could play with the Tar Heels. The game went back and forth until Carolina finally pulled away and took a 75–62 lead with a little more than three minutes left. Somehow, helped by Carolina missing several free throws, State rallied—the beginning of a pattern that would continue until the national championship game. Even so, with the score tied at 77, Sam Perkins launched a long jumper from the left wing at the buzzer to try to win the game. The ball went in and out, and the teams went to overtime.

"I thought it was in," Lowe said. "I watched Sam's follow-through and I could tell he thought he made it. To this day, I'm honestly not sure how it stayed out." He shrugged. "Meant to be, I guess."

"Amazing," Whittenburg said. "The shot's halfway down—at least. If it stays in we go to the NIT and I'm honestly not sure that V still has a job when the season's over. Think about it—we would have been to one NCAA Tournament in three years. Even though my injury *should* have given him a little bit of a break, it might not have. All people would have remembered was that our last important game of the season was *another* loss to Carolina."

Abatemarco never felt as if Valvano's job was in jeopardy. "But you never know," he said. "Willis [Casey] was an unpredictable guy. If one of the big Wolfpack Club guys, or a bunch of them, had gone in to him and said, 'Get that Italian guy from New York out of here,' it could have happened."

It never became an issue because State, after trailing by 6 early in the overtime, rallied again, then made all its free throws in the final minute and won the game, 91–84. Instead of exiting with yet another loss to the Tar Heels, the Wolfpack now had won two in a row against them.

Even with Smith inside Valvano's head.

"I've always liked Dean," Valvano said years later. "I respected who he was and the program he built. But there was never a possible angle he wouldn't play if he thought it would help him win. It was part of why he was so damn good. But I can also understand why he made guys like Lefty and Terry Holland crazy. There was never any letup."

The win over Carolina put State into the tournament final against Virginia—a team it had already lost to twice, including the night Whittenburg was injured. A tense, seesaw game turned when Virginia assistant coach Jim Larrañaga was—shockingly— called for a technical foul with 5:15 left and State up 71–66. Whittenburg's four free throws made it 75–66, and Virginia, which very much wanted to win the game because it was Sampson's last chance to win an ACC Tournament, never caught up. Hanging on for dear life in the final seconds, State won, 81–78.

The Wolfpack was in the NCAA Tournament. Valvano didn't have to worry about his job. And, as it would turn out, he was also about to make Mike Krzyzewski's job safer—even if that was never his intent.

13

Mike Krzyzewski has given a lot of thought to the events of March 1983. Even now, after becoming the first coach in the history of men's college basketball to win a thousand games, he thinks about what might have been—or, more specifically, what might not have been.

"I think you can make the case that Jim Valvano saved my job that year," he said on an unseasonably warm October afternoon more than thirty-one years later. "I know Tom [Butters] has said he never would have fired me, and I absolutely believe that he believes that. But there were a lot of angry people around here after Atlanta.

"Everyone expected Carolina to go deep into the tournament, so the local media was already geared up for that. The only real surprise was that they ended up *not* making the Final Four. The shock was that State kept winning and advancing. And they played the entire tournament out west, so the local news departments had to send people out there to cover them."

He smiled. "That gave me and, by extension, Tom, cover. The media was so focused on what State was doing that we were out of sight, out of mind. At that point in time, that was the absolute best thing for us. The less people talked about us, wrote about us, even thought about us, the better off we were."

There weren't many in the Triangle expecting much more from N.C. State once the tournament began. As impressive as their ACC Tournament weekend had been, it wasn't that uncommon for upsets to occur in the conference tournament, where everyone knew everyone and if any team—even the best teams—had any sort of weakness, the opponent knew exactly what it was.

One example: Whenever North Carolina played Virginia, Dean Smith told his players to back way off Ralph Sampson early in the game and give him room to shoot from the perimeter. Sampson was a reasonably good shooter, especially for someone who was seven foot four.

"We always hoped he'd make his first one," Smith said. "Because if he did, he'd stay out there and keep shooting. Where would we rather have him, outside or inside?"

On the flip side, when teams outside the conference encountered Carolina's run-and-jump trapping defense, they frequently had trouble handling it. ACC teams, having seen it in the past, not only knew it was coming but almost always knew *when* it was coming, rendering it far less effective.

That was one reason Virginia had won the ACC tournament as a number-six seed in 1976 and then, so euphoric about its victory, had lost to DePaul in its first NCAA Tournament game a week later. A year later, Virginia had been the number-seven seed and had come within a whisker of *again* winning the tournament, losing to top-seeded North Carolina 75–69 after leading late in the championship game. Three years later, Duke had also won the ACC Tournament as a number-six seed. State winning the 1983 tournament as a number-four seed was a surprise but not a shock.

That 1977 championship game had really been the start of Terry Holland's simmering feud with Dean Smith. Holland's best player was Marc Iavaroni, a hard-nosed six-eight forward from Long Island, who would go on to play and coach in the NBA. Iavaroni wasn't afraid to mix it up, and Smith didn't like the way he pushed his big men around in the low post. At halftime, Smith confronted Iavaroni on the way to the locker rooms, planting himself in front of him and pointing his finger up into his face to tell him to lay off the physical stuff.

Iavaroni was hardly bothered by Smith's indignation. He laughed and continued to the locker room. Terry Holland—and his wife, Ann—were not amused.

"I was only a few yards away in my seat," Ann Holland said.

"I looked up and saw Dean pointing up at Marc, clearly lecturing him. I wanted to run down there and tell him to stop, but of course I couldn't."

Had Terry Holland been a little bit closer, he undoubtedly would have told Smith to stop. "I was stunned," he said. "I just couldn't believe any coach, much less Dean Smith, would behave that way."

Actually, Smith yelling at opposing players was, as longtime UNC play-by-play man Woody Durham, a close Smith friend, would say years later, "a bad habit." For all the intensity of the Duke–North Carolina rivalry, Smith—for some reason—held a special place in his heart, not a good one, for Virginia.

Dan Bonner, who went on to become one of college basketball's best analysts, recalls Smith being infuriated when Bonner had two of his best college games against Carolina in his senior season (1975)—including scoring twelve points when Holland's first team stunned Carolina late that season in Charlottesville.

"I just don't think Dean believed I was worthy of being on the same court with his players," Bonner said years later. "If truth be told, he was probably right. But it *really* made him angry when I actually played well against them. And yes, I did get kind of physical at times. I was playing against Mitch Kupchak and Tommy LaGarde. I had *no* chance if I tried to finesse them."

Smith's dislike for the state of Virginia extended beyond the basketball court. He honestly believed there was at least one Virginia state trooper who would lie in wait for him when he would drive back down Route 29 from Charlottesville after his team had played there—which it did every season.

"It's always the same guy," Smith said, standing in the hallway outside his locker room in Virginia's old gym, University Hall, just prior to his final game there in 1997. "He sees my [North] Carolina plates go by and he pulls me over. He knows the number— I guarantee it. Last time we lost here, I rolled down the window and he said, 'Tough loss tonight, Coach, license and registration, please.'"

Smith was a notoriously fast driver. Apparently the thought of perhaps slowing down a little until he was safely across the state line hadn't crossed his mind.

Smith's biggest blowup because of his habit of yelling at players took place in 1995, when he and Rick Barnes, then the coach at Clemson, had to be held apart by referees Rick Hartzell and Frank Scagliotta during an ACC Tournament game. Late in a Carolina rout, Smith began yelling at the Tigers' Iker Iturbe for the same reason he had yelled at Iavaroni: he thought Iturbe was trying to hurt one of his players.

"If you have a problem with one of my players, you talk to me," Barnes yelled at Smith that night after seeing Smith pointing and yelling at Iturbe.

Smith began walking in Barnes's direction, telling him he needed to coach his players to not play dirty. Barnes yelled and Smith yelled back.

"Do you want to hit me, Rick?" Smith said. "If you want to, go ahead and hit me."

That's when Hartzell got between the two men.

There was another argument after a game at Clemson a year later when Barnes was convinced Smith was yelling at another of his players, Billy Harder. Gene Corrigan, the ACC commissioner at the time, finally decided enough was enough and ordered the two coaches to his house for a meeting.

"They both walked in carrying film," Corrigan said. "Dean said he had proof Clemson was playing dirty; Barnes said he had proof Carolina played dirty. I said, *'We are not looking at any film!'* Then I handed them the press release we were putting out the next day in which they both were going to say it was all behind them and they had great respect for each other.

"Next time either one of you says a word about the other you're suspended," Corrigan said. "I probably should have done it already. No questions, no excuses. Period."

Corrigan then suggested everyone have a drink and relax for a few minutes. Things became almost collegial, and Corrigan pulled out an old scrapbook from his playing days (lacrosse) at Duke and his days as Virginia athletic director to show Smith and Barnes. Some were of Smith and Corrigan together. Just when Corrigan thought all was well and he'd taken back control of his league, Smith pointed at one of Corrigan's old Duke photos and said, "I guess you're kind of enjoying this, aren't you, Gene?"

Corrigan was genuinely baffled. "Enjoying what, Dean?" he asked.

"Well, you being a Duke guy and Carolina being in the middle of all this . . ."

Corrigan threw his hands up and said, "*Stop,* Dean. I'm begging you, *stop.*"

A year later, in Chapel Hill, Barnes asked John Dubis, who was assigned to escort visiting coaches from the floor to the locker room and back in the Dean Dome, if the Carolina fans truly hated him. Dubis tried to be polite about it, but when Barnes asked him again he nodded and said, "Yes, Coach, these people hate you."

"Do they hate me as much as they hate Mike Krzyzewski?" Barnes asked.

"Oh no, Coach," Dubis said. "It's not even close."

—

No one in Chapel Hill hated Krzyzewski in 1983. At that point, he was an afterthought.

They were, however, beginning to notice Valvano, especially after his team took away Carolina's opportunity to win a third straight ACC Tournament title. Even so, the expectation was that the Tar Heels would breeze through the Eastern Regionals—St. John's was considered the only serious threat— and go to Albuquerque to play in a third straight Final Four.

N.C. State was sent to Corvallis, Oregon, as the number-six seed in the West Region. The number-one seed out west was Virginia. State drew a first-round game against Pepperdine. If the Wolfpack were to win, it would face Nevada–Las Vegas, the number-three seed. The Rebels had a first-round bye since there were still only fifty-two teams in the tournament. It would be two more years before the tournament would expand to sixty-four teams, meaning everyone played a first-round game.

Valvano met with the media before his team flew to Corvallis and made a comment that was little noted then but is long remembered now: "We'll probably be so flat [against Pepperdine] that we'll probably lose," he said. "But if we can get by somehow, some way, I think we'll win it all."

He also pronounced his team to be on "a divine mission."

Most of it sounded like classic Jimmy V bluster—with the protective caveat that his team would probably lose to Pepperdine coming off the draining weekend in Atlanta, not to mention having to fly to Corvallis to play.

It turned out Valvano was about 99 percent right in his predictions. The Wolfpack should have lost to Pepperdine. The team came out flat—as predicted—and missed twelve shots in a row to start the game, three of them air balls. Pepperdine led from start to—almost—finish.

Twice in the final minute, Dane Suttle, an 85 percent free-throw shooter for the Waves—which put him in the top ten nationally—went to the line to shoot one-and-one with a chance to ice the game. Twice, he missed. In the first overtime, Pepperdine led by six with twenty-four seconds to go. State tied the game again and pushed it to a second overtime.

The rules back then did not include the double bonus, which was adopted in 1991 in an attempt to keep teams from fouling on every possession when trailing. Back then, no matter how often you fouled, a nonshooting foul was one-and-one, meaning you had to make the first to shoot the second. If the double bonus had been in effect back then, Valvano's strategy—foul as soon as possible when trailing—might not have worked.

"If the double bonus existed back then, no way do we win," Terry Gannon said. "Of course if it had, V probably would have figured something else out."

State finally got past Pepperdine, 69–67, in double overtime.

That set up a second-round game against a heavily favored UNLV team that was 28–2 and, in the minds of most, underseeded at number three—behind Virginia and UCLA—in the West. With eleven minutes left, the Rebels led 52–40. State began chipping away—and Valvano started fouling. Three times, UNLV players missed the front end of one-and-ones, including Danny Tarkanian, Coach Jerry Tarkanian's son, who was a 90 percent shooter. In all, the Rebels made 2 of 5 in the last three minutes and left 3 more potential points on the court when they missed the front end of one-and-ones.

State ended up with the ball with under ten seconds to play. Lowe put up a jump shot from the left wing that missed but Bailey out-leaped everyone in the scramble for the rebound and tipped the ball in just before the buzzer. State had escaped again, this time 71–70—the identical score it had beaten Wake Forest by in the first game of what was now becoming a "survive and advance" run of miracles. The team that had appeared NIT bound was now bound for Ogden, Utah—and the Sweet 16.

"By then it was more than just a feeling that we were going to win," Whittenburg said. "We had reached the point that no matter how far down we got, no matter what the circumstance was, we believed we were going to win. We figured if we were good enough to beat Carolina and Virginia back-to-back we could beat anyone. We also figured if we were lucky enough to beat Pepperdine, we were bound to get out of any corner we were in—somehow, some way."

There were all sorts of slogans associated with that N.C. State team: "Cardiac Pack" and "Team of Destiny," among others. But it was Valvano—naturally—who came up with the catchphrase that stuck: "Survive and advance." It was simple, it was obvious, and it became the title of his post-championship book.

The Wolfpack flew straight from Corvallis to Ogden, Utah, the site of the West Regional.

Since it had played on Sunday and the round of sixteen began on Thursday, there didn't seem to be any point in flying all the way back east and then west again on Tuesday night or Wednesday morning to be at the mandatory practice/media session on Wednesday afternoon. Virginia, which was on spring break that week, went directly from Boise, Idaho, to Ogden.

Not everyone was as lucky. Boston College, which had also advanced through Corvallis, had to fly home and then back to Ogden. Gary Williams, who was the BC coach back then, still hasn't completely gotten over it. "We lost to Virginia by three," he said years later. "We actually had a chance to tie the game in the last few seconds and one of our guys stepped on the baseline going in to dunk the ball. Would the game have been different if we hadn't flown all the way home and back? I have no idea. But I *do* think about it."

Valvano spent three days in Ogden entertaining the media. None of the North Carolina media went home either. Which was just fine with Mike Krzyzewski. Those who weren't in Utah were in Syracuse with North Carolina. The Tar Heels had beaten James Madison in the second round (by 19, a much easier victory than the year before when they had won 52–50 on their way to the national title) and would play Ohio State in the Sweet 16.

On Thursday night, after Virginia had escaped from Gary Williams's slightly jet-lagged BC team, N.C. State faced Utah. The good news was that the Utes had upset second-seeded UCLA. The bad news was the game was in Utah.

"Didn't really bother us," Sidney Lowe said. "Dereck, Thurl, and I had been playing on the road in the ACC for four years. There was no way that crowd was going to bother us."

The Wolfpack broke the game open early in the second half, building a double-digit lead before coasting home to a 75–56 win. It was the first game since the regular season finale against Wake Forest where they hadn't had to sweat out the final seconds. They were now one game from the Final Four. Standing in their way—again—was Virginia.

This was Ralph Sampson's last go-round. In 1979, as a high school senior in Harrisonburg, Virginia, he had arguably been the most highly recruited player of his generation. He had been the first high school player whose press conference to announce where he was going to college had been televised live—which it was, in Kentucky, North Carolina, and Virginia. Those three state schools were the finalists. Sampson said "Virginia" and they danced in the streets of Charlottesville. When Roger Bergey, Sampson's coach at Harrisonburg High School, called Holland just before the press conference to tell him it was Virginia, Holland's first words were, "Can I kiss you?"

He might not have been thinking that during Sampson's freshman season, when the Cavaliers went 7–7 in the ACC and lost their first-round ACC Tournament game to Clemson—meaning they were consigned to the NIT. Most ACC fans believed that NIT stood not for National Invitation Tournament but Not Invited Tournament. When fans really wanted to mock a struggling team during the ACC Tournament they often chanted "NIT, NIT" in their direction.

Holland was normally about as easygoing and cooperative with the media as any coach in college basketball, and the Virginia locker room was a reporter's delight, filled with bright kids who were willing to talk honestly about the games and themselves.

It all changed when Sampson arrived in the fall of 1979. He was shy by nature, and often felt awkward about being seven foot four. It was understandable. One night during his freshman season, Sampson granted a rare one-on-one interview to a *Washington Post* reporter. As Sampson stood in line at a cafeteria close to the UVA campus to get dinner, a woman standing behind him began screaming, *"Oh my god, it's you. Of course it's you. Who else could it be?"* When Sampson turned to politely say hello she looked straight up at him and said, *"No one can be that tall! You can't possibly be that tall!"*

Sampson was that tall and had to deal with moments like that all the time. He and his teammates also had to deal with the notion that Virginia was now a national power because of his presence. The Cavaliers already had three very good players before

Sampson's arrival in point guard Jeff Jones and forwards Jeff Lamp and Lee Raker, meaning it was supposed to be automatic that they would compete with North Carolina, with Bill Foster's last Duke team, and with Maryland at the top of the ACC. Only it wasn't that simple. Some nights, the Cavaliers were all-world. Other nights they weren't all-Charlottesville.

When they lost, the Virginia media wanted to know why—and so did the public. As the season lurched along and no long winning streak occurred, everyone became more uptight. Relations with the media were so bad that Todd Turner, the sports information director, would stand in the middle of the locker room after games and literally count down the minutes left until Virginia (under ACC rules) was allowed to close the locker room.

"Five minutes left," Turner would bellow. "Four minutes . . ."

It made for an almost openly hostile atmosphere. Finally, just prior to the regular season finale at Maryland, Holland decided to take care of that problem: he put his players off-limits to the media. If that made the players less uptight, it didn't show on the court: they lost badly at Maryland and then almost as badly in the first round of the ACC Tournament.

A year later, Sampson had become a dominant player, winning the national player of the year award. The Cavaliers made it to the Final Four in Philadelphia, but Carolina's Al Wood had a career game—thirty-nine points—in the semifinals and the Tar Heels, after losing to UVA twice in the regular season, won to advance to the championship game.

That weekend provided a window into Dean Smith's constant search for an edge. On Friday, before facing Virginia, he explained at great length to the media why there was no doubt that Virginia had a psychological edge going into the game. "They beat us twice," he said. "They should feel very confident."

On Sunday, prior to facing Indiana in the championship game, Smith insisted the Hoosiers had a psychological edge because they had *lost* to Carolina during the regular season. "They're going to want to get even for what happened in December," he said. "That gives them a psychological edge."

If North Carolina had been facing Boy Scout Troop 23 from Libby, Montana, Smith would have insisted the scouts had a psychological edge because they could get a pup tent up faster in an emergency.

Holland and the Cavaliers weren't worried about any mind games prior to playing State. They were worried about Bailey, Whittenburg, and Lowe and the fact that there was no reason for State to fear them.

"They knew us and we knew them," Holland said. "Every game we'd played them had been tough. We were hoping it would help us a little that there was no three-point line."

The ACC had used that experimental three-point line during the regular season, but it wasn't in play during the NCAA Tournament. UVA had good shooters in Othell Wilson, Jim Miller, and Tim Mullen. But it didn't have anyone as consistently good from outside as Whittenburg, or Gannon.

The game wasn't that different from the ACC Tournament final, but the absence of the three-point line, and what was at stake, slowed the pace considerably. With twenty-three seconds left and Virginia leading 62–61, Lorenzo Charles was fouled. Virginia called time-out. Valvano then gave Charles a pep talk that all his teammates remember to this day.

"Okay, Lo, make these and we go to Albuquerque," Valvano said. "Miss and you're going back to Brooklyn. What do you think, Lo, Albuquerque or Brooklyn?"

Charles smiled and said: "I got it, Coach. Albuquerque. I got these."

And then he made both free throws, for a 63–62 lead. There was still the not-so-small-matter of stopping Virginia from scoring in the final seconds. Sampson already had 23 points and 12 rebounds, and everyone in the gym knew the ball was going to him. Valvano decided to gamble, switching to a 1-3 zone defense with Lowe playing man-to-man on Virginia point guard Othell Wilson. That meant Bailey and Cozell McQueen could shade in Sampson's direction at the back of the zone. It also meant someone from Virginia would be open.

Wilson dribbled the ball to the right of the key looking for an opening to get Sampson the ball. But his passing lane into the low post was cut off. With Lowe in his face, Wilson swung the ball to the top of the key, where Tim Mullen was open. Mullen had no choice but to shoot. The ball hit the back of the rim as the buzzer sounded. Sampson was right under the basket and the missed shot landed in his hands. He promptly slammed the ball through the net but it was a futile gesture—nothing more. State had won.

A day earlier, Lowe had talked about how remarkable it was that his team's season had come full circle—back to Virginia and North Carolina. "In Atlanta, we had to beat Carolina and then Virginia," he said. "Now it's the other way around: Virginia first and then Carolina. We just have to make sure it's us going to play them [UNC] in Albuquerque. That's our focus right now."

State had made it to Albuquerque. A day later, shockingly, Carolina did not. After beating Ohio State, the Tar Heels had expected a rematch with St. John's—the team they had lost to on opening night way back in November—in the regional final. But Georgia had upset the Redmen.

Carolina knew little about Georgia. Dean Smith was familiar with Coach Hugh Durham—having lost to a Durham-coached Florida State team in the 1972 Final Four—but his players knew almost nothing about the Bulldogs. And, in an almost shocking slip of Carolina basketball decorum, Sam Perkins admitted during the off-day press conferences that he knew nothing about Georgia, saying he didn't even know what conference the Bulldogs played in.

Twenty-four hours later Perkins may or may not have known that Georgia played in the SEC. What he *did* know was that *they*, not Carolina, would be going to the Final Four. Georgia was a veteran team led by a veteran coach and had a very legitimate star in

James Banks. The Bulldogs stunned the Tar Heels, 82–77, meaning they would be the team N.C. State would play in the national semifinals the following Saturday.

The other semifinal would match Houston, now known as Phi Slama Jama, against Louisville, known as the Doctors of Dunk. That game was expected to be one of the great exhibitions of above-the-rim basketball ever seen. It was also expected to decide the national championship. Georgia and N.C. State were both nice stories, but that game was the undercard merely deciding who would get to lose to Houston or Louisville on Monday night.

That scenario was just fine with Jim Valvano. In fact, it was perfect.

14

It was Lorenzo Charles who dunked the basketball on the final play of the championship game. It was Dereck Whittenburg who got the ball into the air on that play so Charles could dunk it. It was Sidney Lowe who ran the offense on every possession. And it was Thurl Bailey who kept Hakeem Olajuwon under wraps for most of forty minutes that night.

But the 1983 Final Four in Albuquerque belonged to James Thomas Valvano.

The days when college basketball's premier event would still be played in real basketball arenas were beginning to dwindle. A year earlier the Final Four had been held in the New Orleans Superdome. In 1984 it would be played in Seattle's Kingdome. By 1997, abandoning any pretense that the last weekend of the college basketball season was about anything but money, the NCAA Basketball Committee would pass a rule that no building with fewer than thirty-five thousand seats need apply to host. In 2009, it would go a step further, moving the court from one corner of the football playing field in the selected venues to the middle of the field—creating more seats to sell and terrible viewing angles for almost everyone in the building.

That included those sitting on the team benches since they were *below* court level. A coach's reward for getting his team to the Final Four became a little stool he was given so he could sit at court level and not have to look *up* at the action like everyone else.

But this was 1983, and the Pit, as the University of New Mexico's basketball arena was fondly called by everyone, was one of college basketball's legendary locales. The building seated 17,327, and the court was located well below street level—although street level in Albuquerque is 5,312 feet above sea level. To get to the court, teams walked down a steep ramp into a cauldron of noise. Then, at halftime, they had to walk back *up* the ramp to get to the locker rooms. That alone gave New Mexico a home-court advantage. When visitors walked into their locker room they were greeted by signs warning them of the hazards of playing in thin air.

"Welcome," the signs all said, "to the Legendary Pit."

For one week, Valvano made the Pit—its actual name was University Arena but *no one* called it that—his home. By Friday night, he was sick, running a fever but undeterred. He had won a dance contest one night and talked repeatedly about how fortunate the Wolfpack was just to be playing and, wow, beating Georgia would be hard enough, but Houston or Louisville? . . . Gosh.

As it turned out, Georgia's run was done. The Bulldogs, having upset both St. John's and North Carolina the previous weekend in Syracuse, were just happy to be in Albuquerque. State, now very much on Valvano's "divine mission," won the opening semifinal with relative ease, 67–60. That set up the feature attraction: Phi Slama Jama against the Doctors of Dunk.

Houston had emerged as a truly great team during the regular season. The Cougars were led by Olajuwon and Clyde Drexler, both future NBA Hall of Famers, and guard Michael Young, who was their leading scorer and also a future first-round draft pick. They were deep, they were experienced, and they had dominated opponents for most of the season. They had beaten a good Villanova team, 89–71, in the Midwest Region final and arrived in Albuquerque with a 30–1 record and a 25-game winning streak.

They had been dubbed Phi Slama Jama in January by Thomas Bonk, then the basketball writer for *The Houston Post*. Bonk called them "The Tallest Fraternity in Texas" in giving them their name. Although Phi Slama Jama remains an iconic nickname to this day—it even has its own Wikipedia page—and Houston made millions of dollars selling Phi Slama Jama gear, Bonk didn't get a nickel out of his creation.

"They gave me a jacket," he said. "With the logo on it."

Louisville also played consistently above the rim. The Cardinals had won the national championship in 1980, and Denny Crum, who had once been John Wooden's top assistant at UCLA, consistently recruited top players to Kentucky's "other" basketball program. Louisville was in its fourth Final Four in Crum's twelve seasons as coach and, perhaps even more important, had beaten Kentucky in overtime in the Mideast Region final.

Kentucky had refused to schedule Louisville for more than twenty years, and the chance to play and beat the Wildcats in the NCAA Tournament meant almost as much to Louisville people as winning the national title had meant three years earlier.

For two hours, the two teams flew up and down the court, making one spectacular play after another. Houston finally wore Louisville down and pulled away in the final minutes for a 94–81 win that would have left everyone in the building breathless even if they weren't a mile above sea level. In all, Houston had 14 dunks in the game, including 8 in a row during one breathtaking stretch in the second half when they Phi Slama Jammed the game away.

Roger Valdiserri, Notre Dame's associate athletic director, who had worked as a volunteer public relations assistant at the Final Four for more than twenty years, summed the game up best: "Welcome," he said, "to basketball in the twenty-first century."

There was little doubt in anyone's mind that Houston's performance had been the climax of the basketball season. Just as N.C. State had been forced to go through the ritual of beating Marquette on Monday night in 1974 after its climactic double-overtime win over UCLA on Saturday, Houston would have to make its crowning official by beating—in a small twist of irony—N.C. State on Monday night, nine years later.

On Sunday, Valvano told the media he completely understood that thinking. "If we get the ball first," he said, "we may hold it until Tuesday. We certainly don't want to get into an up-and-down game with them."

Coaches always sing the praises of an opponent (see Smith,

Dean E.), but Valvano's words that Sunday made sense to everyone. Dave Kindred, the distinguished *Washington Post* columnist, who had worked for years in Louisville and knew great basketball when he saw it, wrote this in his Monday column: "Trees will tap dance and elephants will drive in the Indianapolis 500 before N.C. State beats Houston on Monday."

No one knew it that day, but the trees were trying on their tap shoes and the elephants were warming up their engines.

—

"There is no way we're not attacking this team. We're going after them right from the start."

Not long after he had told the media about his plans to play keep-away, to slow the game to a walk, if not a halt, Jim Valvano told his players they were going to do no such thing. This was on Sunday afternoon, just before the Wolfpack practiced in the empty Pit. Unlike the Friday practices that were open to the media and the public, the Sunday practices were completely closed.

"You could feel the surge of adrenaline in the room," assistant coach Tom Abatemarco said. "All our guys believed we could compete with anyone by that point. We'd beaten Carolina twice, we'd beaten Virginia twice, we'd beaten Vegas, which was twenty-eight and two when we played them. We knew Houston was good, but Thurl Bailey wasn't afraid of Olajuwon. Lo [Charles] and Co [McQueen] weren't afraid of Drexler. V had a plan. At that point if V had said, 'Fellas, we're gonna play standing on our heads,' the guys would have thought it was a brilliant move.

"There was no doubt in the room. And when V said, 'We're going after them,' that was exactly what everyone wanted to hear."

Years later, Sidney Lowe shook his head as if he could hear his coach's voice all over again. "We already didn't like Houston," he said, smiling. "When we were going through our open practice on Friday, they came walking through on their way to the locker room to get ready for their practice. I remember checking them out, and they were all laughing and joking or wearing headphones. They never even looked at us, as if we didn't matter, like we were invisible."

Lowe laughed. "At least that's what we decided they were doing. When Coach V said we were going after them it was exactly what we wanted to hear. The only thing we were disappointed about was that we couldn't go out and play them *right then*. I can tell you for sure we weren't afraid of them."

In the end, N.C. State would dunk the ball twice in the game—once more than Phi Slama Jama. The second dunk, the one that ended the game, has been seen millions of times since that night, Charles somehow rising above everyone to pluck Whittenburg's "pass" from the air. But the first one, by Bailey, forty seconds into the game, was probably just as important.

"It was a message," Whittenburg said. "Not so much to them but to us. It gave us a surge of adrenaline that put us into the game emotionally right away—took away all the jitters."

Valvano never forgot that play either. "Honestly, at that moment, I thought, 'We're gonna win,'" he said. "It wasn't as if I didn't believe we could win before that. I did—absolutely did. But when Thurl went over them all and dunked Sidney's miss that way, I felt this surge go right through my body and I turned to Tom [Abatemarco] and said, 'We got 'em, T, we got 'em.'"

The irony in that comment was never lost on Abatemarco or anyone else on the bench. Valvano and Abatemarco were like a comedy act during games, voice of doom vs. absolute voice of doom.

"Cozell would lose the opening tip and Jim would turn to Tom and say, 'My god, what's going on with that—he's killing us,'" Terry Gannon, who always began the game on the bench, remembered. "Tom would say, 'I don't know, V, I don't. I think he's lost it. Maybe we should get him out.' Remember, this was the first possession of the *game*.

"Then if, say, Whitt missed his first shot, Tom would say, 'He hasn't got it tonight, V, we gotta get him out.' And V would say something like, 'Jeez, we got no chance tonight. No chance.' Usually the score was about two to two at that point."

There was none of that frenetic talk on that fateful April night in Albuquerque. Everyone on the bench was too focused on every possession to let little things bother him. The Wolfpack jumped to a 6–0 lead and was up 33–25 at halftime.

Could they possibly continue to control the game? No. State's shots stopped falling when the second half began, and, as is almost always the case, grabbing rebounds after misses rather than inbounding the ball after makes allowed Houston to find some offensive rhythm. The Cougars began the half on a 17–2 run to take a 42–35 lead, and it looked like the game was over and the dream was dead.

But with State clearly tiring—Valvano played six players, the starters plus Gannon, the entire game, except for the one minute Ernie Myers played—Cougars coach Guy V. Lewis decided to spread the court and kill the clock.

It would turn out to be the most crucial mistake of his Hall of Fame coaching career.

"It gave us life," Valvano would say later. "It gave us a chance to catch our breath a little. And it gave us a chance to foul. If they keep playing, they're probably going to end up with dunks for Olajuwon or Drexler because our guys were gasping a little—especially in that thin air. They were much deeper than we were. Honestly, if they don't spread the floor, we're probably dead. But we weren't meant to die. We were meant to win."

As with all the other teams that had been in position to put the Wolfpack away, Phi Slama Jama couldn't do it. There were more missed free throws, and suddenly Lowe and Whittenburg got their second wind, each hitting a couple of long jumpers to bring the Wolfpack back. With a little more than a minute left, Whittenburg hit again to tie the game at 52–52.

Houston came down, presumably planning to hold the ball for last shot. Valvano wasn't about to let that happen. With 1:08

left, he ordered Lowe to foul freshman point guard Alvin Franklin. Naturally, Franklin missed the front end of the one-and-one. State brought the ball into the frontcourt and called time to set up for a last shot.

"By then we were all so dialed in to what we were doing we didn't even have to think very much," Gannon remembered. "We were on offense so I automatically went to the scorer's table to check in for Cozell without even checking with the coaches. That was what we'd done the whole run at the end of a close game: Co in on defense, me in on offense."

The players knew what Valvano wanted on the final possession: the ball in Lowe's hands once the clock was under ten seconds. Lowe would penetrate and create either for himself or, more likely, for Whittenburg or Gannon, flashing open on a wing when someone collapsed to help on Lowe. Charles and Bailey would try to position themselves underneath for a potential offensive rebound or tip-in, like the one Bailey had gotten to win the UNLV game.

As they came out of the huddle with the national championship on the line, they all caught themselves thinking about the moment.

"I wanted the shot," Whittenburg said. "I always had faith in myself in moments like that. I was ready for it."

Gannon, only a sophomore, wasn't so sure. "I have to admit I thought about Fred Brown," he said. "I said, 'Please, God, don't let me be Fred Brown.'"

Brown had been the Georgetown guard who, a year earlier, had mistaken James Worthy for a Georgetown teammate and thrown him the ball in the final seconds of the championship game with the Hoyas trailing North Carolina, 63–62.

It was then that Guy Lewis sprang a surprise on the Wolfpack—changing his defense to a 2-3 zone, trapping if the ball went into the corner.

"He surprised us with that," Abatemarco said. "It was a good move, and we didn't have a time-out left to get the guys over and call something different against the zone. We had to leave it up to Sidney to make the right decisions."

Lowe kept the ball moving on the perimeter as the clock melted away. But with just under ten seconds remaining, he picked up his dribble and was forced to find Bailey, who had drifted to the left corner. As soon as Bailey caught the ball, Houston trapped. Surprised and a little bit desperate, Bailey threw the ball back in the direction of the key. Whittenburg had rotated in that direction, hoping for a catch-and-shoot pass, but Houston guard Benny Anders saw the pass coming and got his hand on it. He was about a quarter step from a clean steal that might have led to a game-ending dunk at the other end.

But he could only deflect the ball, and Whittenburg alertly chased it down near midcourt. Knowing there were no more than two seconds left, he swiveled, took one quick dribble and, from thirty-five feet, heaved the ball in the direction of the basket.

All the Houston players had reacted to Anders's deflection, and seeing the ball heading toward their basket, they had turned their bodies that way.

"I thought Benny had it," Olajuwon said years later. "I took one step and then realized that Whittenburg had it."

Too late. Olajuwon's one step pulled him just far enough away from the basket that neither he nor anyone else was in position to box Lorenzo Charles out.

As Whittenburg picked the ball up, Gannon was wide open on the right wing with his hand in the air. "I don't think I meant it, though," Gannon said, laughing. "I knew Whitt was going to try to shoot anyway."

Whitt shot. Or "passed."

Left without a man on him because of the Anders deflection, Charles saw the ball in the air and realized it was going to come up well short of the rim. He leaped, grabbed it cleanly, and dunked it as the buzzer sounded.

"I was just trying to get in position for a putback," Charles said later. "Then, when I saw that the ball was short, I went up to try and get it."

"Think about it," Lowe said. "If he grabs it and comes down and then goes back up, the clock runs out. But somehow he had the presence of mind and the athleticism to just grab it and dunk it in one motion. It was amazing. Except, by that point, nothing was amazing anymore."

On CBS, play-by-play man Gary Bender was so stunned, he said nothing for a moment, not quite sure what had happened—which was completely understandable. It was analyst Billy Packer who first understood that the clock was at zero and N.C. State had won. "They did it!" he screamed. "They did it! They won!"

Pandemonium broke out on the court. As the Houston players stood, sat, or kneeled in complete shock, Charles was mobbed by his teammates. Valvano, not knowing how exactly to react to having his life's dream realized at the age of thirty-seven, began running around the court looking for someone to hug.

"Whitt was my designated hugger," he would say later, retelling the story—joking, but not joking. "I couldn't find him. I couldn't find anyone, so there I was just running around in circles."

It may be the most iconic run to nowhere in sports history. It is replayed throughout the basketball season hundreds if not thousands of times every winter.

It was Valvano's run to nowhere, the ultimate moment of joy for any college basketball coach. Moments later he would do what he had fantasized about in his mind and pretended to do at the end of clinics since the day he had started coaching: he would cut down the final net.

And then his run to nowhere would begin again.

15

When the North Carolina State basketball team flew into Raleigh-Durham International Airport on the night of April 5, 1983, a crowd that police estimated to be about five thousand people was waiting to greet the team. As Jim Valvano exited the plane, a local police officer was waiting for him.

"Coach, don't worry," he said. "There's a back exit over here where I can take you and get you out of here without fighting your way through this crowd."

Valvano looked at the cop as if he had lost his mind.

"Are you kidding?" he said. "No way am I passing up all of this. I want every hug and every kiss. I want to savor this for as long as I can."

The cop shrugged. "Whatever you say, Coach."

And with that, Valvano led his players and coaches into the adoring crowd. He savored every hug and every kiss and every pat on the back and every "I love you, Coach." And then, when he was finished, he circled back to where he had started and waded slowly through the crowd for a second time. When the bus carrying the team arrived on campus later that evening, Valvano did the same thing—this time circling back so he could reboard the bus and come out the front door for a second time.

"He was the first guy in and the last guy out," his brother Bob said. "He'd actually done that before. When he was a senior and Rutgers made it to the NIT semifinals, the team would bus back to campus after each game and they'd be met by the cheerleaders and the band and a lot of the students. Jimmy would jump off the bus first, go through the crowd, and then circle back and get on the bus through the emergency door so he could also be the *last* guy off. There was never too much love to go around for Jimmy."

—

Bob Valvano is fifty-nine years old now, twelve years older than his brother was when he died in 1993. Bob was the third of the three Valvano boys, eleven years younger than Jim and fifteen years younger than Nick. "I think it's fair to say I was something of a surprise," he said with a laugh, sipping a cup of coffee on a cold February morning in Charlottesville, Virginia.

The night before, Bob Valvano had flown into Charlottesville to broadcast a basketball game and rented a car at the airport.

"Valvano," the man at the rent-a-car desk had said, recognition in his voice and his eyes. "Jim Valvano. Wow. Great to meet you, Coach."

Several lines ran through Bob Valvano's head, not the least of which was, "If Jim is here, we've got a hell of a story to tell."

Instead, he just smiled, pointed at his driver's license, and said, "Bob. It's Bob Valvano."

Bob Valvano is a slightly rounder version of his older brother. He has the same jet-black hair, the same easy smile and heartfelt laugh that Jim had. If you close your eyes when he's talking, you might swear you were listening to Jim.

"The difference is that even though I'm funny, I'm not as funny as Jim," Bob said. "No one was as funny as Jim."

When Bob was little, he shared a room with Jim. Nick left for college by the time Bob was four, so it was Jim who Bob grew up with. "He was my hero," Bob said. "He was my hero when I was a kid, he was my hero when I became an adult, and he's my hero now."

Bob has talked about his brother so often since his death that he can do so most of the time without getting emotional. He even wrote a book called *The Gifts of Jimmy V.* But there is still some pain that's evident, especially when he talks about his boyhood and about the direction Jim's life went after he won the national championship.

"Nick always told me that Jim was a star right from the beginning, from those first days when the nuns took him around school to do his Durante impression."

When Bob was old enough to play ball, Jim would play with him. By then he was a high school star in football, basketball, and baseball. "We'd play basketball and he'd do play-by-play during the game. He'd always let me get close to winning and then he'd crush me. He'd say things like, 'And poor Bobby has absolutely no chance. He's being humiliated yet again. It's over for Bobby, it's over!'

"I'd run inside crying and my mother would say, 'If he's going to do that why do you keep playing with him?' I didn't have an answer for that other than, 'Why would I *not* play with him? It's *Jim*. It's my big brother—my hero.' I'm not sure I consciously thought any of that, but there's no doubt that's the way I felt."

Bob wasn't as good a player as Jim, who went to Rutgers as a recruited walk-on and became the starting point guard as a sophomore. Bob played at Division III Virginia Wesleyan. He then followed Jim into coaching, mostly at the Division III level. Like Jim, Bob has a lightning-fast sense of humor and a knack for storytelling. He also has vivid memories of his brother's remarkable rise to coaching stardom and what happened after Lorenzo Charles dunked the ball that night in the Pit.

"Jimmy always talked about cutting down the last net," Bob said. "That was his dream from the first day he got into coaching. He never doubted that he could do that. He was a coach's son who wanted to follow in his father's footsteps first but always believed he could outcoach anybody. As much as he respected Dean and Mike there was never any doubt in his mind that he could outcoach them. If he'd coached against Wooden, he would have felt the same way, and he worshipped Wooden.

"I guess some of that was ego. It has to be if you want to be good at something. But it was more than that: it was his feel for the game. People act sometimes as if Jim didn't study the game. He did—all the time. But he also had a feel for the game that was pretty close to unique. There were times he'd do something in a game that was the exact opposite of what should have been right—and he was right. The Houston game, going out and attacking them, was a perfect example.

"But it was always about cutting down the last net. Whenever he gave clinics, he'd talk to the kids about that. Then, at the end, he'd make them all carry him on their shoulders, and he'd cut down the net. It made Garf [Five-Star Camp owner Howard Garfinkel] crazy because he always had to pay for a new net. He'd tell Jimmy not to do it again and Jimmy would do it again. Garf would get angry, scream at Jimmy, and then say, 'So, when are you coming back?' Because no one ever put on a better clinic for the kids than Jimmy, and Garf knew that.

"When Iona beat Louisville in the Garden in eighty, Jimmy had the team cut down the nets. That team might have been good enough to win the whole thing if they'd gotten on the kind of roll State got on in eighty-three.

"Then, almost overnight, Jim goes from being a rising young coach, who was always entertaining and funny, to being a flat-out rock star. He went from coaching in Dean's shadow to overshadowing everyone. He wasn't going to walk away from coaching, because he loved basketball and he loved the pressure and intensity of the games. Never practice—the games. Other guys like Dean and Mike will tell you they loved practice first and foremost. Not Jim; he always lived for the games.

"Then he won the ultimate game. He had just turned thirty-seven and he had lived out his dream. Jim always loved basketball, but he wasn't basketball obsessed. He woke up after Albuquerque and the thought in the back of his mind was, 'I'm thirty-seven, I've cut down the final net. I've done coaching. *Now* what do I do?' "

Valvano was the seventh-youngest coach to win a national title—a little more than six years older than Branch McCracken, who was thirty-one when he won at Indiana in 1940. No one as young as Valvano was in 1983 has won a title since then. Dean Smith was fifty-one when he won for the first time. Mike Krzyzewski was forty-four. In fact, no coach under the age of forty has won a championship since Valvano.

For a while, Valvano did what came naturally: He was a star. His speaking fee skyrocketed, and he could have spoken 365 days a year had he wanted to. He didn't fall that far short. He was on TV all the time. For a while he flew to New York on Sunday nights, did *The CBS Morning News* on Monday morning, then flew back to Raleigh. He hosted a truly terrible TV show called *Sports Bloopers,* and he frequently guest-hosted for Bob Costas on his national radio show. He even did color on games for NBC during the season, often coaching a game on Saturday and then flying somewhere to talk about someone else's game on Sunday.

"He was so good hosting my show I thought the network might make him the host and let me guest in his place on occasion," Costas said. "He was a natural."

Which is why the *Sports Bloopers* show was so bad. It was scripted, and the scripts weren't funny. If Valvano had been allowed to wing it the show would have been much better.

"You couldn't script Jim," Nick Valvano said. "You just had to let him go."

Valvano also did a daily five-minute radio commentary every morning on a local Raleigh station. The station set up a special phone line in Valvano's office that allowed him to call into the station and tape the commentary with studio-quality sound at any hour of the day or night. He never wrote a script. He would call the designated number, look at his watch, and talk for exactly five minutes about whatever was on his mind.

One morning, after a game, he drove home at about two A.M. and went to bed. "At four thirty I sat bolt upright in bed and realized, 'I didn't do the radio bit,' " he said. "It's supposed to air at seven thirty. I can't do it from home; I gotta go to the office. I get out of bed, get in the car, and drive back to campus. I get to the turn onto campus and the light's red—it's one of those long left-turn arrows. It's five o'clock in the morning so I just make the turn. Sure enough, there's a cop right there. Pulls me over right away.

"He comes up to the car, points the flashlight at me, and recognizes me. He says, 'Coach, you ran the light back there.' I tell him, 'I know and I'm sorry.' He says, 'Coach, have you been drinking?' I tell him, no, that I'm coming from home to do the radio bit. He looks at me like I'm crazy and says, 'Come on, Coach, you gotta do better than that—get out of the car.'

"I said, 'Gladly,' and got out. I was in my pajamas. I said, 'Now do you believe me?' He couldn't stop laughing. He just waved at me to get back inside and walked back to his car."

Valvano kept his life filled to the brim but not with anything that made him feel fulfilled the way the crusade to cut the final net had kept him fulfilled.

"He never thought of himself as just a basketball coach," Pam Valvano Strasser said. "He was an English major in college. He was a reader, a real reader. He liked talking to smart people who weren't in basketball. It was almost as if he had to prove to himself that he could succeed in something other than basketball. He'd already done that."

Or, as Valvano would frequently say late at night—or very early in the morning—"What am I going to be when I grow up?"

Valvano would always gather friends in his office after games. Like most coaches, he couldn't sleep after a game; there was just too much adrenaline pumping. Most coaches use that time and energy to review game tape, sometimes until dawn if a loss has been especially aggravating. Valvano wasn't much for late-night tape watching. For one thing, he could still see almost every play in a game in his mind's eye, so there wasn't much need. He almost always knew why his team had won or why it had lost.

"Easiest thing in the world is to come up with reasons why you lost a game," he often said. "The officials screwed you; a player had a bad night; someone messed up a critical play. I've got a million excuses. Here's the bottom line: a W is a W and an L is an L. None of the rest of it matters. None of it."

And so, rather than rehash the game, Valvano and his assistants and invited friends would order pizza and wine, and Valvano would hold court. Time would pass. Pam would call to find out when Jim was coming home. He would tell her, "Soon," and resume storytelling because he wasn't close to being ready or able to sleep. People would drift out, and often Valvano would stretch out on the couch in the office amid the now-empty pizza boxes and wine bottles and turn reflective.

"Dean will coach forever," he often said. "So will Mike. They like almost everything about the job. Dean would rather not deal with the media, but he does what he has to because he loves the rest of it so much. Mike was born to be a coach. He loves it so much that while he's hating a loss he's finding a way to use it to get better. That's one reason why he's so good.

"I'm not like that. We lose and I'm pissed off. I don't question the outcome—because that's pointless. I question myself: Did I recruit the wrong players? Am I not coaching them as well as I should? Do I have the right assistants? What'd I do wrong? Where'd I go wrong?

"And then I say, 'What the hell am I doing this for? What do I love about this job? The money—yup, love the money. Never *ever* thought I'd make this kind of money. Practice? Not so much. Recruiting? God no. Dealing with the media? It's okay, I'm good at it, but if I never did it again would I miss it? Maybe a little. Maybe a couple of guys. But not much.

"I love the games. I *love* the damn games. I love the forty minutes. I love the spotlight and I love the pressure and it's *real.* The rest of it—what's real about it? Nothing. And most of it I can do blindfolded. But not the forty minutes. The forty minutes is really hard and I love it. But how many times a year do I get to do it? Thirty-five times—maybe. In a good year. That's less than ten percent of a year. Is that enough? I don't know."

In truth, it wasn't enough. Which is why Valvano wandered. His wanderings—and wonderings—didn't really hurt the team on the court. State's miracle run, combined with the likeability of the players on that championship team and Valvano's newfound fame, had allowed Valvano to get into the home of almost any recruit in the country. If you were a big-time player, N.C. State was now on the list of schools you had to consider. And once Valvano was inside the door—or had a recruit on campus—he was going to win recruiting battles more often than he lost them.

He put together a film to show to recruits and their families when they came to campus that made it almost impossible for anyone to say no to him—or what he was selling, which was supposed to be N.C. State but in reality was Jim Valvano.

The film began in a darkened gym that slowly lightened to show a mist and a fog billowing through. Then came the sound of someone dribbling a basketball. The sound grew louder and louder until Valvano appeared out of a cloudy mist wearing N.C. State sweats quoting Carl Sandburg, Shakespeare, and John Greenleaf Whittier: "For of all sad words of tongue or pen, / The saddest are these, 'It might have been!' "

Valvano didn't need a teleprompter; he knew all the quotations by heart. After quoting Whittier, the camera dissolved to show highlights from the championship run: Mullen's miss; Charles's dunk; Lowe, Bailey, and Whittenburg making plays; Valvano looking for someone to hug, and, finally, hugs—lots of hugs. By this moment the thought that one might *not* play for Valvano at N.C. State had to be completely gone. What would Whittier have said about such a decision? Finally, the camera came back to Valvano looking into it as the fog and the mist and darkness began to roll back in saying, "Dream the dream . . . at N.C. State." With that, he turned and walked back into the darkness.

Where do I sign?

The Wolfpack dipped a little bit in 1984 after the departures of Whittenburg, Lowe, and Bailey, but the season was a joyride anyway, an ongoing celebration of the previous spring. Valvano got a commitment that winter from six-foot-eleven Chris Washburn, the most highly rated big man in the country. Charles was now a star and, like Gannon and McQueen, would be back for another season.

In both 1985 and 1986, the Wolfpack came within one win of going back to the Final Four—losing in the Elite Eight to St. John's and then, a year later, to Kansas in a tense game played in Kansas City, a virtual home court for the Jayhawks.

Valvano was despondent after that loss. He had believed his team was going to win the game. "I thought we had them by the cojones," he said afterward. "One play, two plays, but what the hell—*all* the plays went our way in eighty-three. I guess I got every break that year, so now God is evening things up." He shrugged. "I guess he's entitled."

Good players—very good players—were still going to N.C. State. Things had changed in the Triangle, though: Duke was now a factor. In fact, on the cold January afternoon in 1986 when North Carolina opened its new basketball palace—the 21,000-seat Dean E. Smith Center—North Carolina and Duke were ranked first and second in the nation.

Even so, Valvano managed to steal some of the thunder surrounding that game and the announcement that the building was going to be named for Smith. Two weeks earlier, the Wolfpack played the last game in Carmichael Auditorium, losing 90–79. The buildup to the Carmichael finale had been hyped in the North Carolina media a little bit less—not much, though—than man's first landing on the moon.

Would the Tar Heels' last memory of Carmichael be a win? Who would score the first basket of the last game? Would Dean Smith start his seniors in their last game in Carmichael? (No, just joking.) Who would score the last basket?

Valvano had the final word on the final game. After he had shaken Smith's hand, he had someone throw him a basketball. By then, everyone from Carolina had left the court and all eyes and cameras were on Valvano. He walked to one end of the court and softly tossed a layup through the basket.

"Now everyone knows the answer," Valvano said. "I scored the last basket in Carmichael."

With that, not unlike Elvis, he left the building.

16

If Jim Valvano and North Carolina State had won the national championship in 1983 *before* Dean Smith and North Carolina won the title in 1982, there might have been some unhappy rumblings among the Carolina faithful.

After all, the notion that both mean, in-your-face Norman Sloan and funny, outgoing Jim Valvano could win national titles in Raleigh while the iconic Dean Smith couldn't win one in Chapel Hill might have been more than Tar Heel fans could bear.

Fortunately, that issue didn't exist. What's more, the Tar Heels appeared to be loaded—again—going into the 1983–84 season. Michael Jordan was now a junior and, unquestionably, the best player in the country. Sam Perkins was a senior and a lock All-American, and Matt Doherty was also a senior, the kind of player every college coach would love to have on his team. Brad Daugherty had a year of experience. Steve Hale wasn't Mark Price, but he was a very solid ACC shooting guard.

Additionally, there was—naturally—another outstanding freshman class, led by a guard from New York named Kenny Smith who quickly lived up to his nickname: the Jet. Depth? Buzz Peterson, who had been the sixth man on the '82 championship team, was still coming off the bench as a junior. And there were two freshmen big men, Dave Popson and Joe Wolf. Neither was seven feet (of course) but both were talented. Only one player who had played any serious minutes the previous season had graduated: Jim Braddock.

The three best players on N.C. State's championship team were gone. So was Ralph Sampson. Maryland had a solid team led by Len Bias and Adrian Branch but appeared to be light-years behind the Tar Heels. The same was true of Georgia Tech, which had come on strong at the end of the previous season. Duke would be better if only because it couldn't possibly be any worse.

"I think we all thought everything was in place for us to win again," Roy Williams said. "You never know what's going to happen in March, but if we stayed healthy we all thought we were going to be tough to beat. We had size, we had experience, and we had depth." Williams smiled. "We also had Michael."

Jordan had become an iconic figure in North Carolina after his title-winning shot in New Orleans. With Worthy gone and Dean Smith's freshman shackles removed, he had emerged as a star during his sophomore season. The three best players in the country as the season began were Jordan and two great centers: Hakeem Olajuwon at Houston and Patrick Ewing at Georgetown.

Smith, as always, tried to downplay expectations. But even he had to admit this was a team that had the potential to be great—better even than the '82 championship team.

At the other end of I-40, Valvano knew he might be in for a relatively difficult season. He had never coached a game at State without Sidney Lowe, Dereck Whittenburg, and Thurl Bailey. It wasn't as if State was without talent: Lorenzo Charles, Terry Gannon, and Cozell McQueen were now the heart of the team, along with Ernie Myers. In fact, the Wolfpack opened the season by easily beating Houston in the Tip-Off Classic in Springfield in a "rematch" of the championship game.

"I didn't just lose my three best players," Valvano said. "I lost the heart and soul of my team. It wasn't like we didn't have good players—we did. But those three had become special in a lot of ways."

Valvano wasn't that worried. He knew he had a big-time recruiting class on the way and all his key players would be back the following season. Plus, the Wolfpack could have gone 0–33 and Valvano still would have been a hero in Raleigh. The days of worrying about getting a win over Carolina were completely forgotten.

Mike Krzyzewski had no such luxury. He had *no* luxuries. There would be only one year left on his contract at the end of the season, and he knew anything resembling the 10–17 and 11–17 of the previous two seasons would make it almost impossible for Tom Butters to continue defending him—or employing him.

During the postmidnight meeting at Denny's in Atlanta the previous March, Bobby Dwyer had mentioned the fact that Tom Sheehey, who had verbally committed to Virginia, might be having second thoughts and perhaps it might be worth seeing if he would take a late look at Duke.

Krzyzewski had cut him off in midsentence. "No, we're not doing that," he said. "First of all, we don't do that sort of thing. Second, if we can't win with these freshmen and Amaker, then we should get fired."

Amaker was Tommy Amaker, the little point guard Krzyzewski had fallen in love with two summers earlier while watching him play in the Jelleff League. Amaker had once dreamed of playing at Maryland but had changed his thinking for several reasons: Lefty Driesell was more interested in Keith Gatlin, a six-foot-five point guard from North Carolina; he loved the idea of pairing in a backcourt with Johnny Dawkins; and he and his mom had both become enamored of Krzyzewski.

"I think more than anything it was his passion," Amaker, who is now the basketball coach at Harvard, said many years later. "My mom liked him right from the start. He looked you right in the eye and there was never any doubt in his voice when he spoke. Plus, it was apparent how much he wanted me at Duke. My mom loved the idea because she loved him but also because it was such a good school academically."

Amaker made an early decision to go to Duke, and throughout the long winter of 1983, the thought that Amaker could take over for Dawkins at the point and allow Dawkins to move to shooting guard was often a ray of hope for Krzyzewski and his coaches.

"We get better at two positions when Amaker gets here,"

Krzyzewski would often say during late-night film sessions at his house. "He's a better point guard than Johnny, and Johnny's a better shooting guard than anyone."

By then, Krzyzewski's staff had changed. At season's end in 1983, Bobby Dwyer decided he'd had enough of the life that had to be lived to be a big-time recruiter. He was getting married, he wanted to start a family, and he was worn out by the road and the cutthroat nature of recruiting.

"I felt like Chuck [Swenson] and I had finally gotten Mike into the homes we needed to get him into with the Dawkins class," he said. "It was the right time for me to get off the road."

Dwyer left to take a Division III job at Sewanee College in Tennessee. At the same time, NCAA rules had changed (again) to allow schools to hire a part-time coach and a director of basketball operations. Tom Rogers, the retired army colonel who had talked Krzyzewski out of taking the Iowa State job, was going to be the director of basketball operations.

That meant Krzyzewski had two coaches to hire. Pete Gaudet, who had succeeded him at Army, had struggled to win games and was out of a job. Krzyzewski knew that Gaudet was as good as anyone in the country coaching big men. Plus, he thought Gaudet's experience—Gaudet was four years older than he was—was something he could use on the bench. Dwyer's job was filled by Bob Bender—meaning one coach's son replaced another coach's son. Bender had played on Bill Foster's Final Four team in 1978 and had been working for Tom Butters. He wanted to coach. Krzyzewski offered him the chance.

"I remember people saying to me, 'What are you doing? You'll be looking for a job in another year,'" Bender said. "I wanted to coach and I'd been around Duke watching Mike work, and I thought he knew what he was doing. I was single. I figured I'd give it a shot."

The best news for Krzyzewski when practice started was that he no longer had to deal with a divided team. The seniors had graduated and Dawkins, Mark Alarie, Jay Bilas, and David Henderson were now the clear leaders of the team, along with junior Danny Meagher, the hard-nosed Canadian who had been the best player in the '81 recruiting class.

Meagher wasn't a star but he was an important player. He was physical and fearless, something Duke needed. And, a bonus, his style of play drove Dean Smith crazy. Meagher reminded Smith of guys like Dan Bonner and Marc Iavaroni. He complained to the officials about him all the time and insisted on referring to him in public as "May-har," even though his name was pronounced "Mu-har," and Smith knew that because Smith knew everything.

Once after a game, Smith referenced the fact that May-har would be playing the following summer on the Canadian Olympic team. "I really feel badly for my good friend Bob Knight having to play against May-har," Smith said. May-har loved hearing that sort of thing.

Knight, who would be coaching the U.S. team in the '84 Olympics, was probably not losing a lot of sleep at the thought of facing May-har or Meagher or anyone else playing for Canada. Smith thought he was a nightmare, which made Krzyzewski smile.

More important was the improvement of the sophomores. Duke didn't have an especially challenging preconference schedule, but that didn't mean it was going to win all those games (see Wagner). The opener *was* a difficult one. Vanderbilt had beaten Duke two years in a row, soundly a year earlier in Nashville.

The game was tight throughout, and it came down to Amaker standing at the free-throw line needing to make two shots to clinch the victory. He made both. Afterward, as Amaker was standing in front of his locker talking to the media, Krzyzewski walked by with a wide grin on his face. He patted Amaker on the shoulder and whispered in his ear, "I told you I'd make you a star."

The second game of the season was even tougher than the first. Bruce Parkhill had put together a very solid program at William and Mary and had talked Krzyzewski into playing a game in Williamsburg—not normally a road trip that an ACC team would make. The game was every bit as difficult as the Vanderbilt game, if not more difficult. Duke survived, 70–68, when David Henderson hit a fifteen-foot jump shot with two seconds to play.

"In a funny way that was one of our biggest wins," Krzyzewski said. "We had gotten into the habit of folding when things got tough. There was always an excuse. The year before it had been that the freshmen weren't ready yet. Well, now they were sophomores. Amaker was never really a freshman—never played like one anyway. Hanging on to win against Vanderbilt was good, but winning a tough game like that by making a big shot on the road was better. It really gave us a boost."

—

The Blue Devils charged through December and went to Hawaii for the Rainbow Classic with an 8–0 record. They lost their opening game, 78–76, to a very good SMU team and then won the next two games they played on Oahu. By the time conference play began they were 11–1. That was also a nice boost—especially considering the win totals of 10 and 11 the previous two seasons—but everyone knew the test would come once ACC play began.

Things started well enough—very well, in fact. With Amaker playing almost flawlessly against Virginia's veteran backcourt of Othell Wilson and Ricky Stokes, Duke beat Virginia 78–72 in Charlottesville. Ralph Sampson was finally in the NBA, but Virginia still had talent—enough talent that the Cavaliers would make it to the Final Four three months later. Sampson had been 9–0 against Duke, and it was Krzyzewski's first win against Terry Holland and UVA.

Which meant it felt like a breakthrough. Two more nonconference victories raised the overall record to 14–1, but then the backsliding began. First came a home loss to Maryland in Cameron, an ugly game punctuated by the students taunting Herman Veal, a Maryland player who had been accused of sexual assault. The students went over the line from funny to tasteless, throwing women's underwear at Veal and chanting "R-A-P-E" at him throughout the game. All their behavior did was fire up a Maryland team that was probably ready to be taken down.

Three days later, the Blue Devils lost on the road to a very good Wake Forest team that would reach the Elite Eight of the NCAA Tournament in March. Even so, the 97–66 margin was embarrassing.

And then, Carolina came to town.

Duke hadn't beaten Carolina since Krzyzewski's first season, in the "Gene Banks game" that had led to Linnea Smith's concern about her daughter's future and the conception of Jamie Krzyzewski.

Carolina was 13–0 and ranked number one in the country. A week earlier, the Tar Heels had won at Wake Forest, winning by 8 on the same court where Duke would lose by 31 four days later.

On the day prior to the North Carolina game, Duke president Terry Sanford had written an open letter to the student body that appeared on the front page of *The Chronicle*. The students had—deservedly—taken a pounding in the media following the Maryland game, and Sanford decided enough was enough.

"We should be funny, but not tasteless," he said. "Treat our opponents with respect but try to help the team win." He signed the letter "Uncle Terry," which was the way he was thought of by the student body.

The students responded. They showed up for the game wearing halos, lest anyone think they were less than angelic. When Carolina came onto the court to warm up, they held up signs that said "Welcome Honored Guests." When Dean Smith walked to the bench, the Blue Devil mascot was waiting for him with a dozen roses.

Smith wasn't amused. He had never found the Duke students funny.

When the game began, the students abandoned the profane "Bullshit" cheer that had become—and, sadly, still is—a staple in student sections around the country. Instead, when they didn't like a call they chanted, "We beg to differ." And, when a Tar Heel went to the free-throw line, instead of waving their arms as a distraction they held up signs that said "Please Miss."

It was arguably the greatest performance by a student section in history.

Their team was almost as good. The game was filled with the kind of fury and intensity that can happen only in a rivalry involving teams and coaches who know one another well. The Duke players were tired of being embarrassed by North Carolina. The Carolina players weren't about to let their undefeated run end against Duke.

The building was hot, the two coaches hotter. At one point, when the men working the scorer's table didn't notice a Carolina player trying to check in to the game and failed to hit the horn to alert the officials to the sub, Smith sprinted angrily to the table and tried to hit the horn himself. He missed—instead adding ten points to his team's score. The crowd was booing, the scorer's table crew was screaming at Smith, and Smith was screaming right back at them—accusing them of cheating.

No one was angrier, though, than Krzyzewski, who couldn't believe Smith hadn't been given a technical foul when he tried to hit the horn.

"They had to tee him up then," he said many years later. "You can't let a coach do that. It doesn't matter if he had a legitimate complaint or not. He got away with it because he was Dean Smith."

Carolina got away with the win because Michael Jordan played for Dean Smith and Duke couldn't stop him in the final minutes.

"There were a lot of reasons that game was important," Jay Bilas said. "The biggest thing was it was the first time we walked into the locker room after losing to those guys and we were pissed. The year before, I don't think we believed we could compete with them. We were almost in awe of them even before tip-off. They were just *so* good.

"But after that game in Cameron, we weren't intimidated anymore. It wasn't as if we didn't think they were great—we did. We just thought we were good enough to beat them."

Krzyzewski was convinced they would have beaten them if Smith hadn't been able to intimidate the officials. With eleven seconds left in the game and the Tar Heels in control, Krzyzewski called time-out for one purpose: to get a technical foul.

"If they weren't going to give Dean one," he said, "I figured they might as well give me one."

Krzyzewski never stepped into his team's huddle during the time-out. He railed at referee Mike Moser, repeatedly saying, "These kids deserved to win this game. *You* took it away from them." Moser knew what Krzyzewski was doing and tried to wait out the rant. That wasn't going to happen; Krzyzewski was going to make his point. When Moser finally teed Krzyzewski up, the students erupted in mock cheers: the officials, in their mind, had finally gotten a call right.

It didn't end there. Even after winning, Smith was noticeably upset during his postgame press conference. When someone asked him about the behavior of the students, he waved a hand in disgust. "The schedule says we have to come over here and play once a year," he said. "We do that, try to win like we did tonight, and go back to Chapel Hill. I don't pay any attention to what they [the students] are doing."

Years later, when the subject of that night came up, Smith was still upset.

"Maybe they were funny on occasion, but more often they were rude," he said. "They treated our players badly a lot of the time, went over the line, and I didn't forget that. They liked to call attention to themselves. I never thought that was the right way for fans to behave."

Krzyzewski's view of the events of the evening was, not surprisingly, different. He had no issues with the students or with his team's performance. He was angry at Smith and angrier at the officials.

"There's a double standard in this league," he famously said. "One for Dean Smith and one for the rest of us. It's not right."

The "double-standard" comment caused a furor. Most of the media in North Carolina—not surprisingly—raced to defend Smith. One columnist called Krzyzewski a "classless loser." Others speculated that he was a desperate man who saw his job slipping away. About the only columnist who didn't side with Smith was the *Durham Morning Herald*'s Keith Drum.

He wrote that both coaches had behaved badly. Smith, he said, had no right to charge the scorer's table and hit the horn the way he had and certainly should have been teed up—at least once. Krzyzewski, he said, was out of line by claiming the officials had somehow stolen the game for North Carolina. "Michael Jordan," he wrote, "beat Duke last night. He wore Carolina blue—not stripes."

Drum must have gotten it right because *both* coaches called him the day after the game to complain about the column. Smith accused him of being pro-Duke because he had defended Krzyzewski. This was a major crime to Smith since Drum had gone to North Carolina. Krzyzewski, after debating with Drum at length, finally concluded, "Aah, you're just another Carolina guy."

Drum was fine with that. He was just another Carolina guy to the Duke coach and pro-Duke to the Carolina coach. All in all, a good day's work.

—

While the "double-standard" debate raged—almost all of it in-state anti-Krzyzewski and pro-Smith, Krzyzewski had a bigger problem: his team was now 1–3 in the ACC with N.C. State coming to town on Thursday. The Wolfpack wasn't anywhere close to being as good as the year before but was still good enough to be a tough out for Duke.

"What made Duke good, really good, was their ability to take you out of your offense," Tom Abatemarco said. "They would play passing lanes, get out after your guards, extend their defense.

Especially once they got Amaker, it was really hard for a point guard to get a team into its offense. So, we didn't run any offense."

Actually, State had one offensive set: use Amaker's aggressiveness against him, get the point guard into the lane, and dish to the wings when Duke's inside help came after the point guard. On occasion, Amaker would upset that strategy by stealing the ball or deflecting a pass. But, often as not, someone from State would end up with an open outside shot.

"And we could shoot," Abatemarco said. "We could always shoot."

There was also another issue for Duke—the students . . . again.

They were up to their old tricks when the Wolfpack showed up. Lorenzo Charles, the dunking hero of Albuquerque, had been charged during the off-season with holding up a Domino's Pizza delivery man. He hadn't stolen any money—just pizza—but, not surprisingly, the story of his arrest received a good deal of attention.

And, just as unsurprisingly, the Duke students weren't going to pretend the incident hadn't happened. Shortly before tip-off, a Domino's pizza delivery man showed up at the State bench with an armful of pizzas ordered, he claimed, by a Mr. Charles. Valvano quickly defused that by paying for the pizzas and then handing them out to students sitting a few rows behind the bench.

Naturally, the students weren't finished. When Charles was introduced, they filled the air with empty Domino's boxes. Nowadays, the boxes never would have gotten inside the building.

"It was a huge mistake," Mark Alarie said, able to laugh about it many years later. "I took one look at Lorenzo when we lined up for the tip and said, 'Uh-oh.' He had this look on his face that told me I was in for a long night."

Charles had added ten pounds of muscle to his frame during the summer and had become N.C. State's best player. That night, guarded by a very good defender (Alarie) he was unstoppable. Every time State needed a basket, he got it, either out of the offense or on an offensive rebound. He finished with 35 points and 11 rebounds and State won, 79–76.

"We had Domino's on the bus ride home," Valvano would joke. "If I'd had three game balls that night I'd have given one to Lo, one to Domino's, and one to the students."

The Duke players agreed. "Sometimes you should let sleeping dogs lie," Alarie said. "The 'Please miss' signs would have been a much better call."

Duke was now 14–5 overall but 1–4 in the ACC, with a 4-game losing streak. The Iron Dukes and other alumni and fans were now in full cry. Clearly, they believed, Krzyzewski wasn't ever going to be able to win in the ACC—with or without any double standard.

17

Tom Butters was in his office early on the morning after the loss to North Carolina State.

He hadn't slept much thinking about what his next step should be. He poured himself coffee and walked from his office across the Cameron Indoor Stadium lobby and down the narrow hallway to Mike Krzyzewski's office.

He wasn't surprised that Krzyzewski wasn't in yet. He imagined his coach had probably been up until dawn looking at tape to try to figure out what had happened the previous night. The answer, of course, was simple: Lorenzo Charles and pizza boxes had happened.

"I usually liked to meet with my coaches in their office," Butters said. "Me walking in and sitting down, I thought, felt less threatening than 'Come to my office.' That morning, though, I left word that I wanted Mike to come to my office as soon as he got in."

Krzyzewski was in by midmorning. The team had to leave that afternoon to bus to Clemson for a quick turnaround game on Saturday afternoon. In addition to everything else, the schedule wasn't doing him any favors. Clemson was usually a very solid team, and at home, even in years when it wasn't good, the Tigers were always difficult to beat.

Krzyzewski looked tired when he walked into Butters's office and even a little bit apprehensive. "When Mike's uncomfortable, he'll narrow his eyes a little bit," Butters said. "Maybe he was tired, but maybe he was a little worried too. I'm not sure I'd called him into my office since I'd hired him."

Krzyzewski didn't think Butters was going to fire him. "I honestly didn't know what it was about," he said. "If I hadn't been so tired, maybe I'd have been worried. All I was thinking about that morning was trying to figure out a way to beat Clemson. We needed to win a game."

When Krzyzewski sat down, Butters told him he'd been thinking about what was going on with the basketball team a good deal.

"Me too," Krzyzewski said, forcing a smile.

"I've got three problems right now," Butters said. "First, I've got an alumni base that doesn't think I've got the right coach in place. Second, I've got a lot of media who want to believe I don't have the right coach and are going to keep saying and writing it until you prove them wrong once and for all."

He paused. "I can handle all that. But here's my biggest problem. I've got a coach who doesn't know how good he is and he's doubting himself. So, there's really only one thing I can do about it."

With that, he pushed something across the desk in Krzyzewski's direction. Krzyzewski picked it up and looked at it. It was a new contract—a five-year extension.

"I don't want you or anyone else thinking there's any chance you aren't going to be coaching here for a long time," Butters said. "So let's lay that question to rest once and for all."

Butters thought he saw Krzyzewski's eyes glisten just a little.

"It was an incredible thing for Tom to do, especially on that morning," Krzyzewski said. He smiled. "I told him later it was also a *smart* thing for him to do. But I can see why that wasn't exactly the focus in the media or among the alumni when he made the announcement."

In fact, Butters was skewered both in the media and by Duke people—many of them major donors to the athletic program—after the announcement. He didn't take much of it too seriously, even the notes that said, "If you don't fire Krzyzewski someone might kill you," until one night when he and his wife, Lynn, came home to find their teenage daughter, Jill, in tears.

"There had been a phone call," Butters said. "Whoever it was said he was going to come to the house and hurt me if I didn't get rid of Mike right away. *That* bothered me. My daughter shouldn't have had to deal with that."

Butters kept the letters—almost all of them signed. Today, they sit in a box with letters written several years later, many by the very same people, telling him he *had* to make sure Krzyzewski didn't leave Duke to coach in the NBA. "Same people, no sense of irony," he said. "None of them ever said, 'I guess I was wrong back in eighty-four.'"

When the team gathered on that Friday afternoon for the bus ride to Clemson, Krzyzewski told them about his new contract.

"If any of you were worried about this—don't," he said. "Mr. Butters just gave me a five-year contract extension. I'm going to be here after you've all graduated."

That was a big deal for the players.

"We had talked about it," Jay Bilas said. "We read the papers; we knew what was going on. We'd seen the looks on people's faces after the game in Atlanta. I think we all felt the same way: our loyalty was to Coach K. He was the reason we'd all come to Duke. We had never stopped believing in him. I'm pretty sure if they'd fired him, most of us would have left.

"To hear him say, 'I'm not going anywhere,' was a huge relief for all of us. It meant we could just worry about winning basketball games and not worry about whether we were going to have to be thinking about where to go to school the next year."

Coincidence or not, the Blue Devils won two close games on the Saturday–Monday road trip, winning exactly the kind of games they had been losing. First, they beat Clemson, 67–65, and then, two nights later in Atlanta, they beat Georgia Tech, 69–68. They went on an eight-game winning streak that included a win at Maryland and a win at home against Wake Forest—the team that had beaten them by 31 a month earlier. It was Krzyzewski's first win (0–8 until that night) against Carl Tacy and the Demon Deacons, and it came when Alarie hit a jump shot in overtime after Duke had blown a big lead at the end of regulation.

When Alarie hit that shot, with five seconds left, Mickie Krzyzewski was sitting in her husband's office. The game wasn't on TV so she listened, hoping to hear a roar that would mean good news. She had left her seat at the end of regulation because she couldn't bear to watch the overtime.

On March 3, Duke went to Chapel Hill with a 7–6 conference record to conclude the regular season against North Carolina. The Tar Heels were attempting to finish the conference season with a 14–0 record. They had finally lost—by one—at Arkansas with Kenny Smith out injured and were 25–1 overall. Even after their loss, they had still been ranked number one because their résumé was so impressive.

Other than the fact that Smith still wasn't 100 percent (he had broken his left wrist, so he could play once the cast was off even though he wasn't completely healed), the Tar Heels appeared to be virtually unbeatable. Michael Jordan was going to be the national player of the year and Sam Perkins was a first-team All-American.

"I've only had a handful of teams I looked at and said, 'Yes, this team should win the national [championship] if we stay healthy,'" Smith said years later. "If Kenny hadn't been hurt, who knows? But even with him playing at less than one hundred percent, it was still a team that was good enough to beat anybody."

Carolina was great. Duke was unafraid.

And Carmichael Auditorium was a cauldron, the Tar Heel fans having not forgotten Krzyzewski's "double-standard" comments six weeks earlier.

Amaker and Dawkins were well prepared to handle Carolina's run-and-jump pressure defense. Time after time they beat the trap and set up Duke baskets. On the other hand, Duke didn't have any answers for Jordan, in large part because no one really had an answer for Jordan. He finished with twenty-five points. So did Perkins.

At one point, after Jordan had soared over everyone for another basket, Pete Gaudet turned to Bob Bender on the Duke bench. "It's really not fair," he said. "He can't be guarded."

He was guarded just enough that Duke had a two-point lead with the clock dwindling in regulation after an Alarie three-point play; Carolina setting up for a tying basket. Steve Hale missed a shot from the corner and Dawkins corralled the rebound and took off, heading for the Duke basket with no one in his way. He was one on zero. This was before there was a three-point shot and before the rule had been put in place stopping the clock in the final minute of a game after a made basket. Dawkins was going to dunk the ball and Duke was going to win the game.

Except that there was a whistle. Very smartly, Matt Doherty had grabbed Danny Meagher away from the ball. The foul had nothing to do with the play, and normally a good referee would have looked away and let the play continue.

Hank Nichols was a good referee—one of the best ever. For some reason, at that moment, he called the foul. Instead of Dawkins going in for an uncontested dunk, Meagher went to the foul line to shoot one-and-one.

Meagher, a 64 percent free-throw shooter, missed. After a Carolina time-out, Doherty hit a spinning off-balance jumper at the buzzer and the game went into overtime.

Piss factor.

It took two overtimes before the Tar Heels finally pulled away and won, 96–83. Krzyzewski wasn't even that angry after the loss. Disappointed, sure. Upset with Nichols, absolutely. But he had seen something during the first forty-five minutes—regulation and the first overtime—that made him feel good.

"I remember in the locker room he was clearly proud of the way we'd played," Mark Alarie said. "Not in the sense of any sort of moral victory, coming so close to beating them in Chapel Hill, but in the sense that 'Hey, guys, we *are* this good.' He remembered how one-sided the games had been the year before, and he knew that us coming close in Cameron wasn't the same as us just about winning in Chapel Hill. We'd come a long way. He knew we were good enough to beat them."

Jay Bilas goes a step further. "*That* was the game that was really the turning point for us, not just in terms of Carolina but in where we had progressed to as opposed to where we'd been as a team and as a program. There was no doubt in our minds that we could walk on the court and look Carolina in the eye when we played them. The year before, we didn't think we belonged on the same court with them and, being honest, we probably didn't. After that game in Chapel Hill, we knew we could play with them."

In his column the next day, Keith Drum wrote that "the best team wasn't the winning team in Carmichael Auditorium yesterday."

Just as in January, both coaches read Drum's column. This time, though, only one of them was upset about it.

—

With the win over Duke, North Carolina finished the regular season 14–0 in ACC play. In what was a deep and balanced league, that left the Tar Heels a remarkable five games ahead of second place Maryland, which had finished 9–5. Wake Forest and Duke had tied for third at 7–7 with Georgia Tech and Virginia a game back at 6–8 and N.C. State seventh at 4–10. The Wolfpack's record was four games worse than it had been a year earlier, but no one was expecting another miracle run as the eight teams—Clemson had finished last at 3–11—assembled in Greensboro.

The feeling going into the tournament was that Carolina, Maryland, and Wake Forest were all locks to make the NCAA Tournament—Carolina, at 26–1, clearly, as a number-one seed. Duke, Georgia Tech, and Virginia were on the bubble, each needing at least one win to secure a bid. Duke and Georgia Tech would meet in the first round in what appeared to be an unofficial knockout game: winner shows up in the NCAA bracket on Sunday night, loser heads for the NIT.

Most people were conceding the tournament to Carolina. It wasn't just that the Tar Heels hadn't lost in conference play and their only loss all season had been by one point, on the road against a ranked team with Kenny Smith not playing; it was Jordan.

Although he had averaged "only" 19.8 points per game—which created the never-ending joke about Dean Smith being the greatest defensive coach in history because he was the only coach to ever hold Jordan to under twenty points a game—Jordan was clearly the best player in the country. NBA scouts, who loved big guys, were talking up Houston's Hakeem Olajuwon, Kentucky's Sam Bowie, and Sam Perkins as *the* players to watch in the draft, but those who had watched Jordan closely knew they were looking at something truly special.

Smith knew Jordan wasn't coming back for his senior season. He had always counseled his players to leave if they were guaranteed to be among the top five players chosen in the draft. The only player who had ever refused this advice was Phil Ford, who had told Smith he didn't care, he wanted to come back for his senior year. It worked out fine—Ford was the number-two pick after his senior season in the spring of 1978.

Jordan wasn't coming back, which was why Smith badly wanted this team to win the national championship. The Tar Heels would still be competitive the following year, but with Perkins and Doherty graduating and Jordan leaving, they wouldn't be nearly *this* good. Smith had long since given up the notion of convincing anyone that Jordan was just another very good Carolina player. Even so, he still had what everyone in the Carolina family called his "Dean" moments.

One had come in January, when Carolina had pulled away late to win a heated game with Maryland in College Park. In the final seconds, with Carolina up 72–62, Jordan made a steal and went in unmolested for a dunk. But he didn't just dunk the ball. Wanting to send a clear message to the now-defeated Maryland fans, Jordan rose into the air, cupped the ball below his waist, and then reached his arm back as far as he could and tomahawk-slammed the ball through the hoop just before the final buzzer.

For a split second there was silence. Then the entire building erupted; no one had ever seen a dunk quite like that one. Maryland fans were high-fiving one another because they knew they had just seen something extraordinary—and it had the bonus of not affecting the outcome of the game.

As the jubilant Tar Heels raced to the tunnel, Eddie Fogler spotted a reporter he knew and waved him over.

"Ever see anything like that?" Fogler asked.

"Have you?" the reporter answered.

Fogler shook his head. "Nope. I gave it a nine point nine."

He was wrong. It was an absolute ten.

Of course Smith didn't want to hear about it. "Spectacular" wasn't his thing. When someone asked him about the dunk during his postgame press conference he shrugged and said, "We'll take the two points. A layup would have been just as good."

The next day, when Smith saw Fogler quoted as saying he'd given the dunk a 9.9, he berated him for making it a bigger deal than it should have been. And, when Carolina fans tuned in to *The Dean Smith Show* that weekend, no doubt hoping to see the dunk either again or for the first time, they were disappointed. It didn't make the highlights.

"Why should it?" Smith said years later. "It had no effect on the outcome of the game."

—

Duke barely beat Georgia Tech in the unofficial knockout game on Friday. It took an Amaker fifteen-foot jump shot late in overtime and a missed Mark Price jumper—which was a shock since Price never seemed to miss when it mattered most—to allow the Blue Devils to escape, 67–63, against another young team that was clearly on the rise.

North Carolina had easily beaten Clemson that afternoon, setting up a third Duke-Carolina game in Saturday's first semifinal. Beating Georgia Tech had relieved some pressure for the Blue Devils because they now knew they were in the NCAAs and because the Yellow Jackets and Bobby Cremins had now clearly established themselves as an up-and-coming threat in the ACC. Duke–Georgia Tech was rapidly becoming a very good rivalry—on the court and in recruiting.

Even so, the Blue Devils were thrilled to get another shot at Carolina—no one more so than their coach. Before they left the locker room on Saturday afternoon, he delivered a stern message: "When we win the game, I don't want to see anyone hugging or jumping up and down," he said. "Just do what we do after any other game—walk off the court. Don't act as if you didn't expect to win, because *I* expect you to win and you should feel that way too. You're the better team. Now go out and prove it."

Needless to say, proving it wasn't easy. By now, Amaker and Dawkins were so comfortable against the run-and-jump that they were able to use it against the Tar Heels, finding Bilas and Alarie open for layups so frequently that Smith finally backed it off.

Duke led for most of the afternoon before the inevitable Carolina rally led to a tie game with a little more than three minutes left. A noncall on what appeared to be a Meagher foul with the game tied sent Smith into a tizzy and led to a David Henderson basket that put Duke ahead for good. When Perkins's desperation seventy-foot shot went wide left as the buzzer sounded, Duke had won, 77–75.

"I was nervous until I saw Sam's shot fading left," Bilas said. "They were Dracula. You felt at times like you needed an actual wooden stake to put them away. As soon as I heard the buzzer, I started to walk off the court, just like Coach K had told us to. No celebrating because we expected to win. Then I looked at center court and there was Coach K *hugging* Dawkins."

It was true. As soon as the buzzer sounded, Krzyzewski had walked down for a brief—and uneventful—handshake with Smith and then charged Dawkins.

"I couldn't believe it when I saw him," Dawkins said, laughing at the memory thirty years later. "I think we all remembered what he said about not celebrating. He wrapped me up in this hug and

I said, 'Coach, I thought we weren't celebrating.' He said, 'Aah, f—— it.' So then we all celebrated."

Krzyzewski smiles when the subject comes up but doesn't find it quite as funny as his players still do.

"It was a moment I loved and one I cherish, because that was a *great* Carolina team and beating them, especially in the ACC Tournament, was a huge step for that team and that group of kids," he said. "But, looking back, it was a learning experience for me as a coach. I made a mistake. I reacted emotionally because it was a big win, but we had another game to play the next day. We ended up running out of gas because it *did* feel like we had won the tournament or something very important at that moment. If I'd handled it differently, we might have beaten Maryland the next day."

Seven years later, when Duke pulled off one of the biggest upsets in college basketball history by beating a 34–0 Nevada–Las Vegas team in the national semifinals, Krzyzewski raced onto the court at the final buzzer with his palms pointed to the ground, screaming, "Calm down, calm down!" even as his players were starting to hug one another.

"What I learned from eighty-four is that you never celebrate when there's another game to play," he said. "After that Vegas game, we still had to beat Kansas to win the national championship. If we had lost to Kansas, the win over Vegas would have been hollow. We all make mistakes. The important thing is to learn from them."

That afternoon, very few people from Duke thought it was possible to celebrate too much. Some Duke fans were so ecstatic about the win that they had bumper stickers made up that said simply: Duke—77, North Carolina—75, March 10, 1984.

Krzyzewski wasn't thrilled when he saw them. "You don't build a program based on beating one team—any team," he said. "You get bumper stickers made up for winning a championship, not for winning one game."

While Krzyzewski was still hugging Dawkins and his team-mates, Dean Smith stalked down the steps to the hallway area just outside his locker room and lit a postgame cigarette. He was angry about the outcome, angry about losing to Duke and Krzyzewski. He was still angry about the whole "double-standard" imbroglio. Standing there, he spotted Keith Drum coming down the steps heading to the interview-room area, which was down the hall from the Carolina locker room.

Tossing his cigarette, Smith walked across the hall and cut Drum off. Hand extended, he said, "Congratulations. I'm sure you're very proud of the way your team played today."

Smith was still seething from the "better team lost" column that Drum had written a week earlier and from his refusal to take a clear stand against Krzyzewski—as most columnists in the state had done—after the "double-standard" game. Drum had gone to the University of North Carolina. In Smith's mind, his "siding" with Krzyzewski in any way, shape, or form was a betrayal. Sarcasm was almost always the way he showed his anger—whether in person or in practice or during a game.

"He never raised his voice or used profanity in practice," Buzz Peterson remembered. "But he could cut you down in a second. I might take a shot and he'd blow the whistle and say, 'Tell me, Buzz, how good a shot do you think that was? Was it the best shot we could have gotten right there? Let's ask your teammates what they think: Anyone think that was the best possible shot we could have gotten?' And you'd stand there wishing a hole would open in the court and swallow you up."

Often the sarcasm came in response to someone not playing as hard as Smith thought he should be playing. "He'd say, 'Eddie, is that as hard as you can go after a loose ball?'" Eddie Fogler said. "'Are you okay? Do you need a rest?' There was never any doubt about the message he was sending."

Now Smith was standing in front of Drum, smiling, hand extended, clearly sending him a message.

"That was Dean," Drum said. "If you knew him, you knew

that was just him being hypercompetitive. I've never met a great coach who wasn't. The difference was Dean tried to sound as if he wasn't being that way when, in fact, there was never anyone alive more competitive than he was." Drum smiled. "Only guy I ever knew well who was as competitive was Krzyzewski. Which probably explains a lot about their relationship."

Indeed.

18

The 1983–84 season didn't end especially well for any of the teams in the Triangle.

North Carolina State's season fell apart midway through February. The Wolfpack was cruising along at 19–7 and appeared to be—at worst—an NCAA Tournament bubble team, just as it had been a year earlier. Given the departure of Sidney Lowe, Dereck Whittenburg, and Thurl Bailey, making it back to the tournament would have been a major achievement.

Two losses, one not at all surprising, the other stunning, turned the season around. On February 18, State was pummeled 95–71 in Chapel Hill. This surprised no one, least of all Valvano, since the Tar Heels were pummeling just about everyone at that point.

"They were as good a college basketball team as I'd seen since the Wooden [UCLA] teams," Valvano said years later. "I think the only person more shocked that they didn't win the national championship than me was Dean."

Five nights later, Duke came to Raleigh and won, 73–70, in overtime.

"That was the loss we never got over that year," Tom Abatemarco said. "By then, we knew they were good and we didn't expect to win easily anymore. But we did expect to *win*."

As it turned out, State didn't win again for the rest of the season. It lost in the first round of the ACC Tournament to Maryland and then sleepwalked through a 74–71 first-round NIT loss to Florida State. That was the team's seventh straight loss, and it was pretty apparent that *no one,* including the head coach, had any interest in playing in the NIT.

"We'd won the whole thing a year earlier," Valvano said. "At that point in my life did I have any interest in cutting down the last net in the NIT? Did any of our guys? Of course not. The only thing that would have been worse than losing to Florida State would have been winning and having to play another game."

Once a team and a coach have tasted the NCAA Tournament—much less won it—playing in the NIT is very difficult. For smaller schools, it can still be a big deal. But if you are from the ACC or one of the other major conferences, it is a place you go only after a lost season. A year after Valvano made his only NIT appearance as a coach, Bob Knight and Indiana played in the NIT after Knight's worst season ever in the Big Ten. The Hoosiers were 7–11 in league play during a winter lowlighted by Knight's infamous chair throw.

Somehow, the Hoosiers pulled together to make it to the NIT final—perhaps because in those days coaches were allowed to make their team practice until the Final Four was played, and Knight's players preferred playing games to facing Knight in practice day after day with no games to break up the anger and the monotony.

After Indiana had beaten Tennessee in the semifinals, Bill Raftery asked Knight during a postgame TV interview what he liked most about his team at that point in the season.

"The fact that I only have to watch it play once more," Knight said without a hint of a smile.

Watching that interview, Valvano, never a fan of Knight's, could relate. He was more than happy to pack up the basketballs after the Florida State game. As had been the case two years earlier, he had his three best players—Lorenzo Charles, Terry Gannon, and Cozell McQueen—coming back as seniors, and he was going to add Chris Washburn, the most highly touted big man to come out of high school since Ralph Sampson.

Valvano didn't enjoy losing seven straight games to end the season, but he looked at it as a blip. He was right. His next five teams all made the NCAA Tournament.

—

It turned out that Krzyzewski's on-court celebration after the win over North Carolina was his last chance to enjoy a win that season. Duke lost to Maryland in the championship game the next day when the Blue Devils wore down midway through the second half after building an eight-point lead and Len Bias, voted the tournament MVP, ran amok in the final eight minutes.

"The guy was the closest thing to Jordan I ever saw in a college game," Mark Alarie said. "He jumped so high and shot it so softly he was almost impossible to stop."

Two years later, when Duke had a truly great team and Alarie and Bias were both seniors, Maryland came in to play at Duke. Krzyzewski knew how good (great) Bias was, but he was also stubborn about not double-teaming *anyone* unless he had absolutely no choice.

"We don't double-team at Duke," he said, stalking into the locker room prior to the game. He looked directly at Alarie and Jay Bilas. "Which one of you is guarding Bias? Which one of you is up to the challenge?"

Alarie pointed at Bilas. Bilas pointed at Alarie.

"It ended up being me," Alarie said. "Jay had put on a lot of muscle in the off-season and wasn't as quick as he'd been, so I got Bias. It might have been the best defensive game I've ever played. I was all over him, never lost him on a switch, contested every shot. We won the game because our other four were a lot better than their other four, but I was really proud of the way I kept him under control.

"We got in the locker room and I grabbed a box to see what I'd held him to." Alarie paused and smiled. "He only got forty-one."

Bias "only" got 32 in the '84 ACC championship game, but that was enough for Maryland to pull away and win, 74–62.

Maryland's win meant that, in his fifteenth season, Lefty Driesell had *finally* won an ACC championship after losing the title game five times. It also led to one of the most widely misquoted lines in basketball history. Speaking to the media after the game with the championship trophy right next to him at the lectern, Driesell said, "When I was younger, I'd'a probably taken this trophy, attached it to the hood of my car, and driven all around North Carolina, pulled into every driveway, honked my horn, and said, 'Come on out and look what I got.'

"Now, though, I'm too old for that. I'm just gonna take it home and get some rest."

To this day, Driesell is still quoted as saying he was going to take the trophy and attach it to the hood of his car.

Krzyzewski had no trophy to take home or put on the hood of his car. Instead, he and his team were sent to Pullman, Washington, for the second round of the NCAA Tournament after receiving a first-round bye. It was hardly an ideal draw because their opponent was the University of Washington. Even though Duke was the higher-seeded team, it had to play on what amounted to a home court for the Huskies because so many of their fans could drive to the game. Durham is a long drive—2,097 miles—from Pullman. Seattle wasn't exactly around the corner—284 miles—but Washington had fans across the state.

Duke ended up losing, 80–78, the game ending when Johnny Dawkins caught what looked like a perfect alley-oop pass from Tommy Amaker and appeared to get undercut as he tried to control the ball and put it in the basket.

"*Appeared* to get undercut?" Dawkins said thirty years later, smiling but still clearly not over it yet. "Go back and look at the tape. These days, it would have been two shots and the ball."

In those days, in Pullman, it was no shots and a long plane flight home. Even so, a corner had clearly been turned. Duke finished 24–10, winning more games than it had won in the previous two seasons combined. The win over North Carolina and the return to the NCAA Tournament after a four-year absence calmed the waters in Durham considerably.

"The angry letters stopped," Butters said. "It wasn't as if people were writing to say, 'Okay, Tom, you got it right,' but at least they weren't saying I was a complete idiot anymore."

One place where they had never thought Butters was a complete idiot was in the basketball offices located on the concourse level of Carmichael Auditorium. Dean Smith and his staff had always believed Krzyzewski could coach but had wondered if he'd be able to survive those first rocky years.

"We always knew Jimmy [Valvano] was a threat but we also wondered how long he'd stay or want to stay, especially after he won the championship," Roy Williams said. "With Mike, once he had turned that corner in eighty-four, we were pretty sure he was going to be around for the long haul. He was always the bigger threat if only because we always recruited against Duke and rarely recruited against State.

"Coach Smith knew how good he was. But there's also no doubt that the whole 'double-standard' thing really set a tone for their relationship that never completely went away as long as they were coaching against one another. Some of the hostility was inevitable because of who they were and the setting they were coaching in against one another. But at that point, there's no doubt it got to be a little bit personal." Williams smiled. "Probably a little more than a little bit."

No one from Carolina was worried about Krzyzewski or about double standards when the Tar Heels traveled to Atlanta to play Indiana in the East Region semifinals after a relatively easy second-round win over Temple in Charlotte the previous Saturday.

No one believed that Indiana was any kind of a serious threat in the round of sixteen. Bob Knight had probably done one of his better coaching jobs getting that far into the tournament. His team was built around Uwe Blab, the seven-foot-three German who had been a part of Duke's lost recruiting class of 1981, and Steve Alford, a freshman guard who could catch-and-shoot about as well as anyone in the country but, at six foot one, with little ability to create his own shot, appeared to be eminently guardable.

No one was more convinced about that than Knight. On the afternoon of the game, after the team's pregame meal, he pulled Alford aside for a rare game-day one-on-one talk. Knight usually reserved his private meetings with players for practice days. He made an exception because he believed this was an exceptional situation.

"If Dean is smart tonight, he's going to put [Michael] Jordan on you man-to-man the whole game and you'll never touch the ball," Knight told Alford. "But I think he's going to stick to his system because he thinks they're so much better than us, it doesn't matter." What Knight didn't say to Alford at that moment was that he agreed with Smith—Carolina was almost certainly much better than Indiana.

Then he continued. "What that means, Steve, is they're going to trap the ball and double-team all over the place. Which means you *should* get open shots all night." He looked Alford in the eye. "If I'm right about that, you better make those shots."

Knight was right. Carolina came out in the run-and-jump, and Indiana, which had practiced against the run-and-jump for four straight days, was ready for it. Alford did get open shots. And, even though he wasn't guarding Alford, Jordan picked up two fouls in the game's first eight minutes and was consigned to the bench for the rest of the first half.

If there was ever a game in which Knight should have considered a zone defense, it was on that March evening in Atlanta's Omni—a building that no longer exists. He stuck to his man-to-man, assigning six-foot-five-inch junior Dan Dakich to guard Jordan. Dakich, who is now one of ESPN's lead college basketball analysts, was a hard-nosed, blue-collar kid from Merrillville, Indiana, which isn't far from Chicago and is a suburb—for lack of a better term—of Gary, Indiana. He was slow, he couldn't jump, and he wasn't much of a shooter. He was also fearless—and funny.

When he was asked after the game what his first thought was when Knight had told him he would be guarding Jordan, Dakich said, "I went to my room and threw up." That was true—he'd been sick and had made the mistake of thinking he could eat his way out of his nausea with spaghetti. Dakich's understanding of dietary matters was always questionable. A couple of years later, when he was a graduate assistant coach at Indiana, Dakich and a friend decided to go on a diet by having lunch every day at a Chinese restaurant in Bloomington that served an all-you-can-eat buffet.

Dakich told the media he'd thrown up at the thought of guarding Jordan for one reason: "I thought this was the only chance I'd ever have to make [*Sports Illustrated*'s] 'They Said It,'" he admitted years later. "I was right."

Jordan actually scored the first four points of the game, and Dakich, doing some quick math in his head after Jordan's second basket, realized that if that pace continued the final score would be Jordan: 160, Indiana: 0.

"I figured I needed to start doing better."

Helped by Jordan's absence the last twelve minutes of the first half, both Dakich and the Hoosiers got much better. Indiana led at halftime, 32–28. That was hardly reason for Carolina to panic: they were only down 4 even though Jordan had been on the bench.

Indiana's view of the first half was simple: we can play with these guys. Stew Robinson, a sophomore guard, was having the game of his career, consistently breaking Carolina's pressure to score 14 points and set up Alford and the other Indiana shooters. Dakich picked up his fourth foul early in the second half, but Knight left him in the game, figuring he was smart enough to know how to play effectively with four fouls.

Indiana began pulling away, stretching the lead at one point to 61–48. Alford would finish the game 9 of 13 from the field, consistently getting open shots against the Carolina pressure. He was also 9 of 10 from the foul line, finishing with 27 points. After making his first two shots, Jordan was 4 of 14 the rest of the night and ended up scoring 13 points in what turned out to be his last college game. Carolina made a late run—aided by Indiana missing a slew of free throws—but never got even. Indiana won, 72–68, in one of the more shocking upsets in college basketball history.

The loss stunned the Tar Heels—from Smith down. In the locker room, Matt Doherty, who had also played his last college game, shook his head in disbelief. "That number eleven [Dakich] is someone I'm not sure would get picked by anyone in a school-yard game," he said. "I'm still not sure how he was able to guard Michael."

Through the years, there have been numerous jokes made about the fact that it was Smith, by choosing to bench Jordan for those twelve first-half minutes, who stopped Jordan. But Jordan played eighteen minutes in the second half and never got going. Dakich had plenty of help from his teammates because Indiana's man-to-man defense has a lot of zone principles in it, but he was the one who faced up to Jordan each time he caught the ball.

Later, Smith would admit it was one of the most disappointing losses of his career. He knew how good his team was, and when he teared up a little in his postgame press conference talking about how much he had wanted to win, "for the seniors," he knew that Jordan—at least in basketball terms—was one of those seniors.

Indiana went on to lose in the Elite Eight to a Virginia team that North Carolina had beaten twice during the regular season. A year after failing to make the Final Four with Ralph Sampson starting at center, Terry Holland made it back with Kenton Edelin, a onetime walk-on, as his starting center.

Smith flew to Seattle to attend the annual coaches' convention at the Final Four. Standing at the rent-a-car counter, he was handed the keys to a compact car.

"A compact?" asked someone standing nearby.

Smith shrugged and smiled wanly. "I didn't rent until the last minute," he said. "I thought I'd be on a bus out here. My team's bus."

19

By the time the 1984–85 season rolled around, the dynamic among the three Triangle coaches had changed, in large part because Dean Smith's early prediction—that if Mike Krzyzewski could survive the trials of his first few seasons he'd be around for a while—had proven true.

The three games the two teams had played in 1984 had made the Duke–North Carolina rivalry real again. During Krzyzewski's first three seasons, there had been moments—the angry nonhand-shake/handshake between the two coaches at the 1980 Big Four; Duke's only victory in Gene Banks's final home game—when the intensity flared, but they had been few and far between for the simple reason that the programs weren't on a level playing field.

That had changed. All three games in 1984 had been memorable for different reasons: Krzyzewski's "double-standard" comments after the game in Cameron; Duke's belief that it should have won the game in Carmichael; and, finally, Duke's win in Greensboro. Smith's anger—his sarcastic comment to Keith Drum, his not-at-all-subtle shots at Danny Meagher, aka "May-har"—made it clear how badly he wanted to beat Duke and, perhaps more significant, Krzyzewski.

Smith had always seen Duke as North Carolina's primary and most dangerous rival. As good as N.C. State had been at times, especially during the David Thompson era, he rarely recruited against Norman Sloan or Jim Valvano. On the other hand, he almost always had to recruit against Duke. The two schools—regardless of who was coaching at Duke—were selling essentially the same thing: big-time basketball and a primo liberal arts education for anyone who decided to pursue it in those hours when he wasn't working at becoming an NBA player. Very few players who had the chance to play in the ACC were thinking about any postcollege career other than basketball.

Additionally, it was a simple, ironclad fact that Duke people and North Carolina people looked down their noses at State. To them, it was the "cow college"—it had been founded as an agricultural school—and the Raleigh campus, while nice enough, couldn't compare with the aesthetics at either Duke or North Carolina.

One of the Duke students' more enduring obnoxious chants was always directed at the Wolfpack—especially when the Wolfpack was whipping the Blue Devils throughout the 1970s: "If you can't go to college, go to State," they would begin. And then, just to be certain they sounded like spoiled, arrogant kids, they would add: "If you can't go to State, go to jail."

Of course they never brought that chant out for Carolina. They viewed the Tar Heels as near equals—an attitude that infuriated Smith. He was constantly researching studies that showed Carolina to be superior academically to Duke—which it was in any number of ways. One of those was the presence of a journalism program. While Duke had produced some prominent journalists—most notably *Time* magazine editor Clay Felker—it couldn't begin to touch the list of prominent UNC journalists, among them *The New York Times*'s Pulitzer Prize–winning columnist Tom Wicker; Vermont Royster, who became the editor of *The Wall Street Journal;* and Jeff MacNelly, the Pulitzer Prize–winning cartoonist.

The sports world was filled with prominent writers who had Carolina diplomas on their walls. The best of them were Peter Gammons, who had been on the team bus that fateful night in 1965 when Billy Cunningham pulled down the effigy; Furman Bisher, who wrote superbly in *The Atlanta Journal-Constitution* for more than sixty years; and Mark Whicker, who started at the *Winston-Salem Journal* before moving on to Philadelphia and Los Angeles. Many talented UNC graduates remained in state: Ron

Green and Bob Quincy, columnists for *The Charlotte Observer;* Lenox Rawlings at the *Winston-Salem Journal;* and Drum, who worked in Durham until he became an NBA scout.

There were also many UNC graduates who worked at papers in North Carolina and, unlike Drum, remained loyal-to-the-core Tar Heels. That was often reflected in both their reporting and their writing, causing Krzyzewski to say often, "No matter how much we might win, I know I'm always going to be working as the minority in this state. I'll never outnumber them, so I have to outwork them."

Duke's breakthrough season in 1984 had put Krzyzewski's job on firm ground and had also put him into a position where he now believed he could take Smith and North Carolina on in an area where the Tar Heels had been virtually untouchable: recruiting.

For many years, Duke and North Carolina had gone head-to-head in recruiting on a regular basis. One of the turning points for Smith had come in 1964 when he convinced Larry Miller, a six-four forward from Allentown, Pennsylvania, to turn down Duke and Vic Bubas to go to North Carolina. That had started a twenty-year run during which Smith won most of his recruiting battles while encountering Duke less and less.

In fact, when Krzyzewski first arrived at Duke, he and his assistants quickly figured out that trying to beat Smith for players, especially in the state of North Carolina, was going to be a waste of time more often than not.

"If you think about it for a minute, it made perfect sense," said Chuck Swenson. "Carolina was *the* state school, and they'd been great for a long time. If you were a kid in state, unless you had some connection to N.C. State, you grew up a Tar Heel fan. If you could play basketball, you grew up wanting to be a Tar Heel. Even when Duke was good, it was always going to be viewed in state as the northern school. Even before the end of our first year, we'd figured that out.

"In a lot of cases, Bobby [Dwyer] and I honestly believed that if we could get Mike into a kid's home, there was a good chance we'd get him. Even back then, he was that good. But there were certain homes where, no matter what he said, no matter how much he impressed the kid and his family, he just wasn't coming to Duke. Our job was to find the kids who we had a break-even chance with starting out. When that was the case, we had a shot. We learned early that almost none of those kids were going to be from North Carolina. We needed to go north and we needed to go west."

Danny Ferry was from Annapolis, Maryland. He was six foot ten, could pass and shoot, and had about as good a basketball pedigree as one could hope to find. His father, Bob, had played in the NBA for nine years and was general manager of the Washington Bullets. Danny's older brother, Bobby, was ten inches shorter than Danny but still a good-enough player—and student—to be Harvard's point guard. Ferry played at DeMatha High School—coached by Morgan Wootten, the same Morgan Wootten who had turned down N.C. State prior to the hiring of Jim Valvano and would later become the first high school coach voted into the Basketball Hall of Fame.

By the time Ferry was a DeMatha sophomore, he was being targeted by the top basketball schools in the country as a must-get recruit. DeMatha was literally two miles down US-1 from the Maryland campus, and Lefty Driesell was willing to do almost anything to keep Ferry home. Dean Smith knew that a player with Ferry's skill and basketball smarts would fit his system perfectly. And Mike Krzyzewski believed that Ferry would be a great addition to an already very good team in 1986 and then could be Duke's next key player once his first great senior class—Johnny Dawkins, Mark Alarie, David Henderson, Jay Bilas, and Weldon Williams—graduated.

When Harvard, led by Bobby Ferry, came to play Duke during the 1984–85 season, the Duke students were more than ready to let him know how much they wanted his little (though much taller) brother to come to Duke. Throughout warm-ups, they chanted "We want your brother!" in Ferry's direction. They were prepared to give him a standing ovation, unheard-of for a visiting player, when he was introduced with the other four Harvard starters.

Sure enough, Ferry was the last player introduced. When longtime Duke PA announcer Art Chandler got to Ferry—"A six-foot senior from Annapolis, Maryland, Bobby Ferry!"—the students were on their feet. And then, they stopped—stunned into complete silence. The player who trotted onto the court when Ferry was introduced was Dane Hudson.

Dane Hudson was African American.

"Might have been the only time I've ever seen the students not have any answer at all," said Tommy Amaker—now Harvard's basketball coach. "They had no idea what to do."

"Arguably the best performance by a visiting player in the history of Cameron Indoor Stadium," Krzyzewski said.

Even though Bobby Ferry outwitted the Duke students, it might have been their sense of humor that ultimately drew his brother to Duke. The Ferrys get their sense of humor from their father, who was known around the NBA for his keen wit. It would follow that his sons would also enjoy a good laugh.

While Ferry was trying to decide where to go to college, North Carolina, Maryland, and Duke were all having very good—if not great—basketball seasons.

There was nothing Smith savored more than to play the role of an underdog—something he rarely got to do. But with Michael Jordan, Sam Perkins, and Matt Doherty gone, Carolina wasn't picked to win the ACC. In fact, the Tar Heels weren't even picked second. Georgia Tech and Duke were the favorites, each having a plethora of returning talent. Of course Carolina, with Brad Daugherty, Kenny Smith, Joe Wolf, Dave Popson, Buzz Peterson, and Steve Hale all still around, wasn't exactly dealing with a bare cupboard.

In fact, almost everyone in the ACC appeared loaded. Maryland still had senior Adrian Branch and junior Len Bias, who had emerged as a star during his sophomore year. North Carolina State might have had more talent than anyone. In addition to seniors Lorenzo Charles, Cozell McQueen, and Terry Gannon, Ernie Myers was now a junior. Chris Washburn, the number-one rated recruit in the country, had run into trouble—stealing a stereo—so he wasn't eligible to play. But Valvano had added Nate McMillan and Vinny Del Negro, who would both go on to very productive NBA careers.

Del Negro hadn't been recruited very heavily, and during the preseason, someone asked Valvano if it was true that he had recruited Del Negro because the kid was Italian.

"Absolutely not," Valvano said. "I recruited him because *I'm* Italian."

He had recruited him because he could play.

So could Spud Webb, although he certainly didn't look like a player. Webb was five foot seven (maybe) and weighed 138 pounds (maybe). Valvano had been very skeptical about recruiting a player that small to play in the ACC, but after N.C. State won the national championship, Tom Abatemarco had convinced him to at least take a look at Webb and meet him. As it turned out, Webb, who had just graduated from Midland Junior College, visited campus before Valvano had a chance to see him play. When Valvano and Abatemarco went to the airport to pick him up, they had trouble finding him.

Finally, they went to the baggage-claim area, where they found a lone passenger from Webb's flight standing forlornly by himself, looking lost.

"He looked about fifteen," Valvano said later. "I said to Tom, 'If that's Spud, you're fired.'"

It was Spud. Abatemarco wasn't fired. Webb ended up taking over the point guard spot from Sidney Lowe. Not only did Webb have a stellar two-year career at State, he played in the NBA for thirteen years. As an NBA rookie in 1986, he won the Slam Dunk Contest at the All-Star Game.

In 2015, most of those who were the ACC's best players in 1985 would have been long gone to the NBA. But back then, great players almost always stayed in college for three or four years. The league—like all of college basketball—was dominated by juniors and seniors.

In 1985, no one from the ACC made the Final Four. But Georgia Tech, North Carolina, and N.C. State reached the Elite Eight; Maryland got to the Sweet 16; and Duke—with Mark Alarie injured—lost in the round of thirty-two. Those five teams finished within a game of one another during the ACC regular season. Georgia Tech, North Carolina, and N.C. State were 9–5 in league play; Duke and Maryland were 8–6.

"Those two years, 1985 and 1986, the league was unbelievable," Krzyzewski remembered. "It seemed like everyone, even the teams near the bottom, had very good players and, of course, some of us had great players. The experience and the depth were amazing. You don't see college basketball teams like those teams anymore because the best players don't stay in college."

Duke ended up 23–8 that season, losing in the ACC semifinals to Georgia Tech after Alarie was hurt in an opening-round win over Maryland. The NCAA Tournament expanded to sixty-four teams that season, meaning there were no byes and everyone played in the first round. The Blue Devils managed to win their first-round game against Pepperdine but were then upset in the second round for a second straight season, losing to Boston College. Now Duke fans had a different complaint about Krzyzewski: he couldn't win in postseason.

Valvano had no such problems. Two years after the "survive and advance" miracle of 1983, the Wolfpack almost went back to the Final Four, losing to top-seeded St. John's in the West Region final. Valvano had been convinced his team was good enough to win the tournament again.

"I remember there was a time-out with about twelve minutes left in the St. John's game," he said. "We were up, I think, four. I got in the huddle and said, 'Guys, we're twelve minutes away from the Final Four.' I looked at the seniors and said, 'Are you ready to do this again? You *know* how to do this.' I was convinced we were going back. But [Chris] Mullin wouldn't let it happen."

Mullin, the player Krzyzewski had coveted during his first season at Duke, had become a first-team All-American at St. John's. He was every bit as good as Krzyzewski had believed he was going to be when he had recruited him. Down the stretch against N.C. State he made several critical shots and went 7 of 7 from the free-throw line when Valvano began fouling. He finished with 25 points; St. John's won 69–60 and went to the Final Four for the first time since 1952—when Frank McGuire was the coach.

Valvano went home as disappointed as he could remember being at the end of a season. "It was a little bit like my last season at Iona because I believed we were good enough to beat anybody we played," he said. "The difference was in eighty-five we were *so* close to going back [to the Final Four]."

Valvano was lying on his office couch as he spoke. It was three years later and his team had just lost a home game to Georgia Tech. He sat up on the couch and took his last sip of wine. "Now, if I was Dean, I'd tell you I was really disappointed that day for my seniors. Don't get me wrong—I loved all three of them [McQueen, Charles, and Gannon], but, what the hell, they'd already won a national title. They were fine.

"Come to think of it, after a while I was fine too. I knew we were going to be good again the next year. Some years the breaks go your way, some years they don't. In eighty-three *all* the breaks went our way. It was as if God said, 'Everything that's ever gone wrong for you, I'm making up for it all at once.' Then, after we won, he said, 'Okay, we're even now.'"

As hard as Valvano took losing in the short term, he didn't dwell on tough losses. He put on his "a W is a W and an L is an L" face and moved on. Smith and Krzyzewski didn't dwell on that sort of loss either. Krzyzewski's oft-repeated motto became "Next play." Regardless of what happened—win, lose, play well, play poorly—you had to move on. Smith had no mottos but he never had trouble getting wound up to compete again.

"Actually the *waiting* to compete is what's hardest for me," he said one night, pacing a hallway prior to a game at Virginia. "If I had my way, we'd play every game at noon." He smiled and added, "Not any earlier than that, though. I'm not really a morning person. Actually, one o'clock might be better."

Smith's last loss in 1985, like Valvano's, came in the Elite Eight. Prior to the season, if someone had told Smith his team would advance to within one game of the Final Four, he undoubtedly would have signed up for that. But Carolina had played so well in the games leading to the Southeast Region final that everyone, from Smith down, was convinced they were going to the Final Four.

"He was as good that year as he's ever been," Roy Williams said, talking about Smith's coaching job. "He always loved a challenge, especially when outsiders doubted him—or, more importantly, doubted his team. He wanted to show people that, even though we'd lost Michael and Sam and Matt, we could still be very good. That was always his greatest strength—he didn't believe in down years. *Every* year was an opportunity as far as he was concerned."

Villanova was a team that had been close to making the Final Four on several occasions under Rollie Massimino. It had been to the Elite Eight three times since he had become the coach on Philadelphia's Main Line—losing to Duke in 1978, North Carolina in 1982, and Phi Slama Jama in 1983. The presence of the Wildcats in the Elite Eight was a surprise to most. They had lost ten games in the regular season and had barely squeezed into the tournament as a number-eight seed.

The committee's opinion of them was pretty evident when they were sent to play Dayton in the first round—on Dayton's home court. They somehow got out of that game, winning 49–48, then played a textbook game in the second round to beat top-seeded Michigan before taking out Maryland in the round of sixteen. Villanova's strength was that it was old. Three starters were seniors, two were juniors. What's more, they had played in the Big East, a league good enough to produce four Sweet 16 teams that year—including Georgetown, the defending national champions.

The game was played at Villanova's pace: slow, slower, slowest. Senior point guard Gary McLain was able to handle Carolina's pressure, and in college basketball's final season without a shot clock, the Wildcats milked the game clock throughout. Carolina had played thirty-four games to that point and had scored fewer than 60 points on three occasions. On that Sunday afternoon in Birmingham, they managed to score 44. Villanova broke open a tight game late, made all its free throws in the final minute, and won, 56–44. In the last thirty seconds, with the game no longer in doubt, Smith ordered his players to back off and not foul. That allowed Massimino, his coaches, and his players, to drink in what they had just accomplished as the seconds ticked down to zero.

"That's a memory I'll never, ever forget," Massimino said years later. "To stand there and look around the arena and realize we were going to the Final Four; to be able to hug my son [R.C., a Villanova walk-on that year] and just drink it all in. I'll be forever grateful to Dean for backing off that way. A lot of coaches wouldn't have done that."

Even though a loss, especially in a game he believed his team was good enough to win, always left Smith despondent—and, as Keith Drum could attest, often angry—he believed it was important to be gracious in defeat. This was certainly one of those occasions.

The 1984–85 season was best described by Bill Guthridge as he sat on a chair outside the locker room that day: "Great year, terrible ending," he said. "One of those days at the worst possible time."

Three Big East teams made it to Lexington and the Final Four that spring. Villanova beat Memphis in the first semifinal and then shocked Georgetown in the championship game, shooting an otherworldly 79 percent from the field in one of the most memorable championship game upsets in history. It ranked right up there with N.C. State's win over Houston two years earlier.

Seven years after the championship made him an almost godlike figure in Philadelphia, Massimino fled Villanova for, of all places, Nevada–Las Vegas. To those who followed college basketball, the irony was inescapable: two years earlier, also seven years after becoming an iconic figure, Jim Valvano had left N.C. State.

The circumstances were entirely different except for one thing: the change of life brought on by the championship and the newfound stardom were impossible to resist—and to overcome.

20

On the morning after Villanova's remarkable victory over George-town, Danny Ferry announced where he was planning to go to college. The choice was Duke. This was a major breakthrough for Mike Krzyzewski because, for the first time, he'd won a head-to-head recruiting battle with Dean Smith. For Smith, it was a loss, but hardly a crippling one. Not only did he have Brad Daugherty returning, but Carolina was clearly the leader for both J. R. Reid and Scott Williams, who were considered to be among the best big men—or, in the case of Reid, *the* best big man—in the high school class of 1986.

Even so, Ferry's decision got people's attention.

"For a long time, Carolina seemed to have the market cornered on the 'great player, good student' market," Valvano said several years later. "The Dawkins class was a huge breakthrough for Mike. But Dean didn't go after any of those kids. Usually, when Dean wanted a kid like that, he got him."

Even Smith, who rarely talked about recruiting or in any serious way about having any sort of rivalry with another coach, admitted several years later that Ferry's decision got his attention.

"By then he [Krzyzewski] had it going," he said. "When Danny went there I remember saying to myself, 'Time to make some extra phone calls.'" As in phone calls to recruits, their families, and their coaches. Smith had always made the calls that Eddie Fogler and Roy Williams asked him to make, but it was not his favorite sport.

"Sometimes he would say, 'Is this really important?'" Williams remembered. "If I said it was or Eddie said it was, he did it without asking any other questions. But we tried to ask him to make those calls only when we knew it was necessary."

The requests from Fogler and Williams became more frequent. Sometimes, Smith didn't need to be asked.

Ferry had grown up as a North Carolina fan and, for a long time, dreamed of playing for Smith and the Tar Heels. But Krzyzewski changed his mind. "In the end, he was the reason for my decision," Ferry said. "I was bowled over by his intensity and by the clarity of his plan for the program and for me as part of the program.

"There were other factors: I liked the idea that I'd be playing with a group of really good seniors for a year and then, after that, there would be big opportunities for me after I'd had a year to learn. Plus, I loved the idea of playing on the same team as Johnny Dawkins. I'd played against him when I was a freshman and he wasn't just a really good player, he was cool. The way he played, the way he was as a person was cool. I loved that about him then." He paused. "I love that about him now. He's *still* cool."

Morgan Wootten never asked a player where he was going or even where he was leaning. He wanted to be able to tell college coaches that he had no idea where a player was thinking about going and to be telling the truth when he did so. In fact, as he and Ferry walked across the gym floor at DeMatha to the press conference for Ferry to make his announcement, Ferry asked him if he wanted to know where he was going to college.

"I'll find out here soon enough, Danny," Wootten said. "I'm fine."

But he had a feeling that he already knew. "Once Danny said it wasn't going to be Maryland, I just had a sense that he liked Mike a lot. It wasn't that he didn't like or respect Dean, I just felt a connection there. As it turned out, I guess I was right."

Lefty Driesell had pulled out every trick he had in his playbook to try to get Ferry. When Ferry made his official visit to Maryland, Driesell sent a helicopter for him. Ferry's house was a twenty-five-minute drive from Maryland's campus. Lefty sent the helicopter anyway—to no avail.

—

It can be argued that the 1985–86 ACC was the deepest league in the history of college basketball. Three teams—North Carolina, Georgia Tech, and Duke—took turns being ranked number one in the country throughout the regular season. North Carolina State, with Chris Washburn eligible and playing center, was probably a half tick, if that, behind the top three. Virginia had a big-time frontcourt led by Olden Polynice and the onetime would-be Duke recruit Tom Sheehey plus a plethora of guards who could shoot. And Maryland also had a solid backcourt and Len Bias, who had become virtually unguardable, as Mark Alarie would learn during the course of the winter.

North Carolina opened its new basketball palace on January 18. From the moment the announcement was made that the building would be called the Dean E. Smith Center, it was dubbed the "Dean Dome" by everyone in the ACC. Only those who worked for the school ever referred to it as the Smith Center.

The man for whom the building was named never referenced it that way, but he did notice the bust of him in the main lobby. Walking past it one afternoon, he stopped and pointed it out to a visitor. Not the bust—the writing on it.

"Look," he said. "It says, 'Dean E. Smith, 1931 to.'" He laughed. "I guess they're just waiting to fill in the second date."

Years later, when the building was renovated and the bust was moved to a spot right outside the basketball offices, the writing was removed. Apparently Smith had pointed it out to enough people that it had been decided there was no need for *any* writing at all.

The opening game in the Dean Dome was—not coincidentally—against Duke. Construction delays had pushed back the opening. Originally the plan had been to open the season and the building with a game against UCLA on November 24.

When it became apparent that the Dome wouldn't be ready for the UCLA game, the decision was made to not rush the finishing touches and to open it in January against Duke.

The game would have been hyped under any circumstances. As luck—or the basketball gods, as Krzyzewski often liked to say—would have it, Carolina was 17–0 and ranked number one in the country and Duke was 16–0 and ranked number three. The media was calling it one of the biggest regular season games in college basketball history. Smith, naturally, didn't want to hear it.

"Every conference game is a big game," he said. "Of course the pressure's on us since we're playing at home."

Krzyzewski didn't mind the hype at all. "It wasn't that long ago that we didn't belong in the same sentence with Carolina," he said. "This is exactly the kind of game we wanted to be good enough to play in. I just hope we *are* good enough to play in it."

They were good enough to play in it—but not good enough to win it. Both teams loved playing up tempo, and there was little need for the forty-five-second clock that had been introduced to college basketball at the start of the season.

The building was electric from the start and both coaches were clearly wired. Smith certainly didn't want his team's unbeaten skein to end against Duke and Krzyzewski in a building newly christened in his name. Krzyzewski wanted nothing more than to ruin Carolina's opening-day party.

Late in the first half, Krzyzewski got into it with referee David Dodge, believing that the entire officiating crew was falling prey to the "double-standard" syndrome. Unlike two years earlier in Durham, it had nothing to do with Smith's bench decorum. It had strictly to do with the way the calls were going.

Dodge didn't want to hear it. Krzyzewski continued to let him hear it. Dodge teed him up. Krzyzewski got angrier. Dodge teed him up again. Back then, it took three technicals to get a coach ejected—it is two now—so Krzyzewski wasn't thrown out of the game. His assistants came to the rescue and got him away from Dodge before he could get technical number three.

Carolina led the entire afternoon, but Duke never went away. The final was 95–92. Carolina ended up extending its record to 21–0 before losing at Virginia. Duke had to play at Georgia Tech three nights later and lost to the Yellow Jackets, 87–80. That would be the Blue Devils' last loss for more than two months. Even so, years later, Krzyzewski still hadn't completely gotten over the loss in the Dean Dome opener.

"We could have won if we'd played a little better and if we'd gotten a couple more calls," he said, smiling. "Just a couple. I believed then that, one way or the other, we weren't going to be allowed to win that game. I don't think there was any conspiracy at all. I just think it was a very tough game to officiate. I wouldn't have wanted to be the refs that day." He shook his head. "Of course being the visiting coach that day wasn't easy either."

There were very few easy games for anyone in the ACC that winter. A little more than a month after Duke failed to get a win in the Dean Dome, Maryland did—in overtime. Len Bias stole the ball from Steve Hale at midcourt and went in for a dunk to tie the game in the final seconds, and Maryland went on to win 77–72 in overtime. It was one of the rare nights in which Maryland coach Lefty Driesell won a tight game against Smith.

Just as Krzyzewski carried some angst from the Dean Dome opener with him for years, Smith did the same with his team's first loss in the building. Years later, when the subject of that game came up, Smith shook his head and said, "You know, I was looking at the tape of that game this summer [this was in 1997, eleven years after the game] and Bias double-dribbled on the play where he stole the ball from Hale."

When it was pointed out to Smith that it had been eleven years since the game had been played *and* that Len Bias had been dead for almost as long, Smith nodded. "I know that," he said. "But lots of dead men have double-dribbled."

He wasn't smiling when he said it.

Several years later, when Smith had retired from coaching, he traveled with North Carolina to Maui for the annual pre-

Thanksgiving tournament played there. Hank Nichols, who had been one of the referees in the 1986 game, was having dinner at Roy's, one of the better-known spots on the island. When he saw Smith walking in, he went over to say hello and introduced him to the woman he was going out with at the time, his wife having passed away a couple of years earlier.

"I introduced her to Dean," Nichols said. "He looked at her, smiled, said it was very nice to meet her, and then said, 'You know you're with someone who missed a key double-dribble call twenty years ago.'"

Elephants—and coaches—never forget.

———

The Duke team that Danny Ferry joined had come a long way since the humiliation in Atlanta in 1983. Not only had the Blue Devils reached back-to-back NCAA Tournaments, they had started the season by winning the first preseason NIT, becoming the first Duke team to ever win a national tournament of any kind.

They were, to paraphrase the Blues Brothers, on a mission from Krzyzewski. The four freshman starters of 1983—Johnny Dawkins, Mark Alarie, Jay Bilas, and David Henderson—were now senior starters. Tommy Amaker, the only nonsenior starter, had become everything Krzyzewski believed he could be when he had first seen him that night in the Jelleff League. There was also depth: Ferry and fellow freshman Quin Snyder and two talented sophomores, Kevin Strickland and Billy King, a lockdown defender.

The entire league was filled with the kind of experience that no one in today's basketball world would even dream about having. North Carolina's seniors were Brad Daugherty (who would be the number-one pick in the NBA draft) and Steve Hale; Georgia Tech's seniors were John Salley, who would be taken with the eleventh pick in the draft; and Mark Price, who would be picked twenty-fifth and go on to be an All-Star. Maryland had Len Bias, who would be the number-two pick in the NBA draft in June and would die tragically that night from a cocaine overdose. N.C. State didn't have the senior experience of some of the other teams, but it did have Chris Washburn, who, after one year of college play, would be the number-three pick in the NBA draft. Dawkins and Alarie (number ten and number eighteen) would also be first-round picks.

In short, this was a loaded league.

"I'm not sure there's ever been a league that was as experienced, as talented, or as deep as the ACC was in eighty-six," Krzyzewski said. "It wasn't just that there were a lot of guys who would go on and be very good NBA players or high draft picks, it was the league was *old*. There were very few teams starting freshmen or sophomores. Danny Ferry was a very good basketball player, even as a freshman, but he didn't start for us. The top teams were all that way."

When the dust cleared, the team sitting on top of the league was Duke. In 1985, the Blue Devils had hosted Carolina in the last game of the regular season with a chance to tie for the conference title. They hadn't handled the pressure that day and had gone from a tie for first to a tie for fourth. A year later, with the five seniors—Weldon Williams was the fifth—facing their last home game, the circumstances were similar. If Duke won, it would finish 12–2 and win the regular season conference title outright, something Duke hadn't done since 1966. If Carolina won, there would be a three-way tie at 11–3 among Georgia Tech, Duke, and the Tar Heels.

"We didn't want to lose our last home game, and we especially didn't want to lose it to Carolina," Mark Alarie said. "In a lot of ways, that game felt like a culmination of our four years, especially given where we had been as freshmen. We felt like we could have won the game in Chapel Hill in January and didn't. We *had* to win this game."

Jay Bilas, Alarie's close friend then, as now, agreed. "We did a lot of very good things that year," he said. "Winning the conference tournament, getting to the Final Four. I'm not sure there was a more memorable day than that last home game against Carolina. It was as if this was the way it was supposed to happen: all of us celebrating on the court after winning the conference title."

It's also a fond memory for Krzyzewski. "It was the first accomplishment we'd had that was a season-long thing. Beating Carolina in the ACC Tournament in eighty-four was important; winning the preseason NIT was a big deal; and getting back into the NCAAs was a big deal too. But we went twelve and two in a loaded league and we beat the team that had been on top forever to win that title." He smiled. "And Dean always said the regular season title was more important than the tournament. I know he wanted to share first place and to keep us from winning it by ourselves. I'd be lying if I said that didn't matter too."

Not that Krzyzewski wanted to bask in the victory for very long. In fact, the next afternoon as the team began preparation for the ACC Tournament, he threw the team out of practice en masse. They hadn't practiced badly or been flat, but Krzyzewski had decided beforehand, as he occasionally did, to throw them out regardless.

"Sometimes you do it just to make a point that this isn't a time to relax," he said.

The players knew that. They knew the "tantrum" was premeditated. They had seen it before.

"Remember, we were a very experienced team," Bilas said. "We knew the drill. But we also knew exactly *why* he did it. He was making a point. I think we got the point."

—

The following Sunday, they won the ACC Tournament, surviving a riveting game against Georgia Tech. After Tech's Craig Neal had missed a jump shot with nine seconds left and Duke leading 66–65, Johnny Dawkins coolly (of course) made two free throws to clinch the win. Tech's last basket—there was no three-point shot—made the final 68–67.

The tournament victory was, for Krzyzewski, cathartic. He understood what winning the regular season meant, but the tournament was hugely symbolic and important for any ACC coach. Lefty Driesell, who had lost the championship game five times before winning it in 1984, admitted that afternoon that he'd lost many hours of sleep over not having taken the trophy home— *without* putting it on the hood of his car—even though he had won the regular season title on two occasions.

That same day, when Mickie Krzyzewski had congratulated Joyce Driesell on her husband's victory, Joyce had said to her, "I just hope you don't have to wait as long as we did."

Driesell had won the tournament in his fifteenth season at Maryland. Smith's first tournament championship had come in his sixth year. Valvano had done it in his third season. Krzyzewski was in his sixth at Duke. At that point in time, Smith had won nine ACC Tournaments. More important to Krzyzewski, Valvano and Cremins—the other two "young guns"—had already won it once. He still trailed the other two: Valvano had a national title and Cremins had taken Georgia Tech to the Elite Eight in 1985 after winning the conference tournament. This, though, was a major step in the right direction.

Duke finished the regular season 32–2 and went to the East Regionals as the number-one seed. Georgia Tech was a number-two seed—in the Southeast Region. North Carolina was sent to the West as a number-three seed—along with Maryland as a number five—and North Carolina State went to the Midwest as a number-six seed.

"If we had ended up with four ACC teams in the Final Four that year I wouldn't have been shocked," Krzyzewski said. "I thought all five teams who made the tournament had a chance."

Among the ACC five, only Duke made it to Dallas, and it had to survive a first-round scare against sixteenth-seeded Mississippi Valley State just to get to the second round. Maryland lost in the second round to UNLV in what turned out to be the last basketball game Len Bias ever played. North Carolina was beaten in the round of sixteen by Louisville. Georgia Tech also went out in that round, stunned by eleventh-seeded LSU in Atlanta.

That left Duke and N.C. State still alive in the round of eight. Valvano had become the King of March by now. Going into the regional final against Kansas—in Kansas City—his NCAA Tournament record dating to 1983 was 12–1. This was the Wolfpack's third trip to the Elite Eight in four years. Valvano would tell anyone who would listen that he had a simple formula for success: "You schedule a bunch of directional schools early [home games against weaker teams]; play a couple of TV nonconference games and hope you steal one; go 7–7 in the ACC; and you're in the tournament. Then, once you're there, all bets are off."

The winter of 1986 had gone just as Valvano drew it up: the Wolfpack was 7–7 in the ACC, 18–12 overall, plenty good enough to make the tournament. Then, once postseason began, they played their best basketball, beating Iowa, Arkansas–Little Rock (which had shocked Notre Dame), and Iowa State (which had upset Michigan) to again reach the Elite Eight.

Valvano would admit in later years that he was on semi–cruise control as a coach at that stage of his life. Coaching had become easier for him because his fame and the popularity of the 1983 team—all seven of the core players were eminently likeable young men—had made recruiting a lot less challenging. Valvano still had all his charm and humor, but now he was also Jimmy V.

"It wasn't just that kids wanted to play for him," his brother Bob said. "It was that parents wanted to hang around with him, especially the dads. They wanted to say, 'Hey, I was having a beer with Jimmy V and he told me . . .'"

Valvano was in a position not unlike the one Smith had found himself in: his job was to select as much as it was to recruit, because so many good players wanted to come to State every year. There was one major difference: Smith was working harder than ever because he heard Krzyzewski's footsteps. Valvano was working very hard too—but it wasn't always at coaching. He was all over the map, doing TV, speaking, selling blue jeans (seriously) and artwork (seriously). When he focused on coaching he was as good as anyone. But his focus was often someplace else.

Larry Brown, who was coaching at Kansas, found that out firsthand the day before their teams played each other for a trip to the Final Four.

"I was sitting in the holding area with my players waiting to do our press conference on Saturday," he said. "Jimmy was going long—of course—and I could tell he was on a roll because all I could hear coming out of the room was nonstop laughter. Finally he finished and the NCAA guy came to get my guys [players] to get them on the podium.

"Jimmy came walking through on his way out and when we shook hands he said, 'Come over here a second, I need to talk to you, it's important.' I couldn't imagine what was going on. To tell you the truth, I was kind of worried something might be wrong.

"He says to me, 'Listen, I've got a deal with this guy who does these lithographs. They're really well done. He's going to do one of the eight coaches in the Elite Eight. Each of us will sign a couple hundred of them and then he's going to sell them for a lot of money. We should each make about two hundred and fifty thousand dollars. It'll take you an hour or so to do it—at most.'

"Finally I jumped in and stopped him. I said, 'Jimmy, we're playing tomorrow to go to the Final Four. Can't this wait?' He looked at me like I was nuts or something, like, 'Why should this wait?' He started explaining to me again how easy it would be, and finally I said, 'Jimmy, I gotta go, they're waiting for me inside.'"

Kansas won the game, 75–67, after State led deep into the second half. Valvano was disappointed because, like the year before, he believed his team was good enough to win the whole thing. Had the Wolfpack won, it would have played Duke in the national semifinals.

"We probably would have lost to Duke anyway," he said later. "They'd beaten us twice that year and both times I thought we should win. They were one of those teams that you looked at and said, 'They aren't that good,' and then they'd beat you. By then, Mike had become a great coach. That team was the epitome of who he was. They were tough, they guarded like crazy, and they didn't make mistakes. I was shocked when they didn't win it all."

Not as shocked, in the end, as Krzyzewski.

Valvano didn't have time to dwell on the loss to Kansas. He was on his way to Dallas—to do TV work for NBC and a couple of speeches. The money was still pouring in. He was still winning a lot of games. And he was still searching for The Next Thing.

21

The Mississippi Valley State game had proven to be the toughest test Duke faced in the East Regionals. Johnny Dawkins had taken over the game in the final eight minutes and Duke had hung on for an 85–78 win. The Blue Devils beat Old Dominion easily and advanced to the Sweet 16 in the Meadowlands. There, they eased past twelfth-seeded DePaul in the regional semis, setting up an Elite Eight matchup with Navy.

"Navy," Krzyzewski said, laughing when the subject came up. "I'm a believer in the basketball gods and I think they have a sense of humor, but this one didn't seem funny to me at the time. I mean, here I am one game from the Final Four for the first time in my coaching career and we're playing Navy? I remember lying awake in bed the night before the game and thinking, 'If I lose to Navy to go to the Final Four I will never, ever live it down. I'll never be invited to an Army alumni function for the rest of my life."

Krzyzewski's fear of losing to the Midshipmen was understandable. They were led by David Robinson, who had been recruited by Navy as a gawky, six-foot-seven-inch engineering wonk. When Navy coach Paul Evans visited his house, Robinson had no interest in talking about basketball or how he might fit in with the basketball team at the academy.

"All he wanted to do was show me the TV set he'd built," Evans said. "Then he explained how he had built it. I promise you I've never had a home visit quite like that one."

Robinson might have been interested in going to George Mason, which in Fairfax, Virginia, was right down the street from his home. The Patriots had a better basketball program than Navy at the time.

"We never recruited him," said Jack Kvancz, who was Mason's athletic director at the time. "We didn't think he'd be good enough to play for us."

Robinson eventually decided to go to Navy because his dad was a retired naval officer and he was interested in engineering. Evans was glad to have him because at six-seven he would be one of his tallest players and he thought he had potential because he could run the floor and was clearly smart enough to learn the game.

Robinson averaged 7.6 points per game coming off the bench as a freshman. That summer, he grew *six* inches—but lost none of his athletic skill. He became a star as a sophomore, leading Navy to a first-round upset of LSU in the NCAA Tournament. Evans had recruited some solid players by then, notably point guard Doug Wojcik and Vernon Butler, a rugged six-foot-seven-inch forward who could shoot the ball from outside and mix it up inside.

At the end of Robinson's sophomore season, many civilian schools tried to recruit him. At all the military academies, any student can leave before the start of his or her junior year and not pay any financial penalty for the two years of free education. When one returns it is called "Two for Seven," because he or she is committing not only to two more years at the academy but to five years in the service after graduation.

Robinson had become a clear-cut NBA prospect. Many schools figured he would want to leave Navy to avoid serving when he graduated. As a first-round NBA draft pick, Robinson would make millions. As an ensign in the navy, he would make $690 a month. Kentucky went so far as to tell Evans it would seriously consider him for its vacant coaching job *if* Robinson came along. Evans wasn't playing that game.

Robinson stayed and Navy was 30–4 going into the regional final. It had beaten Tulsa, Syracuse—on Syracuse's home floor in a blowout—and Cleveland State to reach the regional final. Prior to the game, Krzyzewski gave what his players later called the greatest pregame talk of his life.

"I want you guys to know something," he told them in their small locker room, which was just a few yards down the hall from the Navy locker room. "There is no team in the country I respect more than that team down the hall. What they've done to be in this game is unbelievable. It's almost impossible. I'd like to give every one of them a hug when the game's over and tell them how proud I am of what they've accomplished because I understand it in a way none of you guys can."

He paused for a moment. "But let me tell you one more thing: *They* are Navy. *I* am Army. I cannot tolerate the thought of *not* beating Navy. I live to beat Navy."

One more pause. The room was deadly quiet.

"So here's the deal. If you do not go out there and completely and utterly kick their blue-and-gold butts, don't even come back in here. Don't ever think of speaking to me again. You will be dead to me—dead. *I'm* Army. *They're* Navy. I don't lose to Navy. And that means that *you* don't lose to Navy."

Most of the players can repeat that speech word for word to this day. "I have never been so ready to play in my life," Tommy Amaker said. "I can still hear those words in my head: '*I'm* Army. *They're* Navy. I don't lose to Navy.' I'm honestly not sure if he meant it when he said he'd never speak to any of us again, but none of us wanted to take that chance."

Whether they were inspired—or frightened—by Krzyzewski's talk, the Blue Devils really never let the Mids into the game. They led 34–22 at halftime and pulled away steadily in the second half to win, 71–50. The game's signature moment came midway in the second half when Dawkins went down the lane and Wojcik decided to try to stop him. Dawkins simply jumped *over* Wojcik and dunked the ball.

"Stupidest thing I ever did on a basketball court," Wojcik said. "I had no chance."

It was at that point that the Duke students, sitting in the

upper deck thanks to the generosity of the NCAA, began chanting, "Abandon ship!"

The Mids went down with the ship—Robinson scored twenty-three of his team's fifty points and declared after the game, "We played like girls."

Krzyzewski, who *did* hug all the Navy players when the game was over, would have disagreed. "They gave it everything they had," he said. "We were just better."

And now, they were going to the Final Four.

—

Duke had been in the Final Four four times in the past—three times under Vic Bubas, once under Bill Foster. The Blue Devils would play Kansas in the second semifinal after Louisville played LSU, the surprise team in the group, in the first game.

Duke and Kansas had played in the preseason NIT championship game in early December, and Duke had won, 92–86. But a lot had happened since then, including sophomore Danny Manning emerging as the star everyone had expected him to become when he first arrived at Kansas. Manning had grown up in Greensboro and had been the subject of an intense recruiting battle between North Carolina and N.C. State.

But prior to his senior year, his recruiting path took a turn—west. Larry Brown had taken the Kansas job in the spring of 1983. While putting his staff together he decided to hire an old teammate from his playing days in the ABA, Ed Manning, who also just happened to be the father of the number-one rising high school senior in the country. Brown never pretended that Danny wasn't a factor in Ed's hiring, but he also resented people saying it was the *only* reason he hired him.

"Ed was a friend for a long time, someone I could trust," Brown said. "Did it help that he was Danny's dad? Sure. But a lot of college coaches hired kids' high school coaches or AAU coaches strictly as a quid pro quo. That wasn't the case with Ed and Danny."

Needless to say, people in North Carolina didn't see it that way when Danny Manning transferred to Lawrence High School for his senior year and announced soon after that he would enroll at Kansas. Brown became something of a pariah in the state where he had played college basketball, something that pained him but didn't change the fact that he would have done the exact same thing regardless of how people in North Carolina felt about him for doing it.

Manning was a shy, often reticent youngster who probably would have been a perfect player in Dean Smith's system because it didn't put the focus on one player and because he would have played for a coach who completely understood Manning's dislike of the spotlight. Brown ran the same system, but where Smith used sarcasm to motivate, Brown used anger.

"There were times," Manning would admit later, "when I hated him."

But, like most players, Manning also learned from him. The Kansas team that showed up in Dallas was now Manning's team, although it had other very good and experienced players in Ron Kellogg, Cedric Hunter, Calvin Thompson, and Greg Dreiling. All five Kansas starters started in all thirty-eight games—except for Kellogg, who had missed one game with a minor injury. Duke was similar: Dawkins, Mark Alarie, David Henderson, and Tommy Amaker started all thirty-nine games for Krzyzewski. Only the center position, where the starts had been split between Jay Bilas and Danny Ferry, had any volatility. The only player in either starting lineup who wasn't a junior or a senior was Manning. Duke was 36–2; Kansas 34–3.

It had been only eight years since Duke had played in a Final Four, but there were just two people on the Duke bench who had been part of Bill Foster's Final Four team in 1978 who were in Dallas in 1986: trainer Max Crowder and assistant coach Bob Bender.

Bender had been Duke's sixth man in 1978, playing substantial minutes at the point-guard spot.

He had graduated in 1980 shortly after Krzyzewski arrived at Duke and, after spending a couple of years working for Tom Butters as a fund-raiser, had joined Krzyzewski's staff when Bobby Dwyer left shortly after the Virginia debacle in Atlanta.

Bender had known Krzyzewski since his senior year of high school. In those days, anyone on a coaching staff could go out and recruit and there were no limits on the number of times a coach could see a player. Bender was a senior at Bloomington (Illinois) High School. Krzyzewski was a graduate assistant on Bob Knight's staff and Bender was one of the players he was assigned to recruit.

"I loved him, thought he was a great guy," Bender said. "But my parents *really* loved him. They thought he was exactly the kind of person they would want me to have as one of my college coaches. He was smart, direct, and honest. Of course I never got to play for him."

Bender chose Indiana, but by the time he got there, Krzyzewski had been hired as the head coach at Army. Bender was part of the undefeated national championship team as a freshman, but a year later, when it became apparent he wasn't going to play much as a sophomore, he transferred to Duke. There, under Bill Foster, he flourished.

Like everyone else at Duke, Bender wasn't shocked when Foster left in March of 1980 for South Carolina. And, like everyone else, he figured the Durham paper had it right when it said the new coach's last name would start with a W—Wenzel, Webb, or Weltlich. And so, when Tom Butters called the apartment Bender shared with Mike Gminski and said he'd like them to come and meet the new coach—even though they wouldn't be playing for him—Bender thought the new coach might be Bob Weltlich.

"I knew Bob because my year at Indiana was his last year on the staff before he took the Mississippi job," Bender said. "In fact, when I decided to transfer, that was where Coach Knight told me I should go. He was a big pecking-order guy. I knew Tom [Butters] respected Knight, and I figured if Knight was pushing him, he'd have a good chance to be the coach."

Knight had pushed Weltlich. But he wasn't the new coach.

"We were all waiting outside Tom's office," Bender said. "There was a mail slot in the door. I leaned down and looked through it and saw Mike standing there. I turned to everyone and said, 'Holy shit, that's Mike Krzyzewski. He's hired Mike Krzyzewski.'

"They all looked at me and said, 'Who?'"

Three years later, when Dwyer decided to leave to coach at the University of the South, Bender, who had been working as Butters's number-one fund-raiser, went to Butters and said, "I want to coach. My dad was a coach and I think this is what I want to do."

Krzyzewski interviewed Bender three separate times before hiring him. "I think he wanted to be sure this was what I really wanted to do," Bender said. "Not just something I wanted to try."

Bender knew he was going to work with a coach who many thought was on shaky ground. It didn't bother him, because he believed Krzyzewski was doing the right things.

"There were people who said to me, 'You better be ready to look for another job next year,'" Bender remembered. "I knew what the deal was, but I looked at the four freshmen who had started the year before and I *knew* we were going to be better."

The faith had paid off, and three years later, as Bender and Pete Gaudet sat down on the bench as the teams lined up for the opening tip, Bender felt Gaudet elbowing him softly.

"Look behind you and to your right," Gaudet said, indicating the area in the stands where college basketball's most prominent coaches were seated. "Dean Smith is there. So's Bob Knight. You know what they're doing right now? They're watching *us* in the Final Four."

Gaudet, whose only college coaching experience prior to coming to Duke had been at Army, was just a little bit in awe of where the program had come since he and Bender had joined the staff.

"I always told Mike that Bob and I turned it around for him," Gaudet said, laughing, many years later after he had retired from coaching. "Of course I conceded that the players he'd recruited might have had a little to do with it too."

For the next two hours those players were involved in one of the better Final Four games anyone in Reunion Arena had seen.

Kansas blew to an 11–2 lead, and Krzyzewski, remembering something Knight had told him—"Don't be afraid to call an early time-out if you need it"—did so. Duke calmed down, and the game became one of those wars of attrition where every possession feels as if it is the one that will decide the game.

Alarie might have played the greatest defensive game of his career. He held Manning to four points on 2-of-9 shooting, consistently denying him the chance to set up in the places he was most comfortable shooting from. "I can't remember ever being quite so exhausted and drained after a game," Alarie said. Remembering how hard he had worked to "hold" Len Bias to forty-one points earlier in the season, Alarie shook his head. "Manning was very good. Bias was, well, Bias."

Dawkins scored 24 points, but it was Ferry, chipping in 8 critical points off the bench, who came up with the offensive rebound and putback that decided the game in the final minute. Duke hung on to win, 71–67, meaning it would meet Louisville, which had won against LSU with relative ease, in the championship game.

The two teams also met—sort of—on Sunday, an afternoon that began to set a tone for Krzyzewski's program that would linger for many years.

—

College basketball's national championship game has been played on a Monday night since 1973. NBC took a chance on moving the game from Saturday afternoon to prime time, hoping to take advantage of the UCLA dynasty. The Bruins were on their way to winning a seventh straight national championship that year, and they didn't let the network down. Bill Walton produced one of the great performances in college basketball history, shooting 21 of 22 from the field (the miss was an attempted tip-in) on his way to 44 points as UCLA routed Memphis State.

Dean and Jim share a pregame laugh—no surprise. Eddie Fogler is sitting next to Dean, and Roy Williams is next to Jim. *Robert Crawford*

Moment of pure joy . . . Dean Smith celebrates the 1982 national title with (from left) a very young Michael Jordan, Sam Perkins, and James Worthy. *Heinz Kluetmeier*/Sports Illustrated/*Getty Images*

Valvano finally finds his designated hugger—Dereck Whittenburg—after his run to nowhere in 1983. *Greg P. Hatem*

Dean and Mike pose together before a game. Note the forced smiles.
Robert Crawford

The author, Lefty Driesell, and Valvano. Two of the great talkers in college basketball and look who is talking. *Courtesy of the author*

Krzyzewski's first national title team in 1991. In a twist, Jim Delaney— North Carolina graduate—had to present the trophy as NCAA basketball committee chairman. *Duke Athletics*

Krzyzewski with one of the five nets he cherishes most.
Duke Athletics

The author and Dean about twenty minutes before a game. Dean was never looser than during pregame warm-ups. *Courtesy of the author*

Dean, Mike, and Jim sign autographs together at a charity function . . .

The Herald-Sun/*Harold Moore*

Christian Laettner releases the shot that beat Kentucky in 1992.
Note the time on the clock overhead. *The Herald-Sun/Chuck Liddy*

Title number three. Back on top six years after the fall of '95 . . .
Duke Athletics

A rare, genuine Michael Jordan moment. This was during the one hundredth anniversary celebration of UNC basketball.

Robert Crawford

At least he listens on occasion: Mike Krzyzewski with the author.
David Bradley/Duke Blue Planet

Dean and Krzyzewski at one of Dean's last public appearances.
Charles Scott, North Carolina's first African American player, is sitting
next to Dean. *Duke Athletics*

Forty-three years later, college basketball people refer to "Monday Night" as if it were a holiday—which it is—the highest holy day of the year in the sport. Every coach aspires to coach at least once in his life on Monday Night.

Part of playing on Monday Night is dealing with Sunday afternoon. That's the time when the two teams that will play in the championship game meet with the media for ninety grueling minutes apiece. First, the coaches and the five starters sit up on a dais and take questions. Then, the coach stays on the dais while the players are taken to separate rooms for what are called "breakdown sessions." Often a star might have two hundred reporters in his breakdown session, while the fifth starter who averages six points and four rebounds a game might have three—or fewer—in the room with him.

Louisville went first on Sunday afternoon in 1986 because it had played in the first game. Coach Denny Crum had been through this once before, in 1980, when the Cardinals had beaten UCLA in the national championship game. His players hadn't seen anything quite like it. Most of their answers were brief, sometimes halting. As with many—if not most—college athletes, there were a lot of "you knows" in their answers. Nothing unusual.

Then came Duke. This was their first time on this stage too—for all, including their coach. But there were two things that made them different from Louisville: Four were seniors, one a junior (Louisville's best player, Pervis Ellison, was a freshman). And, having played in the ACC, they were constantly exposed to the media. In fact, the ACC had very specific rules about media access that made it a given that players from all teams would be exposed to the media from day one and game one of their careers.

"After what we'd gone through as freshmen and even the next couple of years, this was easy," David Henderson remembered. "We were having fun."

"Why wouldn't you have fun?" Jay Bilas said. "We were playing for the national championship. We'd won thirty-seven games after winning eleven when we were freshmen. It was a joy ride."

And so, for the first half of the media session, the five Duke players entertained the media. They were bright, confident, and articulate. And funny. When someone asked the players if they aspired to play in the NBA—two of them, Dawkins and Alarie, would be first-round draft picks and Henderson would also play in the league—Bilas was the first to respond.

"I'd give my left arm to play in the NBA," he said. "But last I looked there isn't a lot of call for one-armed players in that league."

It went on that way for forty-five minutes. Most of the media were charmed by the Duke players and found their candor and humor refreshing. But not everyone.

Standing in the back of the room, Mike Lupica of the New York *Daily News* decided he'd had enough. "What are they, the Cosby kids?" he said, referencing what was then the number-one-rated TV show in the country. "Are we all supposed to love them because they're from a rich kids' school?"

Lupica is a columnist who has always worn his biases on his sleeve. He and Larry Brown were close friends—they had run together the previous morning prior to the game. Lupica was convinced that Kansas had been jobbed by the officials at the end of the game, and he was venting.

Charlie Pierce, then of the *Boston Herald-American,* had no such biases. But he didn't like the Duke kids' act either. "White America's team," he said. "So they speak in complete sentences. I'm supposed to like them more because of that?"

Neither Pierce nor Lupica was shy about sharing his feelings with others in the room. Only a handful bought in that day, but it was the beginning of a trend in the media's reporting about Duke that's never really gone away. The "white America's team" label really rankled Krzyzewski, especially since Louisville had one white starter in the room that day and his team had two.

"I'm supposed to apologize because our kids sounded smart?" he said. "I'm supposed to feel bad because all five of those kids got degrees in four years and have gone on to be very successful? I'm not going to sit in judgment of anyone else's players because

I don't know them as people. But I'm not going to apologize for my players coming across as smart and appealing. If people are bothered by that then *they* have a problem."

True or not, fair or not, the label stuck. Duke has had a lot of very good white players in the last twenty-five years, among them Bilas, Alarie, Ferry, Bobby Hurley, Christian Laettner, Mike Dunleavy, J. J. Redick, and Kyle Singler. But it has also had plenty of African American stars, including Amaker, Dawkins, and Henderson from the '86 team and players like Billy King, Robert Brickey, Alaa Abdelnaby, Grant Hill, Thomas Hill, Elton Brand, Chris Carrawell, Shane Battier, Jason Williams, Carlos Boozer, Chris Duhon, Shelden Williams, Nolan Smith, and the one-and-dones Kyrie Irving (a number-one NBA draft pick who played all of eleven games as a Duke freshman), Jabari Parker, and Jahlil Okafor.

That's a lot of African American players for white America's team. But people latched on to the easy stereotype because Duke was winning a lot and they were looking for a reason *not* to like Krzyzewski and *not* to like Duke. Pierce and Lupica helped launched the myth that Sunday afternoon in Dallas.

—

Louisville won the national championship the next night, beating Duke 72–69. Ellison was the star, scoring 25 points and pulling down 11 rebounds. CBS's Jim Nantz wondered in the postgame if America had just witnessed the beginning of the "era of Never-Nervous Pervis." Ellison never played as well again in the next three years as he played that night.

Duke's biggest problem on that Monday Night was Kansas. The draining game with the Jayhawks had left the team tired, specifically Alarie and Henderson. They had spent most of forty minutes on Saturday chasing Manning and Ron Kellogg, and they both had tired legs. They struggled to shoot throughout the night, and, more than anything, that proved to be the difference.

"It was my fault," Krzyzewski said. "I had never been in that situation before, and I didn't do enough to keep them fresh. The next time we went through something like that, I was better prepared, but that night I didn't completely understand that I needed to get them more rest both before the game and during the game."

Dawkins, who finished with 24 points, and Amaker, who had 11 points, 7 assists, and 7 steals, almost saved the Blue Devils. In fact, Duke had a 68–65 lead with a little more than two minutes left when Louisville point guard Milt Wagner drove the baseline. Bilas came over to take a charge and appeared to arrive before Wagner—who had four fouls. Referee Pete Pavia didn't see it that way. He called Bilas for a block.

"I thought I was there, but I'm a bit of a biased observer," Bilas said with a wry smile many years later, the play still clear in his mind's eye. "If it goes the other way, Wagner's out of the game and we've got the ball with a three-point lead."

Instead, Wagner stayed in the game and made two free throws to cut the margin to one. The game came down to a possession in the final minute with Louisville leading 70–69. The Cardinals ran the shot clock down but couldn't get a good shot as it wound to zero. Finally, Jeff Hall launched an air ball that was so short that it went right to Ellison, who was boxed out by Bilas but in perfect position to grab the woefully short shot.

This was the first year of the forty-five-second clock, and the rule then was that the shot simply had to be launched before the shot-clock buzzer went off. Under today's rules, where the ball must hit the rim, Louisville would have been guilty of a violation. But in 1986, Ellison grabbed the ball and laid it in for the clinching basket—it was also the last season without a three-point shot—before Bilas or any of the other Blue Devils could move.

It was a crushing loss, not only because the national championship was at stake but because the Duke players believed they were better than Louisville. Still, as Valvano might have said, the L was an L, and nothing could change that. To this day, when the final buzzer sounds in the national title game, Bilas doesn't watch the winners celebrate—he watches the losers.

"I know exactly how they're feeling and what they're thinking at that moment," he said. "You move on in life, we all do, but that's not something you ever completely get over."

Bilas was an assistant coach when Duke won the national championship five years later. So was Amaker. In 2001, Dawkins was on the staff when Krzyzewski won his third national title. All enjoyed cutting down the nets and being a part of a national championship team. All say the same thing about those victories: "It was nice, but it couldn't compare to how it would have felt to win one as a player."

Krzyzewski understands that and, for all his subsequent successes, still broods about that night in Dallas. "I'll always feel as if I let those guys down," he said. "I learned some lessons that night that I was able to use later. But it couldn't bring that night back."

Because an L is always an L.

22

During one of the Final Four press conferences in Dallas, Mike Krzyzewski had talked about how much it meant to him to have made it to the final weekend of the college basketball season. "You never know if you'll get here again," he said. "We've got four great seniors on this team. But you never know. Maybe Tommy [Amaker] will average thirty-five a game next season and we'll get back."

Amaker didn't average 35 a game the following season, but Duke got a lot closer to the Final Four than anyone—including perhaps Krzyzewski—might have expected.

"In a lot of ways that season might have been the most important one in his career," Keith Drum said about the 1986–87 season. "Most people thought that Duke would be a one-shot wonder, that once those seniors were gone, they'd back up and that Carolina and State would continue as top programs. Winning twenty-four games and going to the Sweet Sixteen that next season was a big deal. It showed people that Duke wasn't going away."

In fact, when the great Al McGuire had come to town prior to the '86 Final Four to tape a piece for his Final Four special on NBC, he had urged Krzyzewski to enjoy the coming week because it might never happen again.

"He came to the house one night and said, 'What you've done this year is special,'" Krzyzewski remembered. "He told me to enjoy it because it was really hard to do it twice, especially at a place like Duke."

North Carolina was back on top of the ACC that next season, going 14–0 for the second time in four years, led by a backcourt of Kenny Smith and Jeff Lebo and a frontcourt of senior big men Dave Popson and Joe Wolf and freshmen big men J. R. Reid and Scott Williams. N.C. State had lost Chris Washburn to the NBA but still had Charles Shackleford and Vinny Del Negro. Even so, the Wolfpack had a tough regular season, going just 17–13 and finishing 6–8 and in sixth place in the ACC—one game shy of Valvano's stated goal of 7–7 in conference play.

Valvano had become State's athletic director in 1986 after Willis Casey retired. He took the job in part because he didn't want to take a chance on State hiring someone he didn't like. He also took it because the school's other coaches pleaded with him to do it—for similar reasons. "I might be the devil," Valvano joked, "but at least I'm a devil they know." The last reason he took the job was probably the most important—and the worst reason to do so: he was bored, still in search of The Next Thing.

His sense of humor hadn't changed even a little bit. In the summer of 1986, he got his first look at the Dean Dome. State hadn't played there the previous winter because it had played the last game in Carmichael. On a hot July morning, Valvano walked inside to scout the National Sports Festival, an annual event that featured top high school athletes. It was taking place in Chapel Hill that summer, with the basketball games being played in the Dean Dome.

Valvano walked in, looked around at all the seats and then at the rafters. There is no building in college basketball with more banners hanging in it than the Dean Dome. There are national championship banners, Final Four banners, ACC Tournament championship banners, ACC regular season championship banners, NCAA Tournament banners, NIT banners, and "honored"—not retired—numbers. It appears that about half the players who ever put on a Carolina uniform are "honored."

Valvano looked at all the banners and pointed at one that said "ACC Champions" in huge letters.

"What's that writing at the bottom?" he asked. "I can't read it."

The writing at the bottom said "Regular Season Tie."

"So let me get this straight," Valvano said. "They *tie* for a regular season title and they put up a banner?"

When this was confirmed, Valvano smiled. "Okay, now I've figured out what I'm going to do. I'm going to put up a banner for 1985 that says 'National Champions!' Then at the bottom, in tiny little letters, I'll put 'almost.' After that, I'll do the same thing for 1986. Damn, I just won my third national championship . . . almost."

For all the humor and the "almost" national championships, those around Valvano knew he wasn't especially happy with his life. In fact, when stories coming out of New York reported that the New York Knicks were interested in hiring him to coach, Keith Drum suggested Valvano take the job *and* keep coaching at N.C. State.

Pam Valvano was concerned when her husband took the AD's job. "It just felt like too much," she said. "The [basketball] team was still winning, but he was pushing himself too hard, trying to be in three places at once all the time. I knew him well enough to know that he was going to try to be the best AD he could be. That was going to take time—more time than he really had."

Valvano was still a master recruiter but, because he was involved in so many other things, he often left the hard part of recruiting—scouting—to his assistant coaches. He didn't get to know the players as well as he had in the past. "I'm the closer now," he said after State had gotten commitments from Chris Corchiani and Rodney Monroe, two superb guards, in the fall of 1986. "They [the assistants] set things up for me and I come in and close the deal."

The system worked fine except for the fact that some of the players Valvano was closing on were, to put it kindly, questionable students. Chris Washburn's presence at State had raised eyebrows, but it had been overlooked by many because he was too good a player to say no to if he wanted to come. But when other players with questionable academic records who weren't as good as Washburn began showing up, the ice began to get thinner.

"The worst thing I did," Valvano said in 1989 after the NCAA had come to town to investigate allegations against the program, "was not pay enough attention. We didn't break rules; we didn't cheat. But I didn't pay enough attention."

Even in 1987, after a mediocre regular season, Valvano and State were able to get their act together in the ACC Tournament. They were the number-six seed, and, much like in 1983, they went into the tournament knowing they had to win three games or face the purgatory of the NIT.

On opening night, State beat Duke in overtime. The next afternoon, they beat Wake Forest (which had pulled an upset the first night, beating number-two-seeded Clemson) again in overtime—double overtime. And, on Sunday, facing a North Carolina team that was 29–2 and had beaten the Wolfpack by 18 and by 17 in the regular season, Valvano slowed the pace, his team played a perfect game, and they pulled off the shocker of the season, 68–67. Carolina had scored 96 points in each of the regular season meetings when State tried to play up tempo. Valvano turned the tables by playing walk-it-up basketball all afternoon.

"If we played ten times, they'd win nine," Valvano said. "But we got our one at just the right time."

Unlike in 1983, though, when the Wolfpack was an excellent team that had hit a bump because of Dereck Whittenburg's injury, this was still a flawed team. Paired against ole Norman's very good Florida team in the first round of the NCAA Tournament, State went out quietly, 82–70. There were no missed free throws at the end, no miracles, no surviving and advancing. Just the end of a 20–14 season, salvaged only by three days in Landover, Maryland—which was the site of the ACC Tournament that year.

Duke's season ended a few days later, but—in spite of the disappointing overtime loss to State in Landover—the feeling was completely different. The Blue Devils had gone 9–5 in the ACC, finishing third behind Carolina and Clemson. They had lost both regular season meetings to the Tar Heels but had come closer than anyone to beating Carolina.

The game in Durham had been especially frustrating to Krzyzewski because it had turned on two crucial calls made by veteran referee Paul Housman—an official Krzyzewski liked and respected.

"If I missed either one," Housman said while Krzyzewski was barking at him about the second call, "I'll buy you a Coke."

"I don't want a f——ing Coke," Krzyzewski answered. "I want to win the f——ing game."

He didn't. Before he went in to talk to the media, Krzyzewski went to his office, which back then was only a few yards from the media room, to look at replays of the two calls. "Go to the officials' locker room," he told one of his managers, "and tell Housman I said he owes me *two* f——ing Cokes."

By then, the Duke-Carolina rivalry and the Smith-Krzyzewski rivalry had truly been joined. Smith was still the King, the icon, but the Prince of Durham had made inroads. The Ferry recruitment had been one step, and now the two coaches were both recruiting a talented big man from outside Buffalo named Christian Laettner. There was also a guard from New Jersey named Bobby Hurley, who was only a sophomore, but already drawing attention. Smith was still winning more than his share of recruiting battles: Krzyzewski would have loved to have been able to get Jeff Lebo, and J. R. Reid had been the most sought-after big man in the country. But Smith was no longer a lock to get everyone he wanted, even though, by his own admission, he was making the extra phone calls.

With the four seniors from the 1986 team gone, Danny Ferry had emerged as a star. Amaker was still the glue, but Ferry, Billy King, Quin Snyder, and Kevin Strickland were now stepping into major roles. Only Amaker was a senior. Duke made the NCAA field easily and opened with wins over Texas A&M and Xavier, putting it into the round of sixteen against Indiana—the number-one seed in the Midwest Region and a heavy favorite to make the Final Four for the first time since 1981.

Knight and Krzyzewski were still close at the time. In fact, Knight had spent the entire weekend in Dallas the previous spring wearing a "Go Duke" button on his sweater. Neither man wanted to face the other even though the matchup was made in heaven for the media. The entire week became a teacher-pupil lovefest.

There was far more pressure on Knight and Indiana to win than on Duke and Krzyzewski. By reaching the Sweet 16, Duke was playing with house money. Indiana had been ranked number one for a good portion of the season. Steve Alford and Daryl Thomas were the team's senior leaders, and Knight, who had started recruiting junior college players a year earlier, had added two good ones—Keith Smart and Dean Garrett—to what was already a talented, experienced team.

Duke stayed in the game all night, cutting the gap to two at 78–76 with three minutes left. But Alford hit a key shot and the Hoosiers made their free throws down the stretch to win, 88–82. They would go on to win the national championship—Knight's third.

Knight said all the right things about Krzyzewski and Duke after the game. He talked about how proud he was of Krzyzewski and the program he'd built at Duke, emphasizing that the game had been between "two teams that do things the right way, with good kids who graduate."

Krzyzewski was happy with all the bouquets being thrown in his direction but couldn't help but wonder how Knight might have handled a loss. "I'm not sure he would have been able to be quite as gracious," he said.

It would be several years before he learned just how prescient he had been.

———

As it turned out, the fall of 1987 was not an especially happy time for Dean Smith. On October 15, the first day of practice, Smith got a phone call from the police in Scott Williams's hometown in California. Both of Williams's parents had died that day. His father had shot and killed his mother in the family's garage and then killed himself.

It was Smith who had to deliver the news to Williams, who was about to start his sophomore season. Many years later, Smith still wasn't comfortable talking about that day. "My only concern was for Scott at that point," he said. "I think it's fair to say that, of all the things I've ever done as a coach, giving him that news was the most difficult. There was very little I could say to comfort him other than telling him we would all be there for him."

Not long after the Williams tragedy, Smith began to experience nosebleeds. He thought perhaps it was stress and went to see his doctor. The doctor told him stress might be involved, but the real issue was his smoking. All the nicotine he had inhaled had affected his nasal passages. He had to stop smoking—period.

Smith did, but it wasn't easy. He began popping Nicorette constantly and never stopped. In 2009, he sat behind his desk one afternoon during a lengthy interview, reaching into his pocket for Nicorette again and again. "There's not a day that goes by," he said, "that I don't want to smoke a cigarette. And it's been almost twenty-two years."

Carolina would go on that winter to win another ACC regular season title. North Carolina State finished second and Duke finished third. Oddly, N.C. State beat Duke twice in the regular season, North Carolina beat N.C. State twice, and Duke beat Carolina twice. It was the first time since 1980, Bill Foster's last season, that Duke had beaten Carolina twice in a season and the first time since 1966 that Duke had swept both regular season games with the Tar Heels.

The Blue Devils went on to beat both State and Carolina in the ACC Tournament, finally slowing the freshman guard duo of Corchiani and Monroe just enough to get a 73–71 win over the Wolfpack. By then, Duke's signature move on defense had become for all five players to slap the floor to show their unity on an important defensive possession. Valvano loved to make fun

best regular season in Valvano's ten years. The Wolfpack won the regular season title, going 10–4, meaning it was an NCAA Tournament lock going into the ACC Tournament. It was a classic case of a team being able to use an "us against the world" mentality to play well.

In February, Simon & Schuster, which had been scheduled to publish the book, announced that it had decided not to publish it because there were issues with Golenbock's sourcing—specifically Simonds. There were other issues since the book was based almost entirely on anonymous sources. When a number of State players from the 1987 season—which was the focus of the book—came out and said they had never spoken to Golenbock, the author said that he had *told* players whom he had interviewed that they should deny that they had spoken to him.

Book or no book, the issue wasn't going away. The NCAA was coming to town to investigate, and *The News & Observer* also had several reporters looking into the charges.

"Regardless of how much of the book jacket was true or untrue, it awoke the *N&O* to the fact that there was a possible story that needed to be checked into going on at N.C. State," said Liz Clarke, who was an education reporter at the *N&O* at the time. "In the end, a lot of what was claimed turned out not to be true. The violations that the NCAA found were relatively minor. If all of this had happened in today's world, it would have been looked at as almost nothing. But it was 1989 and Jim Valvano was a very important person in the state of North Carolina. The story couldn't be ignored."

There were, of course, those who saw the *N&O*'s pursuit of the story as an anti-State/anti-Valvano crusade. One of those who saw it that way—and still does to this day—was Mike Krzyzewski.

"Jimmy was a threat to Carolina," he said. "A lot of those people saw this as their chance to get rid of him and remove that threat. In the end, they succeeded."

The executive editor of the *N&O* in those days was Claude Sitton, a Pulitzer Prize–winning columnist who had graduated from Emory University. He was an old-school newspaper man who could not have cared less about whether the story involved North Carolina State, North Carolina, Duke, or anyone else that the *N&O* covered on a regular basis.

Many who worked in Sitton's newsroom were graduates of North Carolina's School of Journalism. Most of those who worked on the N.C. State story weren't sportswriters. After the story broke, Sitton decided he needed reporters who covered education and politics involved because most on the sports staff knew Valvano too well and had been charmed by him through the years.

There was no doubting that Sitton was right about that. *Everyone* who covered Valvano had been charmed by him.

Twenty-five years later, in the academic scandal surrounding UNC's Department of African, African American, and Diaspora Studies, the *N&O* broke many of the key stories—stories that embarrassed the school, the football program, and the basketball program. It also brought the NCAA to Chapel Hill. The writer responsible for most of the important stories was Dan Kane, a graduate of St. John Fisher College in Pittsford, New York, who also worked on the news side as an investigative reporter.

As Mike Cragg, who has worked at Duke for twenty-seven years and is now Mike Krzyzewski's chief fund-raiser, put it, "When the news side people get involved, that's when you've got a problem."

In 1989, regardless of whether they had any biases or not, the news side people from the *N&O* were involved. If truth be told, there are very few major college football or basketball programs that don't have blemishes of some kind. Once a major newspaper with good reporters starts looking under all the rocks and inside the crevices, they are almost bound to find something.

As Clarke points out, what the *N&O* learned and what the NCAA also learned about N.C. State would barely be worth reporting these days. Some State players had sold sneakers and other gear that they'd been given by the school and had scalped some of their tickets to games. There was little doubt that admissions standards had been compromised—although *that* charge could be made to one degree or another against any big-time school.

The most damning stories didn't involve any rule breaking. The *N&O* found a clear pattern of what can best be described as academic manipulation. Back then, there were no NCAA rules on academic progress like the ones that exist now. As long as an athlete didn't flunk out of school, he could remain eligible under NCAA rules. A number of State basketball players—many— would sign up for a full load of classes, then drop any class it appeared they were going to flunk before the end of the semester. Often, they would sign up for the exact same class the next semester and, given the advantage of having taken it once, pass it. Or, if need be, drop it again. In short, many basketball players were staying eligible but weren't making much progress at all in the direction of the degree.

"They were gaming the system," said Clarke, who wrote or cowrote many of the stories. "They didn't break any rules, they just used the rules to their advantage to keep players on the court helping them win games for as long as possible. The simple fact is this: Jim Valvano's job description, in reality, was simple: win games. Never once did he fail to live up to his job description."

In the charged atmosphere of 1989, the story became in many ways a UNC vs. N.C. State story. The state legislature, populated with many UNC grads, became involved. Sweeping changes to the entire academic system at State were recommended. Bruce Poulton, the chancellor, who was close to Valvano, was forced to resign in the summer of 1989. Even Valvano, who often joked about the paranoia State people had about North Carolina, was swept up in it.

"It isn't a coincidence that most of the people who wield power in this state, who are now insisting on a complete revamping of our academic standards, are UNC grads," he said one night. "If I thought it was a coincidence at this point, I think I'd be naïve."

Golenbock's book was finally published by Carroll & Graf in

September 1989 with one of the longest and most convoluted titles in history: *Personal Fouls: The Broken Promises and Shattered Dreams of Big Money Basketball at Jim Valvano's North Carolina State*.

The book cover was one of the few places in the book that contained no misspellings or factual inaccuracies. The book was riddled with them. At one point, Golenbock had Thanksgiving falling on a Friday. At another, he wrote "Kryzewski—tough name to spell," misspelling it in that sentence. For these reasons, the book was widely panned by critics and its accuracy was questioned by many. But it had already done crippling damage to Valvano if only by "awakening," as Clarke put it, the *N&O*'s news staff.

The title of the book Valvano cowrote in 1991 (ironically enough with a North Carolina graduate) summed up the entire affair quite well: *They Gave Me a Lifetime Contract, and Then They Declared Me Dead*.

—

Jim Valvano's last appearance in an NCAA Tournament took place on a rainy night in East Rutherford, New Jersey, on March 24, 1989.

N.C. State had advanced to the round of sixteen to play top-seeded Georgetown with wins over South Carolina and Iowa. In the opening game that night, Duke had beaten Minnesota to advance to the Elite Eight for the third time in four seasons. Duke's presence in the East Regional and in the Meadowlands had enraged Dean Smith and most living, breathing North Carolina fans.

Duke and North Carolina had finished tied for second in the ACC during the regular season—a game behind N.C. State. They had split their regular season meetings, each winning on the other's home court. Duke's three wins against UNC the previous season, including in the ACC title game, and the fact that Christian Laettner, the gifted center from Buffalo, had chosen Duke over North Carolina had ratcheted the rivalry up even more than in the past.

Carolina hadn't won an ACC Tournament since 1982—the year it had won the national championship—and it hadn't been back to the Final Four since then either. In that span, Duke had won two ACC Tournaments and been to two Final Fours. The only hole in Krzyzewski's résumé at that stage was the lack of a national championship.

"We weren't hearing footsteps at that point," Roy Williams said. "They were there, right next to us. It wasn't as if we'd gone backwards; they'd just come charging forward. I think it made Coach Smith even more intense about beating them when we played—if that was possible."

There had been more tension between the two schools and the two coaches during that season. In January, North Carolina came to Cameron. Duke had started the season 13–0 and was ranked number one in the country. North Carolina was a mere 14–3 and ranked number thirteen. Jeff Lebo, now a senior, had been injured three nights earlier in a loss at Virginia.

In short, the perfect Dean Smith setup. He could tell his players quite honestly that they were underdogs—playing on the road, with their point guard injured, against an undefeated, top-ranked team. Of course Smith always liked to say that a team could produce one excellent performance after the loss of an injured player. He probably neglected to mention that in the buildup to the game.

Carolina blew Duke out of the building, 91–71.

Unfortunately, that wasn't Smith's focus after the game. He had spotted a sign somewhere in the student section that said "J.R. Can't Reid."

The sign wasn't funny, it wasn't accurate, and it was mean. There was also a racist tinge to it, and Smith, rightly, was furious. The fact that he couldn't stand the Duke students to begin with may have added to his anger.

The problem was, he couldn't let it go. Krzyzewski also

denounced the sign and said he didn't believe it was in any way a reflection of the way those in the Duke student body felt. "Someone was trying to be funny and failed," he said. "It was just in poor taste."

That didn't assuage Smith. When the teams were getting ready to play in Chapel Hill, he brought it up again. This time he referenced the fact that his two African American big men, Reid and Scott Williams, had a higher combined SAT score than Duke's two white big men, Danny Ferry and Christian Laettner.

Smith's anger was genuine. He had always been sensitive to racial stereotypes—especially truly dumb ones. But he had gone too far in bringing up anyone's SAT scores, especially those of two players at another school. "I know their scores because I recruited them," Smith said.

Which was exactly the point. Smith had been given Ferry's and Laettner's transcripts in confidence and had broken at least part of that confidence. What's more, both would have been accepted at North Carolina and, like Reid and Williams, would have done just fine academically. Finally, if *anyone* understood how incomplete SAT scores were in judging someone's academic potential, it was Smith.

Duke won the game in Chapel Hill, and Smith and Krzyzewski barely looked at each other during the postgame handshake. Krzyzewski believed Smith was trying to embarrass Duke by keeping the story alive. Smith wouldn't back down even a little bit.

"I call it competitive anger," said John Thompson, the former Georgetown coach who was very close to Smith and knows and likes Krzyzewski. "You get two guys who are that good at something and are always competing, there are going to be moments like that. Neither one was ever going to back down from a fight."

That was the setting as the eight ACC teams headed to Atlanta for the conference tournament. Sitting on his bench not long before Carolina played its first game on Friday afternoon, Smith still insisted he was only trying to bust racial stereotypes.

Someone asked Smith if he had successfully recruited Ferry

and Laettner, and Reid and Williams had somehow landed at Duke, if he would have brought up the SAT scores.

"If our students held up a sign like that, absolutely," he said. "But *our* students would never do something like that. I wouldn't allow it."

The implication was clear: Krzyzewski, somehow, should have prevented the sign from ever appearing. The competitive anger was as high as it had ever been.

—

In the opening game of the tournament, N.C. State, the top seed, was stunned by eighth-seeded Maryland, losing 71–49 in about as shocking an upset as anyone had ever seen in the thirty-six-year history of the tournament. Duke and Carolina ended up facing each other in the final. Walking into the building that day, Krzyzewski was so wound up that he walked right past his wife without even noticing that she was standing there.

"I think Mike has his game face on," Mickie Krzyzewski said dryly.

Early in the game, Krzyzewski and Smith had a brief shouting match with each other after Smith encouraged the officials to give Krzyzewski a technical foul while he was arguing a call. Krzyzewski responded by encouraging Smith to shut up, and the two men took a few steps toward each other, pointing and shouting. A few moments later, when Smith was convinced the officials had given Duke a couple of calls to shut Krzyzewski up, he turned and kicked the scorer's table in frustration.

No one had ever seen *that*. The message was clear: Smith was tired of all the fawning over Duke in the national media and he absolutely did *not* want to lose another ACC championship game to Krzyzewski.

He didn't. Carolina made just enough plays in the endgame to hang on and win. On the game's last play, with his team down 77–74, Ferry launched a shot from just beyond half-court that went all the way around the rim and finally spun out.

"If that had gone in," Smith said later, "I'm not sure the old coach would have been around for overtime."

It was as close as Smith had ever come to admitting that he *really* wanted to win a game.

With the victory, Smith was convinced his team would be sent to the East Regionals, meaning it would play its first two games in Greensboro and then go to the New Jersey Meadowlands. When the brackets were unveiled that evening, *Duke* was in the East as the number-two seed and Carolina was in the Southeast as the number-two seed.

Smith was furious. As luck would have it, Tom Butters, the Duke athletic director, had gone on the basketball committee that year as the ACC's representative. Smith was 100 percent—at least—convinced that Butters had manipulated the selections to send Duke to Greensboro and back to the Meadowlands—a place from which it had already advanced to the Final Four twice in three years.

Naturally, the committee's version was different. It had placed Carolina in the Southeast Region as a reward for its victory over Duke. The number-one seed in the East Region was Georgetown. Even though the committee didn't formally rank the four number-one seeds back then as it does now, Georgetown was overwhelmingly considered the number-one seed in the tournament. Oklahoma was the number-one seed in the Southeast, and the consensus in the committee room was that it would be tougher for a number-two seed to beat Georgetown to get to the Final Four than to beat Oklahoma to get to the Final Four.

Smith, needless to say, wasn't buying it. He was convinced that Butters had gotten his school a spot in Greensboro and then, if it advanced, in East Rutherford—both in buildings that were homes away from home for Duke.

Duke almost didn't make it to East Rutherford, having to beat a very good West Virginia team in the second round. Carolina beat Southern University and UCLA in Atlanta, meaning it would play Michigan, the number-three seed in the Southeast, in

Lexington, Kentucky, in the round of sixteen. Duke did *not* have to play Stanford, the number-three seed in the East. The Cardinal was upset in the first round by Siena, which then lost to Minnesota, the number-eleven seed. Smith spent most of the next week explaining how he would have *much* preferred playing Minnesota than Michigan.

He was right. Duke cruised by Minnesota. Michigan, which would go on to win the national championship, beat Carolina. Glen Rice, Michigan's senior guard, was on a shooting tear. Rice would become famous in a nonbasketball way many years later when reports would surface that he'd had a fling with a young sportswriter named Sarah Palin when Michigan played in the Great Alaska Shootout.

After the loss to Michigan, Smith was his usual self, saying he wasn't disappointed for himself but for the team's seniors, Jeff Lebo and Steve Bucknall. He also knew—without saying it—that J. R. Reid, then a junior, had played his last game at Carolina, since he would be turning pro.

Once his press conference was over, Smith stood in a Rupp Arena hallway and talked to some of his local writers about the season. When he was finished, several of them thanked him for his help and cooperation throughout the winter. This is a ritual beat writers and coaches go through after a team has played its final game.

As Smith shook hands with Ron Green, Jr., of *The Charlotte Observer* (a non-Carolina graduate) he looked at Green and said, "I wish we could have played Minnesota."

To Smith, that was the season's legacy.

Several hours later, with Duke having already beaten Minnesota, N.C. State and Georgetown battled late into the night for the right to play the Blue Devils on Sunday. Valvano's team had been rejuvenated in the tournament, and he was completely convinced they could beat Georgetown and *would* beat Duke, given the chance to play Krzyzewski's team for a third time.

With a little under two minutes to play, Georgetown led

64–61. The Wolfpack's Chris Corchiani caught the ball on the left side of the lane and drove to the basket, appearing to slide between two Georgetown defenders—one of them star center Alonzo Mourning, who had four fouls. The ball went in the hoop and, on TV, Billy Packer said, "There it is," referring to Mourning's fifth foul. It appeared that Corchiani would go to the line with a chance to tie the game—and Mourning on the bench.

It didn't turn out that way. Rick Hartzell, an ACC official who had advanced to the Sweet 16 for the first time, looked at Corchiani, looked at Mourning, and then—remarkably—signaled that Corchiani had traveled.

"No way was that a travel," Packer said as CBS showed a handful of replays.

The only real question was whether there was a foul. The basket clearly should have been good. Ten rows up from the court, Fred Barakat, who was the ACC's supervisor of officials at the time, buried his head in his hands when he saw the call. Hartzell would go on to become one of the better officials in the country. But that night—and that call—has haunted him.

"I've never looked at a replay, too painful," he said. "Fred let me know afterwards in no uncertain terms that I'd missed it. What was worse was Lou Bonder, who was the officiating supervisor at the Meadowlands, telling me in the hallway that, if not for that call, Tommy [Lopes], [Jim] Bain, and I were going to the Final Four. We'd had a very good game up until then. Those five seconds are pretty painful to think about for me, even now."

The next season, the first time he worked an N.C. State game, Hartzell sought out Valvano and Corchiani before the game and apologized for the mistake.

"They both couldn't have been classier about it," Hartzell said. "I thought the right thing to do was to tell them how sorry I was and they both accepted the apology. That made it a little bit easier to take."

Three years later, only a few months before Valvano died,

Hartzell ran into him in an airport. He went over to say hello and ask how Valvano was doing.

"It was just the two of us," Hartzell said. "I couldn't help but think about the call in the Meadowlands. I started to say, 'I hope you know that I'm still sorry—' I never finished the sentence. Jim put up his hand and said, 'Stop. I don't want you to ever think about that again. I mean that.' Then he gave me a hug. That's a moment I'll never forget."

There was, of course, no guarantee that State would have won the game, even if Hartzell had called Mourning for his fifth foul and counted the basket. Best-case scenario, the game would have been tied with 1:46 left in regulation. But the traveling call, for all intents and purposes, ended the game. State had to foul. Unlike in 1983, their opponent made the free throws it had to make. The Wolfpack didn't score again. The final was 69–61.

An hour after the game had ended, well after midnight, Valvano walked through the bowels of the arena with his head down, unable to hide the pain of this particular L.

"I thought we were going to win, I really did," he said. "I can't tell you for sure we'd have beaten Duke on Sunday, but we'd have had a hell of a shot at it. We know how to play them." He paused and looked at the rain beating down on the team bus, which sat waiting for him on the ramp leading to the parking lot.

"Everything that could go right when we *had* to have it go right happened for us in eighty-three," he said one more time. "Since then, when we've been close . . ." He stopped for a moment and smiled. "You know, *almost* . . . We haven't caught a break."

He sighed and pulled his coat tighter. "Maybe I used 'em all up that year. I hope not but you never know." He forced one more smile and then—as he did often—quoted from *The Godfather*.

"Michael," he said to an invisible Michael Corleone, "this is the business we've chosen."

24

Two days later, with Jim Valvano watching from his living room and Dean Smith not watching at all ("It was a nice day," he said later. "I went out and played golf."), Duke beat Georgetown, 85–77, to reach the Final Four for the third time in four years.

The star of the game was Christian Laettner, who scored 24 points and completely outplayed fellow freshman big man Alonzo Mourning, who was held to 11 points. As it turned out, that game was Laettner's coming-out party as a great player. A month earlier, Duke and Arizona had played in the same building—a made-for-TV game that was scheduled in part because both had become national powers in the mid-eighties, but also to showcase the country's two leading candidates for player of the year: Arizona's Sean Elliott and Duke's Danny Ferry.

Ferry won the battle, Elliott and Arizona won the war. With Arizona leading 77–75 and eight seconds remaining, Laettner took the ball on the right wing, drove to the basket with one second left, and, just before he released a shot, was fouled. He went to the foul line, needing to make both ends of the one-and-one to send the game to overtime.

He missed the front end. As soon as the buzzer sounded, Krzyzewski raced onto the court and grabbed Laettner by the jersey. "Listen to me," he shouted up at him. "I want you to remember one thing: You didn't lose the game. You gave us a chance to win the game. Hold your head up."

Al McGuire was doing the game on NBC. From the TV announcer location, only a few feet from where Krzyzewski and Laettner were standing, he heard exactly what Krzyzewski said to his freshman center. Later that night, McGuire made one of his classic Al statements while having dinner with Dick Enberg, his close friend and TV partner. "That was one of the most brilliant coaching moves I've ever seen," McGuire said. "I'll bet you that kid never misses another big shot."

Laettner missed almost no shots in the Georgetown game, going 9 of 10 from the field and 6 of 7 from the foul line. The victory put Duke into the Final Four for the third time in four years, meaning that Krzyzewski was now clearly one of the game's elite coaches.

A week later, in Seattle, Duke lost in the national semifinals for the second straight season. The Blue Devils jumped to an early 26–8 lead over Seton Hall but began to come apart when Robert Brickey, who had become a key inside player, went down with a leg injury and couldn't come back. Seton Hall ended up blowing the game open, winning 95–78. The loss was a big disappointment for Duke and a major relief in Chapel Hill.

"As long as Krzyzewski doesn't win a national title, he's still not on par with Coach Smith," wrote one local columnist. "With any luck, that day will never come."

For Krzyzewski, much like Smith, the most disappointing aspect of the loss was that it was the last game for his seniors: Ferry and point guard Quin Snyder, whose last loss took place in his hometown. Still, a team that had looked extremely vulnerable at times during the season had made it to the Final Four. Snyder was graduating, but Krzyzewski had successfully recruited Bobby Hurley, a hard-nosed coach's son from New Jersey, to be his next point guard. Two other talented guards—Billy McCaffrey and Thomas Hill—had also committed.

Duke would be good again. So would North Carolina. It had become a given that both teams would be stocked with very good players. The biggest off-season question in the Triangle, though, had little to do with talent or recruiting. It had to do with Jim Valvano.

—

Even though it could be argued that Valvano had done his best coaching job in 1989—the miracle of 1983 aside—there was little doubt that the wolves were baying at the door of N.C. State's lead wolf.

Personal Fouls had finally been published in September. *The News & Observer* was still looking into all the academic question marks. State legislators and faculty members were calling for major reforms. And the bad guy in all of it was the same guy who had been both a local and a national hero less than seven years earlier.

"The whole thing wore him out," Pam Valvano Strasser said many years later. "He felt let down by the school and by people he had thought were his friends. He stopped being Jim. When he was funny you could almost see him forcing it, trying to keep other people from being depressed about what was going on."

She stopped for a moment, hands folded calmly in her lap. But her voice lowered as she continued. "There are doctors who believe that stress, great stress, can lead to cancer. There's no way to prove what happened that last year at State had anything to do with Jim's cancer. But you can't say it isn't at least possible."

One of the people Valvano talked to quite a bit during that season was Krzyzewski. The rivalry between the two had always been intense but never contentious the way it was with Krzyzewski and Smith. The two men's public personas were very different: Valvano the class clown, Krzyzewski the serious bookworm—ironic since Valvano was a voracious reader and Krzyzewski rarely finished a book. In private, Valvano sometimes mocked Krzyzewski's superserious approach.

"I guess they didn't play *Duke* basketball," he would say after his team had beaten Duke, a reference to Krzyzewski frequently telling the media that his team needed to play "*Duke* basketball," to be successful.

Krzyzewski simply said, "That's not who I want to be," when Valvano's name would come up. Mickie, on occasion, referred to "Valvano world," because clearly it was an entirely different place than where she and Mike lived.

But the two respected each other as coaches and liked each other. On occasion, the Krzyzewskis and Valvanos would have dinner at the ACC meetings and there was always a lot of laughter. "Jimmy did a killer Dean," Krzyzewski said.

"I think, even though there was always a rivalry between Mike and Jim, they were bonded by trying to figure out a way to beat Dean," Bobby Cremins said. "All of us felt it but Mike and Jim were right there, surrounded by it every day."

Krzyzewski knew what it was like to get pounded by the sports media in North Carolina. Many—if not most—of the state's columnists had made fun of his hiring and then reveled in his early failures. Almost all of them had sided with Smith during the "double-standard" debate. There was an odd double standard of a different kind. The small handful of Duke graduates in the sports media were always—*always*—labeled as pro-Duke by most in the Carolina media whenever a Krzyzewski-Smith controversy broke out. No one ever put the same label on the Carolina graduates, at least in part because there were so many of them and there wasn't the time or space to do so.

"I think I can say with a lot of confidence that there's no coach who has had success who's done it under the circumstances I did," Krzyzewski said. "Usually—always—if you are a winner you are *the* program in your area and the media is on your side. We've always been the minority here—and always will be. Private schools are almost always the minority because they have fewer alums, but it's especially true here because our number-one competitor is a state school that's had huge success and is ten miles away from us.

"But what Jim went through was different because it wasn't just sportswriters writing columns saying he was a bad coach or even a bad guy—the kind of thing I went through early. He had people writing that he'd lost control of his program and that it had run amok."

What hurt Valvano the most during this period was that he hadn't run a perfect program, especially after 1983. He had stopped paying attention at times, and as a result a number of players who really couldn't do the work academically had been taken into the program. That led to, as Liz Clarke called it, the "gaming of the system" academically to keep many of those players eligible. Once the NCAA came to town and once the state began investigating, a happy ending was almost impossible.

In August, eight months after the initial book-jacket story, Valvano was forced to resign as athletic director. The publication of Golenbock's book in September brought another round of bad publicity. Then, on December 12, the NCAA announced that it was putting N.C. State on probation for two years—including one season in which it would not be allowed to participate in post-season play. State had already announced self-imposed recruiting sanctions, and the NCAA used that as an excuse not to ban the Wolfpack from TV. The real reason for the non-ban was that the networks and the ACC didn't want to lose State—or Valvano—from TV for the rest of the season.

The "major" violations cited by the NCAA were all connected to players selling sneakers—valued then at seventy-five dollars a pair—and their complimentary tickets to games.

Things got worse in February, when allegations surfaced that Charles Shackleford, who had turned pro after the 1988 season, had been involved in point shaving. Although that was never proven, it did come out later that an agent and a booster had paid him about sixty thousand dollars while he was still in school.

By then, Valvano knew he was done. Between the sanctions, the recruiting restrictions, and all the allegations swirling, it was going to be nearly impossible to rebuild the program. State still had some very good players, among them Chris Corchiani, Rodney Monroe, Tom Gugliotta, and Vinny Del Negro, but the weight of all the various investigations was finally kicking in.

The players knew their coach was in trouble. As far back as August, on the day Valvano stepped down as athletic director, Raymond C. Long, the chairman of the N.C. State Faculty Senate, had said he believed Valvano's resignation as athletic director

Coach Jim Calhoun. They had won the Big East Tournament and arrived at the Meadowlands with a record of 30–5, the clear favorites to come out of the East and go to Denver for the Final Four.

Except that they almost lost to Clemson. After leading by as many as 19 points, the Huskies missed a number of key free throws down the stretch and appeared dead when Clemson took a 70–69 lead on a three-point shot by David Young with twelve seconds to go. But UConn got one more chance after a missed Clemson free throw with one second on the clock. Scott Burrell—who was also a baseball pitcher—threw a perfect length-of-the-court pass to Tate George in the right-hand corner. With the Clemson defenders backed off so as not to foul, George managed to catch the ball, get into a shooting motion, and swish the shot. In today's world, the officials would have gone to replay to see if he had released the ball in time, and it might not have counted. In 1990, the shot counted, and the UConn players piled on top of George in celebration.

Two days later, George was again involved in one of the game's critical plays. Duke and Connecticut had swayed back and forth for nearly forty-five minutes—forty minutes of regulation and almost five minutes of overtime. Abdelnaby had played the game of his life, with 27 points and 14 rebounds, but had missed a short jumper that could have won the game in regulation. Hurley hadn't made a shot from the field—0 of 9—but had done a superb job running the offense against Connecticut's stifling pressure defense. He had 8 assists and only 2 turnovers.

Connecticut led 78–77 and had the ball with the shot clock and the game clock running down. With two seconds on the shot clock, Chris Smith missed a jumper and Laettner rebounded. He quickly pitched the ball to Hurley, who began pushing it upcourt with the clock winding toward five seconds. Seeing Phil Henderson on the left wing, Hurley tried to whip a pass in his direction. Henderson already had 21 points, and a last-second shot taken by him, or even a drive to the basket with UConn scrambling to get back, seemed like a good idea.

But Hurley hadn't seen George sneaking up on Henderson like a cornerback jumping a passing route. George stepped in front of Hurley and had his hands on the ball in full flight. Had he caught the ball cleanly, he would have been able to dribble out the clock before anyone from Duke got close to him. But he bobbled the ball. There's a photo of Krzyzewski, standing just a few feet away in front of the Duke bench, giving a traveling signal—knowing, no doubt, that if George gained possession, an unlikely traveling call was Duke's only chance.

The ball bounced off of George's hands and shoulder and went out-of-bounds—rolling into the Duke bench. There were 2.6 seconds left. Krzyzewski called time to set up a final play.

The play he called made sense. Laettner would inbound. Abdelnaby would set a screen on the baseline, and Henderson would try to go around it and come open in the near corner. If the pass reached him, he would have time to shoot while Abdelnaby tried to get to the basket for a possible rebound or tip-in.

But as the teams came back onto the court, Krzyzewski noticed that Laettner was unguarded. Calhoun wanted an extra defender inside the key to cut off the kind of screen that Krzyzewski was hoping would spring Henderson. Krzyzewski made a snap decision. "Run special!" he yelled at Laettner and at Brian Davis, standing a few feet away near midcourt.

Special was a simple short-clock play. Laettner would inbound to Davis and, unguarded, cut in the direction of the key. Davis would pass it right back to him, and if all went well, Laettner would have about a second to release a shot before anyone from UConn could get close to him.

Krzyzewski didn't even have time to let the other three players on the court—Abdelnaby, Hurley, and Brickey—know that he'd changed the play. Which was probably a good thing since all three carried out what had been called convincingly enough that the Huskies believed the ball was going to Henderson.

Laettner flipped the ball to Davis, left open near midcourt since he was a nonshooter. The ball came right back to Laettner doesn't know the secret. Only God and Mike Krzyzewski know the damn secret and *it's killing me!*"

The Virginia game was one of those rare days when Krzyzewski couldn't find the secret. But he damn well wasn't going to let his players think they could get away with allowing it to happen again.

Hill's injury was the price paid—mostly by Hill—for the punishment practice. But everyone got the message the coach was trying to deliver. Four nights later, a ranked Georgia Tech team, still led by Kenny Anderson, came to Cameron. Duke won 98–57, a game that caused Bobby Cremins to wonder if this might be Krzyzewski's best team.

"They were still young," Cremins said. "That eighty-six team were all seniors [except for Amaker, who was a junior]. This team had no seniors, but boy were they talented."

Actually, there were two seniors on the team. One, Greg Koubek, had been put into the starting lineup after the Virginia game even though Brian Davis was likely to play more minutes most nights. The other, Clay Buckley, came off the bench to play serious minutes inside only if someone got in foul trouble. The heart of the team consisted of juniors Laettner and Davis; sophomores Hurley, McCaffrey, and Thomas Hill; and freshman Grant Hill—broken nose and all.

The Georgia Tech game began a skein of twelve wins in thirteen games, including a 74–60 win in Cameron against North Carolina. The Tar Heels had come to town with a 13–1 record, riding an 11-game winning streak. Duke blew open a close game down the stretch. Four days later, they lost at N.C. State, which still had Chris Corchiani, Rodney Monroe, Vinny Del Negro, and Tom Gugliotta. Like Jeff Jones, Les Robinson won his first encounter with Krzyzewski. Although Krzyzewski didn't go to a Denny's and vow never to forget that night, he did win his next twelve encounters with Robinson.

As it turned out, Duke and Carolina both arrived in Chapel Hill on March 3 for the regular season finale with conference records of 10–3. There was good reason to believe that the Tar Heels, playing at home, would win the game and the championship. Valvano was undoubtedly in a TV studio that day wondering if Krzyzewski might hang a banner that said "ACC Regular Season Champions—Almost."

He needn't have wondered. Duke stunned Carolina and the 21,000 fans in the Dean Dome by winning the game, 83–77. It was the third time in four years that Duke had made the ten-mile trip south down 15-501 and then come back north with a victory. It also meant Duke got to take Friday off because of Maryland's absence from the ACC Tournament. Duke beat N.C. State on Saturday, and North Carolina beat Clemson on Friday and Virginia on Saturday, meaning the two teams would meet in the championship game for the third time in four seasons.

One of Dean Smith's many mantras was that it was very hard to beat a good team three times in the same season. He usually rolled it out when his team was about to play a team it had already beaten twice. This time, though, it worked in reverse. The Tar Heels crushed the Blue Devils, avenging the loss a week earlier in Chapel Hill by a final score of 96–74. The game probably wasn't even that close.

As pleased as he was with the win—it was his eleventh ACC Tournament title—Smith couldn't resist getting in a little postgame dig at Krzyzewski and Duke.

"I just asked Mike in the hallway if he had talked to Tom to find out where we might both be going," he said to open his postgame press conference.

Two years later, Smith was still smarting from *not* getting to play Minnesota in the NCAA Tournament. Tom Butters was still on the committee. Smith was making a very pointed point.

Krzyzewski shrugged off Smith's crack. By then he knew what John Thompson liked to call a "Deanism" when he saw or heard it. His concern was the way his team had played that afternoon. They had spent most of two months steadily improving—peaking in the win a week earlier in Chapel Hill—and then had landed with a thud in the championship game. If Krzyzewski had decided to put up one of Valvano's "almost" banners, it would have said "Not So Almost" if it was going to be accurate.

As he walked to the bus, Krzyzewski felt he needed to do something to light a fire under his players right away. He didn't want to wait until the brackets were announced (he had *not* spoken to Butters, so he had no idea where his team was going) or until practice the next day. He also didn't think yelling at them was the right thing to do at that moment—he'd already spent most of the afternoon doing that to try to break them out of their malaise. So he went in the opposite direction.

He walked onto the bus, and instead of sitting in the first row on the right the way he always did, he told the driver, who normally started moving as soon as he sat down, to hang on for a minute. He walked back a couple of rows and stood in front of his team.

"Fellas, that was a bad day, you all know it," he said. "But I'm telling you something right now. We're going to win the national championship. I know how good you are. Now you guys have to find out how good you are. When you do, we're going to win."

It was an audacious thing to say, not only because his team had just suffered through a 22-point loss but because everyone in the sixty-four-team bracket was going to be looking up at Nevada–Las Vegas, which was 30–0 and had played only one game in which it hadn't won by double digits. The Rebels' average margin of victory was 29 points. They were being touted as one of the greatest teams in history.

"Remember, we're going to win the national championship," Krzyzewski said one more time—and sat down.

A few hours later, Dean Smith got what he wanted—and deserved—when the brackets were unveiled. North Carolina was sent to the East Regional as the number-one seed—meaning its road to the Final Four would go through Duke's "home" court in East Rutherford. Duke was sent to the Midwest as the number-two seed behind Ohio State. Six of the seven ACC teams eligible for postseason made the tournament. N.C. State was also sent to the East as the number-six seed, meaning it could meet North Carolina only if both made the regional final. The Wolfpack lost to Oklahoma State in the second round. Valvano had gone to the NCAA Tournament seven times in ten seasons. Les Robinson was now 1 for 1. Few in Raleigh would have imagined at that moment that it would be eleven years before State would make the tournament again.

Duke and Carolina both blew through the first weekend easily. In the East, the number-two, -four, and -five seeds failed to make it to the Meadowlands. Syracuse, the number-two seed, lost in the first round to Richmond—which became the first number-fifteen seed to win an NCAA Tournament game. In six years, number-fifteen seeds had been 0–24 before Richmond's upset. To get to the Final Four, the Tar Heels had to beat twelfth-seeded Eastern Michigan and tenth-seeded Temple in East Rutherford. They hammered EMU, 93–67, but didn't have nearly as easy a time with Temple, which was one of those sleeper lower-seeded teams. Mark Macon, who had played so poorly in the 1988 regional final in the same building against Duke, was now a senior. He kept making shots in the second half, finishing with 31 points on 12-of-23 shooting to keep the Owls close before Carolina finally prevailed, 75–72.

It was an important win for Smith. He had not been to the Final Four in nine years, a fact made far more significant by State's title in 1983 and, perhaps more important long term, Duke's four trips in the previous five seasons.

"On the one hand, I never really worried about what other teams were doing," Smith said several years later. "As long as we were good, I was happy. But they *were* only a few miles away from us. They were always our number-one rival, even during State's glory years. They were always going to be the number-one threat long term. And he clearly had it going by then. But that day, after we beat Temple, I was just pleased to be going back to the Final

Four. It felt as if it had been a while. We'd gotten a little spoiled during that stretch when we went a lot."

That stretch, from 1967 through 1982, had included seven Final Four trips and a national title.

A little more than two hours after the Tar Heels cut down the nets in the Meadowlands, Duke did the same thing in the Pontiac Silverdome. The Blue Devils' 78–61 win over St. John's in the Midwest Region final was never in doubt. In four tournament games, Duke had won by an average margin of 19 points. Its closest game had come in the regional semifinals when it beat Connecticut, 81–67, in a sort-of rematch of the previous year's regional final. The teams were very different and so was the setting. The result, ultimately, was the same.

St. John's had upset top-seeded Ohio State just prior to Duke's win over UConn. But the Redmen simply couldn't play with Duke, which jumped to an early lead, built the margin to 40–27 at halftime and never looked back. Two hours after celebrating their return to the Final Four after a nine-year absence, North Carolina fans looked up to see that Duke was also going—for the fifth time in six seasons.

While the nets were coming down, Mickie Krzyzewski stood next to the Duke bench with a huge smile on her face. "Dean may be going back to the Final Four," she said gleefully. "But he's *not* going unaccompanied."

He wasn't. But there was one consolation for Carolina: Smith would be facing Kansas—coached by Roy Williams—in the first semifinal. Duke would then play Nevada–Las Vegas. The Rebels were 34–0. They were trying to become the first team since Indiana in 1976 to go undefeated.

Almost everyone in college basketball awaited their coronation.

26

Indianapolis was hosting the Final Four for the second time. The NCAA had first brought the event there in 1980. Market Square Arena, which seated 16,530 people and was the home of the Indiana Pacers, had been the venue when Louisville had beaten UCLA for the championship.

UCLA was nowhere near the Final Four in 1991, and Market Square Arena had been replaced as the venue by the Hoosier Dome—home of the Indianapolis Colts—which would seat 47,100 fans for basketball. When the NCAA first started playing in domes, it made a minor accommodation to fans by putting the court at one end of the building so that it was possible to get more fans closer to the action. It was only in 2009 that it moved the court to the middle of the football field so it could sell every possible seat even if most of the sightlines were awful.

The Final Four had a very ACC feel to it, even smack in the heart of Big Ten country. North Carolina and Duke were both playing and so was Kansas, coached by former Smith assistant and acolyte Roy Williams. The only true outsider was the team everyone expected to walk off with the trophy on Monday night: Nevada–Las Vegas.

Vegas had become a rock group in basketball uniforms, traveling with a huge entourage, various roadies, and groupies—not to mention their richer-than-rich fans. The Rebels returned all the key players from the team that had destroyed Duke in the national title game a year earlier. They were, of course, facing NCAA sanctions, but even the NCAA seemed to understand how popular the Rebels had become. It had decided to hold off on handing down punishment to UNLV until *after* the '91 season was over. That was a huge relief to CBS, which built most of its regular season schedule around the Rebels and promoted them so shamelessly that some started to refer to CBS as "the official network of the Runnin' Rebels."

For Duke, the Final Four run was considered a bonus. Next year, with Christian Laettner, Bobby Hurley, and Grant Hill all returning, would be the school's chance to finally win a national championship. Vegas would lose its key players and the Blue Devils would all be a year older. There was no talk in those days of anyone leaving school early for the NBA.

Krzyzewski, though, saw it differently. He hadn't come off the notion he had voiced to his players as their bus pulled out of Charlotte, that they were going to win the national championship. His initial plan that week was not to even look at the tape of the previous year's game. But he changed his mind—watching it with his coaches first and then showing it to his team.

"As good as they were, I wanted our guys to see how many times we had chances to stay in the game," he said. "We were washed out that night. I looked at myself on the bench and I saw no emotion, nothing. I looked at the players and saw the same thing. Vegas was *great*. We could have played our best game and lost. But we didn't even come close."

Vegas's mascot was a giant shark—in honor of Jerry Tarkanian, aka "Tark the Shark." After being hounded by Vegas's pressure defense in the championship game, Bobby Hurley had admitted he'd had nightmares in which he was being attacked by sharks. Now he would be facing those same sharks again.

But Hurley was a very different player. Midway through his sophomore season, Krzyzewski had asked Pete Gaudet to put together a tape showing Hurley's various on-court reactions to bad calls (or what he thought were bad calls), bad plays by teammates, and bad plays of his own. Gaudet was the king of the video machine. He was always putting together specialty tapes. Most of the time, though, they were of an opponent running a certain offense or of the shooting technique of a Duke player who was struggling. This was different.

Hurley looked at the tape and was shocked.

"His basic reaction was, 'Is that really me?'" Gaudet said. "He was stunned that he looked that way on the court. I told him it wasn't so much about his facial expressions but about what those facial expressions said to teammates, to officials, and to opponents. I told him I thought it was probably pretty hard for him to move on to the next play if he was still sulking about the past."

The "whine" tape, as Krzyzewski called it, changed Hurley's demeanor—and his play. There were still moments, but far fewer of them. As his confidence grew, his teammates' confidence in him grew. The Hurley who arrived in Indianapolis wasn't having nightmares about sharks; he was dreaming about beating them.

Most years, a matchup between two glamour teams like North Carolina and Kansas, especially one that had a teacher-pupil coaching matchup, would have been CBS's prime-time game. But Vegas was *the* story, the one team that truly drove ratings. The fact that it was matching up with the team it had hammered a year earlier in the title game made that game the more appealing one for TV.

Kansas was a wonderful story. Roy Williams had succeeded Larry Brown in the spring of 1988 after the Jayhawks had won the national title, and Brown, who couldn't stand being happy for too long, decided to leave to return to the NBA in San Antonio. About fifteen minutes after Williams arrived, he found out that Kansas would be ineligible to play in postseason in 1989 because of violations that had occurred on Brown's watch. In his third season, Kansas had upset both Indiana and Arkansas in the Southeast Regionals to make the Final Four.

Kansas outplayed Carolina in the second half to win the game, 79–73. Unfortunately, the Jayhawks' remarkable trip to the championship game was completely overshadowed by the events of the game's final minute.

Kansas led, 76–71, with thirty-five seconds left when Rick Fox fouled out, fouling to stop the clock. Dean Smith had been dueling with referee Pete Pavia for most of the evening. Pavia had teed Smith up in the first half when he had argued a foul called on Pete Chilcutt. Now Smith slowly walked Kenny Harris, who was subbing for Fox, in the direction of the scorer's table. As he did, he repeatedly asked Pavia, "How much time do I have?"

The third time Smith said it, Pavia—who had worked games for Smith long enough to know Smith's sarcasm when he heard it—gave him a second technical, which meant automatic ejection. The entire building was shocked.

Pavia was an experienced and respected referee. But he probably shouldn't have been working that night. At fifty-three, he was battling cancer and, as a result, was taking a good deal of medication. Colleagues had noticed that he'd become short-tempered on the court and wondered if the meds were affecting him. Three nights earlier, working the NIT championship game, he had tossed Oklahoma coach Billy Tubbs.

A sweet and gentle man by nature, Pavia had developed a reputation for being quick on the draw when it came to technical fouls. Everyone wanted to overlook his temper because they knew what he was going through, but he probably shouldn't have been working such a high-stakes game at that point in his life.

What's more, like a lot of officials, Pavia wasn't a fan of Smith's sarcasm. They'd all heard it. Lenny Wirtz, the veteran ACC official who had dueled with Smith for years, had once teed him up for telling him that North Carolina's record in games Wirtz worked was worse than with any other official. After that game, Smith had said, "You know, Lenny and I have been together for twenty-five years. I think we're entitled to a divorce."

Pavia knew Smith wasn't asking how much time he had because he needed to know. "You think for one second Dean Smith didn't know a rule?" Pavia asked a year later, shortly before he died. "He was trying to give me a hard time but wasn't going to get in my face because he didn't want to get tossed. The second time he said it, I put up my hand to say, 'That's enough, Dean.' Then he said it again."

Later, Jim Delany, the chairman of the basketball committee—and UNC grad—would claim Smith had been ejected for leaving the coaches' box when he had walked Harris to the scorer's table. Technically, Pavia had the right to tee Smith up for leaving the coaches' box, but that wasn't why he did it. If Smith had simply walked Harris to the table without saying anything, nothing would have happened. He knew Smith was walking with Harris for the express purpose of getting close enough to him to say something.

After getting tossed, Smith went down the length of the Kansas bench, shaking hands with Williams, his staff, his players, his managers, and perhaps the mascot, before finally leaving.

As the officials walked in the direction of the tunnel leading to the locker rooms after the game had ended—the same one Carolina was using—Bill Guthridge started screaming angrily at Pavia. "That was bush league!" Guthridge screamed. "Bush league!"

When Guthridge walked closer to Pavia to continue yelling, security stepped in to intervene. They needn't have bothered. Carolina SID Rick Brewer already had an arm on Guthridge and wasn't going to let him get any closer to Pavia.

In all, it was embarrassing for Smith and for everyone involved. It was only the third time in thirty years Smith had been ejected from a game.

"The worst part is that all you guys are going to want to talk about is [Smith's ejection]," Williams said. "We should be talking about how well our guys played."

He was right. It wasn't going to happen.

In the Duke locker room, Mike Krzyzewski was sitting in the coaches' locker area watching the game's final minutes. His thoughts weren't about Smith's ejection: they were about Carolina's loss. Like most people, he had expected the Tar Heels to win the game.

"I realized when they lost that I felt a sense of relief," he said later. "If we won, we wouldn't have to play them in the champion-ship game. The pressure—on both teams—if that game happened would be unbearable. Beyond that, if we *didn't* win against Vegas, I wouldn't have to sit and watch them play in the game.

"It occurred to me that if I was thinking that, the players were thinking that too. I felt like I had to deal with it right away."

Krzyzewski walked into the main area of the locker room. It was not the time he would normally talk to his players.

"Guys, listen up a second," Krzyzewski said. "Carolina's just lost. Let's not pretend that doesn't matter to us. It does. Okay, think about it for a second: Carolina's out. Now, *flush it*. What just happened doesn't matter. We have to go out ready to play Vegas."

With that he walked out.

—

They were ready to play. With Hurley handling the Vegas pres-sure and Laettner getting off to a fast start, Duke jumped to a 15–6 lead, making its first five shots from the field. The Reb-els dug in after that and began to pound Duke on the boards. The two teams seesawed to halftime, UNLV leading 43–41 at the break. The feeling could not have been more different from what it had been a year earlier in Denver when Duke had been lucky to be down only 12 at halftime.

This time the sense in the locker room was, "Coach was right, we can beat these guys."

Down the hall, there was tension in the Vegas locker room. Prior to the game, CBS's Billy Packer, one of the few members of the national media who had publicly said that Duke could win the game, made an important point: "If Duke can take this game down to the final minutes, the pressure will all be on Vegas," he said, adding, "and they haven't played in a down-to-the-wire game all season."

The Rebels didn't want to play in one now. After Anderson Hunt had made a steal and layup early in the second half to give his team a 4-point lead, he turned in the direction of the Vegas fans, who were mostly sitting on their hands, and began waving his arms, imploring them to somehow push his team to the next level.

They couldn't do it. The game stayed close—neither team leading by more than five points. But when center George Ackles tipped in a Hunt miss with 2:15 left to give UNLV a 76–71 lead, it appeared that Duke would walk off the floor after a gallant effort that just wasn't quite good enough. Krzyzewski stood to signal time, knowing his team needed to regroup and take a deep breath. It had been a draining game, physically and emotionally.

Nowadays, as soon as Krzyzewski signaled for time, it would have been granted. Back then, though, someone on the court had to actually ask for a time-out. Hurley had dribbled quickly into the frontcourt and didn't see his coach trying to call time-out. Neither did his teammates. Seeing an opening, Hurley quickly stepped into a seam and drained a three-point shot with 2:14 left.

That summer, when Krzyzewski spent time with the great Coach Pete Newell, who in many ways had become his mentor at that stage of his life, Newell said to him, "The Laettner kid was great in Indy, but Hurley hit the most important shot of your career."

As soon as Hurley's shot swished to make it 76–74, Krzyzewski got the time-out.

Hurley's shot changed the feeling in the building—and on the two benches. Duke *wasn't* going to go gently into that good night. Vegas had *not* yet survived its most difficult test. They were now in the danger zone that Packer had talked about prior to the game.

"There's no underestimating how important Bobby's shot was," Krzyzewski said. "It was as if we all got a shot of pure adrenaline at that point. The game was like a heavyweight fight." He smiled. "It was like *Rocky*, where Rocky and Apollo keep landing haymakers and neither one of them will go down. Just when it looked like we might go down, Bobby hit that shot. We went from on our heels to feeling like we had them on *their* heels."

Vegas *was* tired. Duke was the deeper team, the younger team, the team playing with house money. The Rebels couldn't find an open shot and were called for a forty-five-second shot-clock violation with 1:24 left. With the entire building standing, Duke came down, everyone expecting the ball to go to Laettner. But Brian Davis caught a pass on the wing and went to the basket, surprising the Vegas defense. The shot went down and Davis was fouled. He made the free throw with 1:02 to go and, stunningly, Duke was in front, 77–76.

Vegas didn't wait long to shoot. Stacey Augmon drove to the basket and missed, but Larry Johnson—who had been outscored 26–12 by Laettner to that point—grabbed the rebound and was fouled. Clearly feeling the pressure, Johnson missed the first shot. Then he missed the second. But there was a whistle.

Johnson had a hitch in his free-throw shooting motion. He would bring the ball up, seemingly start into his motion, and then stop. Then he'd reload and shoot. It almost looked like a Harlem Globetrotters move—act as if you're going to shoot and then hold on to the ball. Needless to say, opponents knew about the hitch, and players were told not to move on Johnson's first motion. But with all the raw emotion in the building at that moment, Thomas Hill forgot for an instant about the hitch. When Johnson made his first nonshooting move, he stepped into the lane. Granted a reprieve and a third shot, Johnson finally made one to tie the score at 77–77.

There was a five-second difference between the game clock and the shot clock, so Duke couldn't play for a last shot. Krzyzewski didn't want to call time-out because that would give Tarkanian a chance to set up his defense.

Thomas Hill flashed open fifteen feet from the basket and fired a jumper with the clock just under fifteen seconds. It rimmed out, but Laettner was right there for the rebound. As he went up with the ball, UNLV'S Evric Gray fouled him with 12.7 seconds left. Tarkanian called time to let Laettner think about the free throws. Krzyzewski—perhaps channeling Al McGuire—didn't even think about the possibility of Laettner missing either shot.

"Okay, after Christian makes these, this is what we need to do," he said as his players leaned in to listen. What he didn't want was Hunt, who had been UNLV's best player all day, with twenty-nine points, getting any kind of look at the basket. In fact, he much preferred allowing Johnson to have the ball because it was clear to Krzyzewski that nerves were affecting UNLV's star. He saw no such sign of nerves in Hunt.

The teams came back on court. Neither of Laettner's free throws hit anything except the bottom of the net. Down 79–77, suddenly facing defeat, Vegas pushed the ball into the frontcourt. Hurley and Grant Hill both attacked Hunt, forcing him to give up the ball. It swung on the right wing to Johnson, who, for a split second, had an open three-point shot. Johnson froze. Laettner got out to him and Johnson had to pass. By now, though, the clock was under two seconds. Desperate, Johnson reversed the ball to Hunt, who was a good twenty-five feet from the basket with Hurley in his face. Hunt had no choice but to heave a shot in the direction of the rim. It hit off the side and bounced to Hurley as the buzzer sounded.

Hurley dropped the ball and began leaping in the air, arms over his head, celebrating. He jumped into Grant Hill's arms as everyone in blue began to hug one another.

And then they stopped.

Krzyzewski had rushed onto the floor at the final buzzer—but not to hug anyone. This wasn't 1984 in Greensboro against North Carolina or even 1986 in Dallas against Kansas.

"*Stop!*" he screamed at his players, his palms down in the "cool it" signal. "*Stop!* We haven't won anything yet!"

They stopped. They went and lined up and shook hands with the stunned UNLV players. Krzyzewski hugged Tarkanian, who was clearly in shock.

Up in the stands, John Wooden, who had won seven straight national championships at UCLA between 1967 and 1973 and coached four undefeated teams, stood up and turned to Quinn Buckner, who had played on Indiana's undefeated team in 1976.

"You know something, Quinn," he said. "A lot of great teams have won one in a row."

The two men made their way out, both with broad grins on their faces.

—

There was, of course, the not-so-little matter of beating Kansas in the final. The Jayhawks were on an impressive roll. They were a veteran team led by center Mark Randall and two superb guards, Adonis Jordan and Terry Brown. There was also the added twist of Roy Williams—the same Roy Williams who had been so stunned when Krzyzewski refused to shake his boss's hand for a moment the first time they'd met more than ten years earlier—being the one coach left standing between Krzyzewski and a national championship.

Krzyzewski wasn't concerned about Williams or any twists of history. He really didn't care that Saturday had been arguably the worst day in North Carolina basketball history. Not only had Carolina lost a national semifinal, Dean Smith had been ejected and *then* Duke had pulled one of the great upsets in the history of the tournament. The hopes of all Tar Heels now rode on Roy Williams, UNC class of 1972.

Krzyzewski's concern was with his team—and his players. Laettner and Hurley had both played forty minutes against UNLV. Laettner had been banged around by the Rebels' big men and was sore and tired. Hurley, who could run forever, appeared to be fine.

But Krzyzewski was just as worried about his team's mind-set. No matter how many times he told them that the job wasn't done yet, he sensed a feeling of accomplishment he didn't like. They had taken down the team that had humiliated them the year before, the team that had already been crowned as champion in the minds of most people.

It was en route to practice on Sunday that Krzyzewski found a way to get his team's attention. When he walked onto the bus he noticed that Greg Koubek and freshman Marty Clark had apparently done some shopping. They were both wearing brand-new cowboy hats.

Not for long.

Krzyzewski took the hats off their heads and stood in the front of the bus.

"Let me tell you guys something," he said. "Yesterday is yesterday. It's done. Over. Kansas could give a damn that you guys beat Vegas. Frankly, right now, I could give a damn that you guys beat Vegas.

"I don't like the way you're walking or the way you're talking right now. I don't like the looks of satisfaction on your faces, and I *really* don't like the way"—he paused to glare at Koubek and Clark—"you're dressing right now. I'm gonna tell you this right now and I'm not gonna say it again: When we get to the arena, you better have forgotten yesterday. You better be totally focused on tomorrow night. Because if you're not, we'll lose the game. And if we lose the game, none of you are gonna want to be around me."

He sat down. The cowboy hats had given him exactly the excuse he was looking for to rip them.

"It was actually perfect," he said later. "I mean, what was I going to yell at them for? They'd just beaten Vegas. I had been telling them they needed to put it behind them, but, I mean, what the hell, they'd just *beaten Vegas.* But the cowboy hats were proof—tangible proof—that they thought they'd become God's gift to basketball. It was just what I needed."

Championship Monday is the longest day of the year for the teams playing in the game. Because Indianapolis is in the Eastern time zone, tip-off wasn't until nearly 9:30. It was Krzyzewski's third championship game in six years, so he had the hang of it.

The second championship was entirely different from the first. Duke was picked number one in preseason and had become college basketball's most polarizing team. The Blue Devils were the heavyweights now, favored to win every game, expected to win every game *easily.* Laettner and Hurley were at the center of all the emotions directed at the team. They were the two best players *and* they were white. Even though the other three starters—Grant and Thomas Hill and Brian Davis—were African Americans, Duke was again labeled by many as "white America's team."

Much of the invective directed at them came from white people—moneyed fans and students at other schools who could accept the notion that an African American was a great player but didn't want to deal with the notion that two baby-faced white kids could kick their team's butt.

Many assumed that Laettner, with his boyish good looks, was a rich kid: in fact, his parents were both printers at the *Buffalo Evening News.* Hurley was the son of Bob Hurley, one of the best high school coaches in the country. Bob Hurley, Sr., coached at St. Anthony's, a tiny Catholic school in Jersey City, New Jersey. For most of his coaching career he supplemented his income by working as a probation officer.

Even so, the image stuck. In 1992, after winning an unlikely national title a year earlier, Duke was the most beloved and the most despised team in the country.

"It was like traveling with a rock band," said Mike Brey, now the coach at Notre Dame but a Duke assistant back then. "Everywhere we went, we heard screams—some of adoration, some of hatred. It was tough for some people to accept the fact that a bunch of smart kids—white or black—played basketball that well."

By the time the Blue Devils got to Chapel Hill the first week in February, they were 17–0 and the only close call had come at Michigan against the group that would come to be known as "the Fab Five." That game went into overtime and, as it turned out, was the closest the five Michigan freshmen—Chris Webber, Juwan Howard, Jalen Rose, Ray Jackson, and Jimmy King—would come to beating Duke.

North Carolina was 15–3 and ranked ninth in the country when Duke came to town, but the feel in the building was that it would take a huge upset for the Tar Heels to win.

"They're already planning bonfires on Franklin Street [the main drag in Chapel Hill]," Jim Heavner, the longtime owner of the North Carolina radio network, said shortly before tip-off. "It's full role reversal. Duke has become North Carolina."

That night might have been the first time that the Dean Dome felt like Carmichael Auditorium. After losing to Duke at home for the third time in five years the previous March, Smith had told his "bosses"—Smith didn't have any real bosses at Carolina—that he wanted some students close to the court, not just the rich boosters who tended to sit on their hands. And so a couple of thousand students had been moved downstairs—mostly in the corners and behind the baskets but close to the court nevertheless. The difference was noticeable.

The game rocked back and forth. Carolina led for most of the second half, but part of the role reversal was that it was now *Duke* that never seemed to be out of a game. The Blue Devils rallied to cut the margin to 75–73 and, with the clock ticking toward zero, came downcourt with a chance to tie or win the game. The ball swung to Laettner, who appeared to be open for a three at the top of the key. But Laettner opted to pass up the three and drove the lane. His shot from the right side fell off the rim as the buzzer sounded, the students stormed the court, and Smith heaved a huge sigh of relief.

"If Laettner takes that three and it goes in, Dean might never have coached again," Keith Drum said afterward. "They worked so hard to win that game and deserved to win. If Duke had somehow stolen it the way Dean always stole games, I'm not sure Dean could have handled it."

Years later, when Drum's comments were repeated to him,

Smith smiled. "Keith might have had that one right," he said. "If Duke had won that game, they might have gone undefeated."

Left unsaid was the rest of the sentence: and *that* might have killed me.

Hurley was injured late in the game and, as it turned out, missed the next seven games. Krzyzewski moved Grant Hill to the point and Hill played well there. Even so, with Antonio Lang starting in Hill's place at forward, Duke was weaker at two positions.

"The fact that we only lost one game during that stretch [at Wake Forest] tells you how good we were," Krzyzewski said. "Before Bobby got hurt in the Carolina game, we were playing about as well as you could hope to have a team play. Without him, we were still good, but not as good."

They were good enough to go to LSU three days later and beat a Shaquille O'Neal–led team, 77–67, with Laettner outplaying O'Neal for the second year in a row. The previous season, in Cameron, the Blue Devils had humiliated the Tigers, 88–70. This win—on the road, without Hurley—was more impressive.

With Hurley back, Duke beat Carolina, 89–77, in the regular season finale to finish 25–2. The mind-set of the players was apparent when Laettner spoke to the crowd after the game during the Senior Day speeches. "Now listen, you guys, we still have nine games left to play," Laettner said. "And even though we're not playing here, we need to know you're all behind us and you're back here partying it up after we win."

Nine games would mean playing three games in the ACC Tournament and six in the NCAA Tournament. Clearly, that was the plan.

—

The ACC Tournament wasn't that big a problem. Duke eased past Maryland and Georgia Tech and, after a tight first half in their fourth final in five years against UNC, blew the Tar Heels away in the second half, winning 94–74. The 20-point margin was almost identical to Carolina's 22-point margin in the final a year earlier. That had been the day Krzyzewski had told his players they were going to win the national championship. They had done that. The win over Carolina meant their record since the "bus speech" was 34–2.

The Blue Devils won their first three NCAA Tournament games by double digits, making it look easy except for one second-half stretch against Iowa—whom they played in the second round for the second straight season—when they let the Hawkeyes' press get to them for a while. They recovered in time to win, 75–62.

As it turned out, their difficulties with Iowa's style proved to be a harbinger. The opponent in the regional final was Kentucky. Rick Pitino had become the coach three seasons earlier in the wake of NCAA sanctions that came about after the infamous Emery air express envelope containing a thousand dollars, which had been mailed from the Kentucky basketball office to the father of a recruit, fell open.

Eddie Sutton was fired at the end of the 1989 season and Pitino was hired to rebuild. He had recruited superbly, convincing Jamal Mashburn to leave New York (Pitino was also a New Yorker, growing up on Long Island) and adding two excellent guards, Sean Woods and Dale Brown. They had combined with four seniors, most notably John Pelphrey, to make Kentucky into a power again during the 1992 season.

What's more, Pitino's aggressive, ninety-four-feet-of-pressure defensive style was tough to play against and to prepare for, especially on a two-day turnaround, which is what teams get between the round of sixteen and the round of eight in the NCAA Tournament.

For the first time since 1985, the East Regionals were *not* being played in the Meadowlands. They were in the Philadelphia Spectrum, the same building that had been the site of Bob Knight's first two national titles at Indiana. It had also been the site of one of the more comic scenes of Knight's career. As he was about to walk into the interview room after his team had beaten LSU in the first semifinal in 1981, Knight was stopped by a security guard.

"You can't go in there without a credential," the guard said.

For once, Knight was momentarily speechless. Then, actually thinking the guard was kidding, he started to walk past him. The guard—who wasn't kidding—blocked his path.

"I told you, sir, you can't go in there without a proper credential."

Knight actually smiled. "Look, pal, believe me, I'd be very happy to not go in there," he said. "But if I don't, *you* are going to have to explain to everyone in there why I didn't show up."

At that point, an NCAA official arrived to explain that Knight did *not* need a credential. No one will ever know what might have happened next had he not intervened.

There were no security issues on the night of March 28, 1992. Just what has since been called "the greatest college basketball game ever played."

The game was a track meet from the start. It went back and forth, neither team able to get control or able to stop the other for more than a couple of possessions at a time. Duke led 50–45 at halftime but couldn't widen the lead. The Wildcats pushed in front, then Duke led again. Midway through the second half, a play happened that Kentucky people and anti-Duke people wail about to this day. During a skirmish under the basket, UK backup center Aminu Timberlake hit the floor. As he lay there, Laettner very clearly stepped on him. He didn't *stomp* his foot but he did step on his chest. Timberlake was completely unharmed. He jumped up right away and laughed at Laettner, who was instantly called for both a personal foul and a technical foul.

Perhaps if Timberlake had rolled on the floor in pain, Laettner would have been ejected. But he didn't and, since it was clear to the officials that Laettner's act had been more stupid than violent, he was given the technical foul—which meant he had four personals—and the game moved on. They went to overtime, tied at 93. The extra five minutes swayed back and forth, one team scoring, the other team answering. Finally, after Laettner had put Duke ahead 102–101, Sean Woods drove to the basket and somehow banked in a shot high off the backboard over Laettner's reach to put Kentucky ahead, 103–102, with 2.1 seconds to go.

Krzyzewski called time. His team had to somehow go the length of the court and score or the dream of back-to-back titles would be gone. Almost everyone in the building was standing.

"I'll never forget the first thing Coach said when we came to the huddle," Hurley said. "He just said, 'We're going to win the damn game.'"

Then he drew up the play that he believed would win the damn game. Earlier in the season, trailing Wake Forest by two points, the Blue Devils had run a play in which Grant Hill, who had the strongest and most accurate arm on the team, had thrown a pass to Laettner near the top of the key. If Laettner could catch it, he would have time to turn and—at six-eleven—shoot over anyone guarding him. But the pass had faded just enough to the left that Laettner hadn't been able to catch it cleanly. Still, Krzyzewski knew it could work, and given that Laettner had not missed a shot in the game—he was 9 of 9 from the field and 10 of 10 from the foul line at that moment—this was clearly Duke's best chance.

As the teams walked onto the court, no one from Kentucky was guarding Hill. Krzyzewski was surprised and thought Pitino was going to call time to reset his defense now that he had seen how Duke was lining up. Most coaches, when a team needs to throw a long pass from the baseline, will stand someone in front of the inbounder to make it harder to throw the pass. Dean Smith always sent his tallest player into the game in those situations— even if he hadn't played a single second—to force the passer to throw the ball over him. The higher the pass, the more time there was for someone to intercept it or at least deflect it.

There was no time-out. With no one on him, Hill was able to stand still and line up his pass. Laettner came to the top of the key and the ball reached him on a string. Once he had it, the Kentucky players were helpless. They'd been told not to foul, especially Laettner, so they more or less stood and watched as Laettner, knowing that 2.1 seconds was plenty of time, took one dribble to balance himself, turned, and shot an eighteen-footer, a shot he had taken in practice hundreds of times.

It was actually an easier shot than the one he had hit in the regional final two years earlier against Connecticut because then two UConn players had come at him and forced him to shoot slightly off-balance, his left leg flying outward as he released the ball. The buzzer went off with the ball in the air and it splashed cleanly through the net as players on *both* teams fell to the floor in shock.

Thomas Hill didn't fall down, but he burst into tears, completely drained by the entire experience of playing in the game, and wept on Pete Gaudet's shoulder. Krzyzewski went to shake hands with Pitino and then walked over to Richie Farmer, one of the four Kentucky seniors, who was still lying on the floor in shock. He helped Farmer up, then hugged him.

"There was nothing I could say to him," Krzyzewski said. "I think I just wanted him to know how much I respected everything they had accomplished. I felt the same about Rick."

He also felt that way about Cawood Ledford. Laettner's basket was the last play Ledford would call after thirty-nine seasons as the radio voice of Kentucky basketball. He had announced earlier in the year that he was retiring. Krzyzewski walked over to where Ledford and partner Ralph Hacker sat and asked if he could come on the air for a minute. He then delivered a tribute to Ledford, talking about what he had meant to basketball, and urged Kentucky fans to be proud of their team and the game they had just played. "I would be proud of my team even if it had lost tonight," he said. "It was a great game, one worthy of Cawood's career."

It is likely that no coach, before or since, has done anything like that for an *opponent's* broadcaster.

"I just thought it was the right thing to do," Krzyzewski said. "I didn't think about it, I just did it."

A few yards away, Bob Ryan of *The Boston Globe* was standing, watching the Duke celebration. "When Laettner's shot went in, I leaped to my feet," Ryan said. "It wasn't because I had a rooting interest one way or the other, it was just that I was amazed by what I'd just witnessed. It was a leap of 'Oh my god, that was incredible' more than anything. But when I realized I was standing, I was embarrassed. You aren't supposed to do that on press row—no matter what. Then I looked around me and saw that everyone else was standing too. Then I felt better. It was a moment when we all became human, when we all recognized that we'd seen something truly special. It was worth jumping to your feet, not just for the shot, but for the entire game."

—

Having beaten Kentucky in a game that would be talked about and written about forever—the game has spawned both books and documentaries—Duke now faced the not-so-small task of playing Indiana in the national semifinals in Minneapolis.

It was the first time Knight and Krzyzewski had faced each other since the Sweet 16 in 1987. Then the circumstances had been very different: Indiana was a clear favorite as the number-one seed in the Midwest Region. Krzyzewski was just coming off his first Final Four and was many rungs below Knight on the coaching ladder.

Five years later, Knight was in the Final Four for the first time since Indiana's championship run in '87. Duke was in the Final Four for the fifth straight year and was going for a second straight title. Knight still had more titles—three to one—but Krzyzewski had actually surpassed him in Final Fours—six to five. Just before the tournament began, Alex Wolff of *Sports Illustrated* had written a lengthy piece on Krzyzewski with the headline "Blue Angel," wondering if the pupil had surpassed the teacher.

The story essentially said that Krzyzewski had evolved into about the best thing going in college basketball. One of the reasons he had become so good was that he was *not*—as he had been portrayed for so long—a Knight clone or even necessarily a disciple. Knight wasn't going to like any story that implied someone, especially an ex-player/ex–assistant coach for whom he had once been the ultimate authority figure, might be a better coach than he was.

Krzyzewski certainly never implied that in any way, but he did admit he grew weary at times of hearing that everything he was and had become was because of Knight.

"I value Coach Knight very much," Wolff quoted him as saying. "He's been a tremendous influence on me, mostly in good ways. There are also some things I don't do as a result of being influenced by him. But to keep bringing him up doesn't give credit to others who have helped me: my mom, my brother, my wife, my AD, my assistants, my buddies. I've been a head coach for sixteen years and I don't go over every game plan with Coach Knight."

Saying that others had been important in his life hardly sounded like an insult. Saying that, after six Final Fours and a national title, he was a pretty good coach in his own right hardly sounded out of line either. The implication that maybe he didn't copy everything Knight did not only made sense but was one of the reasons for his success.

Knight, naturally, didn't see it that way. This was an act of disloyalty in his view, and in the week prior to the Final Four, he sent Krzyzewski a note telling him that. Krzyzewski really wasn't bothered by it that much because, to some degree, it was just Knight being Knight, and because he thought Knight might be trying to get inside his head before they faced off again.

Whether Knight had gotten inside Krzyzewski's head hardly seemed to matter during the first half of the game. Someone had gotten inside Laettner's head. The same guy who literally couldn't miss in the Spectrum couldn't throw it into any of Minnesota's thousand lakes while playing in the Metrodome. He was 1 of 5 from the field in the first half and even missed the front end of two one-and-ones after having made twenty consecutive free throws in the tournament.

Indiana appeared to be on the verge of blowing Duke out of the building. But Hurley wouldn't let them. Every time Indiana seemed ready to go on a run, he buried a shot—four of them from three-point range. The Hoosiers led 39–27 with 4:20 to play, but Hurley hit his fourth three and Grant Hill and Thomas Hill chipped in with baskets to cut the margin to 42–37 at the break.

"We should have been down more," Krzyzewski said later. "We were lucky—especially lucky that we had Bobby on our side."

Having missed their chance to take control of the game, Indiana came out firing blanks at the start of the second half. In the first ten minutes, the Blue Devils outscored IU 21–3, meaning the run over two halves was 31–6. Knight didn't help his team's cause at all by drawing a technical foul early in the half from referee Ted Valentine. "TV Teddy," as Valentine was known, had a quick draw when it came to techs, but Knight got in his face anyway.

To their credit, the Hoosiers rallied late, but even with both Brian Davis (ankle) and Grant Hill (knee) hurt, the Blue Devils hung on to win, 81–78. That put them in the championship game against the tournament darlings, Michigan's Fab Five.

Krzyzewski was hardly jubilant after the game. For one thing, Davis's injury made it unlikely that he could play very much—if at all—on Monday night. Hill would be able to play but might be hobbled. And there had been an ugly postgame incident with Knight.

It had started with the postgame handshake. Knight had done what coaches call a "blow-by" with Krzyzewski, not even slowing down as the two men passed. Then he made a point of wrapping Colonel Rogers in a hug to show that he wasn't so much mad at the loss as at the Duke coach. Everyone saw that.

What they didn't see was what took place right after Indiana's press conference ended. The losers always come in to talk first after the second game on Saturday night at the Final Four because the winners have TV obligations. Knight and his players had come off the podium and were in a curtained-off area that led back to the locker rooms. As Krzyzewski, Hurley, and Laettner passed Indiana's representatives—Knight, Alan Henderson, and Calbert Cheaney—everyone slowed down to exchange handshakes. Knight wished Hurley and Laettner good luck in the championship game. Krzyzewski, trailing his players, figured Knight was over his seconds-after-the-game funk and walked up to Knight with his hand out.

Knight walked right past him—never so much as looked at him. Krzyzewski was devastated. It was the beginning of nine years when the two men didn't speak to each other.

Two nights later, Krzyzewski became the first coach since John Wooden to win back-to-back national championships. After another sluggish first half, the Blue Devils blew the Fab Five out of the gym, pulling away for a 71–51 win. Laettner finally found his shot midway through the second half, and Hurley was voted Most Outstanding Player.

Krzyzewski now had one more national title than Smith—and Valvano. It was Pitino, appearing on CBS, who summed up the way Krzyzewski was now viewed by his fellow coaches. "Simply the best," Pitino said. "Simply the best."

That summer, Bob Knight came to North Carolina to play golf with Dean Smith. He made certain the Carolina media knew he'd been there—and that he hadn't bothered to so much as call Krzyzewski. One member of the local media, an older man who saw only good in Smith and only evil in Krzyzewski, wrote rapturously about the two great coaches playing golf together: "I can't help but think that as they made their way around the golf course, the two greatest basketball coaches of all time were enjoying one another's company."

Perhaps. But the coach with the back-to-back national titles wasn't there. He didn't play golf.

28

Jim Valvano was on a trip to Europe, working World League of American Football games for ABC in the spring of 1992, when he began to experience serious back pain. His first thought was that he was just sore from doing gigs on the sideline, during which he had to stand for most of a three-hour football game, and from long plane flights.

It had been a hectic, busy, and enjoyable year for Valvano. In December, he had almost become coach of the New Jersey Nets. The Nets, struggling as always, were planning to fire Bill Fitch and contacted Valvano to see if he was interested in taking over the team. He was, so much so that he called younger brother Bob to tell him he wanted him to be one of his assistant coaches.

The Nets told Valvano they wanted him to take over after the Christmas holiday. They thought it would be in poor taste to fire Fitch, a distinguished NBA coach, just before Christmas. But the deal never happened, because the story leaked.

Valvano was convinced that someone at ESPN overheard him talking to someone about the job on the telephone and made a phone call to a friend who covered the Nets for a New York newspaper. Once the story leaked, the Nets backed away.

"Part of it was that they had this fractured ownership," Bob Valvano said. "Several of them really wanted Jim for the job. Others wanted to wait until the end of the season. The ones who wanted Jim had the upper hand until the story leaked."

One person who wasn't disappointed that the deal fell through was Pam Valvano. "It was New York, so I would have been okay with the move," she said. "But if he never coached again, that was more than fine with me."

In January, Valvano had been awarded a CableACE Award for his work on ESPN, a sign of how quickly he had become a star in television. No one who knew him had expected different, but the award was a tangible sign that he was probably on his way to big things in TV.

"If he had decided to put his heart and soul into TV for a number of years, he would have ended up hosting *The Tonight Show* or something along those lines," Mike Krzyzewski said. "No way sports would have been enough for him."

At that point, though, Valvano wasn't certain if TV was really The Next Thing. It was almost too easy. He missed the W's, and to a lesser extent he even missed the L's. That was why he had been ready to take the Nets job. He was a natural on TV as long as no one tried to script him. But there was no real challenge there for him. Hosting *The Tonight Show* might have been fun someday, but it wouldn't have been comparable to cutting down the final net.

Which may explain why he was intrigued—more than intrigued—when he got a call in March from Wichita State University. The school was looking for a new basketball coach. Eddie Fogler, Dean Smith's former assistant, had left for Vanderbilt in 1990 and had been replaced by Mike Cohen.

Cohen had very little success, going 32–56 in three seasons. Wichita State is very much a basketball school with a lot of tradition. That sort of record wasn't going to come close to cutting it. Cohen was fired.

Doug Elgin, the commissioner of Wichita State's league, the Missouri Valley Conference, brought up Valvano's name to Wichita State athletic director Tom Shupe. Elgin had been the sports information director at Virginia during Valvano's early years in the ACC and still had friends in the league who had told him that Jim was interested in coaching again.

"He was interested—very interested," Pam Valvano Strasser said. "It was because he hadn't left N.C. State on his own terms. It was more about closing the loop than anything else. He didn't like the way it felt when he left, that people thought he had failed in some way or had won because he didn't do things the right way. He knew how good a coach he was, and he didn't like the feeling that some of that had gotten lost when he left State."

Valvano flew to Wichita and met with school officials. They were very eager to hire him and offered him a five-year contract for $500,000 a year. There were schools that might have paid more, but that was still very good money. Jim flew home and sat down with Pam.

"He wanted to do it," she said. "He didn't necessarily want to do it forever or even for ten years. It might have been five years. But he wanted to leave coaching with a good taste in his mouth, not a bad one."

As with the Nets, Jim had talked to his younger brother about joining him. As with the Nets, it never happened. This time, the reason was Pam.

"I told him I just couldn't do it," she said. "It wasn't so much about moving to Wichita, although that would have been tough because I wouldn't have known a soul. New York would have been different—it was home, we both had family there. This would have been a whole new world.

"But that wasn't really it. I had moved before. I knew how to do that. But I really liked the life we were leading. There were no downs. People will say, 'Didn't you miss the highs when he wasn't coaching?' Honestly, there weren't *that* many highs. Most of the time, after a win, he'd just start getting ready for the next game. The only exception to that was in 1983, and that was a once-in-a-lifetime experience. Every coach's wife I've ever known says the same thing: the losses hang around; the wins go away quickly.

"I didn't want that life again. I didn't want the never-ending recruiting cycle. Not only had I been there, done that, but I *liked* the way we were living at that point. So I finally said to him, 'I understand if you feel the need to do this, but I'm not going with you.' I told him I'd visit, that we'd spend time in the off-season, but I wasn't moving. He looked at me and said, 'If you feel that strongly, then I'll turn it down.'

"And he did. It was actually one of the great moments of our marriage. If I'd ever had any doubt that Jim loved me, it went away then. There had been times in the past where basketball had come before family for Jim. But when push really came to shove, he put his family first. I can't tell you how much that meant to me."

Jim went back to television, working through the Final Four. Then, when ABC asked him to be a sideline reporter for a few World League of American Football games in May, he said yes. That was when his back began to bother him.

By the time he got home from his last game in Barcelona, the pain was so acute and persistent that he began to think it was more than just stiffness. He had just turned forty-six. He'd been on long plane flights for years and never felt anything like this.

"He called me after he got back from Europe and said he was going to go in and have some tests done," John Saunders said. "He said, 'I've probably got cancer.' I said, 'Shut up. That's not even a little bit funny.'"

Valvano wasn't joking. He didn't necessarily believe he had cancer, but he was concerned. "It wasn't so much that we thought about cancer," Pam Valvano Strasser said. "It was that we couldn't figure out what it was. And that was a little bit scary."

The doctors ran various tests to see if Valvano had somehow injured himself or even if he had some kind of virus that might be causing the pain. They found nothing. Finally, they decided to do an MRI on Valvano's back to see if there was anything they might have missed.

There was.

"It was actually one of the radiologists who showed us the test," Pam said. "He said he really wasn't supposed to show us, but the doctor was tied up with some kind of emergency and he thought we should know what was going on. So he showed it to us."

Later, Jim would tell friends the story about seeing a huge black area on the film the technician put up on a wall for them to look at.

"What's all that black?" he asked.

"Coach," the radiologist answered. "That's cancer."

One of the people Valvano told that story to was Saunders. Twenty-one years later, Saunders couldn't retell the story without tearing up. "I think at that moment he knew he was going to die," Saunders said. "There was an odd dichotomy to the whole thing. On the one hand, Jimmy was very much at peace with his fate. On the other hand, right until the very end, I think he was convinced he was going to find a way to beat it. To some extent, we all believed that. I mean, how could Jim Valvano possibly die?"

That was the way Mike Krzyzewski felt. "There was no way he was going to die," he said. "And yet, you could see very clearly that he was dying."

When the Valvanos did talk to the doctor, they learned that Jim had something called metastatic adenocarcinoma, which in English is a tumor that springs from the glands. Where it started, why it started, when it started was a mystery. But it was pretty far along.

"They said a year," Pam said. "Turned out, they were being optimistic."

The next morning Valvano called Saunders. "I was sitting on the edge of my bed when he called," Saunders said. "He said, 'I've got cancer.' I guess because it was Jim, I just didn't believe him. I said to him, 'Will you please shut the f—— up with the cancer stuff. I told you it's not funny!'

"He said, 'John, I know it's not funny. I'm not joking.' That's when I started to cry."

On June 18, ESPN's Bob Ley made the announcement on *SportsCenter*. "There is only one way to break this news and it is the way Jim Valvano would want us to do it," he said soberly. "Jim has cancer."

The news stunned everyone who knew Valvano. Of course the first questions asked were, "How serious is it? How early did they catch it?"

The answers were "Very" and "Not early."

Initially, Valvano went to New York to Sloan Kettering for treatment. Sloan Kettering is one of the leading cancer centers in the world. The chemotherapy was awful. His hair didn't fall out, but he had all the other side effects, notably the nausea. Saunders remembers going to visit him and how upsetting it was to see him so weak and sick.

But it was also inspiring.

"I went to see him one evening and Pam and the girls were there," he said. "I knew how much Jim traveled and I knew how guilty he felt at times about not being there for the four of them more often. But the closeness they felt, the bonds that were so strong, were really something to see.

"My wife and I had been talking about having a second child. I didn't want one. I thought one was all I could handle. Seeing Jim and Pam and the girls turned me around completely. I was driving home from the hospital that night [Saunders lived in Westchester] and I pulled off the road to a phone booth. I called my wife and said, 'I've changed my mind. I think we should have another child.'"

Saunders smiled at the memory. "She said, 'I'm so glad you feel that way, because I'm pregnant.'"

The child, born two months before Valvano's death, is named Jenna Tiana Vanessa Saunders.

Valvano's health slid quickly. Not surprisingly, the chemo treatment made him sick. Eventually he and Pam decided he should be treated at Duke Hospital, if only because it was easier on Jim to drive twenty-five miles to Durham rather than fly to New York when he needed treatment.

There was no doubt that Valvano was going to keep working for as long as possible. "If he had just been sitting around the house, I think he'd have lost his mind," Pam said. "He needed to get out and see people. The support he was getting was keeping him going. And, by then, he loved going to the games. It was his therapy."

When Valvano started treatment at Duke, he had a frequent visitor: Krzyzewski. Whenever he was going to be at the hospital, Valvano would let Krzyzewski know, and unless he was on the road, Krzyzewski would come and spend time with him when he was getting a chemo treatment. Sometimes, Valvano would come to watch Krzyzewski's team practice, and on some of those occasions, Krzyzewski asked him to speak to his team.

Few people understood just how sick Valvano was until Gary Smith wrote a lengthy *Sports Illustrated* story on what Valvano was going through. There was a photo of Valvano on the cover in which he looked about ten to fifteen years older than he had looked prior to his diagnosis and the chemo. The cover line read "I'm Fighting to Live."

In the piece, Smith talked about the battle Valvano was waging with himself.

"The triviality of it just clobbers me," Smith quoted Valvano as saying. "You get this sick and you say to yourself, 'Sports means nothing,' and that feels terrible. God, I've devoted my whole life to it."

As he had always done, Valvano poured all his feelings out in his talks with Smith. Now, though, there was little of the Valvano humor. Only occasionally did the guy who *became* rooms peek out from behind the black curtain. "I've lost thirty-five pounds," he said. "I'm the quickest color commentator going. No one can go around me."

As the basketball season chugged through the winter, Valvano went downhill rapidly. He kept doing games, but each one was more difficult. Walking had become difficult. He couldn't taste food anymore. He was trying experimental treatments—drinking shark's cartilage because sharks never got cancer and there were those who thought that ingesting something from a shark might stop cancer from spreading.

"You could see, very clearly, that he was dying," Pam said. "And yet, I don't think Jim ever really believed he was going to die, and because of that we didn't believe he was going to die. The doctors were going to find *something* in time to save him."

Everyone who knew him well felt that way. "Jim had too much life in him to die," Bob Valvano said. "On the one hand, when I saw him, he looked terrible and felt terrible. On the other hand, he was still Jim. He could still make you laugh in ways no one else could make you laugh."

In early February, Valvano had to skip two games he was scheduled to do on TV because he was too sick to travel. North Carolina State had planned a tenth anniversary celebration for the 1983 team for February 21, when the Wolfpack was hosting Duke on a Sunday afternoon. Valvano had been scheduled to do the game on ABC, but he was so fragile by then that ABC had Terry Gannon on standby in case Valvano couldn't make it to the game.

He made it, walking into Reynolds Coliseum for the first time since he had been forced to resign. Some of his former players hadn't seen him in a long time and they were shocked by his appearance. Remarkably, he hadn't lost his hair in chemo, but he was frail and walking was very difficult for him. But when he was handed the microphone during the halftime ceremony, he was Coach V again.

He hummed the State fight song, talked about how much he had loved coaching at N.C. State. All the anger he had felt when he had been forced out three years earlier was gone. He talked about what he had learned from cancer: "Don't ever, ever give up," and for the first time, he spoke the words that became iconic after his death: "Cancer cannot rob me of my mind, my heart, and my soul."

There weren't many dry eyes in the building by the time he finished. Nine days later, on March 3, Valvano was scheduled to fly to New York to accept the Arthur Ashe Award for Courage at the first ESPY Awards. The ESPYS are little more than a self-promotional vehicle for ESPN, a chance for the network to pat itself on the back and remind everyone how important it has become in the world of sports. The presence of Hollywood stars as presenters and hosts makes for extraordinarily awkward television every year.

That first year, though, Valvano produced eleven memorable minutes on a night when Raquel Welch famously awarded the 1993 ESPY for college player of the year to "Christine Laettner."

The fact that Valvano even made it onstage that night was a miracle in itself. Jim and Pam flew to New York that morning with Mike and Mickie Krzyzewski.

"I didn't see any way he was going to be able to stand up and speak," Krzyzewski said later. "He was *so* sick. I don't mean once or twice, I mean the entire flight."

At one point, thinking he was finally okay, Valvano returned to his seat—and promptly got sick all over Pam's expensive handbag.

"I thought, 'This is crazy, we shouldn't be here,' " Pam remembered. "He couldn't really walk, he could barely talk, he should have been in the hospital, not on an airplane to accept an award."

With Pam's help, Valvano managed to get his tuxedo on, but by the time that was done he had chills so violent that he huddled in bed, under the covers, shivering. John Saunders had come to see him, and when he walked in the room, even knowing how sick Jim was, he was shocked.

"You can't possibly do this," Saunders said. "You can't even get out of bed."

"I came this far, I've been sick all day," Valvano said, shaking as he spoke. "I'm going to do this."

And so he did. Dick Vitale introduced him. Before he went onstage, Valvano told Krzyzewski, "When I finish, you have to come and get me. I'll never make it down the [seven] steps without help."

Somehow, with the lights shining and the spotlight on him, Valvano turned what looked like an L into one of the great W's of his life. He looked both sad and tired as he waited for the ovation he had received while Vitale helped him onto the stage to quiet down. And then, for the last time, he became the room.

He started by blowing a heartfelt kiss to his wife. Then he said, "I'm going to speak longer than anyone else tonight. I don't know how much time I have left, so I'm going to cherish every minute I've got."

He talked about Krzyzewski, saying, "As great a coach as he is, he's ten times a better person."

At length, he retold the story about his first game as a coach—when he had just graduated from Rutgers and Bill Foster had hired him to coach the freshman team. He had read a book on Vince Lombardi in which Lombardi told the story about his first pregame pep talk after he had become coach of the Green Bay Packers.

"Lombardi said he waited until it was three minutes before the team was supposed to go onto the field," Valvano said. "Then he walked in, tore open the door to the locker room, pointed to the tunnel, and then turned and pointed a finger at them and said to his players, 'We will be successful this season if you devote yourselves to three things. First, your family. Second, your religion. And third . . . *the Green Bay Packers!*' The players raced through the door, won the game, and the rest is history.

"So I practiced my Lombardi speech. I was going to tell them, 'First your family, second your religion, and third . . . *Rutgers basketball!*' I paced up and down waiting for the clock to get down to three minutes. Finally, I walked inside and I went to the door to tear it open . . . It was locked. I fell flat on my face. But I got up and I turned to the players and I said, 'We will be successful this season if you devote yourselves to three things. First, your family. Second, your religion. And third . . . *the Green Bay Packers!*' "

He owned the room again.

He went on. He talked about his parents, Rocco and Angelina Valvano. He quoted his late father. And then he talked about his life. "I believe you should do three things every single day of your life," he said. "One, you should laugh. Two, you should think. Pause and think about your life. And third, you should cry. Get yourself into a state of emotion where you shed a tear. If you do all three of those things—laugh, think, and cry—well, that's one heck of a day."

Eight minutes into the speech, Valvano saw "thirty seconds" flashing at him in the teleprompter that he wasn't using. "Hey, look at that," he said. "Thirty seconds. Some guy is telling me I've got thirty seconds left. You think I *care* about some guy telling me I've got thirty seconds left? I've got tumors running all through my body and I'm supposed to care about a guy telling me I have thirty seconds left?"

He cursed in Italian.

By now he had become the room, one last time.

He finished with an eloquent plea to help raise more money for cancer research. "I am very proud to announce tonight that we are launching the Jimmy V Foundation for Cancer Research," he said. "Our motto will be 'Don't give up, don't ever give up.' It may not save my life, but it may save my children's lives."

He paused for the applause to die down. You could hear a pin drop.

"I hope in the time I have left that I can give some hope to others."

And then he repeated what he had said in Raleigh: "Cancer may rob me of my physical powers. But it cannot touch my mind, it cannot touch my heart, and it cannot touch my soul. Those parts of me will live on forever."

The audience stood and clapped and cheered and cried as Vitale and Krzyzewski helped him down the steps. He all but collapsed into Krzyzewski's arms as he reached his seat. When he sat down, Pam leaned over and gave him a kiss.

"Was I okay?" he asked her softly.

"Yes, honey, you were okay."

He closed his eyes, completely drained, and, with the cheers and applause still ringing in his ears, he passed out.

He had finally found The Next Thing. He had eight weeks to live.

29

Five days after the ESPYS speech, Jim Valvano appeared in public for the last time. The final game on his ABC schedule for the season was in Chapel Hill: Duke against North Carolina.

The Blue Devils were the two-time defending national champions, although clearly not the same team with Christian Laettner gone. Even so, they still had Bobby Hurley and Grant Hill, and they were ranked sixth in the country. They had beaten Carolina in Durham in early February, but the Tar Heels had won eight in a row since then and came into the game with the ACC regular season title already clinched and ranked number one in the nation. Dean Smith's team was loaded, led by center Eric Montross, forward George Lynch, and three excellent guards: Donald Williams, Brian Reese, and Derrick Phelps.

Even though there was nothing at stake in terms of the league standings—Carolina was 13–2 and Duke was 10–5—the Dean Dome was electric. Although Carolina had beaten Duke at home a year earlier, the Blue Devils had become the dominant team in the Triangle. They had now won three straight against the Tar Heels—and five of seven—but more important, Krzyzewski actually had one more national championship than Smith. To Carolina fans, that was a horrifying thought. It didn't exactly please Smith either.

Valvano felt very little of this. Much like with the ESPYS, he was there because he refused to *not* be there, even though he felt awful. He knew that there was an excellent chance this would be the last basketball game he ever worked—or, for that matter, the last basketball game he ever attended.

As the teams warmed up, he sat quietly at the announcers'

table, surrounded by security because so many people—especially after the ESPYS speech—wanted to say hello to him or wish him luck or tell him how moved they were by his words. Once, Valvano would have been at midcourt, glad-handing and chatting with everyone in the place. Now he sat with a sad look on his face and said, quietly, "I love being here for a game like this. I just wish I felt well enough to enjoy it. All I can really do is try to get through it."

Early in the game, Lenny Wirtz, the lead official, called Krzyzewski and Smith over to the scorer's table. It was clear to him—and everyone else in the building—that both coaches were wound tight.

"Look, guys, I know it's a big game, I get it," Wirtz said. "You've both got a lot of adrenaline pumping right now. But you've got to give us [the three officials] some space. Let us work the game."

Krzyzewski smiled at Wirtz. "Lenny, there's twenty-one thousand people in here and they're *all* against me," he said. "You three are the only ones I can talk to."

Wirtz smiled, maybe even laughed a little at the joke. Smith jumped in. "Lenny, you can't let him do that," he said. "You can't let him try to get you guys on his side by saying things like that."

Before Wirtz could say anything, Krzyzewski waved a hand at Smith and said, "Come on, Dean, stop it, just stop it."

He turned and walked back to his bench, shaking his head at Dean being Dean—or, as John Thompson would call it, "another Deanism."

"If I ever start to act like him, talk like him in any way," he told his assistants, "don't ask me any questions. Just get a gun and shoot me."

It was a heat-of-the-moment comment, but it reflected just how intense the relationship between the two men still was at that point. Smith had already been in the Basketball Hall of Fame for ten years; Krzyzewski's résumé was clearly Hall-of-Fame ready. But each still burned to beat the other. And Krzyzewski was just beginning to learn what it had been like to be Smith for so many years.

"Look, Dean and I are very different," Krzyzewski said. "I curse. He doesn't curse. I'm in your face, he's the master of the subtle shot. I've always said if I was ever president, I'd want Dean in charge of the CIA. The times we got into it on the court, we were both doing the same thing: trying to win a game *and* trying to protect our players.

"We couldn't *both* win the game. One thing I always knew, every single time I coached against him, was that it was going to be really hard to beat him. He was that good, and most of the time his players were that good. After those first couple of years I had really good players too. I wanted to make sure I did everything I could to give my players a chance to win. I didn't want to miss something or make a mistake that would give Dean and his players any edge, because if I did, we were probably going to lose. I would guess he came to feel the same way."

Smith always felt that way—regardless of the opponent. But, by that March afternoon in 1993, there's no doubt he felt it most keenly when Krzyzewski was on the other bench. Smith's team pulled away late that afternoon to win, 83–69, sending the Dean Dome into the kind of paroxysms of joy that—ironically—had rarely been felt until Duke became the kind of power it had become. Beating teams you beat all the time isn't nearly as much fun as beating teams who are difficult to beat.

As it turned out, that March was the worst one Krzyzewski had experienced since 1983. After the loss in Chapel Hill, the Blue Devils lost to Georgia Tech in the first round of the ACC Tournament—only the second time in ten seasons they'd failed to win at least one ACC Tournament game. The previous time, 1987, they had advanced to the Sweet 16 in the NCAA Tournament. Not this time. With Cherokee Parks, now the starting center and also a key player, hurt, Duke was upset by California—and Jason Kidd—in the second round of the NCAA Tournament.

Duke had been to six Final Fours in seven seasons and had lost in the round of sixteen in that seventh season. The early departure was surprising—but not stunning given Parks's injury and the fact that the team had played inconsistently that season.

"Grant and I had to take on the leadership mantle that season," Bobby Hurley said. "It wasn't always easy. As difficult as Christian [Laettner] could be at times, there was never any doubt about the fact that it was his team and he, almost as much as Coach—sometimes even more than Coach—demanded that we compete at a certain level all the time. That kind of thing didn't come as naturally to Grant and me. We had to take ownership of the team, and at times we struggled to do that."

How deep Duke might have gone if Parks had been healthy is hard to say. California, which would be placed on probation not long after its '93 success, lost in the next round to Kansas—which reached the Final Four.

"We missed Cherokee, but we just didn't have it that year," Krzyzewski said. "Bobby and Grant tried; in fact, Bobby had a great year. It was disappointing for me to see his career end the way it did because he meant so much to me and to Duke."

Krzyzewski broke down in the postgame press conference after the loss to Cal while talking about Hurley. It was only the second time he had cried publicly after a game. The first had come four years earlier after the regional final victory over Georgetown.

"Both times it was about my point guard," he said. "The kids who have played that position, from [Tommy] Amaker on, have always been very important to me. They're my coach on the court, and everything we do starts with them at both ends. I've always been close to them. Quin [Snyder] had gone through a lot to become the player he became. I think that's why I reacted the way I did after the Georgetown game. And Bobby?" He paused and shrugged. "I think I cried just because I realized I'd never coach him again."

—

There were no tears for Carolina that March—or April. Even after losing the ACC Tournament championship game to Georgia Tech—which became the fourth number-six seed to win the event (Virginia, 1976; Duke, 1980; N.C. State, 1987)—the Tar Heels went into the NCAA Tournament with a 28–4 record and were the top seed in the East Region.

They blew through three games before facing Cincinnati in the regional final in the Meadowlands. The Bearcats had reached the Final Four a year earlier and were led by Nick Van Exel, an audacious scorer—and talker. In the game's first fifteen minutes, Van Exel backed up his talk, draining six three-pointers. At that juncture he had outscored the Tar Heels 21–20 and his team led 33–20.

Smith made a defensive adjustment at that stage, telling Derrick Phelps to stay with Van Exel, regardless of what the Bearcats were doing offensively. No switches, no traps. In the game's final thirty minutes, Van Exel made one more basket, shooting 1 of 10 during the second half and overtime. It still took overtime, but Carolina survived, 75–68, meaning Smith would be going to the Final Four for the ninth time in his career.

After the game, the Tar Heels did a very un-Carolina-like thing. They refused to cut down the nets. The only nets they wanted, they all said in the locker room afterward, were the ones that would be used in the Superdome in New Orleans the following week.

"We may regret not doing it if we don't win next week," center Eric Montross said. "But the goal isn't to get to New Orleans, it's to win down there."

They did—and they did cut down the final nets, although it took another classic championship game to get Smith his second national title.

Carolina had to play Kansas in the semifinals, a rematch of the 1991 game in Indianapolis that had ended so disastrously for the Tar Heels—the game lost, Smith ejected by Pete Pavia. This time was different: Carolina controlled the second half and won

78–68, causing Williams to go into one of his third-person speeches, this one about the fact that "any of you who don't think Roy Williams won't be pulling for North Carolina harder than anyone Monday night doesn't know what Roy Williams is all about."

Monday night's opponent was Michigan, the same Fab Five that Duke had blown out in the championship game a year earlier. The Fabs were a year older now and had beaten Kentucky in an electric semifinal on Saturday night. They were as cocky as sophomores as they had been as freshmen. As the Wolverines made their way down the hallway to the court prior to the game, Chris Webber's voice could be heard clearly: "Hey, Michigan, did you hear, we're three-point underdogs. Should we even bother going out there? None of these folks have figured it out yet. They think y'all are going to lose. Are you gonna lose?"

Apparently folks had figured it out—Carolina won, 77–71, meaning those who had given the three points won their bets. Of course it wasn't nearly that simple. The game had gone back and forth. Michigan led 67–63 with 4:32 left, but Donald Williams hit a critical three-pointer to cut the margin to 67–66. The Tar Heels actually went on a 9–0 run to lead 72–67 with just under a minute to play. But baskets by Ray Jackson and Webber cut the lead to 72–71. With twenty-four seconds to go, Michigan fouled Pat Sullivan. He made the first for a 73–71 lead but missed the second. Webber rebounded.

At that moment, the entire Michigan team went brain dead. It began when Jalen Rose, the point guard, ran down the court rather than coming back to take the ball from Webber. Carolina trapped Webber, who, spinning to look for help, traveled. The refs missed it. The entire Carolina bench leaped to its feet screaming.

Webber began weaving his way upcourt, still with no guard help, and, as he got near the top of the key, was trapped again—by Phelps and George Lynch. Once again, he traveled. Once again, no call. But he was still trapped and was going to commit a turnover. Realizing he was in serious trouble, Webber put his hands together to signal for a time-out with eleven seconds left.

Except Michigan didn't have any time-outs left. It had used its last one after Jackson's basket with forty-six seconds to go. As soon as Webber signaled for the time-out, the Carolina players on the court began jumping up and down, making a T sign of their own—for a technical foul. *They* knew Michigan had no time-outs left. Webber, in his panic, had forgotten.

Coming out of the last time-out, Michigan coach Steve Fisher had reminded his players they had no time-outs left. Smith had told *his* players that the Wolverines had no time-outs left. The difference was that Smith's players listened. Listening wasn't really in Webber's repertoire. After the game he said he heard teammates yelling "Time-out!" from the bench. That's entirely possible.

Williams went to the foul line and made both free throws. Then, after Carolina inbounded because it had possession following the technical, Williams was fouled and made two more. Ballgame. Championship. It was Webber's last college game. The Fab Five ended up coming four national titles short of the number each had predicted they would win at the Sunday press conference a year earlier.

Neither Smith nor anyone from Carolina cared very much about that. After having to watch Duke cut down the nets two straight Aprils, it was now—finally—their turn again. Krzyzewski, who was working for CBS that weekend, grabbed a couple of cheerleader pom-poms and helped lead the Carolina students in a couple of cheers.

There was only one small problem: the awards ceremony. In 1991, Duke's first championship season, the NCAA had decided to stage an on-court awards ceremony. In the past, the winning team had simply cut down the nets and, at some point, the championship trophy was shipped to campus.

Now, for the benefit of television, a stage was quickly put together at midcourt and the chairman of the basketball committee presented the trophy to the winning coach with the players standing behind him in NCAA-logo T-shirts and caps that were handed out at game's end with *orders* to put them on instantly.

When the NCAA drones informed Smith that he would be presented with the trophy, he said, "Oh no, not me, give it to the captains."

No, he was informed, that's not the way we do it. Not only will you accept the trophy, you will be expected to say a few words after it is handed to you—and please be sure to thank the basketball committee for doing such a wonderful job putting on the tournament.

"I was actually angry about it," Smith said a few years later. "At the very least, it should have been our option to decide who accepted the trophy." He smiled. "I certainly wasn't thanking anyone other than my players if they insisted I take the microphone."

They did. Smith took the mic and talked for exactly five seconds. "I'm very proud of our players for winning this championship," he said. He turned and handed the trophy to George Lynch, the team's most prominent senior, and all but threw the microphone back to Tom Butters, who—in a twist—was chairman of the basketball committee that year.

In the end, the trophy ended up where Smith most wanted it to be: back in Chapel Hill. No longer did he or any of the Carolina faithful have to hear from the Duke people that Krzyzewski had won more national titles than Smith.

Carolina would return four starters the following season and would add two gifted freshmen, Rasheed Wallace and Jerry Stackhouse. Perhaps the tide had turned—again.

—

One week after (grudgingly) accepting the championship trophy in New Orleans, Dean Smith was in New York. He was there at the request of Jim Valvano.

There was no such thing as a bucket list in 1993—the movie that made the phrase a part of the lexicon wasn't released until fourteen years later—but Valvano had said on several occasions that one of his dreams had always been to throw out a first pitch at Yankee Stadium. Shortly after the ESPYS speech, Valvano was at home one evening talking to his brother Nick when the phone rang. It was George Steinbrenner.

The Yankees owner had heard what Valvano had said and wanted to invite him to come to Yankee Stadium on April 12 to throw out the ceremonial first pitch on Opening Day. The Yankees would begin the season with six games on the road and then return home for Opening Day at Yankee Stadium. Valvano was floored by the phone call. He also knew that the chances of him getting to New York again and making it out to the mound to throw a pitch were somewhere between slim and none—with none the heavy betting favorite. He thanked Steinbrenner and told him he would be there if it was at all possible.

"He hung up the phone and said to me, 'There's no way I can go and do that, you go in my place,'" Nick remembered. "I said, 'That's ridiculous. He invited you. If you can't go, you explain that you can't go, or if there's someone it might mean a lot to, who Steinbrenner wouldn't mind having do it, send him.'"

Valvano knew almost instantly whom he wanted to send in his place: Dean Smith.

Like Valvano, Smith had grown up a Yankees fan even though Emporia, Kansas, was a long way from the Bronx. Beyond that, Steinbrenner had close ties to Carolina: his daughter had gone to school there, he'd given a lot of money to the baseball program, and the Yankees had frequently stopped in Chapel Hill en route north at the end of spring training to play an exhibition game there. Since Smith and Steinbrenner knew each other it made sense to Valvano to ask Smith to stand in for him.

"I think Dean might have been reluctant when Jim first called him," Nick said. "But then Jim said, 'It would mean a lot to me if you did it.' That did it—Dean said yes."

And so, on the twelfth of April, Smith walked to the mound in front of 56,704 fans as Valvano's stand-in. He received a warm, loud ovation—one that he knew was both for Valvano and for him. The Yankees won that day with Jim Abbott pitching a complete game.

Not long before Smith's death, Linnea Smith talked about that afternoon.

"It meant a lot to Dean to have the chance to do it," she said. "Especially to do it for Jim. In our house, we have pictures all over of Dean with children and grandchildren and with former players and close friends. There's only one picture on a wall in the entire house that's just Dean. It's him, throwing that pitch. That's how much it meant to him."

———

By the time Smith threw that pitch in Yankee Stadium, Valvano was in Duke Hospital. He had been there most of the time since the ESPYS speech, going home for brief respites when the walls of the hospital felt like they were closing in on him.

Mike Krzyzewski had visited Valvano throughout the basketball season whenever he was in the hospital. Cameron Indoor Stadium and the hospital were at opposite ends of the Duke campus, but, more often than not, Krzyzewski would walk through campus rather than drive around it to get to the hospital. It gave him time to think—both before he went in to see his sick friend and after he had sat next to the bed for an hour or so and talked or listened or, just as often, laughed.

"Jim never stopped being funny," Krzyzewski said. "He would get going on something, and it was as if he was in front of an audience, even lying there with tubes and machines all over the place. There were times we would laugh so hard and so loud that the nurse would come in and say, 'What's going on here?' We'd just wave her out of the room and Jim would keep on going."

Jim and Pam both recognized the importance of Krzyzewski's visits, especially when the in-hospital stretches became longer than the out-of-hospital stretches. Many years later, Pam Valvano Strasser's voice got very soft remembering those evenings and those visits.

"When Mike came over, for that hour or so when he was in the room, Jim didn't have cancer anymore," she said. "He was a

basketball coach again. He and Mike would sit there and tell stories or Jim would do his Dean imitation [everyone *did* do Dean]
or they'd talk strategy. It had to be Mike in that room. It couldn't
be someone who wasn't a coach, no matter how close they were
to Jim. And it couldn't be just *any* coach, it had to be a truly great
coach, someone Jim really respected, someone who Jim knew had
done everything that he'd ever done and, in Mike's case, more."

John Saunders visited as often as possible. He saw the exact
same thing that Pam saw. "Mike was like an angel who God had
sent to help Jim get through this," he said. "I'm not trying to
sound overly spiritual but his presence was beyond important to
Jim."

Pam remembers sitting in the room one night with Jamie, the
Valvanos' middle daughter, when Krzyzewski walked in. "You
could see the joy in Jim's face the minute Mike walked in," she
said. "We left. I always left the two of them alone when Mike
came, and Jamie said to me, 'What are we, chopped liver?' I had
to try to explain to her that wasn't it. Mike just had a special role,
a very special role, during those days."

Those days were important to Krzyzewski too—although he
didn't fully grasp how important until much later.

"It wasn't something I thought about, as in, 'Oh, I have to go
see Jim,' " he said. "I *wanted* to see him, in part because I enjoyed
it most of the time. When we'd talk, I forgot he had cancer too. He
was still Jim—still funny, still unbelievably smart and thoughtful.
Sometimes we'd laugh and sometimes we'd cry. Jim had moments
when I knew he still thought he was going to beat it somehow,
that he wasn't going to die. I had those moments too. But then
there were times when it hit both of us and we'd sit there and cry.

"But that wasn't really why it was important to me. I was doing
something for someone else for no reason at all other than I knew
he needed me. When you do something like that, when there's no
motive or reason to do it, other than it's the right thing to do, it
means as much to you as to the person you're trying to help."

As much as Valvano clung to hope for a miracle, he continued to plan for the nonmiracle. He made Krzyzewski promise that he would take the lead in making the V Foundation real and viable. ESPN had pledged money and its marketing power to the cause, but Valvano knew his famous friends would have to carry much of the load to raise serious money.

The last time Saunders visited him, most of the visit was consumed with Valvano giving him instructions on who was to be on the board of directors and what role he wanted each of them to play. "At one point he started to talk about Mike," Saunders said. "And he just said, 'You'll never know what he's meant to me,' and he broke down."

The last time the two coaches talked was a few hours before Valvano died.

"The doctor told me before I went in that it was very close," Krzyzewski said. "He said I should walk in thinking this would be the last time I would talk to Jim."

Valvano knew too. He couldn't talk long because he was so weak, but he told Krzyzewski whom he wanted to speak at his funeral and how much he had meant to him in the final months. "We said things to one another that I'm not sure brothers say to each other," Krzyzewski said. "Those last few weeks, that last night make me cry whenever I think of them, but I cherish them too."

On April 28, 1993, on a spectacular spring morning in North Carolina, Jim Valvano died. His family was with him and so was Mike Krzyzewski.

One last time, Krzyzewski made the walk from the hospital across campus and back to his office. He sat in a chair and said quietly, "It's good for Jim that it's over."

What he didn't understand at that moment was that for him, it was far from over. Valvano's death—and the way he died—would stay with him for a long time.

be starting and playing major minutes. On the basis of sheer talent, that was probably true. But Smith wasn't about to take playing time away from juniors and seniors—especially juniors and seniors who had been an important part of a national championship team—in favor of freshmen, regardless of their talent.

At their best, the Tar Heels were very formidable. In fact, they easily won both meetings with Duke that season. But they managed to stumble often enough against less-talented teams that Duke had a two-game lead in the conference standings when the teams met in Durham in the regular season finale. Carolina won the game, 87–77, causing Duke assistant coach Mike Brey to say, "They hate us so much that they forget how much they hate each other when they play us."

Hyperbole? Perhaps—but not by much.

Earlier in the season, when Maryland played at Carolina, Gary Williams had taken his team to the Dean Dome for a game-day shootaround. Carolina was finishing its shootaround as the Maryland players walked in the direction of the court.

"We're coming on while they're coming off," Williams remembered. "As soon as Rasheed [Wallace] hit the tunnel, I heard him say, 'Free at last, free at last.' I didn't have the sense they were a happy group."

If there was one thing Smith disliked as much as losing, it was any kind of dissension within the ranks. Carolina managed to play well in the ACC Tournament, beating Virginia in the final after the Cavaliers had upset Duke in the semifinals. Winning the ACC Tournament made the Tar Heels the number-one seed in the East Region of the NCAA Tournament. Duke went to the Southeast as the number-two seed behind Purdue.

It appeared that Carolina was getting its act together at exactly the right time. Stackhouse had played so well off the bench in the ACC Tournament that he had been voted the MVP. Maybe, the media speculated, Smith had found the balance at just the right time.

He hadn't. Carolina actually struggled for much of its first-round game in Landover, Maryland, against sixteenth-seeded Liberty. Then, facing ninth-seeded Boston College, the Tar Heels fell behind and couldn't make one of their Houdini-like escapes. BC center Bill Curley outplayed all the Carolina big men, with 25 points and 10 rebounds. The Eagles hung on to win, 75–72. It was the first time since 1980 that Carolina had failed to reach the round of sixteen.

In the meantime, it turned out to be Duke that was finding new life at the right time. It hadn't been an easy winter for Krzyzewski. He wasn't feeling especially good because his back was bothering him. His team was inconsistent. The two losses to Carolina rankled, as did the semifinal loss to Virginia in the ACC Tournament. Standing in a corner of his locker room after that game, Krzyzewski said, "Good for the Virginia kids. They deserved to win the game. They showed up to play. We didn't."

But, once again, Duke showed up to play when the bright lights of March were turned on. They hardly looked dominant in a first-round win over Texas Southern, but they played superbly to beat Michigan State in the second round. They moved on to Knoxville, where they beat Marquette—the Warriors had upset Kentucky in the second round, denying CBS a rematch of the Philadelphia Classic of 1992—and then beat top-seeded Purdue in the regional final. Grant Hill outplayed national player of the year Glenn Robinson in the game, but the real differences were Capel, who scored 19 points—11 above his season's average—and Antonio Lang, who also scored 19 and helped Hill hold Robinson to 13 points (on 6-of-22 shooting), which was 18 points below his season average.

Remarkably, Duke was in the Final Four for the seventh time in nine seasons. The Blue Devils went on to beat Florida—which had taken out Boston College in the East Region final—in the national semifinals but came up just short of a third national championship in four years, losing the title game to Arkansas, 76–72.

Even so, Krzyzewski was once again the toast of college basketball. Only John Wooden—who was in another stratosphere when it came to NCAA play—had ever put together a run better than Krzyzewski's. UCLA had not only reached the Final Four eleven times in twelve seasons, from 1964 to 1975 it had *won* on ten occasions. Wooden had been to twelve Final Fours; Smith had been to nine. Krzyzewski was now third in line with seven—and had just turned forty-seven. Smith was still going strong but was sixty-three.

Krzyzewski wasn't sure he was going to come back to go for Final Four number eight. He hadn't been especially happy that winter, in part because of the pain in his back, but also because he—and Mickie—were both hit with wanderlust.

Krzyzewski had given serious consideration to leaving Duke only once. That had been in the spring of 1990, when the Boston Celtics were looking for a coach and Dave Gavitt, who had left his job as Big East commissioner to take over the Celtics, contacted Krzyzewski. Gavitt wanted Krzyzewski to meet with Red Auerbach—the iconic coach, general manager, and then team president—to talk about the job.

The Bulls hadn't been invented as Chicago's NBA team until 1966. By then, Krzyzewski was at West Point. His team as a kid had been the Celtics for the simple reason that they were the NBA's dominant team.

"To be honest, I'd have probably flown to Washington to have the chance to have lunch with Red even if I had *zero* interest in the job," Krzyzewski said. "I did have interest, though, because it was the Celtics, it was Dave, and it was Red."

Krzyzewski asked Auerbach if the meeting could be quiet and private. He didn't want anyone at Duke or in the media getting any ideas until and unless he had serious interest in the job. "He said, 'No problem, kid, leave it to me. I'll pick you up at the airport.'"

Auerbach was as good as his word—at least the part about picking him up at the airport. "He rolled up in a silver Mercedes with a license plate that said 'Celtic' on it," Krzyzewski said, laughing at the memory. "Then he took me to a restaurant where everyone—I mean *everyone*—knew him."

There were few places in Washington that Auerbach could go where everyone didn't know him. He had lived there since getting out of the navy in 1946 and taking the job as coach of the Washington Caps in what was then the fledgling Basketball Association of America—later known as the National Basketball Association. Even after becoming the coach in Boston in 1950, Auerbach and his family had maintained their residence in Washington because Nancy, his oldest daughter, had a serious case of asthma and her doctor did not think she would do very well spending winters in Boston.

Saying no to Auerbach and Gavitt wasn't easy for Krzyzewski. But he felt the job at Duke still wasn't finished, because he hadn't yet won the national championship. And the recent memory of the 103–73 Vegas humiliation was still front and center in his mind's eye. "I couldn't walk away with that loss following me," he said. "If the timing had been different, I don't know what I would have done. But the timing wasn't different."

Four years later, both the timing and the circumstances were different. Krzyzewski had won two national championships. He wondered if maybe he needed to start fresh, find a new challenge. Mickie thought it might be time to leave Duke. She felt her husband was being taken for granted by the people running the school.

"It had gotten to the point where it was, 'Oh, okay, you made the Final Four again—but why didn't you win the national championship?'" she said. "It felt as if they'd forgotten all the work that had gone into getting where we were."

Mickie Krzyzewski was so convinced her husband's time at Duke was over that one of her first comments after the Arkansas game was, "It would have been nice for Mike to win one more championship before leaving."

The offers were certainly there: the Miami Heat wanted him

and so did the Portland Trail Blazers. NBA commissioner David Stern called to encourage Krzyzewski to take one of the two jobs. Mike and Mickie finally went away for a week to talk the whole thing through, take a deep breath, and think about it.

"When I thought about it, I just didn't want to leave," Krzyzewski said. "I realized that Duke wasn't perfect—but neither was I. I love Duke and I love doing the kind of work I do. I like the idea that I can have a positive effect on the kids I coach. If that sounds corny, so be it."

No one at Duke thought it was corny. Tom Butters even got a good laugh out of the whole thing.

"I got all sorts of letters, just like I had in 1990, from boosters telling me I *had* to find a way to keep Mike," he said. "They said, 'Pay him whatever it takes—we'll raise the money for it.'" Butters smiled at the memory. "A lot of those letters came from the same people who had written to me in 1983 and 1984 telling me they'd have my head on a platter if I didn't fire the SOB."

Another smile. "I keep them at home—all in the same box."

—

By the time practice began in October, Krzyzewski's back was so painful he couldn't stand up from the start of practice until the finish. He finally agreed to let the doctors run more tests, and, sure enough, they found a torn disc in his lower back. The only way to fix it was through surgery.

The diagnosis didn't thrill Krzyzewski. He knew he had a team that needed a lot of improvement before the season began. But he also knew he had no choice: he wasn't helping his players by being in constant pain every day. On October 22, he had the surgery. The doctors told him to rest for a month. He was back at practice in two weeks.

"During that whole period, his army mentality kicked in," Mickie said. "He has always believed in mind over matter. If you're sick and you tell yourself you aren't sick, then you won't be sick. If your doctors tell you that you can't stand for two hours a day a few weeks after back surgery, you *can* stand for two hours a day by not thinking about how much your back hurts."

Under the best of circumstances, Krzyzewski knew he was facing a tough season. Grant Hill and Antonio Lang had graduated. Steve Wojciechowski and Trajan Langdon had been added to a solid backcourt of Jeff Capel and Chris Collins, but none of them would have Hill there to take pressure off them on the defensive end and free them for shots on the offensive end. Cherokee Parks was now a senior and he had NBA talent. But he was as easygoing as Laettner had been intense and simply wasn't the guy who was going to win games just by the force of his personality. There were solid role players like Ricky Price, Erik Meek, and Kenny Blakeney, but that's exactly what they were—role players.

There was no one who compared to Laettner, Bobby Hurley, or Grant Hill.

"We could have been a good team that year, though not a great one," Krzyzewski said. "But it was a team that needed me to be one hundred percent every single day. I was never one hundred percent, and in the end I was zero percent."

The Blue Devils were 7–1 and ranked number seven nationally (as much on reputation as anything else) when they went to Hawaii to play in the post-Christmas Rainbow Classic. They lost their first-round game to an unranked Iowa team before winning their two games in the consolation bracket. The loss to Iowa turned out to be the least of Krzyzewski's concerns. On the long plane trip home, he stood most of the way because sitting down was too painful. He was still in mind-over-matter mode, but his mind was starting to lose the battle.

Five days later, the Blue Devils opened ACC play against Clemson and first-year coach Rick Barnes. The students weren't back from break yet, and Cameron Indoor Stadium felt like the Dean Dome Lite. The team needed to get the crowd going and it never did. Clemson won easily—the final score was a deceiving 75–70—one of the worst home losses Duke had suffered in a long time.

By then, Krzyzewski wasn't sleeping at all. He was in too much pain. He had come back too soon and not taken care of himself well enough. Two days after the Clemson loss, Duke was scheduled to practice at one o'clock and then fly to Georgia Tech for a game on Saturday. When Mike came downstairs that morning, he found Mickie waiting for him in the kitchen. The look on his wife's face told him right away that she meant business.

"I've made a doctor's appointment for you at two o'clock this afternoon," she said. "That's the earliest he can see you."

"I've got practice at one and then we're flying to Atlanta."

Mickie took a deep breath. She understood that her marriage of almost twenty-six years had never faced a crisis quite like this one.

"Mike, if you don't show up at the doctor's office, I'm leaving you," she said. "You can't go on like this. You can't keep doing this to yourself, to me, to the girls—to everyone in your life. You aren't well. You can't coach this team in the condition you're in. You *have* to go to the doctor and you *have* to go today. You can't go to Atlanta."

Mike listened, watching his wife's face as she spoke. He knew she wasn't bluffing. "I have to go," he said, not telling her whether he was going to get on the plane or show up at the doctor's office.

At two o'clock, Mickie arrived at the doctor's office, terrified. "What if he didn't show up?" she said. "What did I do then? I didn't want to leave him, but if he went to Atlanta and I didn't do something about it, then where were we? More important, where was he? I didn't think there was anyone else who was going to tell him he couldn't coach. It had to be me."

As she pulled up to the office, she saw something that brought tears to her eyes: Mike's car. He had taken her seriously. Not only did he know she was right, but he loved her enough to not call her bluff. The Blue Devils went to Atlanta without their coach.

They had no idea that he would not coach again that season.

31

The news at the doctor's office that afternoon wasn't very good. Mike's back hadn't healed properly because he had pushed it too hard too soon and because he hadn't rehabbed enough. What's more, he was in a complete state of collapse from lack of sleep, from fighting off pain, and from the tension he had been feeling, knowing that he couldn't coach his team the way it needed to be coached.

He needed more tests, he needed complete rest, and he needed to not think about basketball for a while. How long? he asked.

"The doctor said, 'You won't get better until you stop worrying about your team and just worry about yourself,'" Mickie remembered. "That certainly wasn't the answer Mike wanted to hear."

Duke put out a statement that Krzyzewski hadn't made the trip to Georgia Tech and was taking an indefinite leave of absence because of his health. Pete Gaudet would be the coach until Krzyzewski came back. No one knew when that would be. Krzyzewski went back into the hospital two days after Mickie forced him to see the doctor and underwent a battery of tests to try to find out why he was still in so much pain.

Krzyzewski was convinced he knew the answer.

"I thought I had the same thing as Jimmy," he said. "I was forty-seven; I had terrible pain in my back that surgery hadn't fixed. I was in Duke Hospital and I had three daughters. All just like him. I thought I had cancer and I was going to die, just like Jimmy had."

He didn't have cancer. He simply hadn't allowed the disc to heal completely and he needed to rest it—not a little, a lot—and not for only a couple of weeks.

"For two weeks I kept asking the doctors, 'How soon can I coach again?'" he said. "They kept telling me I had to be patient, it was going to take a while. I didn't have a while. My team needed me."

He was right about that. In Krzyzewski's absence, the Blue Devils lost their next five games, dropping them to 0–6 in the ACC. No Duke team had ever been 0–6 in the ACC. One loss was in double overtime to Virginia. In fact, almost all the games were close, the exception being an embarrassing 77–60 blowout loss at home to N.C. State.

On January 22, the message Krzyzewski's doctors had been trying to get him to understand finally clicked into focus: "I had no chance to get back until I stopped trying to get back," he said. "I had to know in my mind that I wasn't going to coach again that season so I could think about getting better, not about getting back."

That day, on Krzyzewski's orders, Duke announced that he wouldn't coach again the rest of the season. For the first time in more than two weeks, Krzyzewski met with his players to explain why he had decided that he couldn't return that winter. He told them he had complete faith in their coaches—Gaudet, Tommy Amaker, Mike Brey, and Chuck Swenson (who had returned to Duke after a stint as the head coach at William and Mary). The meeting was funereal. There was nothing to be said that would make anyone feel any better.

The person who felt worst was Krzyzewski. This was his fault. He had let his players down. The military training kicked in again. "If the leader can't lead his troops into battle, then he has to step down," he said. "I'd failed my troops. The only honorable thing for me to do was step down—resign."

He went to see Tom Butters, intending to resign. The two men had known each other and worked together for fifteen years. Butters knew before Krzyzewski got to his house that his coach was going to try to resign.

"That's who Mike is," Butters said. "He's the ultimate leader.

Failure always falls on the leader. The Roman generals always fell on their own swords when they'd been defeated. He had left his men on the battlefield without him, and they were getting blown up, beaten up. I knew he felt defeated, I knew he was going to try and fall on his own sword.

"And there was no way I was going to let him do it."

Butters listened while Krzyzewski explained to him why he thought the best thing to do—the honorable thing for him to do—was resign. He had failed his players, he had failed Butters, and he had failed Duke.

"Mike, let me ask you a question: Who do you think I could hire to coach this basketball team, this group of kids, next season who is going to do a better job than you?" Butters asked. "What possible reason could I have to want any coach other than you?

"Your job *now* is to get better. And when you're better, you are the only person I want as my basketball coach."

Krzyzewski was stunned—and touched. He started to cry.

"I honestly thought Tom would accept my resignation," he said. "I thought it just made sense. He was paying me to coach and I couldn't coach. He needed to find someone else to do the job I wasn't doing.

"But when he responded the way he did, I thought to myself, 'He's right. I need to get better and I need to come back and coach my team.' That was the only way to make things right."

From that moment on, Krzyzewski began to get better. He spent many hours with H. Keith Brodie, Duke's president, who also happened to be a psychiatrist. He watched the games on television at home. When Duke finally broke the six-game losing streak with a win at Notre Dame, Krzyzewski got in his car, drove to Cameron, and left a message for the team on the whiteboard in the locker room, telling them how proud he was of them and that good things were ahead.

"I wanted them to know that even though I wasn't physically with them, I was still with them and they were in my thoughts all the time," Krzyzewski said. "That was important to me and, I think, to them too."

While Krzyzewski was away from his team, all sorts of wild rumors circulated: he had cancer; he and Mickie had split; he would never coach again; he'd had a nervous breakdown. Throughout, Krzyzewski took phone calls from a few friends, assured them he was okay and that the rumors weren't true.

"I *am* crazy," he said at one point in early February. "But no crazier than I've been for a long time now."

What had been a fragile team at the start of the season became a broken team. The Blue Devils simply couldn't win close games. They lost twice to Maryland—a team that hadn't beaten Duke since 1988, a fifteen-game streak—each time by two points. They lost by one to Wake Forest, and they lost a classic game to North Carolina in double overtime in Cameron, blowing a thirteen-point lead in the last four minutes of regulation. The players were confused. They had signed on to play for Krzyzewski. He wasn't there. Maybe he was coming back next season or maybe he wasn't.

"The truth is nobody knew," Mike Brey said. "The plan was for Mike to come back, but the plan had also been for him to be healthy after the surgery. I remember one day Dr. Brodie asked Pete, Tommy, Chuck, and I to come to his office to talk. I said to him directly, 'Are you sure Mike K. is coming back?' And he said, 'I can't tell you that for sure.' That was pretty chilling for all of us to hear."

The person who suffered the most through all the losses was Gaudet. He felt as if he was letting Krzyzewski down by not winning more often. "It was a lot to take on," he said years later. "It's not a fluke that Mike has the record he has. We could have used him, especially during those close games. He always brought a unique sense of confidence that the players felt. It mattered.

"Plus, we were all in different roles. The guys weren't used to my voice in the locker room, in the huddles. Mike, Tommy, and Chuck had to do a lot of what I normally did. We were all out of place."

The best example of Krzyzewski's importance in the huddle had been the Kentucky game three seasons earlier. To this day, every player in that huddle with 2.1 seconds left remembers Krzyzewski's first words: "We're going to win the damn game."

Grant Hill still shakes his head at that memory. "We all walked to the bench thinking it was over, we were going on spring break," he said. "He asked two questions: 'Grant, can you make the pass?' I said, 'Absolutely.' Then he said, 'Christian, can you make the shot?' Christian just looked at him as if he couldn't believe he'd even asked. We walked back on the court convinced we were going to win. And we did."

Gaudet was a very good basketball coach. He probably knew as much about coaching big men as anyone in the sport. He's written widely read books on the topic. But, as he himself pointed out, he wasn't Krzyzewski. What's more, with Gaudet in the role of head coach, the staff wasn't as deep as it had been. Everyone's role had changed.

What had become the college basketball program everyone aspired to be for the past nine years was now a soap opera—a bad one.

After the double-overtime loss to Virginia, Doug Collins, the NBA Hall of Famer whose son Chris was a junior, burst into the coaches' locker room screaming at Gaudet for the way he was utilizing his players and for the team's inability to win a close game. Collins's frustration was understandable. But there was no way he would have pulled something like that on Krzyzewski.

"We were hurting in a lot of different ways," Brey remembered. "Not only did we not know if Mike was coming back, we had no way of knowing if he was going to want all of *us* back. You knew watching us lose all those games wasn't making him happy. It couldn't possibly make him happy."

Even Brey, usually calm and mild mannered, lost it on one occasion. "Pete tended to be clinical with the guys," he said. "He would calmly tell them what we needed to do better. There weren't any theatrics the way you got with Mike sometimes.

"One night, we're getting our asses kicked, I can't even remember who we were playing. But he's kind of calmly walking through what adjustments we're going to make and I couldn't take it anymore. I jumped up and said, 'F—— that, Pete, f—— that! Enough with all the whining and feeling sorry for ourselves and making excuses. Go out and play like f——ing men!"

They went out and lost.

And, in fact, the losing did make Krzyzewski angry. He knew if he came back some things had to change. He did think about reshaping his staff. He also thought about reshaping his own life. He couldn't continue to say yes to every request he got, whether it was from the media, from a coach looking for a job, or from a charity looking for a big-name speaker. Things that took up time, like the standard weekly radio show most coaches did, needed to go. His time had to be protected.

"I never wanted to be that guy—the one who always said no," he said. "But I couldn't go on being the guy who always said yes. I had to learn how to say no. It wasn't easy, because it went against my nature."

Other coaches called to check up on him. Bobby Cremins called so often that Mickie finally told him she would call him when there was anything new to report.

"When he wasn't there, the sport wasn't as good as when he was there," Dean Smith said two years later. "We played a great game against them in Durham, but I wanted to beat them when they were at their best. Duke wasn't at its best without him coaching."

That was clear by season's end. The Blue Devils had been 9–3—albeit against a fairly soft schedule—on the morning when Mickie gave Mike her ultimatum. They went 4–15 the rest of the season, finishing dead last in the ACC with a 3–13 record. The same school that had played in the national championship game a year earlier played in the Les Robinson game in March 1995.

Naturally, the game was against Les Robinson's team. Duke won, and Brey joked, "Well, fellas, I guess we can say we made the tournament."

They had made the quarterfinals of the ACC Tournament. A day later, they were blown out by top-seeded Wake Forest and the season came to a merciful end. The overall record was 13–18. It would be the only season in a thirty-two-season stretch, beginning in 1984, that Duke would fail to make the NCAA Tournament.

"It couldn't end soon enough," Tommy Amaker said. "We kept hearing Dick Vitale saying the NIT should take Duke even with a record under five hundred because it was Duke. We'd all scream at the TV set, 'No, no, no. Please let this end.'"

During the ACC Tournament, Krzyzewski, sitting in his house, was piped into team meetings at the Greensboro Marriott on a speakerphone.

"The intent was good," Brey said. "The effect was borderline eerie."

Once the season ended, Krzyzewski returned to work—meeting with the coaches, making preparations for summer recruiting. His back was healed and so were his mind and his heart. He was healthy. And he was angry.

—

Mike Brey's notion that Krzyzewski wouldn't just shake off the losses with a "Nice try, fellas" proved to be correct. The victim of his frustration turned out to be Gaudet. Krzyzewski knew the losses weren't his fault—he'd been thrown into a completely impossible situation. But he also knew that one of the reasons the team Gaudet had coached hadn't been able to handle Krzyzewski's absence was because it wasn't as talented as the teams that had gone to seven Final Fours in nine seasons.

Krzyzewski decided his staff needed to get younger—especially when it came to getting on the recruiting trail.

"Some of it was on me," he said. "I probably hadn't paid close enough attention to who we were taking the way we had in the years past. We had gotten to the point where we were a little bit like Carolina: we had a lot of kids who wanted to come to Duke. In some cases, we didn't do enough research when the kids said they wanted to come. They were all highly rated. Most were McDonald's All-Americans, so we just said, 'Come on ahead.'

"We needed to get back to knowing the players we were recruiting intimately again. And we needed to beat the bushes a little more, find the kid who wasn't that highly rated—like a Thomas Hill or a David Henderson—who would turn out to be a terrific player.

"Pete was hugely important to our success. It wasn't a coincidence that we got good and then got better when he joined the staff. He was my wise old head, the guy who had seen as much or more than me. While I was away it occurred to me that I was the wise old head now. I needed younger guys to push me, keep my energy level up as high as possible. If ninety-five taught me one thing it was that there was no margin for error. If we slipped even a little, people were going to be there to jump on us."

Krzyzewski's decision to let Gaudet go shocked everyone—including Gaudet. It certainly sent a message to everyone in the program that the coach who was coming back wasn't going to be messing around.

Gaudet's departure in May made him the second coach to leave. The first had been Brey, who had accepted the head coaching job at Delaware shortly after the season ended.

While Krzyzewski had agonized about Gaudet, he didn't want Brey to leave. Brey had been with him for eight seasons and, with Gaudet leaving, would be his most experienced assistant—and recruiter.

"When the Delaware thing came up in late February, my gut told me this was the time to leave," Brey said. "It had been eight years and I thought I was ready. Plus, I thought Delaware was a very good job for me."

Krzyzewski didn't agree. He wasn't the least bit happy when Brey told him he was thinking of leaving.

"Part of it was that C. M. Newton [then the athletic director at Kentucky] had been the one who recommended me to [Delaware president] David Roselle," Brey said. "They had a relationship because Roselle had been at Kentucky. Mike likes to be the one who mentors his guys through job decisions. He didn't think Delaware was the right job for me—that I could wait a year and do better. Plus, I think he was nervous about coming back. He had made a decision on Pete, but that was the only change he wanted to make. He didn't want two openings."

Brey and Krzyzewski talked about the Delaware job on a recruiting trip to an AAU tournament in Maryland shortly after the season ended. From there, Krzyzewski flew home while Brey made the drive to Delaware for a final interview.

"I took the job while I was there," he said. "I called Mike to tell him and he said, 'Well, you better come on back and tell the team.' That was it. He was angry. By the time I saw him that summer, though, he was fine. He understood.

"When we won the America East Tournament a couple of years later [1998] to get to the NCAA Tournament, the first voice mail waiting for me was from Mike K. Didn't surprise me. And I know he was thrilled when I got the Notre Dame job. He's changed a lot—evolved—which has kept him fresh and young. But when it comes to relationships, he's never changed."

—

Krzyzewski hired Quin Snyder to replace Brey—actually promoted him. Snyder had been working as a graduate assistant while finishing dual postgraduate degrees: an MBA and a law degree. That meant that both assistant coaches on the road recruiting would be former Krzyzewski players: Amaker and Snyder. As it turned out, Brey was the *last* non-Duke graduate to recruit on behalf of Krzyzewski.

The second hire was Tim O'Toole, who had been a part-time assistant coach under Krzyzewski's friend Jim Boeheim at Syracuse. O'Toole was thirty—twenty-three years younger than Gaudet—and brought over-the-top passion to every room he walked into. Which was what Krzyzewski wanted.

Even so, Duke needed a rebuild—shocking as it seemed—in the spring of 1995.

Krzyzewski's return was a relief for the players, but the team he would coach that fall would be a shadow of what the seven Final Four teams had been. Cherokee Parks, by far the '95 team's best player, had graduated. So had Erik Meek, who had become a very solid inside player in his junior and senior seasons.

Krzyzewski had recruited Joey Beard and Greg Newton in the fall of 1993, with the idea that they would provide depth as freshmen and sophomores and then be ready to step in as stars when Parks and Meek graduated. Both had turned out to be examples of the kind of recruiting mistakes Duke had made in the wake of the back-to-back championships. Beard was a McDonald's All-American and came out of the same high school—South Lakes in Reston, Virginia—as Grant Hill. Comparisons with Hill stopped there. By the end of his sophomore season, Beard had transferred to Boston University having proven he was not an ACC player, much less a star.

Newton wasn't at Duke either in the fall of '95, having been suspended by a Duke student judicial board for cheating on a computer science test. He did return to school and did graduate but, like Beard, never came close to being the player he had been reputed to be coming out of high school.

The absence of Newton meant that freshman Taymon Domzalski had to start eighteen games at center. Domzalski was a solid backup player but certainly not ready to take on ACC centers for twenty-five or thirty minutes a night. Even when Newton returned, the Blue Devils were still woeful inside.

They were left with a team built around three guards: Chris Collins, Trajan Langdon, and Steve Wojciechowski: tough kids, the kind Krzyzewski loved to coach, but hardly future NBA stars or even NBA players.

Still, the season started well. The Blue Devils went to Alaska and won the Great Alaska Shootout, beating Indiana in the semifinals. The win was important for Krzyzewski because Indiana was a solid team, but perhaps more important because it was the first time he had been face-to-face with Bob Knight since the non-handshake in Minneapolis in 1992.

The two men shook hands, but neither had much to say to the other. The three wins in Alaska put Duke back into the national rankings for the first time in almost a year, at number twelve. The Blue Devils lost to two other Big Ten teams—Illinois and Michigan—in December but went into conference play 9–2 and still ranked—at number nineteen.

That didn't last very long. Almost as if the nightmare of the previous winter was being relived, they dropped their first four ACC games—at Clemson, at home to Georgia Tech and Wake Forest, and on the road to Virginia. The first three games were close—margins of three, five, and three. The fourth wasn't—Virginia won easily, 77–66.

On January 18, Duke went to N.C. State with an excellent chance to drop to 0–5 in the conference. The Wolfpack was fighting to save Les Robinson's job and had played well in the non-conference season, going 10–2—one of the losses to top-ranked Massachusetts. But they had started 1–2 in the conference, and another trip to the Les Robinson game was probably going to be his last appearance there. In Krzyzewski's absence, State had swept Duke the previous season. The Wolfpack needed to win the game at least as much as Duke did.

For most of the night it appeared the Wolfpack would succeed. Duke trailed by double digits early in the second half but wouldn't go away. Chris Collins kept making big shots to keep Duke close until finally the Blue Devils got the ball back, trailing 70–68 with the clock under ten seconds. Everyone in Reynolds Coliseum knew Collins was going to shoot—and they were right. With just over five seconds left, he found an opening at the top of the key and shot. The ball hit the front of the rim, crawled over it, sat on the rim briefly—and dropped in. State missed a shot at the buzzer, and Duke escaped with a 71–70 win.

In the basement of the building where Jim Valvano had once been king, Krzyzewski cried on the shoulder of his oldest daughter, Debbie. He was relieved and drained—and, he knew, very lucky.

"That game, that shot that Chris made—they were as big in their own way as any of the famous games we've won in March and April," he said. "That season was a fight, for me, for everyone. That win gave us just enough of a boost to get us back into the NCAA Tournament. The key guy all season was Chris. He was the bridge we needed to get to the next season when we had some reinforcements arriving.

"We've had a lot of great players do great things, but what Chris did that season was as important as anything any of my players has done. That game was critical. We lose that night and I honestly don't know where that season goes.

"It was the first step on the road back."

There was still a long way to travel.

32

Duke's pratfall in the winter of 1995 wasn't greeted with a lot of sympathy around the ACC—especially among those in the media with degrees from the University of North Carolina. The joke many of them seemed to find funny was that Krzyzewski's back had started to *really* hurt after he got a good look at his team. That line was oft repeated throughout the season in ACC media rooms.

Dean Smith didn't have any doubt that Krzyzewski was sick. He would have much preferred to beat Duke with Krzyzewski on the bench than without him. And the team he had almost certainly would have done so even if Krzyzewski had been healthy—although the case might be made that the double-overtime game in Durham might have tipped the other way if Krzyzewski had been in the building.

Carolina was good—very good. The graduation of Eric Montross, Derrick Phelps, Brian Reese, and Kevin Salvadori had relieved a good deal of the tension in the locker room. All were excellent players and outstanding people—exactly the kind of person Smith loved to coach. But the addition of Rasheed Wallace, Jerry Stackhouse, and Jeff McInnis the previous season had destroyed the chemistry of the national championship team. Adding those three and losing George Lynch had ultimately proven toxic.

None of this made Smith happy. He was a true believer in the "Carolina Way"—after all, he'd created it—and having dissension in his locker room was intolerable for him. Once Wallace, Stackhouse, and McInnis didn't have to defer on or off the court, they were much happier. What's more, Wallace and Stackhouse were over-the-moon talents. With Donald Williams and Pat Sullivan still around to provide stability, there was no doubting that this was a team capable of reaching Smith's tenth Final Four.

Not that there weren't headaches. From midseason on, there were widespread rumors that both Wallace and Stackhouse were going to turn pro at the end of the season. Wallace vehemently denied the first report that he was leaving, and his mother vowed he would stay four years.

The Tar Heels were ranked number two in preseason polls, behind defending national champion Arkansas, which returned most of the key players from the team that had beaten Duke in the title game the previous spring. By the time ACC play began in January, they were 9–0 and ranked number one. But they began conference play with a surprising road loss at N.C. State. Then they went on another winning streak, winning their next nine. By the time they beat Duke, 99–86, in the regular season finale in Chapel Hill, they were 22–4 and had finished in a four-way tie for first place ("ACC CHAMPIONS . . . Four-Way Regular Season Tie" reads the banner) with Wake Forest, Virginia, and Maryland.

Even with Duke taking the plunge to ninth place, the ACC was extremely deep. Wake Forest had a superb inside-outside combination with Tim Duncan at center and senior Randolph Childress at point guard. Maryland had Joe Smith—who would be the number-one pick in that June's draft—and Keith Booth. Virginia had three excellent guards and Junior Burrough, perhaps the most underrated inside player in the country.

Carolina and Wake Forest ended up in the ACC Tournament final, Wake winning an 82–80 overtime classic, thanks in large part to Childress's 37-point masterpiece. The Deacons went to the East Regionals as the number-one seed, while the Tar Heels were sent to the Southeast Regionals as the number-two seed behind Kentucky.

All four ACC teams reached the Sweet 16. Maryland lost to Connecticut in the regional semifinals and Wake Forest was upset by Oklahoma State. Virginia, which was the number-four seed in the Midwest, stunned top-seeded Kansas to reach the Elite Eight before losing to Arkansas in the regional final. The Cavaliers played the entire tournament without Cory Alexander, their senior point guard. If they'd had Alexander to deal with Arkansas's vaunted "forty minutes of hell," they might have made it to Seattle.

Carolina did make it there. In the round of sixteen, they had to face Georgetown—another Dean Smith–John Thompson matchup. The Hoyas weren't nearly the juggernaut they had been through most of the 1980s, but they did have Allen Iverson, who had breathed new life into the program after the Hoyas had gone five seasons without getting past the tournament's first weekend.

Iverson and Victor Page formed both a formidable and perhaps unique backcourt: Iverson had been to jail before college; Page would land there after college. They weren't enough though against the Tar Heels, who won 74–64, to advance to the regional final against Kentucky.

The Wildcats had been crushing people with their full-court pressure defense. They were talented, experienced, and deep. When they destroyed a good Arizona State team, 97–73, in the regional semis, *The Washington Post*'s Thomas Boswell was moved to write that there really was no point in even staging the rest of the tournament, that a lot of time, money, and effort would be saved just by awarding the trophy to Kentucky on the spot.

This was pre-Internet. Even so, someone alerted Smith to the column, and by the time the Tar Heels walked into the locker room to prepare for their off-day practice, it was in every player's locker—the key phrases highlighted.

Four minutes into the game, Kentucky led, 8–2. Then the always hot-headed Wallace threw a punch at Kentucky's Andre Riddick and a brief melee ensued. Both players were given technicals but not tossed, and Kentucky went ice-cold for the rest of the half, shooting 9 of 34. Carolina led 32–23 at the break and cruised from there, winning 74–61. After the game, every Carolina player mentioned Boswell's column as motivation.

"No one gave us a chance," was the oft-repeated theme.

Actually, that wasn't true. One writer who didn't cover a lot of college basketball hadn't given them a chance. But Smith had them convinced that *no one* had given them a chance. That was part of Smith's genius: he was a master at convincing people—most important his players—that no one thought the Tar Heels could win.

In 1980, Georgia Tech's first season in the ACC, the Yellow Jackets finished 0–14 in conference play. On the day they came to play in Chapel Hill, *Durham Morning Herald* columnist Ron Morris wrote a piece headlined "Twenty-Five Reasons Why Tech Will Win Today." They were all fabricated. They also could easily have come out of Smith's mouth.

Years later, at a banquet in Hawaii, the night before North Carolina was to face James Madison—then coached by Lefty Driesell—in the opening round of a holiday tournament, Driesell summed up Smith's career by saying, "Dean Smith's the only coach in history to win more than eight hundred games and be the underdog in every one of them."

Hyperbole? Perhaps. Did every coach alive try to downplay his team's talent? Of course. In the fall of 1985, Bobby Cremins told the media prior to the start of the season that his team was "too young" to be ranked number one in the country. The Yellow Jackets started three seniors, a junior, and a sophomore.

But no one—no one—ever figured out how to gain a psychological edge better than Smith.

That was why Krzyzewski has often said he would have hired Smith to run the CIA had he ever been president. "I mean it in a good way," he said with a smile.

Krzyzewski didn't always mean it in a good way—thus the 1993 "If I ever start to act like him, talk like him in any way, don't ask me any questions. Just get a gun and shoot me" remark. And yet, there's no doubt while Smith's mind games often bothered his opponents, most would have copied them, given the chance.

"The sign of being a great coach is how many coaches copy what you do," Gary Williams said. "No one was more copied than Dean—on and off the court."

Since the NCAA had not followed Boswell's advice, Carolina's victory over unbeaten Kentucky put them into the Final Four along with Arkansas, Oklahoma State, and UCLA. The site was Seattle—the city where Smith had been forced to rent a car at the last minute in 1984 when Michael Jordan and company had been upset in the round of sixteen by Indiana.

This time, Smith was on a bus with his team. But he didn't get the result he had hoped for. The Tar Heels lost to Arkansas in the semifinals. Then UCLA, playing without point guard Tyus Edney, beat Arkansas to prevent the Razorbacks from matching Duke's back-to-back titles in 1991 and 1992. It was UCLA's first title in twenty years, dating to John Wooden's last game in 1975.

Smith returned to Chapel Hill with mixed feelings about the season. He was pleased that his team had made it to his tenth Final Four and especially happy with the way they had played to get there. But it had been an exhausting winter. Wallace, Stackhouse, and McInnis were not easy to coach. Not long after the season ended Stackhouse and Wallace—in spite of all the denials put out by Wallace and his mother—both announced they were passing up their last two seasons of eligibility to turn pro.

Smith had two hugely talented young forwards, Vince Carter and Antawn Jamison, coming into the program, but he knew losing Wallace and Stackhouse would leave him with a very young team that would lack depth. Even so, he couldn't honestly say he was sorry to see the two stars depart. He knew 1995–96 might be a long season. He wondered if it might be his last.

—

The only one of the four ACC teams in North Carolina that entered the 1995–96 season with serious hopes of a deep tournament run was Wake Forest, which was always viewed by the three Research Triangle teams as kind of a distant cousin since it was about fifty miles west of the other three schools—give or take a few miles.

The Demon Deacons had Tim Duncan, who probably could have turned pro after his sophomore season à la Stackhouse and Wallace and been the number-one pick in the NBA draft. Duncan was different from most basketball players in that his whole persona wasn't tied into playing in the NBA or becoming wealthy. He had grown up on St. Croix in the Virgin Islands and had actually been a swimmer as a boy before growing to six foot ten and taking up basketball at the age of fifteen.

Wake Forest coach Dave Odom had heard about Duncan from one of his former players, Chris King, who had played in a tournament on St. Croix and noticed the very skinny, gangly kid who ran the floor like a deer but didn't look like he knew much about how to play the game. "He's got potential," King told Odom. "Hard to know how much."

Odom decided it was worth a trip. He had been told that the best players on St. Croix gathered at an outdoor court most afternoons, so he flew down, found the courts, took a seat, and, as the games began, searched for a skinny six-ten kid. No one fitting that description was on the court.

Just as Odom was beginning to wonder if he had bad information, Duncan walked up and sat down next to him. He explained the politics of the courts: older guys played first. Word had gotten around that a big-shot American college coach was in town, so everyone who had ever picked up a basketball was there that day.

"If I insisted on playing the first game because you're here to see me, they'd give me a bad team so I'd lose in the first game and not play for the next hour," he said. "If I wait my turn, I can pick my own team and you'll get to see me a lot."

Odom was instantly impressed with the savvy, smarts, and maturity of this sixteen-year-old kid. When Duncan got on the court, he was more impressed. Duncan was also being recruited by Providence—Coach Rick Barnes had also been tipped off about him—and probably would have gone there if not for the fact that Providence didn't have a scholarship to offer in the fall of his senior year of high school. Wake Forest did—and the rest became history.

Duncan was only seventeen when he enrolled at Wake, meaning he was now a nineteen-year-old junior. But he didn't play or act like a teenager. The Deacons were clearly the ACC team with the best chance to reach the Final Four in 1996—which would be played in the New Jersey Meadowlands and would be the last Final Four played in a basketball arena.

Wake was the odds-on favorite in the league in large part because of Duncan's presence but also because Duke and North Carolina were question marks. Duke was trying to bounce back from Krzyzewski's absence and the bad recruiting decisions that had been made prior to his illness. The Tar Heels had lost Stackhouse and Wallace, and even though they still had talent, they also had continuing issues within the team. Jeff McInnis was talented but a headache. Vince Carter was hugely talented but immature.

Midway through that season, when someone asked Smith how he liked his two heralded freshmen, his answer was quick and instinctive: "Jamison is a joy to coach." He didn't mention Carter.

Carolina was actually 11–2 after Jamison scored just before the buzzer to beat Maryland—at Maryland—88–86 in early January. But nothing was easy from that point on. In fact, by the time Carolina and Duke met in the regular season finale in Cameron, the Blue Devils had rallied from their 0–4 conference start to a record of 8–7. UNC was 9–6, meaning a Duke win would leave the two teams tied for third place behind Wake Forest and Georgia Tech—which was having a resurgent season led by freshman point guard Stephon Marbury.

The game was chippy from the beginning. Both teams and coaches were uptight. No one at Carolina was happy that the team had gone 8–7 since the win at Maryland. That sort of thing just didn't happen in Chapel Hill. Duke and Krzyzewski were relieved that the Blue Devils had won four in a row and had played well enough to have clinched an NCAA Tournament bid—unofficially—but the losing streak against the Tar Heels had reached six after a last-second loss in Chapel Hill a month earlier. That was the longest losing streak for Duke against Carolina since the six-game streak that had started in the dark days of 1982 and ended in the 1984 ACC Tournament hugfest.

McInnis had become the target of the Duke students, who had heard all sorts of stories and rumors about him and, of course, chose to believe them. They had two chants for him, one involving his personal life and the other far more direct: "Asshole," they chanted repeatedly. "Asshole." The fact that McInnis kept repeatedly hitting important shots—he finished the game with twenty-five points—no doubt upped their anger and their angst.

Late in the game, with the Tar Heels in control, Duke walk-on Jay Heaps—a star soccer player—body-checked McInnis into the scorer's table while trying to foul him to stop the clock. McInnis reacted angrily and was hit with his second technical of the game—the first one had been for trash-talking after he had made a deep three-point shot—and was ejected. As he headed to the locker room, the "asshole" chants reached a climax.

Smith was furious with the chant and with the personal digs directed at McInnis that had gone on during the game too. "I would think the faculty at Duke, the *esteemed* faculty at Duke, would be embarrassed by that," he said. "I thought it was over the line."

Krzyzewski wasn't apologetic. "I think the students recognized unsportsmanlike play," he said, "and they reacted accordingly."

Krzyzewski wasn't nearly as political in private. "They saw an asshole," he said, "and they identified him as such accurately."

The sniping between the two coaches continued that week in the lead-up to the ACC Tournament. Krzyzewski accused Smith of trying to put the focus on the Duke students to draw attention from his ongoing feud with Clemson coach Rick Barnes.

That had started the previous year during the ACC Tournament. Barnes had come to Clemson after stints at George Mason and Providence. He had grown up in Hickory, North Carolina, and, like most kids growing up in the state, he was a huge fan of North Carolina and of Dean Smith.

"But I wasn't going to come in and be in awe of him," Barnes said. "Clemson had always had an inferiority complex, especially when it came to North Carolina. I wanted people to know those days were over."

Barnes didn't have the players to compete with Carolina in 1995. The Tigers were in the process of getting blown out by UNC in the first round of the ACC Tournament when Barnes noticed Smith pointing a finger and yelling at one of his players, Iker Iturbe. True to his word, Barnes walked in the direction of Smith, pointing at him and saying, "If you have a problem with one of my players, you talk to *me* about it."

Referees Frank Scagliotta and Rick Hartzell rushed in to calm Barnes. When Barnes told them why he was upset, they decided to defuse the confrontation as quickly as possible.

"Usually the best thing to do in those situations is bring the coaches together, let them tell *us* what the problem is, and get it over with," Scagliotta said years later. "As it turned out, in that situation, it was definitely *not* the best thing to do."

When Smith walked to midcourt, Barnes repeated what he had said about yelling at one of his players. "He's trying to hurt my players," Smith said. "You need to get him under control."

"You need to get you under control," Barnes yelled back, pointing a finger and moving in Smith's direction.

"Why don't you hit me, Rick?" Smith said. "Go ahead and hit me."

At that point, Hartzell and Scagliotta had to push the two men away from each other—both still yelling and pointing.

After the game, Smith said he had simply been yelling "Iturbe" at Iturbe and said, "He's a European player."

Much like with Danny May-har eleven years earlier, he was saying Iturbe was a dirty player.

The angry words had continued throughout the following

season, and, as luck would have it, Clemson and Carolina were paired again a year later in the ACC Tournament. This time, though, Clemson was a much tougher out. In fact, the consensus was that a Clemson win over Carolina would put the Tigers into the NCAA Tournament for the first time since 1990—the year of the buzzer-beating Sweet 16 loss to Connecticut.

Much to Smith's dismay, Clemson won the game, 75–73, on a last-second basket by Clemson's Greg Buckner. It was the first time that Clemson had ever beaten North Carolina in the ACC Tournament, and it did get the Tigers into the NCAA Tournament, even after they lost to Wake Forest the next afternoon in the semifinals.

Smith made a point of stopping in the Clemson locker room to congratulate the players. He made the trip down the hall in the Greensboro Coliseum for two reasons: he knew it was the gracious thing to do and he didn't want to appear too upset by the loss.

Carolina was sent to the East Regionals as a number-six seed. Duke went to the Southeast as a number-eight seed. North Carolina State, after finishing 15–16—in spite of a win in the Les Robinson game—went looking for a new coach. Wake Forest was the number-two seed in the Midwest, which was unfortunate because it meant it had to go through Kentucky, the number-one seed in that region and, by then, clearly the best team in the country, to get to the Final Four.

As it turned out, Duke's season had really ended with the loss to Carolina in Cameron. With two minutes left, Chris Collins had hurt his foot. He hadn't been able to play in the ACC Tournament, and Duke meekly lost to Maryland. The Blue Devils were a fragile team to begin with and Collins had been the glue all season.

A week later, he played in Duke's first-round game against Eastern Michigan but struggled all afternoon, finishing with 11 points. Even if Collins had been 100 percent, Duke probably would have lost to EMU, which was led by five-foot-five-inch Earl Boykins, a whirling, spinning, shooting dervish who would go on to a lengthy NBA career. Boykins scored 23 points and Eastern Michigan won easily, 75–60.

It was the first time Krzyzewski had lost a first-round NCAA Tournament game. In 1984 and 1985, his team had received byes into the second round before losing, and from 1986 to 1994 they had at least reached the Sweet 16 on eight occasions and had lost once—in 1993—in the second round.

Even so, Krzyzewski felt good about the season. He had known it would be a transition year and that his team would not be nearly as talented as the seven he had taken to the Final Four. Help was on the way in the form of what he believed was a solid recruiting class.

"Just as 1987 was important because we proved that what we'd accomplished in 1986 wasn't a fluke, 1996 was important because we made the [NCAA] tournament and I felt comfortable and I felt healthy. I believed we were going to be good again soon. Eastern Michigan was just better than us—simple as that. As soon as we got home from that game I was ready to go. I wasn't tired. I wanted to keep working. I was excited about what I *knew* we were going to be again."

Dean Smith *was* tired when his season ended three days and one round later than Krzyzewski's had. The Tar Heels had easily won their first-round game against the University of New Orleans. That set up a game against Texas Tech, very much a nonbasketball school, but a team that was having a once-in-a-lifetime season under Coach James Dickey.

In the last season of the Southwest Conference, the Red Raiders had won both the regular season title and the conference tournament. They had finished 28–1, which had earned them the third seed in the East. Carolina was no match for them, losing 92–73. A subsequent NCAA investigation into the athletic program would lead to both of Texas Tech's NCAA Tournament wins that season being "vacated"—meaning that, technically, they never happened.

That didn't change the fact that Carolina had lost—and lost

badly—in the second round of the tournament. It was only the second time in sixteen seasons that the Tar Heels had failed to reach the Sweet 16, but the last two months of the season left Smith feeling drained. His team had gone from 11–2 to 21–11, meaning it had limped to a 10–9 record from early January to mid-March.

It wasn't a happy team—in part because of the losing—but there was a chicken-and-egg component to that. McInnis was an issue, and there was bickering in the locker room, something Smith truly hated. The game in Cameron—although a win—left him feeling angry and exhausted, as did the ongoing feud with Rick Barnes. A first-round loss in the ACC Tournament followed by a second-round loss in the NCAA Tournament left him with a decidedly bad taste in his mouth walking out of the locker room in the Richmond Coliseum after the loss to Texas Tech.

"If I had been making a decision about whether I wanted to coach the next season at that moment," he said the following fall, "I wouldn't have come back."

It was the first time in thirty-five years he had felt that way. He had always vowed to never decide to retire right after the end of a season. "No matter what, you're tired even after a great season," he said. "The thought of just being able to play golf and take life a little bit easier can be very appealing at that moment. But I'd never seriously thought about quitting—until 1996.

"I knew I needed to get some rest and see how I felt in October. I had always said that I would know it was time to quit when October came around and I wasn't excited about the start of practice."

When October came, Smith was ready to coach again. He had a nagging thought as he watched his team go through its pre-season routine: Am I here because I want to be or because I didn't want my last coaching memory to be the Texas Tech game?

The truth, he knew, was that he wasn't sure. He decided to see where the season took him and then try to figure out the answer.

33

North Carolina State hired Herb Sendek to replace Les Robinson as coach in the spring of 1996. Sendek was the anti–Jim Valvano, a very serious and studious young man who had worked for Rick Pitino at both Providence and Kentucky before going on to have a good deal of success at Miami of Ohio, winning sixty-three games his last three seasons. A first-round victory over Arizona in the 1995 NCAA Tournament had gotten Sendek on the national radar and—a year later—to N.C. State.

At thirty-three he was a hot young coach. He was also the same age as Krzyzewski had been when he had gotten the Duke job and three years older than Smith had been when he had been promoted to the head coach's job at North Carolina. Now he was being asked to compete with both of them. Given that the two of them had combined to win four national championships and reach seventeen Final Fours, the task had to be daunting.

Smith and Krzyzewski weren't that concerned with Sendek or N.C. State at the moment. They weren't even all that concerned with each other. Each was worried about his own team.

Wake Forest was still the odds-on favorite to be the best team in the ACC since Tim Duncan had again turned down the chance to make NBA millions and had come back for his senior year. Rick Barnes had turned Clemson completely around in two years, and the Tigers were a top-ten preseason pick nationally and generally considered the second-best team in the ACC. Third? Perhaps Maryland, perhaps North Carolina. Duke, Virginia, and Florida State were next in a very strong league. Only Georgia Tech—which had lost Stephon Marbury to the NBA draft not long after he had declared himself "one hundred percent certain" to stay at

Tech for his sophomore season—and N.C. State were not considered serious NCAA Tournament contenders.

The season didn't start especially well for either Duke or North Carolina.

The Blue Devils played in the preseason NIT for the third time, an event that brought back fond memories for Krzyzewski. Duke had won the event in 1985, the first year it had been played, and had gone on from there to Krzyzewski's first Final Four. Five years later, the Blue Devils had finished third—losing to Arkansas in the semifinals. That season had culminated with Krzyzewski—and Duke's—first national title.

The memories this time weren't so fond. Duke beat St. Joseph's and Vanderbilt at home to reach the semifinals in Madison Square Garden. The Blue Devils then beat Tulsa in the semifinals, meaning they would face Indiana in the championship game on the night after Thanksgiving.

The teams had played in Alaska a year earlier, and Krzyzewski and Bob Knight had been barely civil to each other, the memories of 1992 in Minneapolis still lingering. Krzyzewski decided this time would be different. If Knight wanted him to play the respectful pupil he would do just that—at least until the game started.

And so, as the clock wound down toward tip-off, Krzyzewski walked to the Indiana bench and shook hands with all of Knight's assistants. As always, Knight had stayed in his locker room until the last possible moment. Finally, with about a minute on the clock before the starting lineups were to be introduced, Knight came walking toward the floor, the famous horse trainer D. Wayne Lukas at his side.

This was typical of Knight. He can't stand to be alone, so he almost always has someone hanging out with him in the locker room prior to a game. On this night, the designated walk-around guy was Lukas.

Krzyzewski was standing next to the Indiana bench, waiting for his mentor.

"I wanted to be the one to reach out," he said later. "That's why I was going to him, to his bench. All I was going to say was, 'Coach, let's have a great game. I'm glad to be competing with you again because I hope you know how much respect I have for you.'"

He never got the chance. As Knight approached the bench, he saw Krzyzewski waiting for him. He turned his back on him and began telling Lukas some kind of story. Krzyzewski waited. The buzzer sounded for the players to clear the court and the lineups to be introduced. Krzyzewski gave up and walked back to his bench.

The game was at least as aggravating. Indiana pulled away late to win, 85–69. The loss hurt. Knight's behavior hurt more.

"That's the period on the end of the sentence," Krzyzewski said afterward. "I tried. It's been almost five years. Enough. I'm done."

The next two months were a roller coaster. There was an irritating come-from-ahead loss at home to Michigan, followed by a gratifying win at Villanova—which was ranked number four in the country at the time. There was a come-from-behind win in the conference opener at Georgia Tech, followed two days later by a near miss, an overtime loss at Clemson when the Tigers were ranked number five nationally. Then there was another loss to Wake Forest—which was ranked number two nationally—the ninth straight time the Deacons had beaten Duke since 1993.

But the loss that nearly put Krzyzewski over the edge came at Maryland on Super Bowl Sunday. The Terrapins were also a very good team, ranked number seven in the polls at the time. (The ACC would have five teams ranked in the top ten at various times during the season.) Losing to them in College Park, especially in a taut game that wasn't decided until Steve Wojciechowski missed a jumper that would have tied it in the final seconds, was hardly any reason to feel ashamed or down.

Krzyzewski wasn't ashamed and he wasn't down. He was furious. The next morning he lit into his assistant coaches, who he thought—correctly—believed that a 15–5 record (3–3 in the conference) at that point in the season was acceptable.

"The standards have slipped around here," he told them.

"From now on, everyone's going to meet *my* standards, and what we're producing right now isn't close to good enough."

He was all over his players that afternoon. "I know what's going on," he said. "You're walking around thinking, 'Hey, we were one play away from beating a good team on the road yesterday. Nothing to feel bad about.' Well, I'm going to show you *twenty* chances you had in the game to make that one play."

And he did: missed box outs, sloppy screens, failed switches on defense.

When practice began, Greg Newton, who had come to symbolize the slipping of standards in Krzyzewski's mind, got tossed. The assistant coaches worried that their boss was unraveling. They also knew exactly why he was so uptight: the next game was against North Carolina. The losing streak against the Tar Heels was seven—dating, like the Wake streak, to 1993.

After practice on Monday, Krzyzewski stood in front of his team, took out a blue marker, and drew a line on the whiteboard in the front of the locker room.

"If you have any pride at all," he said in a measured voice, "you should be saying, '*That's* the line, Carolina. You aren't crossing it on Wednesday unless you kill me. You'll have to kill me to cross that line.'"

—

Things weren't a whole lot more cheery ten miles down the road in Chapel Hill.

Carolina had started the season 9–1, the only loss coming in the opener against a very good Arizona team. But the start of conference play hadn't gone well at all. Losing at Wake Forest wasn't unexpected, but the game had been an 81–57 blowout.

Then Maryland came to town, and Carolina, even with Vince Carter sitting out with a hip pointer, controlled the game for almost twenty-six minutes. When freshman point guard Ed Cota sliced through the Maryland defense for a layup with a little more than fourteen minutes left, the Tar Heels led 66–44 and the faithful could sit back in their comfortable seats and relax.

Except they couldn't. Over the next nine minutes, Maryland outscored Carolina 28–2. The only Carolina basket in the run was a putback by seven-foot-three-inch senior Serge Zwikker. The Tar Heels couldn't score, the Terrapins couldn't be stopped. Twice Smith did the unthinkable, calling a time-out before the last two minutes of the game. Nothing could stop the onslaught. Maryland outscored UNC 41–9 in the final fourteen minutes and won, 85–75.

Most of the crowd of 21,444 walked out of the building in a state of shock. No one was more shocked than Maryland coach Gary Williams. "It wasn't so much beating Carolina that way or getting on that kind of run in that building," he said years later. "It was beating *Dean* that way. That was what Dean did to you, not what you did to Dean."

That was the first night that the thought that Smith wouldn't coach forever crossed Williams's mind. It wasn't the loss; it was something Smith said to him before the game started. The two men had been chatting casually in front of the Carolina bench when Williams pointed at Carter, who was in street clothes, and asked Smith when he thought he'd play again.

"If this was fifteen years ago," Smith said, "there's a good chance he'd be playing tonight."

Williams was taken aback by the comment. Smith never said anything to anyone that might be construed in any way as a put-down of one of his players. Now he was clearly making a comment not so much about Carter but about the players of the tail end of the twentieth century.

"I looked at him when he said that," Williams remembered. "And for the first time ever it occurred to me that he was starting to look his age. He looked gray and tired, and the important part of the season was just starting."

The loss to Maryland didn't put a spring into Smith's step by any means. But it did get his attention. That Saturday, when the

Tar Heels played at Virginia, he decided to miss his annual date with the Virginia State Police and ride to and from Charlottesville with his team. This group, he had decided, needed as much of his time and energy as he could give them.

The good news was that he saved a few dollars by avoiding the speeding ticket. The bad news was that the final result was a third straight double-digit loss, this one 75–63.

Things got a little better after that with wins over N.C. State and Georgia Tech—the two teams expected to finish at the bottom of the league. But a trip to Tallahassee produced another loss before the Tar Heels played, arguably, their best game of the season, beating Clemson—which came into the Dean Dome ranked number two in the country—61–48. Of course Carolina *always* beat Clemson at home. In fact, after the Tar Heels beat the Tigers in 2014, Clemson's all-time record in Chapel Hill dating to 1926 was 0–57.

Still, Smith felt better about his team after the Clemson game and was looking forward to going to Duke—sort of. He never enjoyed himself in Cameron, except when a game was over and his team had won. The Tar Heels had won three straight there, and Smith's all-time record in the building was 18–17.

"It's a very big game for them," he said the morning the two teams were scheduled to play. "It's always a bigger game for the home team. And I know Mike has to be tired of losing to us."

Mike was very tired of losing to Carolina—and to Smith.

His pregame talk that night was brief. He walked into the locker room and drew another blue line on the board. Then he turned to his team and said, "Let's go."

That was enough. The game was one of those that has made Duke-Carolina the rivalry it has been for so many years. The game rocked back and forth. Carolina's size appeared to be too much for Duke with Zwikker, Carter, and Jamison up front. Much to the dismay of his assistants, Krzyzewski had benched Newton, who he thought was coasting, because he was Duke's only true inside presence and Krzyzewski wouldn't dare bench him. Krzyzewski dared—starting six-six freshman Chris Carrawell in his place. Newton came off the bench and played as well as he had all season. Duke hung on to win, 80–73, and the students stormed the court. There wasn't an undergraduate in the building—including Newton and fellow senior Jeff Capel—who had ever been part of a win over UNC.

Even with the students coming over the scorer's table in droves, Krzyzewski and Smith stopped to talk when they shook hands.

"That was a terrific game," Smith said. "Your guys were great but I'm happy my guys made you work for it."

"I think it will make us both better," Krzyzewski shouted over the din. And, for the first time in seventeen years, they gave each other a tap on the shoulder.

—

As it turned out, Krzyzewski was right. The game in Cameron turned out to be a launching pad for both teams. Beginning with the Carolina game, Duke went on an 8–1 run, the only loss being an out-of-conference road loss at UCLA in late February. A week after ending their losing skein against North Carolina, they finally beat Wake Forest and Tim Duncan—at Wake. They got lucky in a game at Virginia when a late officiating error—it was so bad that the officials in question drew a one-game suspension from the league—allowed them to escape with a 62–61 victory. When they returned from UCLA to beat Maryland at home, they raised their ACC record to 12–3 and clinched the regular season title with one game—at North Carolina—left to play.

They had come a long way since Krzyzewski's forced departure two winters earlier, going from 3–13 and ninth place to winning the regular season for the fifth time in Krzyzewski's career.

"I didn't feel like we were back at that point," Krzyzewski said. "But we were on the *way* back. Jeff Capel struggled early but really turned things around and had a great senior year. We became a good team again, not a great team by any stretch, but a good team."

Prior to the Maryland game, while he was explaining to his players why the regular season title was important, Krzyzewski overheard freshman Chris Carrawell whispering "We're going to win four of them" to fellow freshman Nate James.

Suppressing a grin, Krzyzewski said, "How about you just worry about winning one before you start thinking about four?"

As it turned out, Carrawell knew what he was talking about. Duke won the regular season title outright during all four of his years at Duke.

As well as they played in February, Duke wasn't the hottest team in the ACC—or in the Triangle. After losing to Duke in Cameron, North Carolina stopped losing. They beat all the teams they had lost to on the road when they got to play them at home, and they went to Maryland and beat the Terrapins to exorcise the ghosts of the 28–2 meltdown in Chapel Hill. Their 2–5 start was too much to overcome to catch Duke, but they did beat the Blue Devils on Senior Day in Chapel Hill to finish 11–5, which put them in a tie with Wake Forest for second place.

Many expected Duke and Carolina to rematch a week later in the ACC championship game in Greensboro. Order, it seemed, had been restored. Maryland and Clemson, after their hot starts, had faded to a tie for fourth place.

Except there was another upstart that prevented the third Duke-Carolina meeting of the season: N.C. State. The Wolfpack had improved slowly but surely throughout the season. After going 0–8 the first time through the conference, they had gone 4–4 the second half of the season. That hadn't kept them out of what was still called "the Les Robinson game," but they won it easily and then faced top-seeded Duke the next day.

And won. Duke started fast but faded almost as quickly, clearly shocked by the fact that the Wolfpack kept hitting shots and didn't go away. The loss didn't stun Krzyzewski. He'd had a gut feeling before the game that something wasn't quite right with his team.

"It was as if when we won the [regular season] conference, we were done emotionally," he said. "Our guys had played over their heads for a while. Unfortunately, we came down to earth at the wrong time."

They landed hard. Losing to Carolina in Chapel Hill, especially with the regular season title wrapped up, was neither a surprise nor an embarrassment. Losing to eighth-seeded N.C. State in the first round of the ACC Tournament was both.

As if to prove the win over Duke wasn't a fluke, the Wolfpack beat Maryland the next day in the semifinals before running out of gas in the second half of the championship game—it was their fourth game in four days—and losing to North Carolina.

The Tar Heels had gotten to the final with a surprisingly easy semifinal victory over Wake Forest. Like Duke, the Deacons, who had spent a good deal of the season ranked number two nationally, were also fading. The low moment of that Saturday afternoon for them—and a high for Carolina—came late in the game when Serge Zwikker hit a three-point shot for the first time in his career. The final was 86–73.

The win was Carolina's eleventh in a row since the loss to Duke in late January. The next day's 64–54 win over State made it twelve straight and gave Smith his thirteenth ACC Tournament title. It also vaulted the Tar Heels into a number-one seed in the East Regionals. The number two seed was South Carolina, coached by former Carolina player and assistant coach Eddie Fogler. The thought of meeting one of his pupils with a spot in the Final Four at stake wasn't appealing to Smith.

For the moment, though, he didn't have to worry about that. His team would make a short trip down I-85 and I-40 to Winston-Salem for the first weekend of the tournament. Fairfield awaited as a first-round opponent. So did history.

—

Duke was given a number-two seed in the Southeast Region and sent to Charlotte for the first weekend. Kansas was the number-one seed in the region, but Krzyzewski wasn't thinking about the Jayhawks or Roy Williams. He was concerned about winning his first-round game against Murray State.

Never afraid to try something different, he skipped his usual prepractice talk on Monday. It was a comfortable spring day so he took his players on a field trip across the back parking lot to Wallace Wade Stadium, where Duke played football—very badly—each fall.

He had the players sit in the stands and sent managers out for ice cream. He told them winter was over—check the weather—and it was spring, which meant new beginnings. The NCAA Tournament should be a new beginning, something to get excited about.

"It was worth a try," he said later. "Anything was worth a try."

Nothing worked. The Blue Devils did manage to beat Murray State on Friday night in their opener for their twenty-fourth win of the season. It was their last. In the second round, facing a very talented Providence team, they were beaten handily, 98–87. A season that had started poorly, then taken off in February, had ended with a thud in March: three losses in the final four games. After making at least the Sweet 16 eight years out of nine, Duke had failed to get that far for the third straight season.

"It was a bad ending," Krzyzewski said. "I can honestly say everyone involved tried everything to keep the momentum we'd had in February going. In the end, we weren't good enough to go deep in the tournament. We got exposed a little bit at the end."

The good news was that reinforcements were on the way. Whether it was because the staff was younger or because Krzyzewski had gone back to being the relentless recruiter Eddie Fogler remembered from the early 1980s, Duke had corralled arguably its deepest recruiting class since the freshman class circa 1982. Two highly touted big men—Chris Burgess and Elton Brand—would replace the quirky (to be kind) Greg Newton inside. Shane Battier would join senior Roshown McLeod at small forward. And William Avery, a talented combo guard, would be added to the duo of Steve Wojciechowski and Trajan Langdon. There would be talent and experience.

But that was still a year away.

Twenty-four hours before Duke's season ended in Charlotte, the North Carolina basketball family staged a huge celebration eighty miles away in Winston-Salem.

Carolina's win in the ACC championship game was the 875th of Dean Smith's career. That left him one victory shy of Adolph Rupp's all-time record for Division I coaching wins. Smith actually had mixed emotions about closing in on Rupp.

He *never* liked to talk about it, for several reasons. First, as always, he didn't ever want the spotlight to be on him. What's more, he wanted the focus to be on *this* team and *this* season and the next game. And, finally, he had decidedly mixed emotions about Rupp, whose reputation—in spite of what his apologists said—was as someone who waited as long as he possibly could before racially integrating his Kentucky basketball team.

Earlier in the season, when Carolina had been struggling, many had thought Smith wouldn't come close to Rupp until the following fall. But the ten straight wins had put him on the doorstep, and with the first-round game considered a virtually certain victory, it appeared likely he would be in position to break the record in the second round.

And the opponent looked as if it might be Bob Knight.

In one of those "coincidences" that always seem to happen when the NCAA basketball committee *isn't* thinking about what matchups might be good for TV, Indiana had somehow landed in North Carolina's bracket as a number-eight seed. That meant the Hoosiers would play Colorado in the first round on Thursday night with the winner playing the Carolina-Fairfield winner on Saturday afternoon.

Knight and Smith had met twice in the NCAA Tournament: the 1981 final in Philadelphia and the 1984 round-of-sixteen game—Michael Jordan's last college game—in Atlanta. This was not one of Knight's better teams—thus the number-eight seed—but then again, the '84 team hadn't been one of his better teams either.

The Tar Heels beat Fairfield, 82–74, on Thursday night, and it seemed as if the entire state of Connecticut—including the Fairfield mascot—lined up to shake Smith's hand after the game.

But Colorado upset the committee's (and CBS's) ratings applecart by blitzing Indiana, 80–62. The rout was so embarrassing to Knight that he refused to ride with his team on the bus back to their hotel. Instead, in frigid weather, he walked the two miles, no doubt shocked by the one-sided outcome and angered that he wouldn't have the chance to delay Smith setting the record until the following season.

CBS had already scheduled North Carolina as the early game on Saturday, meaning the entire country would see Smith's attempt to break Rupp's record—regardless of the opposition. The Tar Heels were on a serious roll and they made a good Colorado team look bad. The final was 80–63, win number 877 for Smith.

Terry Holland was the chairman of the NCAA basketball committee that season. Holland had retired from coaching in 1990 at the age of forty-eight because of persistent stomach problems and was now the athletic director at Virginia. He and Smith had been through many battles during the sixteen seasons they had coached against each other. Holland certainly hadn't been happy when Smith waved his finger in Marc Iavaroni's face at halftime of the 1977 ACC championship game, and Smith hadn't been thrilled when he learned that Holland had named a dog Dean who "did whine a lot"—even if the dog wasn't specifically named after the coach.

Time heals wounds and feuds. Even before the game ended, Holland had instructed the security guards in the Lawrence Joel Coliseum to allow anyone who had played for Smith or coached under him into the backstage area under the stands so they could be part of the celebration.

"It was just the right thing to do," Holland said. "I really did want Dean to enjoy that day as much as he possibly could because it was such a remarkable achievement. We'd had our battles but I always respected him and his program."

Smith didn't want to make a big deal out of the record, for all the reasons he never wanted people to make a big deal of him but also because there was still work to do. Carolina was now in the Sweet 16, and Smith was beginning to believe that this team—which had now won fourteen straight—might just be good enough to win a national championship.

It was on a collision course to meet Kansas—yet again—in the national semifinals.

34

North Carolina held up its end of the bargain, beating California and then routing Louisville to win the East Regional. It was the eleventh time Smith had taken a team to the Final Four, and the argument could be made, given the Tar Heels' 2–5 start in the ACC, that this was the least likely team he had coached to college basketball's final weekend.

Kansas, however, failed to make it to Indianapolis. The Jayhawks, who had ended the regular season ranked number one in the country, were upset in the Southeast Region semifinals by fourth-seeded Arizona. The Wildcats then had to go to overtime in the regional final to beat Providence—the same Providence team that had emphatically ended Duke's season a week earlier in the second round of the tournament.

The loss to Arizona was disappointing to Roy Williams, not because it meant he wouldn't get a third Final Four shot at his old boss but because he was now starting to hear—in his ninth season—that he couldn't win the big ones.

"I was walking through an airport the next week on a recruiting trip," Williams said a few years later. "A guy stops me and says, 'Do you know that you completely screwed up my bracket by losing to Arizona? Do you know that?' I should have been polite, but I just wasn't in the mood. I said, 'Screwed up your *bracket*? Your *bracket*? You think I give a flip about your damn bracket? Losing to Arizona screwed up my *life*!'"

Williams would live to screw up brackets another day, but his mentor was headed to Indianapolis—the site of his most embarrassing moment in coaching—to face Arizona. The other semifinal would match Kentucky, trying for a second straight national title, and Minnesota, which would become another team on the long list of teams whose Final Four appearance was "vacated" by the NCAA for rules violations. For those scoring at home, there were four in a five-year period: Michigan in 1992 and 1993, Massachusetts in 1996, and Minnesota in 1997.

Carolina's hot streak came to a screeching halt against Arizona. The Wildcats had a superb backcourt in Mike Bibby and Miles Simon, and they hounded Shammond Williams into his worst shooting day of the season: 1 of 13 from the field. Point guard Ed Cota wasn't a lot better at 2 of 9. Bibby and Simon outscored Cota and Williams by a margin of 44–8, and that allowed Arizona, even with the rest of the team scoring a total of 22 points, to win the game, 66–58.

The loss was crushing for Smith because he really did think the Tar Heels were good enough at that stage to win the whole thing. What's more, the thought that he might have coached his last game crossed his mind as he congratulated Arizona coach Lute Olson.

A month later, the subject of his future came up at the tail end of an interview. The Q&A went like this:

"You said early in the season that the thought of quitting crossed your mind at the end of last season."

"I was frustrated with the way that season ended. It wasn't a fun year."

"And now?"

(Long pause) "I enjoyed coaching this team. I enjoyed the way we got better."

"So right now you think you'll coach next season."

"I didn't say that. I'm sixty-six. I enjoyed this team, but I was very tired when the season ended. I'll see how I feel in October."

"What are the chances you'll coach next season?"

"I can't put a number on it. I really can't." (A smile) "And if I could, I wouldn't tell you anyway."

—

On October 9, Smith answered the question: the number was zero. He had decided to retire.

The entire college basketball world, even his inner circle, was caught off guard. The first person he voiced the possibility to—other than his wife, Linnea—was Bill Guthridge, his hand-picked choice as his successor. Guthridge had been Smith's top lieutenant for thirty years. He had turned down opportunities to be a head coach somewhere else, and Smith wanted him to get his shot at being the boss.

On the afternoon of October 8, Steve Kirschner, Carolina's sports information director, and Rick Brewer, his predecessor, who was still an associate athletic director, began telling media members that there was a press conference the next day and they should probably try to be there. It didn't take long for word to spread that Smith was going to announce his retirement.

When he walked in, Smith had a broad grin on his face. The room was packed with media, his players—past and present—and many friends. Someone asked Smith what he hoped people would say about him in the future. He shrugged. "That he knew a little basketball, did a good job, and lived happily ever after," he said with a grin. "And that he loved his players."

It was only when he talked about the players and how much he had enjoyed his relationships with them that his voice cracked and he shed a few tears.

He certainly wasn't the only one in the room who did that day. When the news reached Mike Krzyzewski, he was stunned.

"The thought had never crossed my mind," he said. "He was as good that last season as he had ever been. That team had talent, but it wasn't always easy talent to harness. He did that. I guess I didn't understand how much those last couple of years took out of him.

"At that point in my life, it was hard to imagine not coaching against him. I knew Carolina would still be good and would always be tough to beat because of what he'd built, but I also knew it would be different. There was only one Dean Smith."

Krzyzewski sent Smith flowers that day. The note wished him luck and said: "I will never forget that I had a chance to compete against the best."

"I meant it," Krzyzewski said. "Life goes on. But I knew I'd miss trying to beat him."

—

Life in the entire ACC changed when Smith retired.

It changed most—but perhaps least—at North Carolina. Guthridge ran the program, on and off the court, the same way Smith had. The two men had worked together for thirty years, so that was no surprise. What's more, Smith had made certain to leave Guthridge with a full cupboard. Vince Carter and Antawn Jamison had come back for their junior seasons. Ed Cota had a year under his belt at point guard, and Shammond Williams—his performance in Indianapolis the previous spring notwithstanding—was still a serious outside threat. Carolina started the season 17–0 before finally losing in overtime at Maryland.

They almost certainly would have run away with the ACC regular season title except that Duke had come all the way back. Even though freshman center Elton Brand missed a month with a broken foot, the Blue Devils were deep, experienced in the backcourt, and led by a coach who hadn't enjoyed the three previous seasons very much.

The ACC regular season title was decided in Cameron on the first Saturday in March. Carolina had easily handled Duke the first time the teams had met in early February, but that was the Blue Devils' only conference loss. The Tar Heels had slipped a week earlier, losing to N.C. State at home. They needed to win to tie for the title and to be the first seed in the ACC Tournament since a win would mean they had swept Duke. Carolina led for most of the afternoon. But Duke rallied behind Brand, who had just returned to the lineup, and Wojciechowski, playing his last home game, and they won, 77–75. For the second straight season, the Duke students stormed the court.

Just as Smith had felt a year earlier that it had taken Duke's best shot to beat the Tar Heels, Guthridge believed that, all things being equal, he had the better team. That was confirmed a week later when they met in the ACC Tournament final and Carolina won easily, 78–63. Both teams went into the NCAA Tournament as number-one seeds, but Carolina went to the East—with the regional in Greensboro, a decided home-court advantage. Duke went to the South, where—surprise—Kentucky was the number-two seed. The committee simply couldn't pass up the chance to reunite the two schools in a potential regional final.

Carolina blew through the East. The Tar Heels' opener was against Navy. The tone for that game was probably best described by Sitapha Savané, Navy's starting center. "We walked onto the court for the jump and I thought, 'Hey, I'm jumping against Antawn Jamison! Hey, look, there's Vince Carter!' I'd seen them play on TV a million times. I didn't know whether to play or ask for autographs."

Not surprisingly, Carolina won, 88–52. In fact, it won all four games en route to the Final Four by double digits, beating Connecticut in the regional final, 75–64. In his first season as a head coach, Bill Guthridge was in the Final Four.

That game was on Saturday. The next day it appeared that, for the second time in eight seasons, both Duke and North Carolina would be in a Final Four. The Blue Devils built a 17-point second-half lead on Kentucky—and then collapsed. UK point guard Wayne Turner kept beating Duke's guards off the dribble and getting into the lane. The Wildcats scored time after time, while the Blue Devils kept missing. The final was 86–84, one of those games Krzyzewski still vividly remembered years later.

"We lost our poise, which isn't something that happens to us very often," he said. "They played great down the stretch—don't get me wrong. But we had control of the game and let it get away."

While Kentucky fans have never been able to let go of Christian Laettner's shot in 1992—to this day they continue to hate him and all things Duke—most Duke people simply saw 1998 as a disappointing loss, nothing more.

By not making it to San Antonio, the Blue Devils weren't around for one of the more embarrassing episodes in North Carolina history—far worse than Smith's ejection in Indianapolis in 1991. It had little to do with the semifinal loss to Utah. It had to do with Makhtar N'Diaye.

Dean Smith had taken a chance on N'Diaye, accepting him as a transfer after he had first committed to Wake Forest before spending two years at Michigan. N'Diaye was six foot ten and weighed 240 pounds. He had grown up in Senegal but had come to the United States in high school, playing at the famous basketball prep school Oak Hill Academy. Smith rarely took transfers— for one thing he didn't need them—but N'Diaye had too much potential, or so it appeared, to pass up.

He never became a starter; in fact, he was known mostly for trash-talking, accumulating fouls and technical fouls. During one stage of that season he had four technicals in three games. But he hit a new low in the Utah game. While in the process of fouling out in fourteen minutes, he had a running verbal, pushing, and shoving battle with Utah's Britton Johnsen. At one point it appeared that N'Diaye had spit at Johnsen, and the two players had to be separated.

After the game, N'Diaye claimed that Johnsen had "repeatedly" called him "the N-word."

It was the second time that season that N'Diaye had claimed to be the victim of racial epithets. The first had come during Carolina's win in Chapel Hill over Maryland, when he had insisted that the Maryland fans sitting behind the visiting bench had yelled the N-word in his direction. No one in the area—including the black players on the Maryland bench—heard any such thing.

When N'Diaye's claim was repeated to Johnsen, he hotly denied it, as did Utah coach Rick Majerus, who said he would resign if the claim proved true. The next day, after talking to Guthridge, N'Diaye apologized, admitting that Johnsen had not used the N-word once, much less repeatedly. He denied spitting on him and didn't actually admit he had lied, saying only, "I said some things I shouldn't have said."

Guthridge also issued an apology. It was a terrible way to end what had been a great season. The Tar Heels finished 34–4, but that record was sullied not so much by losing in the Final Four as by N'Diaye's deplorable behavior. The only good news was that his eligibility was finally used up.

—

As it turned out, Mike Krzyzewski's comeback from the lost season of 1995 wasn't truly completed until April 2001.

In 1999, his team reached the national championship game with a 37–1 record, the only loss coming in November to Cincinnati in the Great Alaska Shootout.

Elton Brand had emerged as a star—he would be the number-one pick in the NBA draft in June 1999—and he had plenty of help from Trajan Langdon, Chris Carrawell, Shane Battier, William Avery, and freshman Corey Maggette. People were ready to label the Blue Devils one of the great teams of all time—a hyperbolic stretch to say the least—before they lost the national championship game, 77–74, to a Connecticut team that was clearly the better team that night.

UConn had been ranked number one for much of the season and came into the title game 33–2, one of the losses coming when two starters were out injured. Coach Jim Calhoun was in the wonderful position of being able to honestly tell his players that no one was giving them a chance to win. The Huskies came out like a team with something to prove—and proved they were the best team.

As with 1986, Krzyzewski pinned much of the blame for a championship game loss on himself. This time it wasn't inexperience—it was health. He was badly in need of hip replacement surgery, and trying to coach when just walking from the locker room to the bench and back was a major effort had worn him down. By the time the championship game was played, he could barely stand up from the bench—Quin Snyder stood to make most of the in-game adjustments—and Krzyzewski had very little of the energy that he felt was important to bring to his team, especially that night.

"I just wasn't all there," he said. "In the championship game, my team needed me to be in their faces, to really get after them. They got behind and started to feel sorry for themselves, and I couldn't grab them emotionally and say, 'Stop it!' They needed a coach who could bring the intensity you should bring to a championship game, and I didn't have it.

"UConn was great that night. Maybe if I'd have been one hundred percent we'd have lost anyway. But maybe not. We'll never know."

A year later, Duke won both the ACC regular season and tournament titles again and extended its winning streak against North Carolina to five straight games over two seasons. At that point, Krzyzewski was 6–2 against Guthridge. In all, he had been 14–24 against Smith—13–16 beginning with the "no-hugging" ACC Tournament win in 1984.

Carolina had lost in the first round of the 1999 NCAA Tournament to Weber State and barely squeezed into the 2000 tournament as a number-eight seed. Ironically, the deciding vote that got the Tar Heels into the field was cast by Les Robinson—who was on the committee as the athletic director at the Citadel. Jack Kvancz, the athletic director at George Washington, who was also on the committee, remembered what happened when it came down to a final decision.

"We were down to three teams for one spot," Kvancz said. "What we do in that situation is we ask the guys in the room who are most familiar with those teams which one they'd like to play *least*. I turned to Les, knowing he wasn't exactly a Carolina fan, and said, 'Okay, Les, which one do you want to play the least?'

"He shook his head and said, 'I wish I could say different, but it's definitely Carolina.' That put them over the top."

Granted that reprieve, the Tar Heels got on a roll and made it to the Final Four for the second time in Guthridge's three seasons. Duke's season ended with a Sweet 16 loss to Florida. At the basketball banquet that spring, Guthridge couldn't resist a jibe: "Duke beat us three times this season," he said. "They beat us in Chapel Hill; they beat us in Durham; and they beat us back home from the NCAA Tournament."

Game, set, match—at least for 2000—to Coach Guthridge.

Two months later, he stopped being Coach Guthridge. He had proven he could coach—winning more games in his first three seasons than any coach in Division I history. He'd gone to two Final Fours and won an ACC championship. But that wasn't good enough for many of the Carolina faithful.

Guthridge wasn't Coach Smith. And, in their minds, he wasn't Roy Williams.

Williams still hadn't won that elusive national championship, but he had produced consistent winners at Kansas. He was also fourteen years younger than Guthridge, someone likely to be around for a long time once he rode in on his white horse to take the reins of the program.

Guthridge knew all this and didn't see any reason to keep winning games and going to Final Fours for a fan base that wanted him gone as soon as possible. So, in June, he announced he was retiring. It was time, apparently, for Roy to come home.

Only Roy wasn't so sure he was ready to come home. He loved Kansas and he badly wanted to win a national title there. After performing several versions of *Hamlet,* he announced he was staying at Kansas—forever.

This stunned Carolinaworld, especially Smith, who had more or less assumed that when he told Roy it was time to come home, Roy would come home.

"Maybe the toughest conversation I ever had," Williams said years later. "I mean, me saying no to Coach Smith? Never in my wildest dreams did I ever dream that day would come. But it did."

The final decision on who would be the next coach was supposed to lie with Smith. No one doubted that. Except, apparently, athletic director Dick Baddour, who seemed to believe he should have some say in the hiring.

After Williams turned the job down, Smith's next choice was Larry Brown, whose coaching odyssey had taken him to Los Angeles by then as coach of the Clippers. Baddour flew to Los Angeles and Brown took him to lunch at Bel-Air Country Club.

"I knew Coach Smith wanted me to take the job," Brown said. "I was dying to take it. It was my dream job. But as we were talking, I had the feeling that Dick didn't want to hire me. Finally, he asked me if I had a résumé I could give him. At that moment, it was pretty clear to me I wasn't the guy he wanted. I called Coach Smith and told him I didn't think I was going to get the job."

He didn't. Neither George Karl nor Eddie Fogler wanted the job either. And so, it fell to Matt Doherty, who was thirty-eight and had one year of experience as a head coach. Doherty had been one of Roy Williams's assistants at Kansas and had become the head coach at Notre Dame a year earlier. His team had a good— not great—season, finishing 22–15 while reaching the NIT final.

Like Guthridge, Doherty got off to a great start. By early February the Tar Heels were 21–2—the only losses coming early to defending national champion Michigan State and to Kentucky. They were 10–0 in the ACC, including a win at Duke. Early on, there had been some apprehension about Doherty. He had insisted on bringing his Notre Dame assistants with him— understandable, since they had been hired only a year earlier— but the move left Pat Sullivan and Dave Hanners, both Carolina grads, and Phil Ford, Carolina icon, out of jobs. There were also changes in the office staff insisted upon by Doherty in the name of having his own people working for him. Guthridge had changed nothing. Doherty changed everything.

Winning cures all. After the win at Duke, Doherty was quickly becoming a star in the Carolina pantheon. *Sports Illustrated* did a lengthy profile on him in which—among other things—he made fun of Duke's cheerleaders. Unlike Smith and Guthridge, his style was in-your-face. Carolina fans loved it.

And then, the winning stopped. Duke came into Chapel Hill on the last day of the regular season without starting center Carlos Boozer and buried one three after another in a 95–81 rout. That left the teams tied for the regular season title at 13–3. A week later, in the ACC championship game, Duke won even more easily, 79–53. The Blue Devils were clearly the hot team going into the NCAA Tournament. They were the number-one seed in the East. Carolina went to the South Regionals as a number-two seed but didn't stay long—losing in the second round to Penn State. Not in football, in basketball.

Two weeks later, Doherty was chosen as the Associated Press's national Coach of the Year, the voting having been completed in the last week of the regular season. The *Boston Herald*'s Mike Shalin wrote a lead on Doherty's award that said: "Matt Doherty, who guided North Carolina from a trip to the Final Four in 2000 to a second-round loss in 2001, was today awarded the AP national-coach-of-the-year award."

As it turned out, the AP award was the last of any kind that Doherty would win at North Carolina.

—

After beating Carolina by twenty-six to win the ACC Tournament for a third straight season, Duke reached the Final Four for the second time in three seasons and for the ninth time in Krzyzewski's career. Once again, the NCAA had, by sheer coincidence, paired Duke and Kentucky in the same region. The fact that the East Regionals were being held in Philadelphia—albeit in a different building, across the parking lot from the Spectrum—certainly didn't influence that decision at all.

This time, though, the committee and CBS didn't get their made-in-TV-heaven matchup, because Kentucky was upset in the round of sixteen by Southern California. The Trojans, who were a number-six seed, had beaten Oklahoma State and third-seeded Boston College before beating Kentucky. Duke had won three games with relative ease, including a second-round win over Missouri, coached by Quin Snyder. The Blue Devils beat USC, 79–69, and cut down the nets. They hadn't cut down the nets after getting to the Final Four in 1999.

"We're going to cut this one down and enjoy it," Krzyzewski said. "We'll worry about the Final Four in a couple of days."

The Final Four was in Minneapolis—the same place where Duke had won its second straight title in 1992. The semifinal win over Indiana that year had been the beginning of what was now a nine-year feud between Krzyzewski and Bob Knight. The 2001 semifinal was against Maryland, a team and a school obsessed with Duke and Krzyzewski.

The teams had already played three times that season. Duke had won in College Park in January, coming from ten points down in the final minute of regulation to win in overtime. A month later, Maryland returned the favor, winning in Cameron on the night that Carlos Boozer had gotten hurt. Boozer's absence had caused Krzyzewski to completely revamp his offense, and the Blue Devils had won eight straight games to get to Minneapolis, including a riveting win over Maryland in the ACC semifinals.

Maryland had never been to the Final Four. Gary Williams had done a remarkable job rebuilding the program in the wake of Len Bias's death and the probation that had come about four years later because of the incompetence of Bob Wade, who had been hired to replace Lefty Driesell in the fall of 1986. The Terrapins had gotten back to the tournament in 1994 and had gone for eight straight years. But, prior to 2001, they hadn't gotten past the round of sixteen. They finally reached the Elite Eight—beating local rival Georgetown in the sixteens—and then beat top-seeded Stanford to make the Final Four.

And who was waiting for the Terrapins there? Duke.

"Of course," Williams said years later. "It was as if it was meant to be. We finally make it and there's Duke." He smiled. "I think I know how Dean felt in ninety-one when he got back for the first time in how many years [nine] and Duke's there too. At least he didn't have to play them in the first game."

Williams had actually beaten Krzyzewski the first time they had met—in a second-round NCAA game in 1985 when Williams was at Boston College. But he was 4–23 head-to-head against Krzyzewski since getting to Maryland, and many of the losses had been painful.

Williams and most Maryland fans were absolutely convinced that one of the reasons Duke won so often was because there was—wait for it—a double standard among ACC officials where Duke was concerned. Williams often joked that if you showed up for a game against Duke and any combination of Larry Rose, Mike Wood, and Duke (not named for the school) Edsall was working, you might as well go home.

Although Williams never went completely public with his feelings about Duke the way Krzyzewski had with his feelings about North Carolina in 1984, Krzyzewski was well aware of them. He knew that Williams wasn't the only coach in the ACC who felt that way either. Four years after Smith's retirement, he realized that in many ways he had *become* Smith.

"Dean had been the target for so many years," Krzyzewski said. "Even when we were good or N.C. State or Maryland or Georgia Tech were good, they were always there. Of all the stats associated with Dean that I ever read or heard, one jumped out at me: they never finished lower than third in the ACC for the last thirty years he coached. *Thirty* years in our league? Are you kidding me?

"When I heard other coaches complaining that we got all the calls or that the league wanted us to win, it made me angry. It wasn't fair to our players—it took away from their accomplishments. Then I took a step back and said, 'Hang on, Mike, isn't that exactly the same thing that made Dean mad?' And, of course, it was. When Carolina was beating us regularly there was one reason for it: they were better. When we started to beat people regularly it was for one reason: we were better. But I can honestly say when it happened to me, it helped me appreciate Dean a lot more."

Krzyzewski had even started to sound a little bit like Smith. After a win over a good Butler team in 2000, he commented that "this is the kind of team we might very well have to play in the second round of the NCAA Tournament." Pause. "If we're lucky enough to make the tournament."

Duke was 21–2 at the time. The next day a friend left a voice mail: "We're rounding up the guns."

Perhaps not surprisingly, Maryland came out of the gate in the Saturday night semifinal like a team on a mission from God. Or at least from Gary. After fourteen minutes, the Terrapins led, 39–17. Krzyzewski called a time-out. The Duke fans were sitting in stunned silence. Many Maryland fans were literally dancing in the aisles at the Metrodome. This was their dream come true—being in the Final Four and kicking Duke's butt all at once.

The dream turned into a nightmare pretty quickly. Duke cut the lead to 49–38 by halftime.

Then Krzyzewski—perhaps on the advice of the referees—made two adjustments. He took the ball out of the hands of his point guard, Jason Williams, and put freshman Chris Duhon on the point. This freed Williams to get open for jump shots and allowed Duhon to run the team without worrying about having to score. At the other end of the floor, Krzyzewski put six-foot-five-inch Nate James on six-foot-one Maryland star Juan Dixon, who had scored 16 points in the first half.

Dixon went 1 of 8 in the second half. Duke took the lead for the first time on a Williams three that made it 73–72. The Blue Devils pulled away in the final minute and won, 95–84. In the last twenty-six minutes of the game, they outscored Maryland 78–45.

Naturally, Maryland's fans were convinced they had been done in by the officials. They weren't the only ones convinced that Duke got all the calls—and all the media love. Lute Olson, who was about to coach Arizona against Duke in the championship game, made reference to "Dukie Vitale" in a TV interview, the implication being that Vitale was another Duke apologist.

Duke beat Arizona in the championship game with most of the building screaming every time a call went Duke's way. Even the normally low-key Billy Packer commented on CBS at one point that "I think a lot of people in this building believe Duke is getting the benefit of a lot of calls."

He certainly wasn't wrong—most people were convinced Duke was getting *all* the calls.

On that night, Krzyzewski really didn't care what anyone thought. All he knew was that Shane Battier had gone out as a national champion; Mike Dunleavy had come through with the game of his life; Boozer had come back from his foot injury to play well; and Williams had hit the dagger three-pointer with just under a minute left in Duke's 82–72 victory.

And assistant coach Johnny Dawkins, who had played on the '86 team that had come up just short against Louisville and had been an assistant on the '99 team that came up just short against Connecticut, finally had a national championship.

"Seeing Johnny getting to cut that net, seeing him kiss the rim the way he did, that might have been my best moment that night," Krzyzewski said. "I was happy for all of us. I may have been happiest for him."

Krzyzewski's third national title put him in esteemed company. It meant that only John Wooden, with ten national titles, and Adolph Rupp, with four, had won more often than he had. He was tied with his former mentor, Bob Knight. And, most important, he had come *all* the way back from the nadir of 1995.

Duke's victory did not, however, bring joy to all.

Ron Green, Jr., had worked for *The Charlotte Observer* for many years and had always had a great deal of respect for Duke and North Carolina and for Krzyzewski and Dean Smith. His father, a superb columnist at the paper, was a North Carolina graduate. Ron Jr. had gone to UNC-Charlotte.

His wife, Tamara, was also a Carolina graduate and was one of those people who considered Duke a four-letter word and found it difficult to stomach the fact that her husband liked Mike Krzyzewski. Ron wasn't covering the Final Four that year; he was leaving to drive to Augusta for the Masters the next morning. He sat and watched the game while Tamara went to bed. When the game was over, Ron turned off the TV and walked upstairs.

"Okay," Tamara said, "tell me who won."

"Duke," Ron said.

"Oh god," Tamara said. "Can it possibly get any worse than this? Now we're going to have to hear from all those Duke people that Krzyzewski has won as many national championships as Coach Smith."

"You won't have to hear that," Ron said.

"Why not?" Tamara asked.

"Because Mike has three now. Dean won two."

Tamara Green groaned and turned over to try to sleep. Apparently, it *could* get worse.

35

Dean Smith had vowed to give Bill Guthridge space when he retired from coaching. He maintained an office inside the building named for him and came in several days a week because he was still bombarded with mail and media requests.

"Now that I'm not coaching," he said one day, "I don't really have an excuse to not do these things."

Reluctantly, he accepted an offer from CBS Sports president Sean McManus (a Duke graduate) to do some studio work for the network during the NCAA Tournament. He couldn't stand it.

"I'm a lot more comfortable in front of a blackboard than in front of a camera," he said. "Plus, they wanted me to critique other coaches. I couldn't do that. It wasn't fair."

He gave up the job after one season and watched most of his basketball from the family room in his house. He went to a North Carolina game only if he was asked to be there to be part of a ceremony of some kind. Often he went, took part in the ceremony, and left. That didn't mean he didn't watch his old team play.

"He would turn on the television and take out a notepad," Linnea Smith said. "Early on, I'd go in and keep him company, but after a while I realized he really didn't want company. He was working."

It wasn't as if Smith was calling Guthridge—or, later, Matt Doherty or Roy Williams—to tell them what he was thinking, but he wanted to be prepared if asked. Guthridge asked often. At that point, Smith's office was right down the hall from the basketball office and the two men talked on a regular basis. After Doherty got the job, amid all the upheaval in the basketball office, Smith and Guthridge moved to the basement of the Dean Dome to a small suite of offices that had no windows and were a far cry from the palatial digs where each had once worked.

"Do me a favor," Smith said to a visiting writer one day. "Don't describe where I am in this story."

The office didn't really bother Smith that much. What did bother him was what had happened to Carolina basketball after Guthridge's decision to give up coaching. Doherty's first season ended up being okay—nothing more—but there were serious problems that continued to grow during his second season.

The off-court issues bothered Smith. But the on-court product bothered him much more. The Tar Heels were awful. After winning twenty-six games in Doherty's first season they won *eight* in his second. They began the season with a loss to Hampton—at home—and were 1–4 after five games. It only got worse after that. There was a humiliating 112–79 loss at Maryland and three losses to Duke, including an 87–58 defeat at home. The score in Cameron was 93–68. The 60–48 final score in the first round of the ACC Tournament almost felt like a moral victory because it wasn't a complete blowout.

The season was even more rock-bottom than Duke's 1995 season had been. Most of the Blue Devils' losses that winter had been close—and frustrating. Many of the Tar Heels' losses in the winter of 2002 were embarrassing.

Doherty did prove apt at one very important aspect of coaching: recruiting. During that disastrous season he managed to get commitments from Raymond Felton, a superb point guard; Rashad McCants, a talented shooter; and Sean May, a gifted big man with soft hands.

In one of those "it can only happen in college basketball" twists, Doherty and Carolina were helped immeasurably in May's recruiting by Indiana's decision to fire Bob Knight in the fall of 2000. May was the son of Scott May, the star of Knight's 1976 undefeated national championship team. If Knight had still been coaching at IU, Sean May almost certainly would have gone there to play for him. Beyond that, Knight told Scott May that if his son went to play for Mike Davis, who had succeeded Knight, he would never speak to him again.

That took Indiana out of the mix.

With the three freshmen in the lineup the next season, Carolina improved: winning nineteen games, beating Duke at home, and reaching the NIT quarterfinals. That wasn't good enough to save Doherty's job. Several players were threatening to transfer if Doherty returned, and he had angered enough people away from the court that there was no groundswell to give him another year, even though the Tar Heels had won eleven more games than in 2002.

Two things sealed Doherty's fate: he had earned Smith's enmity by the decisions he had made about his coaching and office staffs, and, perhaps just as important, Roy Williams was ready to come home.

Williams had been tortured by the fact that he had said no to "Coach Smith" in 2000. Even though he coached Kansas to the Final Four in 2002 and the national title game in 2003, it was clear to those who knew him that if Coach Smith asked him to come home again he wouldn't be able to say no a second time.

And he didn't.

Kansas fans were furious when he announced he was leaving, because he had said three years earlier he would never leave Kansas. But circumstances had changed: his alma mater was floundering and in 2000 Williams had figured that Larry Brown would take the job when he turned it down. He hadn't. Carolina had gone 27–36 in Doherty's last two seasons. That was unacceptable.

"The truth is, when I said I was staying at Kansas forever that was what I was planning to do," Williams said. "I wasn't lying. I wasn't thinking I'd get the call from Coach Smith again three years later." He paused, his voice getting very soft. "The hardest thing I ever did in my life was say no that first time. I wanted to win a national championship at Kansas. I came close, very close. I knew they'd go out and hire a great coach, which they did—Bill Self. I just couldn't say no to Coach Smith twice."

Williams's sentiment was understandable. He was entitled to go back home and rescue the program that had been built by a man who was a father figure to him. In all likelihood, the anger people felt in Kansas would have subsided a lot more quickly if Williams hadn't kept bringing up how much he loved Kansas and everyone who had ever set foot inside the state.

He even went so far as to wear a Jayhawk sticker on his sports coat the night Kansas played Memphis in the 2008 national championship game—two days after beating North Carolina in the semifinals. That didn't thrill a lot of his fans back home. It also became a running joke on the Internet and in the national media. One website carried a photo of the Dean Dome's floor with some "renovations" that Coach Williams had requested. The logo at midcourt was a giant Jayhawk.

—

Because he was so intense and out there with his emotions and because of a habit he had of referring to himself in the third person, Williams was often the object of jokes and scorn. But no one could argue with the results he got.

Krzyzewski, whose relationship with Williams evolved much the way his relationship with Smith had—from sniping back and forth to mutual respect—actually had a routine he did for friends that he called "the Roy Williams coaching clinic."

"In the first session, Roy Williams will talk about competing," Krzyzewski would say, "because *no one* competes like Roy Williams. In the second session, Roy Williams will talk about loving your players, because *no one* loves his players like Roy Williams does. In the third session, Roy Williams will talk about working hard because *no one* works as hard as Roy Williams. And, in the fourth session, which will go on *all night,* Roy Williams will talk about everything he ever learned from *Coach Smith.*"

It was a little bit mean, but a lot funny. And not inaccurate. When Roy Williams wrote his autobiography after winning a second national championship in 2009, the title was *Hard Work.*

At that point, Roy Williams was doing a pretty good job of kicking Mike Krzyzewski's butt. Duke had beaten Carolina twice in 2004 and had gone to the Final Four that season, losing to Connecticut in the semifinals after leading by eight points with 3:30 to play. The Blue Devils also won the first Duke-Carolina meeting of 2005. Most of the next five seasons belonged to Carolina—in almost every possible way. Beginning with a late-rally victory in the regular season finale in 2005—a win that brought back memories of the old "piss factor" days—the Tar Heels won seven of nine games against Duke through the 2009 season.

More important, they won two national championships during that stretch and went to three Final Fours. Duke, having gone to Krzyzewski's tenth Final Four in 2004, didn't come close from '05 through '09, never getting past the Sweet 16. Carolina's NCAA record those five seasons was 20–3. Duke's was 7–5.

Krzyzewski had been very discouraged after the UConn loss in 2004. Losing the lead late and losing the game hurt, especially because he believed the officials had bought into the "Duke gets all the calls" hype and had actually shortchanged his team when the game was on the line.

"We got screwed," were his first words to a friend after he had walked out of his postgame press conference. "Jim [Calhoun] didn't do anything different from what a lot of guys are doing now. From the first minute, every call that went against them he was screaming, 'Oh yeah, I forgot, Duke doesn't foul.' The difference was, these guys bought it."

What frustrated him more, though, was losing players early. Luol Deng, who Krzyzewski had thought would be at least a three-year player because he was an excellent student from a family that seemed to value education, left after his freshman season. Shaun Livingston, an outstanding guard who should have enrolled in the summer of 2004, changed his mind and went straight from high school to the NBA.

"I'm done," he said at one point that summer. "I'm gonna recruit kids who want to play college basketball for three or four years, not kids who are passing through to the NBA. How do you establish a relationship with a kid in one year?" He smiled. "Or in no years."

The notion was noble—the results were not. It wasn't as if Duke was awful the next five years, it just wasn't, well, Duke. The Blue Devils did win three ACC Tournaments (2005, 2006, 2009), but in the tournament that mattered most, they consistently stumbled. In 2005 they lost in the Sweet 16 to Michigan State (preventing another of those Duke-Kentucky regional finals that always seemed to be set up by the committee by "coincidence"). A year later, as a number-one seed, they were stunned in the regional semis again, this time by a less-than-stellar LSU team.

In 2007 they didn't come close to the Sweet 16, losing in the first round to Virginia Commonwealth. This came a week after a first-round ACC Tournament loss to N.C. State. The loss to the Wolfpack meant that Duke wouldn't play in the ACC championship game for the first time since 1997—a run that included seven tournament titles and two losses in the final. The loss to VCU a week later left the Blue Devils with a 22–11 record. It was only the third time since 1984 that a team coached all season by Krzyzewski had lost ten games or more: the '84 team had been 24–10 and the '96 team, the year after the leave of absence, had been 18–13.

Things got a little better in 2008: the team finished 28–6, second to North Carolina in the ACC, before losing in the second round of the NCAAs to West Virginia. A year later the record was 30–7, and for the first time in three years, the Blue Devils returned to the Sweet 16. But they were blitzed there—77–54—by Villanova and then had to watch Carolina cruise to a second national title in five years.

All was well again in the Carolina family. Roy Williams had come home to return the Tar Heels to glory. The evil rat Krzyzewski hadn't been slain, but he'd certainly been wounded. North Carolina State, even though it had gone to five straight NCAA Tournaments under Herb Sendek from 2002 to 2006, simply wasn't a factor—something that so frustrated State fans that they ran Sendek off in spite of the success he'd had. The Wolfpack averaged twenty-one wins a year during Sendek's last five seasons and reached the Sweet 16 of the NCAA Tournament in 2005, after upsetting Connecticut—the defending national champion—in the second round.

But Sendek was caught in the Duke-Carolina/Krzyzewski-Williams crossfire. The run to the Sweet 16 was State's best NCAA Tournament performance since Valvano's last tournament, in 1989. During that sixteen-year period Duke had gone at least that far thirteen times and Carolina at least that far ten times. Duke had won three national titles and Carolina—including 2005—had won two.

State fans, having seen the school win national championships in 1974 and 1983, couldn't understand why their team couldn't get back to that level or at least close to it. There was another reason Sendek fled when offered the job in 2006 at Arizona State: Jim Valvano.

Valvano had left State in 1990 under a cloud, which was why he had almost taken the Wichita State job two years later. But in death, he had become larger than life. His valiant fight the last eleven months he was alive; the speech at the tenth-anniversary game; and, of course, the ESPYS speech had left him with a remarkable legacy. What's more, the V Foundation, his last great coaching job, had raised millions and millions of dollars to fight cancer. There was a V Foundation golf tournament in Raleigh every year and a Jimmy V Classic basketball tournament, staged in New York—usually Madison Square Garden—every December.

Each year during the Classic, ESPN showed the ESPYS speech on an almost nonstop loop. Those who followed basketball at all knew the speech well. N.C. State fans seemed to know it by heart.

"I think it's been very hard for every coach who has followed Jim here," Pam Valvano Strasser said, sitting in her living room shortly after the twenty-first anniversary of Jim's death. "In a very real sense, Jim's still alive to people here. He's a constant presence. Everyone who coaches at State is compared to him—not just in terms of wins and losses, but in terms of personality. That's unfair. There was only one Jim."

Mark Gottfried is now State's fourth coach since Valvano's departure. Les Robinson had one good season and five bad ones. Sendek's last five seasons were very good, but not good enough. The school then brought back Sidney Lowe, in part because he had a good deal of coaching experience, but also to try to rekindle memories of 1983.

"You can't bring back the past," Lowe, now an assistant coach with the Minnesota Timberwolves, said three years after being fired. "Whoever the coach at State is going to be, he's got to not only get good players, he's got to get great players, because those other two guys [Krzyzewski and Williams] are always going to have great players. It's a tough spot to be in." He smiled. "Even if you played for Coach V."

Lowe matched Sendek's first season when he upset Duke in the first round of the ACC Tournament and made it to the final. Like Sendek's team in '97, the Wolfpack of ten years later ran out of gas, losing to (of course) North Carolina in the championship game. That weekend turned out to be the highlight of Lowe's five seasons at State. The Wolfpack made the NIT twice but never had an ACC record of better than 6–10. After a 15–16 season in 2011, new athletic director Debbie Yow fired him and hired Gottfried—who has had more success than anyone since Valvano, reaching the NCAA Tournament his first four seasons and making it to the Sweet 16 in 2012 and 2015.

By almost any standard, Gottfried's 92–52 record is enviable. But, like the other State coaches, he finds himself wedged between two Hall of Famers. And in the lengthy shadow of Jimmy V.

—

In 2010, Mike Krzyzewski turned the tables on Roy Williams—and college basketball—again. And he did it without any one-and-done players.

The phrase "one-and-done" came into vogue in 2007 when

the NBA changed its rules to require that a player be at least one year out of high school before he was eligible for the NBA draft. This meant that players like Kevin Garnett, Kobe Bryant, LeBron James, and Dwight Howard, who had gone straight from high school to the NBA, would not have been allowed to do so. They would have had to spend a year in college—or overseas—before pursuing the big bucks of the NBA.

This created the phenomenon of star players making stopovers in college for a year before turning pro. Kentucky coach John Calipari, who did not—as he frequently points out—invent the rule, soon became the man who perfected it. Every year Calipari recruits five blue-chip players and then instantly begins recruiting their replacements. His sales pitch is simple: spend your one year in college with me and I will prepare you for the NBA. He does that superbly and wins lots and lots of games in the process. Plus, since only a handful of his players return for a second year, he doesn't really have to worry about any pesky questions about academics or going to class.

By 2009, Krzyzewski had figured out that his utopian notion of only recruiting players who were going to stay three or four years wasn't working. He hadn't been to a Final Four since 2004, and Roy Williams was leaving him in the dust. And so, reluctantly, Krzyzewski jumped into the one-and-done pool with everyone else, getting a commitment in the fall of 2009 from a gifted point guard from New Jersey named Kyrie Irving. Krzyzewski knew he'd only have Irving for a year. He took him anyway.

And then, in what might have been a message from the basketball gods in whom Krzyzewski believes so ardently, Duke won a national championship the following spring with three seniors and two juniors in the starting lineup. The seniors—Brian Zoubek, Jon Scheyer, and Lance Thomas—had been freshmen in 2007, the year of the first-round flameouts in both the ACC Tournament and the NCAA Tournament.

None was a star—none was even drafted by an NBA team, although Thomas has played briefly in the league—but along with juniors Kyle Singler (a second-round pick) and Nolan Smith (a late first-round pick), they became a superb defensive unit. They were a throwback Krzyzewski team, one that struggled on occasion to score but was capable of playing shutdown defense for most of forty minutes.

The season turned around when Krzyzewski decided to put Zoubek, a seven-footer who had struggled with injuries and being offensively challenged throughout his career, into the starting lineup. He was the last piece in what became a superb defensive team. The Blue Devils won the ACC Tournament and then won tough games in the regional semis and final against Purdue and Baylor—playing in Houston, a virtual home court for Baylor—to get back to the Final Four for the first time in six seasons.

They played their best game of the season to beat West Virginia easily in the semifinals and then met Butler, the ultimate Cinderella team, in the championship game.

Butler was an amazing story. The Bulldogs played in a one-bid league, the Horizon, and had been the school Krzyzewski had "complimented" ten years earlier when he had said they were the kind of team Duke might play in the second round of the tournament. Now they were playing for the title, Butler having beaten Michigan State in the semifinals.

They were also playing in Indianapolis at Lucas Oil Stadium, which was a little more than 6 miles from the Butler campus—6.4 miles, to be specific, from Hinkle Fieldhouse, the historic old gym where Butler played its home games. When the Bulldogs, coached by thirty-three-year-old Brad Stevens (who looked twenty-three), made the Final Four the national media went wild with *Hoosiers* references.

Milan, the tiny high school that had been the real-life subject of the fictionalized movie, had won the 1954 state championship game in Hinkle Fieldhouse. Bobby Plump, the real-life Jimmy Chitwood, who had made the real-life winning shot against Muncie Central, was a Butler graduate who owned a bar in downtown Indianapolis. Almost every member of the national media made two pilgrimages that week: one to Hinkle Fieldhouse, the other to Plump's bar to hear the real story about the Milan (not Hickory High) Miracle from Plump.

On the first Monday night in April the only thing standing between the college version of *Hoosiers* and the theatrical ending most of America wanted to see was Duke. Who better to play the role of villain than the Blue Devils? Duke had arrived in town on Wednesday to be greeted by a front-page cartoon of Krzyzewski in *The Indianapolis Star* wearing devil's horns—it was not because of the team's nickname—a target on his forehead, and a mustache and goatee. An extremely stupid writer from Miami who had never met Krzyzewski wrote the following paragraph:

> For some reason we know if the devil had a face it would have beady little eyes (like Mike Krzyzewski's). If he had a voice, it would be nasally and annoying (like Krzyzewski's) and if he had a name it would be impossible to spell and the sound would follow no laws of language (like, well, you know).

Funny stuff—if you have a double-digit IQ and think making fun of someone's ethnicity is clever.

What could have been a better setting for the finale than in a 71,000-seat football stadium with about 67,000 of the fans in the building pulling for Milan, aka Butler?

The game was something straight out of a movie. Butler was every bit as good as Duke on the defensive end of the floor. The Bulldogs hadn't given up sixty points to anyone in five tournament games. They contested every pass. So did Duke. They got in the face of every shooter, every ball handler. So did Duke.

Neither team could score much or build any momentum. The biggest lead all night for either team was five points. And, naturally, the game wasn't decided until the buzzer. Duke led 60–59 when Kyle Singler missed a wide-open jump shot and Butler rebounded and called time with thirty-three seconds to play.

This was the moment when Gordon Hayward—aka Jimmy Chitwood/Bobby Plump—would step into the huddle and say to Stevens, "I'll make the shot."

He almost did. Catching the ball at the top of the key, the six-nine Hayward, who had the ball-handling skills of a guard, tried to go left, then veered right and dribbled to the baseline. As Hayward rose to shoot, Zoubek, seeing him leave his feet, ran at him and forced him to lean back just a little bit to get the shot off. It clanged off the rim, and Zoubek, showing remarkable quickness, turned and grabbed the rebound. He was fouled with 3.6 seconds left.

Zoubek was not a good free-throw shooter, but he calmly swished the first shot. Then, in a move that almost changed his coaching legacy, Krzyzewski told Zoubek to miss the second shot intentionally. His thinking made some sense: it is much easier for a team to set up a play to get a last-second shot off an inbounds pass—see Duke-Kentucky circa 1992 as the prime example—than off a rebound.

But 3.6 seconds can be an eternity, especially in a scramble situation off a missed shot.

As ordered, Zoubek missed the second shot. Hayward grabbed the rebound and began sprinting upcourt as 70,931 people stood and held their breath. Singler, who had done an admirable job guarding Hayward most of the night, came to cut him off—not stop him, but force him to swerve to his right to use up time. But before he could get there, Butler's Matt Howard almost blew him into the upper deck with a screen that probably would have been a foul at any point in any game—except in the final seconds of a national title game.

With Singler on the floor checking to see if he still had all his teeth, Hayward charged across midcourt and squared himself to shoot from forty-five feet. The ball was right on line all the way, and for a split second it looked as if it was going in. It hit the glass, then caught the front rim, hung for a moment, and then dropped to the floor.

Everyone in the building gasped. The majority gasped in disbelief and disappointment. The shot had missed going in by an inch—maybe two. The minority gasped in relief.

"From where I was [on the floor] it looked like it might go in," Singler said later.

Krzyzewski thought the same thing. "What a game," he said as he hugged his family—wife, children, and grandchildren. "I've been in eight of these [national championship games] and this one was the best. They were great. We were great. We won but I don't feel as if they lost."

If Hayward's shot had gone in it would have been the greatest finish in college basketball history—perhaps in all of sports history. A miracle shot winning a national championship for a miracle team—against the sport's Darth Vader. Christian Laettner's shot and Jim Valvano's sprint would have been relegated to supporting roles when CBS rolled out highlights every spring. Even though it didn't go in, Hayward's shot still took its place in the pantheon of remarkable NCAA Tournament moments.

If the shot had gone in, Krzyzewski would have been questioned forever about telling Zoubek to miss. It would have been his Bill Buckner moment. (Buckner had 2,700 Major League hits and won Gold Gloves but is only remembered by most for the Mookie Wilson ground ball that skipped through his legs in game six of the 1986 World Series.) If Hayward's shot had dropped through the basket instead of off the rim, Krzyzewski would have been the coach with three national titles, eleven Final Four trips, and a final-second loss brought on by his decision to tell one of his players to miss a free throw.

But it didn't happen that way. Instead, Krzyzewski had his fourth national championship, meaning that only John Wooden, with ten, had more. Adolph Rupp also had four, but those had been won in an era where a team had to win no more than four games to win a title and never had to leave its region of the country to get to the Final Four. The same could be said of nine of Wooden's ten titles, but ten is a completely overwhelming number—

especially since Wooden won them all in a twelve-year period, including seven in a row.

Krzyzewski was now officially on coaching's Mount Rushmore. Most people would agree that Wooden, Krzyzewski, Bob Knight, and Dean Smith belonged there. Some would argue for Rupp, but who would you remove to make a place for Rupp?

Standing on the court in Indianapolis that night, Krzyzewski was a *long* way from the Denny's in Atlanta. He had reached coaching Nirvana.

36

In the summer of 2007, Dean Smith elected to have knee-replacement surgery. He was seventy-six and the pain had gotten to the point that it was difficult for him to play golf at all, much less play well.

"It was elective surgery," Linnea Smith said. "The reason he did it was golf." She smiled sadly. "If we had known what was going to happen, obviously, he wouldn't have had the surgery. But of course there was no way to know what would happen."

What happened was neurological postsurgical damage. Two years earlier, Smith had noticed that his extraordinary memory was beginning to slip a little. "Every once in a while I reach for a name or a date and it's not there," he said. "That never used to happen. I guess when you're seventy-four this starts to happen."

Even so, Smith's memory was still extremely sharp. That was no longer true after the knee surgery. There were whispers in basketball circles that his memory had slipped, but only a close circle of friends knew how much.

By 2009, those friends were concerned because Smith was still driving and would sometimes forget where he was going or how to get there.

"He shouldn't be driving," Bill Guthridge said. "Knowing him as I do, I'm not sure he would mind if his life ended now, given the condition he's in. But the nightmare would be if he got into an accident and hurt or, God forbid, killed someone else. That's what we're all afraid of whenever he gets into his car."

There were still moments when he was the legendary Dean Smith, telling a story in exact detail. In the summer of 2009, he was asked what he remembered about how he met his first wife,

Ann. Without missing a beat he explained their first meeting at the 1953 graduation dance minute by minute. He recalled the evening in great detail, talking about how he and Ann had started courting after that night. And yes, he said "courting." This was 1953.

The subject changed to Bob Spear, the basketball coach at the Air Force Academy who had given him his first college coaching job. Smith and Spear had remained close friends until Spear's death in 1995.

Smith shook his head. "Tell me something about him," he said. "Maybe it will come back."

He was reminded of Spear's role in his life, not only because he'd hired him but because he had helped him get the job as Frank McGuire's assistant coach at North Carolina.

He shook his head again and banged his fist on his desk in frustration.

"There's nothing," he said softly. "Nothing."

Dementia goes in only one direction. The moments when the patient is lucid dwindle as time goes by. In 2010, for the first time, Smith's family acknowledged the illness publicly because there were rumors in the North Carolina media about it. Some reporters knew what was going on but simply chose not to report the story because of their respect for Smith. It was apparent, though, that someone was going to write it or talk about it in the near future. There was no point trying to keep the secret any longer.

Not long after the announcement, Eddie Fogler drove to Chapel Hill from his home in Columbia, South Carolina, to see his old coach. Smith—who by then had stopped driving—was still coming into his office two or three days a week. After returning to North Carolina, Roy Williams had insisted that Smith and Guthridge move out of the basement, and they had been set up in an office suite just a few steps down the hall from the basketball offices. Williams also refused to park in the spot that was reserved for the head basketball coach.

"That's Coach Smith's spot," he said. "Period."

Before Fogler went in to see Smith, he stopped to say hello to Williams. "Eddie, understand, you may walk in there and he'll throw his arms around you and start talking about recruiting you in 1965 and tell you what your mother served for dinner on his home visit," Williams said. "More likely, though, he won't know who you are. You can't take it personally. It's not because he doesn't still love you."

Not long afterward, Fogler was back in Williams's office, tears streaming down his face. "I know it's not personal," Fogler said. "But seeing him that way is just awful."

There were still moments. On February 28, 2013, Smith celebrated his eighty-second birthday. Cake and ice cream were brought into the office, and Williams and his staff went in to sing "Happy Birthday." Williams could tell by the look in his eyes that Smith was in and out, smiling in recognition of what was going on some of the time, his eyes blank at others.

"I was getting ready to leave and go back to my office and I went to say good-bye to him and wish him happy birthday one more time," Williams said. "As I did, he pulled me down so he could whisper in my ear. He said, 'I'm so proud of you, Roy. You're doing a great job.' I couldn't stop crying."

As he retold the story, Roy Williams cried again.

—

Mike Krzyzewski was aware of Smith's health issues long before the public announcement. Even though they are rivals, those who work in the athletic departments at Duke and North Carolina are friends and colleagues, since they often work on Duke-Carolina events together. Krzyzewski had heard from his staffers, from friends, and from the coaching grapevine that Smith was very ill.

"I didn't really know how bad it was," he said. "I knew it was bad, but I didn't know exactly how bad because I hadn't seen him for a while."

On June 30, 2011, Krzyzewski saw up close how bad it was. The North Carolina Sports Hall of Fame had decided to honor

Krzyzewski, Smith, and the late Kay Yow—the longtime women's coach at North Carolina State, who had died two years earlier after a long battle with cancer—with their Naismith Good Sportsmanship Awards.

The ceremony was held on that June night in Raleigh, and it was full of bittersweet moments for everyone in attendance.

The evening began with a moment of silence for Lorenzo Charles, the N.C. State forward who had scored the winning basket in the 1983 national championship, capping the extraordinary run of the Cardiac Pack. Three days earlier, Charles had lost control of the bus he had been driving on I-40 between Durham and Raleigh. He had worked for ten years for the Elite Coach company and was driving an empty bus back to Raleigh.

There was speculation later that he'd had a seizure of some kind that had caused him to lose control, but nothing was ever confirmed officially. He died at the scene at the age of forty-seven—the same age Jim Valvano had been when he died eighteen years earlier. He was buried ten spaces down from Valvano in Oakwood Cemetery.

Kay Yow was represented that night by her sister, Debbie, the athletic director at N.C. State. Smith was helped onto the stage by Roy Williams, who spoke on his behalf. While Williams spoke, Smith sat next to Krzyzewski. When Williams finished, as the crowd stood to applaud, Smith tried to stand up to thank the audience and to thank Williams.

"He was wobbly when he tried to get up," Krzyzewski said. "I could tell he wasn't going to make it. So I stood up to applaud and at the same time I just slipped my arm underneath his so that he could make it to his feet without anyone noticing that he needed help."

One person noticed: Williams.

"I saw what Mike did," he said. "It was one of those very quiet acts of kindness you don't forget."

Krzyzewski knew that night that the Dean Smith he'd known and not loved, and the Dean Smith he'd come to love, no longer existed. He was a shadow of himself. And that made Krzyzewski almost unbearably sad.

"It was the cruelest twist of all," he said. "You're talking about someone who had the sharpest mind of anybody that any of us ever met. To be robbed of his memory—of all things . . ." His voice trailed off. "It was unthinkable."

—

The four seasons following Duke's 2010 national championship were not filled with joy in Durham, Chapel Hill, or Raleigh.

North Carolina did bounce back after its disastrous 2010 season, when the Tar Heels failed to reach the NCAA Tournament, to return to the Elite Eight in 2011. But the Tar Heels lost to Kentucky one step short of the Final Four. Duke had beaten Carolina in the ACC Tournament championship game that March without star point guard Kyrie Irving.

The first of the new Duke one-and-dones had injured his toe in a December game against—of all teams—Butler and hadn't played since then. Irving was able to return in time for the NCAA Tournament, but he had only played eight games and he and his teammates never got comfortable with one another again. Duke was fortunate to beat Michigan in the second round and then was blasted in the Sweet 16 by Arizona.

Debbie Yow had fired Sidney Lowe at the end of the 2011 season and set her sights on Shaka Smart, the VCU wunderkind coach who had taken the Rams to the Final Four that spring, to replace Lowe. She offered him a $1-million-a-year raise—but he turned it down. He had been at VCU for only two years and he vividly remembered how he had felt when his college coach had left after his freshman season.

"I just couldn't do that to my guys," he said later. "The day may come but not now. I wasn't ready."

Left unspoken was the fact that a lot of coaches were wary about going to work for Yow. During her years at Maryland she had developed a reputation for throwing coaches under the bus if they didn't have instant success. And she had fought constantly with her most successful coach, Gary Williams. The relationship between the coach and AD had gotten so bad during Yow's final years at Maryland that when the two of them absolutely had to speak to each other they would call the other's direct line late at night when there would be no answer and leave a message.

Yow eventually was able to hire Mark Gottfried, who'd had success at Alabama and, like every coach who ever lived, gone into TV after being fired. Gottfried wanted to coach again, so he was willing to deal with Yow. At Gottfried's introductory press conference, Yow was asked about her attempts to hire Smart and the lack of interest in the job among other coaches who would have seemed to be prime candidates.

"Well, everyone knows Gary Williams sabotaged my search," she said.

That must have made Gottfried feel great about his new boss.

Whether he was the result of sabotage or not (he wasn't) Gottfried proved that sometimes it is better as an AD to be lucky than good. Not only did State make the NCAA Tournament in his first season, but the Wolfpack reached the Sweet 16.

Which meant it lasted two rounds longer than Duke did. It was the first time since 1985 that State had still been playing in the tournament after Duke had been knocked out.

Duke was stunned—but not truly stunned—by an underseeded Lehigh team in the first round, a number-fifteen seed beating a number-two seed. The Blue Devils hadn't played well down the stretch—losing to North Carolina at home in the regular season finale and then to Florida State in the semifinals of the ACC Tournament. The only real highlight of the season had been a late rally in Chapel Hill that had produced a memorable 85–84 victory when Austin Rivers hit a three-point shot at the buzzer to completely stun the Carolina crowd.

Rivers was that year's one-and-done, having taken the spot vacated by Kyrie Irving when he turned pro after playing eleven games in a Duke uniform. Rivers's one great moment somewhat overshadowed his otherwise spotty play. If there was ever a highly touted player who could have used another year of college it was Rivers—who completed fewer passes than the average third-string quarterback and seemed to think defense was beneath him.

But that didn't stop him from leaving. He was still going to be a first-round draft pick (he was taken at number ten in the first round by New Orleans) and being a one-and-done had, by then, become a badge of honor for top players.

"That's one of the problems with this rule—one of many," said John Thompson, Jr., the Hall of Fame former Georgetown coach. "Are most of these kids ready for the NBA after their freshman year? Hell no. But they have to go. The money is too big and they don't want the stigma of being a college sophomore while all the guys they played AAU ball with are in the NBA."

Krzyzewski certainly feels the same way but feels helpless to fight it.

"I hate it," he said in the winter of 2015, coaching a team with *three* one-and-dones in the starting lineup. "My thing has always been about developing relationships with the guys I coach. You can't do that in one year. But if I don't have these guys playing for me for a year then I'll almost certainly have them playing against me for a year."

Krzyzewski's one-and-done frustration peaked in 2014. Duke had reached the Elite Eight in 2013 with a team that—surprise—didn't have a one-and-done player on it. Duke won a major recruiting battle in the fall of 2012 for Jabari Parker, a highly touted six-foot-eight-inch player out of Chicago. Parker's recruitment was followed so closely that ESPN.com claimed a scoop when it learned not where Parker was going to college but *when* he would announce where he was going to college.

Much to the chagrin of Michigan State coach Tom Izzo—who thought he had the kid—it turned out to be Duke. Even before the season began the TV talking heads were claiming that Parker, Julius Randle of Kentucky, and Andrew Wiggins of Kansas were the three greatest freshmen in the history of college basketball, perhaps in the history of sports.

None of them quite lived up to the hype. In fact, "led" by Parker and a rare transfer, Rodney Hood, Duke lost in its first NCAA Tournament game for the second time in three seasons. This time the loss was to Mercer, a number-fourteen seed. Parker shot 4 for 14 in the game and was completely outplayed by Jakob Gollon, a sixth-year senior who had missed two full seasons with major injuries. Gollon had 20 points and 5 rebounds and often forced Parker into wild, no-chance shots at the other end. The Bears started five seniors, and when the game was in doubt in the final three minutes they were the team that made all the critical plays.

"They were men," Krzyzewski said after the game—the point being that his players were not. "They never backed down all day."

As he sat and answered postgame questions, Krzyzewski already knew that both Parker and Hood—who had transferred from Mississippi State and was a sophomore—were going to leave to turn pro. When someone asked him if he had any thoughts about next season, Krzyzewski just shrugged.

"I don't even know who's going to be on my team next season," he said. "When I know that, then I can tell you what kind of season I think we'll have."

Krzyzewski had just turned sixty-seven. He was seventeen wins shy of becoming the first NCAA men's Division I coach with one thousand victories. He had decided to stay on as the U.S. Olympic team coach through 2016. So there wasn't any doubt that he was going to continue coaching. There also wasn't any doubt that it wasn't quite as much fun as it had once been.

"I still love it," Krzyzewski said a few months after the loss to Mercer. "I have to be able to adjust to the realities of the game today. What's happened the last three seasons isn't acceptable. That's on me. That's not because of the one-and-done rule. We all have to live with it. I've reinvented myself before; I have to do it again."

—

In August of 2013, Mike and Mickie Krzyzewski rented a house for a week on a small island near Wilmington called Figure Eight. They had rented there periodically through the years when they had some free time in the summer. They were both aware of the fact that Dean and Linnea Smith had a place somewhere on Figure Eight, but they had never crossed paths in the past.

They were taking a walk on the beach one afternoon when they bumped into Kelly Smith, one of Dean and Linnea's daughters. They stopped to talk and Mike finally said, "Do you think there's any chance we could come by the house and see your dad?"

There was a moment of hesitation. "Why don't you call my mom," Kelly finally said. "We're leaving tomorrow morning and I'm not sure about our schedule."

She gave the Krzyzewskis Linnea's cell number. As soon as they were back at the house, Mike made the call.

"Of course," Linnea said instantly. Then she paused for a moment. "Understand, though, that he almost certainly won't recognize you. In fact, he may not know you're here. But if you want to come, you're more than welcome."

Not long after, the Krzyzewskis walked down to the Smiths' house.

"Dean was in a wheelchair," Mickie said. "It was a shock, I think for both Mike and me, to see how far he had slipped. I didn't think he recognized us at all or, as Linnea had said, was really even aware that we were there.

"But Mike, being Mike, he was doing his mind-over-matter thing. So he just kept talking to him as if it was twenty years ago."

Mike talked for a while, looking directly at Dean, about how proud he was that Dean was going to be awarded the Presidential Medal of Freedom by President Obama. "I can't think of anyone who deserves it more," he said, his voice, according to both Mickie and Linnea, soft and filled with sadness. "What you've done as a person is so much more important than basketball."

They lingered for a while. There really wasn't much to say, but Mike and Mickie were both thinking this might be the last time they ever saw Dean.

"He just looked so frail," Mickie remembered. "At one point I thought to myself, 'If we don't leave soon, I'm just going to burst into tears.'"

Finally, it was time to go. Mike walked to Dean's wheelchair and leaned down. He took his right hand and formed it into a handshake, put his left hand on his shoulder, and leaned down to whisper in his ear.

"Coach," he said, "I love you."

At that moment, Dean looked up at him and Mike saw something—he wasn't sure if it was recognition or not, but it was something—in his eyes.

And then Dean Smith took his left hand, placed it firmly on Mike Krzyzewski's right hand, and squeezed it. And then he smiled.

Almost thirty-three years after their angry first handshake in Greensboro, their last handshake brought both Mike and Mickie Krzyzewski to tears.

"I can't even tell you," Krzyzewski said, recalling the moment, "how much that meant to me."

He didn't need to.

—

On the morning of February 8, 2015, Mike Krzyzewski stopped for gas on his way home from church. It was a cold Sunday in Durham, but at least it wasn't snowing.

Krzyzewski's mood was bright. The previous afternoon, his team had hammered Notre Dame, avenging one of his team's three January losses. Exactly two weeks earlier, Duke had beaten St. John's in Madison Square Garden on a euphoric afternoon for Krzyzewski's 1,000th win as a college head coach. The milestones kept piling up. In December 2010, he had won his 880th game, surpassing Dean Smith's 879 career wins. Eleven months later, also in Madison Square Garden, he had won his 903rd game, making him the all-time wins leader in Division I—taking that spot over from Bob Knight.

Knight had been in the building that night, working for ESPN, wearing a garish green sweater on air. The fact that Duke was playing Michigan State, whose colors were green and white, was duly noted by those who understood that it was killing Knight to think that anyone was taking the record away from him—much less his former pupil.

By then, Knight and Krzyzewski had made up. In April 2001, after he had been voted into the Naismith Memorial Basketball Hall of Fame, Krzyzewski called Knight. Their feud had gone on for nine years, so long that neither man was certain exactly what they had fought about.

When Knight answered the phone, Krzyzewski got right to the point.

"Coach, I've been elected to the Hall of Fame," he said. "I really don't care what you're mad at me about or what I'm mad at you about but neither of us is getting any younger and this needs to stop. If I hadn't played for you and coached for you, I wouldn't be going into the Hall of Fame. There's no one other than you who should introduce me at the induction ceremony."

"Mike," Knight said, "I'd be honored."

Hatchet buried—finally.

And so, the two men had hugged after Duke beat Michigan State that night, and Knight—being Knight—had said, "Not bad for a guard who couldn't shoot."

The win over St. John's for win number one thousand had been a joyous day. Dozens of former Krzyzewski players had come to New York hoping to see him achieve the milestone. His entire family—Mickie, the three daughters, the three sons-in-law, and all nine grandchildren were there.

Two weeks later, Krzyzewski and his team were scheduled to

fly to Tallahassee in the afternoon to play on Monday night at Florida State. As Krzyzewski pulled into the gas station, his phone buzzed with a text.

It was from Jon Jackson, one of Duke's associate athletic directors. It was brief.

"Coach," it said, "Dean Smith passed away late last night."

Krzyzewski gasped. "Oh no!" he said out loud, stunned.

"It shocked me," he said later that morning. "Of course I knew how sick he had been, so maybe it shouldn't have been a shock. But it was. It really knocked me backwards. Somehow, I thought Dean Smith would never die."

He paused and there was a quaver in his voice when he continued. "Of course he *won't* ever die. He'll live forever because of all the things he taught people."

Never be proud of doing the right thing; just do *the right thing.*

Ten days later, North Carolina's basketball team made the short trip up 15-501 to Cameron Indoor Stadium to resume college basketball's most intense rivalry. Prior to tip-off, the players from both teams gathered in a circle, knelt, and put their arms around one another for a moment of silence to honor Dean Smith.

Mike Krzyzewski and Roy Williams knelt next to each other, arms around each other. Cameron had never been so silent.

Moments later, the game began. For more than two hours, the two teams fought and scraped and contested every pass, rebound, and loose ball. When it was finally over, Duke had escaped with a 92–90 win in overtime.

"Dean wouldn't have liked the outcome tonight," Krzyzewski said. "But I know he would have been proud of the game."

No doubt he wouldn't have liked all the fuss being made over him either. But, as Krzyzewski had said to him that day at the beach, no one ever deserved it more.

EPILOGUE

For Mike Krzyzewski, 2015 was an emotion-filled year. There were great victories but there was also great loss.

The losses actually began in December 2013, when his older brother, Bill, his lifelong hero, passed away. Bill Krzyzewski had been a fire captain in Chicago and had become the rock in his little brother's life when their father died while Mike was in college.

Bill had been diagnosed with cancer in November, but the outlook had been optimistic after he had surgery just before Christmas. The hope proved to be both false and short-lived. On the day after Christmas, Bill Krzyzewski died.

"I lost not just my brother, but my rock," Krzyzewski said, still unable to talk about Bill more than a year later without choking up. "*No one* ever messed with my brother. He was a big, tough guy, but a gentle, sweet man.

"Losing your parents is difficult for all of us. But when you lose the person you grew up with, someone just five years older than you, it makes you stop and think—a lot. I tried very hard to deal with it, to compartmentalize, to still give my team everything I had the rest of that season. But I failed. I just couldn't do it. They didn't get the best of me that winter and it was my fault."

Mickie Krzyzewski watched her husband struggle with his emotions and felt helpless to make it better.

"Mike always thinks he has to be the one who figures everything out for everyone else," she said. "He's the one who people call when they have a problem. Or he calls them. But this wasn't something he could make better. There was no solution. He was completely devastated, and just telling himself 'You're okay, keep moving forward' wasn't enough. He needed time to grieve and to deal with the loss. You don't get to do that in the middle of a basketball season."

Which is why, when Duke's 2013–14 season ended with the loss to Mercer, Krzyzewski blamed no one but himself. As he had done in the past he looked within for answers and for improvement.

"I went back to the drawing board," he said. "I had no choice. What I was doing wasn't good enough."

Some of the changes he decided to make were hardly earth-shattering. He learned how to get on Twitter so he could follow his players. "In today's world, it's a good way to know what they're up to and what's on their minds," he said.

He worked on his texting skills so he could text with his players at least once a day when they were away from campus.

Beyond that, though, he changed his approach to the one-and-dones. He had four talented freshmen joining the team: highly touted center Jahlil Okafor, forward Justise Winslow, and guards Tyus Jones and Grayson Allen. Okafor was considered a lock to turn pro after his freshman season, Winslow was likely to go, and Jones was about fifty-fifty. Allen was more of an afterthought—at least to the NBA.

"I had to coach them the way I had coached the guys who stayed four years," Krzyzewski said. "I had to be demanding from day one—not coddle them, not worry about whether they were going to stay or go or that they were 'just' freshmen. Today's kids have played much more basketball when they get to college than kids in the old days. They all play all day, all year. I had to work to try to make them better every day with the understanding that my window to coach them might be closing even after it had just opened.

"There's no such thing as a 'young' team anymore. Your team is your team. Period."

With three freshmen starting from day one—and Quinn

Cook the only senior who played at all—Duke was a talented but flawed team—especially at the defensive end of the court. Once, Krzyzewski would have dug in and insisted that his players learn to play his brand of man-to-man defense: attacking the perimeter, big guys flashing to the top of the key to help on screens, trying to turn defense into offense.

But after back-to-back one-sided losses to North Carolina State and Miami in mid-January—the latter at home—Krzyzewski realized this team wasn't able to keep talented guards out of the lane and that the freshmen weren't going to master his defense by March. If they had been planning to become seniors some-day, or even juniors or sophomores, he might have insisted they keep working on becoming good man-to-man defenders. But that wasn't going to happen. And so Krzyzewski did the unthinkable: he began playing zone.

"In truth, our problem was more about offense than defense," he insisted when the season was over. "When we scored a lot of points, which we did often, it took pressure off our defense. But when we began to struggle during that stretch on offense, it affected our defense. Guys weren't focusing the way they needed to focus. Good defense can lead to good offense. But bad offense can also lead to bad defense.

"Playing zone made it a little easier for the guys on the defensive end. Not that they weren't playing hard, but zone is different than man-to-man. And when we started to play man-to-man again, they were more confident and more comfortable with it."

The back-to-back losses came with Krzyzewski stuck on 997 career victories. The questions about the 1,000th win were start-ing to wear on everyone. Then, playing at Louisville, the Blue Devils came out in a zone and stayed in it most of the night. Coincidence or not, they won in one of the toughest road venues in the country.

Two nights later, at home, they blew Pittsburgh out, meaning Krzyzewski would go for win number one thousand in Madison Square Garden.

"The basketball gods do work in mysterious ways sometimes," Krzyzewski said. "The best game I ever played in college was in the Garden [the 1969 upset of South Carolina in the NIT]; the first important tournament we won at Duke was in the Garden [the 1985 preseason NIT]; I went past Coach Knight in the Garden; and now, here I was going for one thousand in the same place."

He smiled. "Of course for a good long while there, it didn't look like the gods were going to let me get it done."

In fact, St. John's led, 61–51, with under ten minutes to play. Then Krzyzewski played a hunch, putting backup center Marshall Plumlee into the game. Plumlee isn't skilled offensively, but he always brings great emotion with him onto the court, and when he makes plays, he seems to give the entire team a jump start. He did just that on that Sunday afternoon in New York. Duke turned the game around completely, finishing on a 26–7 run to win, 77–68.

Even though the thousandth win had been inevitable, actually getting there was both joyful and a relief all at once. No more questions about it; no more planning for how to handle it when it came. There were hugs and kisses all around, and then it was back to work. The Blue Devils were 17–2 at that moment but were still a work in progress.

That was evident three days after the St. John's game when the team traveled to Notre Dame and lost, 77–73. It had been at Notre Dame a year earlier in the conference opener that Duke had blown a big lead by going dry for a lengthy second-half stretch, a pattern that would repeat itself throughout that season.

The loss, though, wasn't the worst part of the trip to South Bend. The day after the game, Krzyzewski announced that he had kicked junior Rasheed Sulaimon off the team. This was stunning, if only because Krzyzewski had never once in thirty-five seasons at Duke thrown a player off the team.

Sulaimon had come to Duke as a heralded six-foot-five-inch forward from Houston. He was a good student—he was on schedule to graduate in the summer after his junior year—and he had an outstanding freshman season, cracking the lineup as a starter from the beginning and averaging 11.6 points a game.

But things began to go south a year later. He came back to school out of shape, lost his spot in the starting lineup, and even sat out an entire game—against Michigan—even though he was perfectly healthy. He still had moments: hitting a winning shot against Virginia (after yet another big lead had been blown) and a stunning three-pointer at Syracuse to send the game into overtime.

But he bickered with his coaches and his teammates and was clearly unhappy with his role. There were rumors he would transfer, but he stayed and had become a productive player off the bench—albeit someone playing a complementary role rather than a starring one. His nonstarting, nonstarring role appeared to be at the heart of his problems, and an incident on the Notre Dame trip—details were never revealed—was apparently the last straw.

Sulaimon's dismissal left Duke with ten players in uniform—eight scholarship players and two walk-ons, whose job was to help out in practice. On the afternoon after Sulaimon's dismissal, Krzyzewski walked into the locker room before practice and went straight to the whiteboard at the front of the room.

He drew an eight on the whiteboard. He then launched into a speech about why eight was "a cool number," making jokes about how one meant you were alone, all the way up to nine, which just didn't look as cool as eight. Then he turned back to the board and said, "This is what eight looks like when it is turned sideways," drawing a sideways eight.

"A sideways eight," he continued, "is what? It's the sign for infinity. So eight can be infinity, which means that eight is all we need. We have all we need in this room to be successful. Fellas, I'm telling you eight is enough."

And so that became the rallying cry for the rest of the season: "Eight is enough."

Two nights later, Duke traveled to Charlottesville and, behind a barrage of late three-point shots, rallied to beat undefeated and number-two-ranked Virginia, 69–63.

Even with the loss, Virginia was still clearly going to be formidable down the stretch in the ACC. Kentucky was the last undefeated team and the clear-cut number-one team in the country. No one, including Krzyzewski, was certain what Duke was going to become in March. Duke hadn't been to a Final Four since 2010. No one was counting on the dry spell ending in 2015.

—

Dean Smith's death on February 7 rocked the basketball world, not because it was a shock but because it was Dean Smith.

Krzyzewski was one of a handful of non–North Carolina people invited to the private funeral for Smith. He arrived wearing a Carolina-blue tie, which he had not bought for the occasion.

"Whenever we're in Las Vegas, I like to go shopping," he said with an almost sheepish grin. "It's one of the places where I can put on some sweats and a baseball cap and walk around and go unnoticed. A few years ago, I was buying myself some ties and I saw this one. I'm honestly not sure why I bought it. I didn't have a specific reason for buying it and I'd never worn it. But when Dean died and I was dressing to go to the funeral, I remembered the tie and I thought putting it on was the right thing to do."

Krzyzewski's genuine grief and the gesture he made by wearing the tie, along with the moment of silence in Cameron ten days after Smith's death, actually brought on a thaw in relations between Duke and North Carolina. It wasn't that the games were any less intense; there was just less hostility than usual coming from the fans.

When Duke went to Chapel Hill for the final game of the regular season, Roy Williams presented Krzyzewski with a plaque commemorating the thousandth victory. The plaque was the idea of Carolina sports information director Steve Kirschner.

"I caught some grief from some people for it," Kirschner said. "But for the most part I think all of our people recognized it was the right thing to do."

Duke won that night, 84–77, meaning it had gone 14–1

since Krzyzewski started to play zone. The only loss had been at Notre Dame, and the most impressive win had been the victory at Virginia.

Looking back at how the season played out, Krzyzewski saw the win at UVA as a turning point. "They were very good," he said. "I mean, they were undefeated, playing at home, and playing with a lot of confidence. But we just kept making plays and shots down the stretch. That was something we hadn't done the year before—closed against a good team. That told me something about this group."

Duke lost to Notre Dame—again—in the ACC Tournament, this time in a semifinal game. The Blue Devils and the Irish met three times during the season. Notre Dame won twice. Duke won the other game by thirty points.

In spite of losing in the ACC semifinals, Duke was given a number-one seed in the NCAA Tournament. A 29–4 record, the win at Virginia, and the 15–2 finish—plus Virginia's loss to North Carolina in the ACC semis—got the Blue Devils the top seed in the South Region.

This time, there were no early struggles. Playing in Charlotte on the tournament's first weekend, Duke blew through Robert Morris and San Diego State—winning by twenty-nine and by nineteen. Then it was on to Houston—the same regional site Duke had gone through in 2010 en route to Indianapolis.

Utah hung in for the entire night in the round-of-sixteen game, but Justise Winslow, playing in his hometown, made several key plays down the stretch, and the Blue Devils hung on, 63–57. Then, playing second-seeded Gonzaga, they blew open a close game late—something they had gotten in the habit of doing—turning a 51–50 lead into a 66–52 win.

And, just like that, Krzyzewski was in his twelfth Final Four—matching John Wooden's record and breaking the tie for second place in the category he had been stuck in for five years with Dean Smith.

Even so, Kentucky was a heavy favorite to win the championship in Indianapolis. The Wildcats had survived numerous close calls, always able to make a key play when they most needed it, to reach the last weekend with a record of 38–0. Their most notable scare had come in the regional final, where they had to come from five points down late to beat Notre Dame.

Thanks to the fact that Kentucky was clearly the marquee team, Duke got to play in the opening semifinal game for the first time since 1990. On seven consecutive occasions, CBS had demanded that Duke play in the second game because Krzyzewski's team drove ratings more than any other.

"I had forgotten what an advantage it is to play first on Saturday," Krzyzewski said. "It means you get to bed at a normal hour. You play that second game, it is always one or two o'clock in the morning before you get your team back to the hotel and to bed. It means your preparation time isn't anywhere close to normal."

There appeared to be a good deal of karma at work. Duke had already won two national titles in Indianapolis—including its first one in 1991 and its most recent one in 2010. Michigan State was the semifinal opponent, a team Duke had beaten in November. Krzyzewski was close friends with Michigan State coach Tom Izzo and had always seemed to have his number. His record against him was 8–1.

"If we lose to Tom," Mickie Krzyzewski said before the game, "I can live with that."

As it turned out there was little reason to worry about losing to Tom. Although Michigan State came out of the gate on a three-point shooting spree and quickly led 14–6, Duke erased that margin in almost no time and, even with Winslow in foul trouble, led 36–25 by halftime. When the Blue Devils began the second half on a 6–0 run to up the margin to 42–25, the game was over. The lead never got below 14 in the second half, and Duke cruised home, 81–61.

Everyone expected the championship matchup to be against undefeated Kentucky. CBS was anticipating perhaps the highest-rated national title game ever. Except someone forgot to tell Wisconsin. The Badgers had lost to Kentucky at the buzzer in the Final Four a year earlier and weren't the least bit intimidated by the specter of the Wildcats. Even after Kentucky had put on one of its patented second-half rallies to turn an eight-point deficit into a four-point lead, Wisconsin didn't blink.

On three possessions, the Badgers forced Kentucky into thirty-five-second violations. "I don't think that's happened to us three times all season," a stunned John Calipari said after the game. "That was shocking."

So was the outcome. After trailing 60–56, Wisconsin went on an 8–0 run, keyed by a Sam Dekker three-pointer that broke a 60–60 tie, and never looked back, ending the game on a 15–4 run and winning, 71–64. While the jubilant Wisconsin players celebrated, thousands of Kentucky fans filed out of Lucas Oil Stadium in stunned silence. They had come to see a coronation. Instead, they had seen a coup.

Krzyzewski honestly didn't care which team Duke faced in the final. He respected what Kentucky had accomplished but didn't fear the Wildcats—they had been proven vulnerable even before the loss to Wisconsin. He also greatly respected Wisconsin and Coach Bo Ryan and knew they were a tough, experienced team.

For almost thirty minutes, it looked like it was Ryan's turn to win a Division I national title (he had won four at the Division III level) and that Wisconsin was the team of destiny. When center Frank Kaminsky made a layup with 13:23 left to give the Badgers a 48–39 lead, Krzyzewski called time-out.

"Desperate times call for desperate measures," he would joke later.

Okafor had four fouls. Winslow had three. Kaminsky, the senior, was schooling Okafor, the freshman. Krzyzewski looked down his bench and saw Grayson Allen.

Allen had become a solid role player as the season progressed, especially after Sulaimon was kicked off the team. He was the eighth man on an eight-man team, but he almost always gave the team a boost when he got a chance to play. He had played well in the Michigan State game and in the first half of the Wisconsin game. Most of his playing time had come in first halves—Krzyzewski getting him a few minutes to keep the starters fresh.

Now, in the second half of the national championship game, Allen found himself on the floor and with the ball in his hands. Never afraid to shoot, he launched a three-pointer. Swish. It was 48–42. Then he dove on the floor and made a steal. After Amile Jefferson missed a shot, Allen got the tipped-back rebound, scored, and was fouled. He made the free throw. It was 48–45.

Suddenly, the Duke bench was alive. Nigel Hayes made a three for Wisconsin, but Allen made two free throws—meaning he had scored eight straight Duke points. The momentum had swung completely.

"I didn't even know what to do next," Krzyzewski said. "Because at that point, I'm not sure I knew what was going on."

What was going on was a remarkable 27–8 Duke run, keyed by Allen. It culminated when Tyus Jones, who would be chosen as the Most Outstanding Player of the Final Four, hit a three with the shot clock running down and 1:24 to go to give Duke a 66–58 lead. Wisconsin gamely cut the margin to 66–63, but Jones made two clinching free throws and the final was 68–63.

"All the years I've coached, I've never had a player do something like that for me," Krzyzewski said months later, shaking his head in disbelief and still becoming emotional when the subject of Allen's performance came up. "What Grayson did was beyond amazing. We've had great players make great plays and huge shots for us in the past, but the way he came into that game and picked us up was . . . I can't describe it. We were dead in the water and he saved us."

The national championship may have been Krzyzewski's most satisfying because he had gone back to square one, looked in the mirror, and rebooted himself as a coach after the Mercer loss. Duke had gone from a bad defensive team in January to a superb one in March and April, and all eight scholarship players had made important contributions.

They had indeed gone to infinity . . . and beyond.

—

Shortly before Krzyzewski and his coaches headed back to the road for summer recruiting, he spent the better part of a day meeting with various media members from around the country. He met first with a large group, then did some TV one-on-ones, and then met with small groups by ones and twos. For four hours he recounted the 2015 season just past and talked about how gratifying it had been for him to see his team evolve into one that had cut down the final net.

No, he said, he wouldn't be going to New York later in the week to see Jahlil Okafor, Justise Winslow, and Tyus Jones all get drafted in the first round.

"That night is for them," he said. "They don't need me there."

When the last interview was over, he sat down in his office and took a deep breath. He had been asked several times during the day how much longer he thought he would coach. Some had thought he might bow out after the 2016 Olympics. Now, with recruits practically lining up outside the door once again, he had no serious thoughts about retirement.

"As long as I'm healthy and enjoying it, I'll coach," he said. "Right now, I'm both."

He was, however, keenly aware of the passage of time and that he wouldn't coach forever.

"When my brother died, I felt very alone," he said. "I know that sounds impossible because I have such a great family and I'm constantly surrounded by love. But when I thought about the family I had grown up in—my mom, my dad, my brother—they were all gone. Where there had been four, there was one. That hit me hard.

"I felt like that—in a different way, but still with a lot of emotion—when Dean died. As hard as he and Jim and I competed against one another we were all *part* of something, part of something special—very special, I think."

He paused and his voice became extremely soft.

"Where once there were three . . . now there's one. I know how lucky I am to still be here, but I still think about both of them, and of those days, often. I know that all things end. That's why I cherish what I'm doing now every single day and why I cherish my memories, different as they are, of the two of them."

He smiled. "What we became, as individuals, but maybe even more as a group, is an amazing story."

And, although Krzyzewski knows that no one lives forever, he also knows what he and Smith and Valvano became. Their intense battles, their friendships, their victories, and their legacies—as coaches, as rivals, and as men—will undoubtedly live forever.

ACKNOWLEDGMENTS

When I first came up with the idea for this book, I knew that two of the three protagonists would not be available to me firsthand, since Jim Valvano had passed away in 1993 and Dean Smith was in the late stages of terminal dementia.

And so, I had to depend on the kindness of others.

First and foremost, I needed the time and cooperation of Mike Krzyzewski, the one member of the troika who was still available to me. I've known Mike for more than thirty-five years, dating to his days coaching at Army, and there are still times when I have to take a step back to understand exactly what he's become within the pantheon of college basketball.

If there is one thing that Krzyzewski, Smith, and Valvano had in common it was this: each was a great basketball coach but, in my opinion, as someone who spent a lot of time with all three, a better person than a coach.

I was reminded of that in my dealings with Krzyzewski throughout this book.

I know what the demands on his time are like. I know that perhaps the most difficult thing he's had to do in the past twenty-five years is learn how to say no to people, because if he didn't, he would never have a chance to sleep. But I counted on a very selfish notion when I first approached him with the idea: he never says no to his friends.

And, yes, we are friends. *Not* because he's the basketball coach at Duke, which happens to be the school I (barely) got a degree from a hundred years ago, but because he's Mike Krzyzewski.

I've been friends with plenty of other college basketball coaches, including Gary Williams, who coached for twenty-two years at a school whose fan base honestly believes Krzyzewski *is* the devil.

As it turned out, my notion about Mike was true. He went above and beyond what I could reasonably have asked for in terms of time and patience throughout the project. He also kept his sense of humor. After we had spent most of two days together during our first lengthy sessions, I thanked him for never once flinching or looking at his watch as I went over events with him in great detail.

"It's okay," he said. "Actually, I should thank you, because, you know, I'm Catholic."

"What does that have to do with anything?" I asked.

"Because now, after these two days, when I die, I can tell God I've already served my time in purgatory."

And more.

Even though I could not put Dean or Jim through purgatory, I came into the book confident I could write about them and their relationships with each other and Krzyzewski for two reasons: First, I had spent a great deal of time with both men through the years, especially in the 1980s, when the three-way rivalry was in full bloom. Second, I believed I would get the help I needed from their families and from former players and coaches.

Fortunately, I was right.

Both Linnea Smith and Pam Valvano Strasser could not have been more gracious with their time or more giving of their thoughts and emotions in talking about their husbands. I know how painful it was for Pam to relive much of what took place during Jim's final years at N.C. State and during the last year of his life. She was remarkable.

So too was Linnea, who was living through the final months of Dean's life when I spoke to her. At one point, she looked at me and said very quietly, "Every single day is excruciating because he can't tell me how he feels about what he's going through."

I remember Linnea choking up when she said that, her voice filled with sadness.

On the morning after Dean died, I heard those words again and, as awful as I felt about Dean's passing, part of me felt relieved for him and for Linnea and for all of those who loved Dean and had to live through those last couple of years.

Long ago, when I covered politics, the Republican gubernatorial candidate in Maryland was a guy named Bob Pascal. Whenever Pascal talked about his wife, Nancy, he called her "my secret weapon."

Mike Krzyzewski has never used that phrase to describe Mickie, but if he did, he wouldn't be wrong. She has truly been his partner in every possible way since the day they got married in 1969—even if she did get him kicked off the Army team bus during his senior year. Whenever I've written about Mike, dating to the first magazine piece I did on him in 1981, Mickie has been *my* secret weapon. Not only does she know and understand her husband better than anyone, she has never been anything less than 100 percent honest about him and about the people in his life—friend or foe. I'm not sure there's any way I can ever repay her for all the time and smart, funny stories she has shared with me through the years.

Jim Valvano's two brothers, Nick and Bobby, aren't as funny as Jim—because *no one* has ever been as funny as Jim. Bob refers to Nick as "the un-funny Valvano brother," which means he's only funnier than about 95 percent of the population. With Bob, the number is closer to 99 percent.

Both could not have been more helpful—and they were also pretty damn funny. I think they probably both came to dread hearing from me: "Have you got a few more minutes? . . . I have just a couple more questions." They never said no.

Those who had worked with Jim or played for him were the same way: Tom Abatemarco, Dereck Whittenburg, Sidney Lowe, Terry Gannon, and John Saunders among them. The same was true for those who had been close to Dean: Roy Williams, Eddie

Fogler, Billy Cunningham, Buzz Peterson, Bill Raftery, John Thompson, Larry Brown, and Bill Guthridge heading the list. I was lucky that I had spent time with Bill before he became ill, when his mind was still sharp as a tack. I would be remiss in not also thanking Linda Woods, Dean's longtime right-hand woman, who helped me track down many of the Carolina people with whom I needed to talk.

The unsung hero of the Duke basketball program is Gerry Brown, who has been to Mike Krzyzewski what Linda Woods was to Dean Smith for more than thirty years now. Like Linda, Gerry helped me track down a number of key people. Among those who spent time with me talking about all three coaches were Lou Goetz and Bob Wenzel (teammates of Valvano, Duke assistants under Bill Foster), Bobby Dwyer, Chuck Swenson, Pete Gaudet, Bob Bender (who first met Krzyzewski as a high school senior when Mike recruited him to play at Indiana), Mike Gminski, Tommy Amaker, Johnny Dawkins, Mark Alarie, Jay Bilas, David Henderson, Billy King, Danny Ferry, Grant Hill, and Bobby Hurley.

Tom Butters and Steve Vacendak were generous with both their time and their memories—both still excellent, I was happy to find—especially in remembering the early dark days of Krzyzewski's time at Duke.

Among those not directly connected to the three coaches who gave me considerable help were Gary Williams; Terry and Ann Holland; the great Lefty Driesell (who *should* be in the Hall of Fame); Ken Denlinger (to whom this book is dedicated); and my pal Keith Drum, who probably understood the three of them better than anyone who covered them on a regular basis back in the 1980s. Thanks also to Morgan Wootten, who, like the three legends, is a Hall of Fame coach, but a better man. And thanks to his son Joe for one of the funnier quotes in the book. Others who were more than helpful included Mike Brey, Jim Boeheim, Fran Dunphy, Jay Wright, Bobby Cremins, Bob Costas, and my friend and colleague Liz Clarke—who was a huge help putting the entire Valvano/N.C. State mess into perspective for me.

The sports information staffs at all three schools all pitched in with whatever I needed: Steve Kirschner at North Carolina, Matt Plizga at Duke, and Annabelle Myers at N.C. State. Special thanks to N.C. State historian Tim Peeler, for digging into his files for old clips I couldn't possibly have found without him.

A word here about Rick Brewer: he has been a friend and a colleague since I was in college. A lot of the reason that Dean Smith came to trust me—in spite of where I went to college—was because Rick told him to trust me, especially early on. As with so many other projects I have worked on, Rick was invaluable on this one. I am forever grateful for his friendship.

This list could have been longer. I've looked back at my early "talk to" list for this book, and it is considerably longer than the above list. There's a reason for that: I realized early on that I had already done a lot of the reporting for the project just by being there throughout the 1980s. I've told many people that I wasn't born to write this book, but I did *live* it. Plus, the people I spoke to were so generous and so detailed in their memories, I realized I had to stop reporting at some point and start writing. I'm sure Jason Kaufman, my editor, was grateful for that, because if I hadn't, he would be working his way through manuscript page 1,000 about now.

Jason was a big believer in this idea from the beginning. Being honest, my agent, Esther Newberg, was not: she's one of those people who can't stand the mention of Krzyzewski's name (she's a UConn fanatic and has apparently forgotten her team beating Duke in *two* Final Fours) and believes the only basketball programs worthy of her attention are the UConn men and women and the Knicks—when they're good.

But to her credit, she understood that this book was "right in your wheelhouse," and admitted when she started reading it that "there *is* a lot in here I didn't know."

I sincerely hope she's not the only one who feels that way.

Jason's colleague, Rob Bloom, a talented editor in his own right, is among the most patient people on earth—believe it or not, I can be a little bit tough to deal with, if only because my knowledge of technology pretty much ends in about 1990—and the same is true of Esther's assistant Zoe Sandler—who has the patience of Job for dealing with Esther *and* me. Thanks also to Bill Thomas at Doubleday and to Kari Stuart, John Delaney, and Liz Farrell at ICM.

And then there are my friends and family, who enable me through each and every one of my books: I usually start with Keith and Barbie Drum, but since Keith was part of this book, I'll just start with Barbie. Thanks also to Jackson Diehl and Jean Halperin, David and Linda Maraniss, Bob Woodward, Matt Vita, Matt Rennie, and Matt Bonesteel—all *Washington Post* editors, believe it or not. More *Post* folks: Sally Jenkins, Marty Weil, Lexie Verdon and Steve Barr (still Posties in my heart), David Larimer, Mark Maske, and Kathy Orton.

Longtime friends: Terry and Patti Hanson, Doug and Beth Doughty, Dob and Anne DeStefano, the wondrous Bud Collins, Wes Seeley, Andy Dolich, Pete Alfano, David Teel, Gary Cohen, Beth Shumway-Brown, Beth Sherry-Downes, Pete Van Poppel, Frank DaVinney, Omar Nelson, Mike Werteen, Phil Hoffmann, Joe Speed, Andrew Thompson, Jack Hecker, Gordon Austin, Eddie Tapscott, Steve (Moose) Stirling, Tim Kelly, Dick Hall, Anthony and Kristen Noto, Derek Klein, Jim (king of the world) Cantelupe, Bob Zurfluh, Vivian Thompson, Mike and David Sanders, Tony and Karril Kornheiser, Mike Wilbon, Nancy Denlinger, Governor Harry Hughes, General Steve Sachs, Tim Maloney, Chris Ryan, Harry Kantarian, Jim Rome, Mike Purkey, Bob Edwards, Tom and Jane Goldman, Mike Gastineau, Dick and Joanie (Hoops) Weiss, Jim O'Connell, Holland and Jill Mickle, Jerry Tarde, Mike O'Malley, Larry Dorman, Marsha Edwards, Jay Edwards, Chris Edwards and John Cutcher, Len and Gwyn Edwards-Dieterle, and, of course, Aunt Joan, Bill Leahey, Andy North, Paul Goydos, Steve Flesch, Bill Andrade, Gary "Grits" Crandall, Drew Miceli, Brian Henninger, and Tom and Hilary Watson.

Thanks to my friends and colleagues at Golf Channel: Kristi Setaro, Matt Hegarty, Eric Rutledge, David Gross, Molly Solomon, Geoff Russell, Mark Summer, Kory Kozak, Adam Hertzog, Jon Steele, Tony Grbac, Courtney Holt, Alan Robison, Frank Nobilo, Brandel Chamblee, Rich Lerner, Kelly Tilghman, Whit Watson, Tim Rosaforte, Mark Rolfing, Notah Begay, Lisa Cornwell, Gary Williams, Damon Hack, Tripp Isenhour, Ryan Burr, George Savaricas, Lisa Cornwell, Jay Coffin, Rex Hoggard, John Feyko, and the world's best-dressed new father, Todd Lewis. To those who came before: Tom Stathakes, Joe Riley, and Dave Taylor.

At CBS Sports Radio: Andrew Bogusch, Max Herman, Peter Bellotti, Dave Mayurnik, Anthony Pierno, and Mike Diaz. At SiriusXM: Scott Greenstein, Steve Cohen, Jeremy Davis, Jon Albanese, Diamond Gray, and Chris Spatola.

Others scattered across the sports world: David Fay, Mike Davis, Mike Butz, Mary Lopuszynski, Pete Kowalski, Craig Smith. It didn't feel like a U.S. Open without Frank and Jayme Bussey. Other golf people: Marty Caffey, Heny Hughes, and Sid Wilson (sigh), Joel Schuchmann, Todd Budnik, Dave Senko, Doug Milne, Chris Reimer, Colin Murray, John Bush, Laura Hill, James Cramer, Joe Chemyz, Phil Stambaugh, Dave Lancer, Ward Clayton, and Guy Scheipers. Denise Taylor commented to me earlier this year that she should be in my will. She's right. Thanks also to Joe Steranka, Pete Bevacqua, Julius Mason, and Una Jones at the PGA of America.

The rules guys: Mark Russell—not to mention Laura Russell and the invaluable Alex, who will be a Democrat someday. Also: Steve Rintoul, Jon Brendle (emeritus), Slugger White, Robbie Ware, Dillard Pruitt, and the great John Paramour.

More hoops people: the world's greatest commissioner (ask him) David Stern. Tim Frank, Brian McIntyre, Lefty and Joyce Driesell, Seth and Brad Greenberg, Jim Calhoun, Brad Stevens, Shaka Smart, Billy Donovan, Larry Shyatt, Tom Brennan, Dave and Lynne Odom, Jim Larrañaga, Mack McCarthy, Pat Flannery,

Ralph Willard, Jim Crews, Zach Spiker, Emmett Davis, Billy Lange, Fran O'Hanlon. Frank Sullivan is still the best.

Docs—a longer list than I'd like it to be, but thankfully most are friends more often than docs: Eddie McDevitt, Dean and Ann Taylor, Bob Arciero, Gus Mazzocca, Murray Lieberman, plus the two men who saved my life, Steve Boyce and Joe Vassallo.

Probably my two favorite guys in basketball: Howard Garfinkel and Tom Konchalski—still the only honest man in the gym.

The swimming knuckleheads, who are *not* aging gracefully (neither am I): Jason Crist, Jeff Roddin, Clay F. Britt, Wally Dicks, Mark Pugliese, Paul Doremus, Danny Pick, Erik (Dr. Post) Osbourne, John Craig, Doug Chestnut, Peter Ward, Penny Bates, Carole Kammel, Mary Dowling, Magot Pettijohn, Tom Denes, A. J. Block, Pete Lawler, and Mike (three-timer) Fell.

The China Doll/Shanghai Village gang: Aubre Jones, Jack Kvancz, Stanley Copeland, Reid Collins, Harry Huang, George Solomon, Geoff Kaplan, and Jeff Gemunder. In absentia but still welcome: Morgan Wootten, Pete Dowling, Joe McKeown, Bob Campbell, and Ric McPherson. Missed always: Red and Zang; Hymie, Rob, and Arnie.

The Rio Gang, where I think I'm finally bringing Tate Armstrong around to the right (actually left) way of thinking. Mark Alarie, Clay Buckley, and Terry Chili remain hopeless, but friends nevertheless.

The Feinstein Advisory Board: Dave Kindred, Keith Drum, Frank Mastrandrea, and—up there somewhere saying, "I told you Coach Cutt would get it done!"—Bill Brill.

Almost last, but certainly not least, my family: Bobby, Jennifer, Matthew, and Brian; Margaret, David, Ethan, and Ben; Marylynn, Cheryl, and Marcia.

And, most of all: my wife and my children light up my life every single day: Christine, Danny, Brigid, and Jane. I could not possibly live without them.

INDEX